M1

The Black Key

Millennium Series

Staci Morrison

First published by Alanthia Publishing 2021

Copyright © 2021 by Staci Morrison

ISBN: 978-1-7365520-3-2

First edition

For Susan, my soul sister, my
friend, and the inspiration to write it.

Table of Contents

Enter the Millennium

The reader will note that years in the text are indicated with ME, Millennial Era, instead of BC or AD. Thus, 999 ME is 999 years into the Millennium.

Character names use a Hebrew construction, whereby 'ben' means child of, so Josiah ben Eamonn means Josiah son of Eamonn.

So, what is the Millennium, and when will it occur?

It is a prophetic time, the next great age. Our world today will not continue ad infinitum. At some point in the future, the Lord will appear in the Heavens and call His church to Himself. This global cataclysmic event is called the Rapture and sets off a series of events that will usher in the Tribulation, seven years of wars, famine, earthquakes, fire, and pestilence; hell on Earth. But in the end, the evil forces are defeated. The Lord returns to rule, ushering in the Millennium, one thousand years of paradise, a return to what was lost in Eden.

"Then I saw an angel coming down from heaven, having the key to the bottomless pit and a great chain in his hand. He laid hold of the dragon, that serpent of old, who is the Devil and Satan, and bound him for a thousand years; and he cast him into the bottomless pit, and shut him up, and set a seal on him, so that he should deceive the nations no more till the thousand years were finished. But after these things, he must be released for a little while."

—Revelation 20:1-3

Prologue

April 30, 985 ME

Prince Eamonn - New City, Alanthia

They were coming to kill him. Blood from Prince Eamonn's manacled wrists dripped to the dungeon floor, a monotonous, hollow sound in the darkness. Sulfur eeked into the dank cell, choking him, a foul stench, rotten. Evil.

Hidden in the bowels of the Palace, he heard a wicked coven preparing a ritual, shouting blasphemies, and crying enchantments. Drunk on the prospect of forbidden power, they inhaled the toxic fumes of their own demise and proclaimed it sweet perfume.

Treacherous fools.

He warned them, nay beseeched them, but their hearts turned to stone, and their feet rushed to do violence. Despite all his efforts, rebellion infected his kingdom.

The Millennium was paradise—until now.

With darkness closing in, he clung to hope, praying the supreme ruler of Millennial Earth, the Iron King, would intervene and avert the coming atrocity. Eamonn raised his chin, drawing himself upright, gathering his courage. He had been placed on the Alanthian throne by the Iron King himself. Thus, no matter how dire his circumstances honor demanded he not falter, that he stay strong. The mantle of responsibility rested on his shoulders. It was his duty. His kingdom needed him. His son needed him…

An image of a brown-eyed boy flashed across his mind, and he threw back his head and howled.

But the cold walls absorbed his anguish, the cry of his soul drowned out by the beat of a sinister drum. No one heard him. No one was coming.

Below, the frenzied ritual changed. Their chants grew softer, chilling. They were singing… it was ancient… haunting. His eyes bulged, discerning the words. They were beckoning evil—by name.

They hid their faces when they chained him in this pit. Beaten and semi-conscious, he smelled their sweat, full of animal aggression, felt their anticipation, saw their lust-crazed eyes. They wanted him to know. They wanted to watch his face when they told him.

He was going to be a sacrifice.

His blood used to unleash Hell on Earth.

Marching feet reverberated up the passageway. Death was on the move.

Fear roared up his spine. In one last futile attempt to break free, he threw himself against the chains, sparking an electrical storm. A lightning strike of pain sizzled down his arms. Blood thundered in his ears as sweat rained off his nose. When the dark storm of shadows reached his cell, hope died.

Time had run out.

They seized him. He fought with the frenzy of a condemned man, nothing to lose. He levied curses on their heads and spat in their faces. Bound and chained, he struggled in vain. A dozen cruel hands restrained him, and a jeweled staff crushed his windpipe, pinning him against the wall. Held still and silent, an injection pierced his right arm.

He hung chained to the dungeon wall like an abandoned puppet. Treachery… betrayal… in his own house.

Sleep beckoned, the blackness a comfort now.

Alanthia's rebellion had begun.

Part 1 - Origins

August 4, 982 ME (2.5 Years Before Rebellion)

Dancing Letters - Alexa and Peter

Princess Alexa ben Seamus found her four-year-old son, Peter, hiding from his tutor–again. Tucked under her dressing table asleep, he snuggled with her ermine trimmed robe, intermittently sucking his left thumb. Korah tried to break him of that habit, but in sleep, Peter forgot his father.

His soft cheeks were flushed. His nanny had dressed him in a long sleeve shirt, and the day had turned warm. A lime-green tie lay in a crumpled heap beside him. Alexa knelt, smoothing a sweaty blond curl out of his eye. He smiled without waking or removing his thumb, her little angel.

Glancing at the door, she saw it was cracked and hurried over, quietly engaging the lock. Chewing her thumbnail, she stared at the connecting door to her husband Korah's suite. She tiptoed across the rug and pressed her ear to the oak panel. Everything was quiet. Using her hip, she nudged a heavy wingback chair in front of it.

There was no lock on that door.

Her shoulders relaxed, and she wiped her palms on

her linen trousers. Korah was having one of his bad weeks. Shrouded in suppressed anger, he became erratic and quick-tempered, unpredictable. Three nights ago, he shocked everyone with the surprise announcement that it was time for Peter to begin his formal education. Alexa glowered at him over her wine glass but held her tongue in front of her brother-in-law, Eamonn, and the rest of the guests.

After dinner, she stormed into Korah's room. "We should have talked about this. He is too young."

Korah scoffed, "You would smother him if I let you."

Their argument turned into a screaming match, a glaring symptom of their failing marriage. They ripped the bandages off old wounds and unearthed buried pain. Shouting accusations, neither gave ground, they simply cast blame.

When Alexa sneered, 'You are acting just like your mother,' Korah erupted.

From there, their fight degenerated, swirling into the muck and mire. Then it turned physical.

Today, standing over her sleeping son, she knew if Korah discovered Peter here instead of the schoolroom, he would conclude she was undermining him; not optimal, given his temper of late.

She sat down carefully, mindful of her sprained wrist, and gathered Peter into her arms. Soft growling nibbles and kisses elicited a lyrical, sleepy giggle, as he snuggled against her. Warm and solid, he emanated the tangy scent of sleeping boy as she buried her face in his neck. "You escaped Mr. ben Merriweather again, monkey."

The little imp stared up at her with emerald eyes haloed by bursts of sunshine. "I do not like school. I like horses."

"I understand, but you are a Prince of Alanthia, and there is much to learn," she said, parroting Korah to present a unified parental front.

Peter narrowed his brows, clearly not happy. "Josiah is the heir. He will be the Ruling Prince, not me. Besides, he is smarter than me."

"Josiah is older than you. That does not mean he is smarter."

Peter gave her a dubious look. "He is, and I do not like the dancing letters."

She tilted her head, uncertain of his meaning. "Dancing letters?"

He nodded solemnly. "They move." Then exhibiting a defiance, she feared would cause him a lifetime of trouble, he snuggled to her breast, and sucked his thumb.

Her heart broke with dawning understanding. "Oh, monkey, do not tell your tutor, for he will be obliged to tell your father, and you know how he can be." Pressing a kiss on the top of his head, she whispered, "It will be our secret, okay?"

Lessons

Peter sulked. He hated school, and his tutor, Mr. ben Merriweather, was a twat. He was not sure what a twat actually was, but the grooms in the stable said it all the time. They were nice. Mr. ben Merriweather was not.

The tutor was mad because he had not come back to class after lunch. So, he ignored him and kept teaching Josiah's lesson, just to punish him. Peter had no idea what they were talking about, and that made him feel stupid. Squirming in his seat, he looked out the window, trying to see the horses. The stables were better than this dumb classroom.

"Peter, perhaps you already know this subject so well, you do not have to pay attention?" Mr. ben Merriweather said, craning his neck and looking down his beaked nose. Peter thought he looked like a stork, a twat stork. "Why do *you* think our forefathers did not recreate computing or transportation technology after it was destroyed in the Great Judgment?"

Peter hunched his small shoulders, refusing to meet those beady eyes. "I do not know."

"Then I suggest you pay attention."

"My father says we should have it," Peter said, knowing this would fluster Merriweather. He was pretty sure the tutor was afraid of his father.

On cue Merriweather flushed. "Your father's opinion on the subject is well known, but that was not the question. Why didn't they rebuild?"

"Because they were stupid." Peter pursed his lips and glared, silently conveying he thought Merriweather was too.

"The men and women who built computers and airplanes were stupid?" Merriweather asked in that condescending voice that made Peter want to punch him.

"They weren't stupid," his cousin interjected. "They chose not to recreate the world they left behind."

Merriweather smiled at Josiah, his prize student. "Very good, and can you tell Peter why?"

"They didn't need it anymore." Josiah shrugged. "And a lot of the people who knew how to make that stuff died in the Great Judgment."

"That's correct, but why didn't they need it anymore?" Merriweather directed his question to Josiah, crossing his skinny legs like a girl.

Sick of being ignored, Peter piped up, "Because you do not need a computer to ride a horse."

Merriweather nodded and looked pleased to see Peter participating. "Or plow a field and pick an apple. Do you think they were concerned about building a computer or a house?"

"They did not have houses?" That surprised Peter.

Josiah rolled his eyes, impatient with Peter, and annoyed they had to take lessons together.

"Not at the beginning, everything was destroyed," Merriweather confirmed.

Peter refused to look at his cousin, actually growing interested in this lesson. "Well, I would build a house first and a stable, because they had horses, right?"

"You are single-minded, Prince d'Or." Josiah threw up his hands.

Merriweather ignored Josiah. "They did have horses, to pull the plows and to ride. After the Great Judgment, men returned to the land and settled in small farming communities. They prospered in health and security, living long lives in peace and harmony."

"They did not live in the cities?" Josiah asked.

"Not at first. People began moving to the cities during your Grandfather Adam's reign, not before."

Josiah rubbed his jaw, thinking. "Interesting. So, the first Millennial generation went from the city to the country, from driving cars to riding horses."

Peter was not clear on what a car had been, so he said, "Everybody likes riding horses." He raised an imperious chin at his cousin, who sighed.

"Josiah, what do you think?" Merriweather asked, smoothing his thin black tie.

"I think it was probably strange for them, but my father told me they were afraid of what recreating technology would do. He said part of the rebellion in the Last Age had something to do with men running to and fro."

"Do you know where that comes from?" Merriweather asked.

Josiah shrugged, looking sulky to be put on the spot. Peter grinned.

"It is a prophecy. Pull out your bible."

Peter, who could not read yet, did not bother. He crossed his arms over his chest and sat stubbornly.

Merriweather turned to Josiah and said, "Daniel 12:4, please."

Josiah flipped over pages in his King James Bible, searching for the text. He knew why they used this version. When the first generation began to resettle the land, this translation was widely printed, so copies were easy to come by. In remote communities, it was often the only book available and became a standard text in schools, used to teach children, not only their faith, but how to read. For generations, English speakers adopted the cadence and word choices in the text. It fell out of fashion early in Grandfather Adam's reign and was now spoken primarily in isolated areas of the kingdom. However, it was still considered proper in courts of law and during state affairs. Josiah's Grandmother Mary had never spoken, what she referred to as common language, insisting they speak properly. But since her death, his father relaxed the standards at home. Now, they only used 'court speech' for official business.

Josiah found the verse and read, "But thou, O Daniel, shut up the words, and seal the book, even to the time of the end: many shall run to and fro, and knowledge shall be increased."

"Very good, Josiah." Mr. ben Merriweather said. "That text supplies the primary reason they did not rebuild transportation and computers. They understood prophecy often has dual applications, so Daniel 12:4 may refer to the end of the Last Age, but it might also apply to our time. The first generation sought to ensure we would not recreate conditions that led to rebellion and another judgment. Do you understand?"

Josiah did not. He could not wrap his head around how knowledge or travel led to rebellion. He needed time to think about this, to ponder in private. Seeking to change the subject, his thirteen-year-old stomach provided the inspiration. "I think they were hungry. They were more concerned about farming, so they could eat."

"I suppose they were hungry, especially in the beginning. They survived a global famine, and in the Last Age, growing food was difficult."

"Things did not grow?" Peter asked in disbelief.

"Not without a lot of work. The ground used to be cursed, Peter. At the beginning of the Millennium, the Iron King lifted that curse, and the earth brought forth every good thing."

Merriweather turned to Josiah. "Put yourself in their place; they lived through the Great Judgment. Imagine what it was like for them to no longer be afraid of being murdered. No one hunted them, and the ground no longer shook with quakes and erupting volcanoes. No hail and fire fell from the sky, the water tasted sweet, not poisoned and bitter. They were finally safe after suffering through war, sickness, and famine."

Josiah drummed his fingers on his thigh, trying to pull it all together, so he repeated what he had been told. "I don't imagine they would want to go back to the way things used to be."

"Exactly. Come up here. I will show you something."

Peter scrambled out of his chair, his shirt tail pulling free from his trousers and flapping behind him as he ran. Josiah followed at an indolent pace, staying outwardly cool, despite being intrigued by the book Mr. ben Merriweather pulled from the shelf.

"Prince Eamonn let me borrow this for our lesson today." Slipping on a pair of cotton gloves, he added, "Neither of you touch it. It is very old."

Peter drew his hand back and grumbled, "It is just a book."

"No, it's more than a book. It is one of the few surviving collections of pictures from the Last Age, which makes it almost a thousand years old." He opened it with great fanfare.

Peter leaned over the picture, blocking Josiah's view. "What is that?"

"A picture of a drought."

"That looks like smoke," Peter protested.

Josiah studied the image of a house about to be enveloped. "Is that dirt?"

Merriweather nodded. "It's a dust storm at the beginning of the Great Judgment. Look at the ground."

"There's no grass, nothing alive." Josiah leaned in closer, noticing the cracked soil.

"No grass? What did the horses eat?" Peter asked.

"Nothing. They died or were eaten for food."

"That is sad," Peter's lip began to quiver. "I do not want to learn about dead horses."

"I understand, but that's not what we are talking about." Merriweather pointed across the classroom. "Go look out the window. Tell me what you see?"

Peter scampered to the window and pressed his nose to the glass. "Green," he declared triumphantly.

"There are a lot of flowers." Josiah said, participating even though he saw where this was going. "And there's Barton walking my dog." He tapped on the glass, but the school-room was too high, neither Barton nor Rex heard.

"What about the mountains over there?" Merriweather asked.

"They are green, too!" Peter said, smiling up at Josiah.

"Exactly. Do you know what they looked like in the Last Age? They were brown and sandy. Men had to bring water up there. Do you think that was easy?"

Peter got a look of intense concentration. "I tried to pick up a bucket in the stable once. Water is heavy. I think that would be hard."

Merriweather laid a hand on the top of Peter's messy blond hair, and said, "You are right. So, what do you think? Do you think men, who once had to carry water and struggle for anything to grow, might have been excited to live in a place where they did not have to do that any longer?"

"I think they were happy. Grass is soft. I think dirt is not."

"I think they thought the same thing, Peter. I truly do."

"Mr. ben Merriweather," Josiah asked after Peter was excused. "I have been thinking about our lesson, and I have a question."

Merriweather nodded. "Certainly."

Josiah tapped his fist against his bottom lip, framing the question. "I sort of understand why they did not rebuild, at first. They were busy trying to stay alive, but why not later?" He sighed and confessed, "I still don't understand why they passed laws prohibiting computers and cars. They did not prohibit other manufacturing. They made tractors. We have glass in our windows, clocks on the wall. My father even permits electricity now. Why are those things okay, but computers and cars are not?"

Merriweather smiled. "They may seem like two separate issues, but they are not. It was about the recreation of conditions that led to rebellion. But let us focus on computer technology for the moment. It was not inherently bad, as a matter of fact, in some ways it did a lot of good. It was what computers enabled that became so destructive, what they did to people and society."

At Josiah's confused expression, Merriweather pulled back on his cotton gloves. "Come here and look."

Josiah suppressed a surge of excitement as Merriweather took the ancient book from the shelf, but he maintained the dignified manner drilled into him since birth. Monarchs were not given over to passions or outward expressions of emotion.

"What do you see in this picture?"

Josiah leaned over the desk. "People sitting and looking at little boxes."

"Do they seem happy?"

Josiah shook his head. "Not really."

"What are they not doing?" Merriweather pressed.

"I don't know, looking at each other or talking?"

"Right. How do they appear to you? Do they look healthy?"

"No." Josiah focused on a pudgy man sitting alone. "What are they holding?"

"Computers."

Josiah squinted. He had never seen a real picture of a computer before. "What's on them?"

"Whatever they wanted. They had them with them all

the time, took them everywhere. They lived their lives watching computers."

"Well, that seems a bit foolish but not bad."

"What if what they were watching was bad?"

This drew Josiah up straight. "Then they should stop looking at it. My father says that we have to guard our eyes, there are some things you cannot unsee." His face flushed because there was a book in the library with paintings of naked women. He looked at it sometimes, purely from an anatomy standpoint, or so he told himself.

"What if they stopped realizing it was bad? What if every day, all day, the information that came across those computers seemed true and good, but was not?"

Josiah gave him a dubious look. "How did they not know good from bad? Everyone knows good from bad."

"I suspect if you tell someone something is good long enough, they will start to believe it."

Josiah shuffled his feet. Each time he looked at the naked ladies he felt a little less guilty. "Is that what happened?"

Merriweather nodded. "Yes, it was. I ask you to consider, Josiah, what if there was a powerful force behind all the lies? How easy would it be to reach people and lead them astray? How much easier would it be to change everything?"

Josiah's mouth dropped open as understanding dawned. "That's why they passed the laws because they knew that wicked men would use those computers."

"Not just men, Josiah. It was not just men."

February 1, 983 ME (Two Years Before Rebellion)

Loss of Innocence - Alexa and Peter

Dark circles and lines of strain creased the delicate skin around Princess Alexa's blue eyes. She would be thirty-six next month, too young to look as haggard as she did. Blending her thick makeup, she concealed a fading bruise with expert skill. She took a sip of hot tea and winced, running her tongue over the lacerated flesh inside her cheek. Her hand shook as she set down the fragile china cup, which clattered in the saucer. She closed her eyes, searching for calm. Everything was falling apart. Korah was not getting better, and she had no idea what to do about it.

Sensing movement behind her, she smiled. Reflected in the mirror, five-year-old Peter stood in the doorway, watching her. She beckoned him forward.

Heartbreakingly beautiful, he strutted in with all the cocky confidence of a young Prince. "Good morning, Mother." He tolerated her too-tight embrace, then broke free, his emerald eyes brimming with excitement. "Look what I found!" he said, producing an ancient hand-held device from his pocket.

"Peter, where did you get that?" Alexa gasped and reached for it.

He snatched it back and scampered out of reach, hiding his treasure behind his back. "It is mine!"

Remaining calm, she delivered an unmistakable maternal command, "Give. That. To. Me."

"No." The blond imp danced further away. "I found it."

Alexa glowered. If she took it, he would throw a tantrum, bringing the servants or worse, Korah. She could not let that happen. So, she settled back in her chair, feigning her normal indulgence, and asked, "Where did you find it?"

He looked away, long golden lashes covering his impudence. "In a drawer."

"Peter, you know you are not allowed in your father's office."

"I was not," he sulked. "I was in the cupboard."

"You are not supposed to be in there either. Those passages are dangerous." Her curious son had discovered a hidden network running behind the walls of the Palace. Though she forbade it, he explored anyway.

He shrugged and set his small shoulders, flashing her a cherubic smile. He charmed his way out of trouble with everyone, except his father. Alexa limited that as much as she could, often at great cost to herself, as the black eye and split cheek attested.

"Listen to me now." The note of fear in her voice caught his attention. "You must give that to me, so we can put it back."

He shook his head, mischief spilling over. "Mother, you should see what I can make it do."

Her hand flew to her mouth. "You made it come on? How is that possible?"

"Magic!" Peter declared in absolute triumph, bouncing on his toes, and keeping the gilded coffee table between them.

Tears burned her eyes, horrified to have her suspicions confirmed. If Korah was in possession of functioning ancient technology, he had moved from idealism to action. He and his brother, Eamonn, battled about it continuously. If anyone discovered Peter with the artifact it would bring down a firestorm.

Alexa had to make him understand. Her breath caught, and she heard the quiver in her voice. "Peter, your father will be furious if he finds out. He is not well. He might kill me for this. He might kill you. We must take it back."

A part of her died as she watched the last innocent love Peter still felt for Korah fade from his emerald eyes.

The Princes of Egypt and Greece

"Okay, boys, it's time for civics," Mr. ben Merriweather said.

Both Princes groaned. Civics made up a huge portion of their curriculum.

"Josiah, read chapter twenty-three on the role and function of the legislature in a hereditary monarchy. I want you to pay attention to the differences between Alanthia and Greece. There will be a quiz."

Josiah hefted his civics book onto the desk with a thud. Merriweather unfurled a map at the front of the schoolroom and motioned for Peter to join him.

Peter scampered up to the map, fixated on the bright colors. "It is like a puzzle. Pretty."

"Indeed, it is. Your uncle commissioned this when your cousin was about your age. Look here, this map shows not only the borders of the ten kingdoms but the dominant trees and native animals who live there."

"There's a lion and an elephant," Peter said, touching the map. A six-pointed gold star in the center drew his eye, and he pointed to it. "That's where we live."

Merriweather shook his head. "No, Peter, that's the Golden City, called Jerusalem in your bible. It is the capital of the world." He pointed to a smaller five-pointed gold star over ancient San Francisco. "We are here." Then he ran his finger around the blue area formerly known as North America. "This is Alanthia."

Peter looked closer, then furrowed his brow and asked, "Where am I?"

The corner of Merriweather's lip quivered. "It's not a map of people, Peter."

"Then who is that?" Peter pointed to the robed figure over the big gold star in the center.

"That drawing represents the Iron King. He gets to be on this map since he ultimately rules all the kingdoms."

Peter put his hand on his hip, skeptical. "Uncle Eamonn rules Alanthia, Mr. ben Merriweather."

"And Josiah will rule one day, too, but everyone is ruled by the Iron King, Peter, including your Uncle Eamonn."

Peter considered, then said, "So, he is like the father, and all the Ruling Princes are like the mother?"

Merriweather chuckled, "In a manner of speaking, yes. I suppose that is right."

"What he says goes, even if the mothers do not like it?" Peter hung his head, directing the quiet question to the floor. "Does he hit them?"

"No, he does not hit them, but they have to listen to him. If they do not, bad things might happen. He is a wise and wonderful King and always knows what is best. Look here."

He pointed to Egypt. "Do you know why it's brown?"

Peter shook his head, glanced at the map, and looked down again.

"Several years ago, the Ruling Prince of Egypt decided not to listen to the Iron King and stopped going up to the Golden City like he was supposed to. Do you know what happened?"

Peter looked up with large green eyes and said, "He got a spanking?"

Merriweather chuckled. "Not in the way you are thinking, but sort of. The Iron King stopped their rain and told the Prince of Egypt that he would not give it back until the Ruling Prince said he was sorry and stopped doing the bad things he was doing."

Peter remembered the artifact he had stolen and grew scared. "What did he do?"

"A number of things. He was already married and took another woman as his wife. He ended all celebrations and holidays the Iron King put in place and started making his own."

Peter felt a measure of relief that the Prince of Egypt had not been playing with ancient technology. "Why did he do that? I like our holidays, especially Sukkot because we get to sleep in a tent."

Merriweather smiled. "I like the Feast of Tabernacles, too, Peter, but the bad Prince of Egypt apparently did not. He began to celebrate other holidays and worship Egypt's old gods."

Peter's eyes widened, even he knew that was a bad idea. "I bet he got in big trouble."

"He did. It is a grievous sin to break the first commandment. Do you remember what that is?"

"Thou shall not murder!" Peter exclaimed, beaming with pride.

"Well, that is one of them, but that is the seventh. Now that I think about it, the Prince of Egypt actually broke the first three." Merriweather named them off counting on his fingers for Peter.

"What does graven mean?" Peter asked.

"It is something like a carved image or a statue that people used to worship."

Peter's mouth fell open. "People worshipped a statue? That is silly."

"I agree, but that is what the Prince of Egypt was doing. So, the Iron King told him to stop, but he felt sorry for the people of Egypt." Merriweather outlined the African continent, then pointed to Cairo. "He mainly withheld rain from here, where the Prince lived."

"For how long?" Peter remembered that picture of the drought Mr. ben Merriweather had shown them. Drought was a very bad thing.

"Forty years. Then the Iron King lost patience, and the wicked Prince died. His son rules now."

"He killed him for being bad?" The color drained from Peter's face.

Merriweather stilled, as if realizing who he was talking to, but said, "To whom much is given, much is required, Peter. Being a Ruling Prince carries great responsibility, not only for the Prince himself, but for everyone in his kingdom."

Peter chewed on his lower lip and glanced at Josiah, deciding in that moment, he never wanted to be the Ruling Prince.

Merriweather pointed to Athens and outlined Greece, Turkey, the Baltics, and the former Eastern Bloc states. "Unfortunately, Monarch Antiochus of Greece is headed down the same path."

"That is not very smart. What does he do?"

Merriweather pursed his lips. "He is being bad."

Peter blinked. "Well, is the new Prince of Egypt being good? Is Egypt okay now?"

Peter glanced over his shoulder at Josiah, who had stopped reading and was listening.

Merriweather shuffled his feet and hedged. "I think he tries to be, but his father had other children by his second wife. That is causing trouble."

Peter leaned in and whispered, "Is that why Uncle Eamonn does not have a wife?"

Merriweather raised a speculative brow at Peter's quick deduction. "Perhaps, but I think your uncle loved his wife very much and does not want another."

"Oh." Peter turned away and trudged back to his desk, surreptitiously and vigorously sucking his left thumb.

April 27, 985 ME (Three Days before Rebellion)

Prince's Study

"Father?" Josiah stood in the doorway of Eamonn's study, dressed casually in khakis and a knit shirt. "May I have a word?"

Eamonn looked up from the papers. "Yes, of course. Come in." He suppressed a smile as his son entered the room. At fifteen, he was a serious young man, deliberate and thoughtful. On leave from the Royal Military Academy, Eamonn could scarcely believe how much he had grown. He was lean, though the RMA fed their cadets well and put them through rigorous physical training, so Josiah was filling out. His jet-black hair and olive complexion came from Margaret, his beloved Italian wife. And for the thousandth time since she died, he wished she had lived to see him, though she might have resented that other than his coloring their son was his mirror image.

Josiah presented himself with a formal bow and stood at attention.

A bit surprised by the formality, Eamonn asked, "What's on your mind, Son?"

Josiah shifted, looking over Eamonn's shoulder at a vase given to his great-great grandfather by the Prince of Asia.

"There were a lot of protestors outside today. I want to ask; do you think it is wise to continue prosecuting technology researchers?"

Eamonn's eyes darted to the hall. He nodded to a footman who closed the door.

"I have struggled with this for a while." Josiah said, holding himself ramrod straight. "There are heated debates all the time at school. Publicly, I support your policies, but I can tell you, that puts me in the minority. Privately, I find I agree with Uncle Korah and think we should lift the ban." A rush of blood ran up Josiah's neck. "As your son, I am honor bound to support you, but I need to know why you are so strongly against it. And I wonder if putting people in jail is the right way to go about it? Doesn't that just make them want it more?"

"I cannot speak to whether it makes them want it more or not, nor am I concerned over how they *feel* about the law. It is my duty to enforce it."

"The people are angry about it." Josiah picked at his cuticle, then met Eamonn's eyes. "They are angry at you."

Eamonn rose from behind the desk and gestured to an embroidered settee. "Being a monarch is not about being popular. It is about doing what is right."

They sat, and he continued, "If I choose which laws the Alanthian government enforces and which ones we did not, we will fall into chaos. What message does it send if I do that? Shall I stop enforcing laws against rape, murder, or theft?"

"But technology research is none of those things," Josiah protested.

"Be that as it may, it is still the law. You cannot pick and choose; it does not work that way." Holding his son's gaze, he added, "Laws are in place for the good of society, Josiah. If you begin to dabble in unlawfulness, you destabilize the very foundation by which kingdoms are governed."

Eamonn rested his arm along the back of the settee, adopting a conciliatory tone. "There may come a time when those laws are changed or relaxed. Your uncle would have me do it unilaterally, but that is not the way our government functions, nor is it the right thing to do."

Josiah started to protest, but Eamonn cut him off. "I plan to take it up at the next Princes' Council meeting in June. There is interest, to be sure, but I don't think any of us are willing to throw away almost a thousand years of legal precedence without due consideration."

"What is there to consider?" Josiah asked, echoing Korah's words.

"The dangers of such a move. What are the consequences?" Eamonn frowned and shrugged his shoulders. "Some we know, some we fear."

Josiah grew impatient. "What is to fear from telephones? I have read about them. They seem marvelous."

Eamonn sighed, besieged on all sides, and it was not getting easier. "You are correct, but there are bigger issues at stake, aren't there?"

Josiah's dark eyebrows drew down into a confused scowl.

Eamonn rubbed his chin and decided it was best to tell him the hard truth. "It is perhaps not for my generation that I am the most concerned, but yours. The end of the age is drawing to a close, Josiah, and everything will change. Already we are seeing disturbing signs and hearing grumblings. The pews are half-empty on Sunday. People are falling away, flirting with outright rejection of the Iron King. When I was a young man, those things were rare, but now it is becoming common."

"But this is happening without technology," Josiah pressed.

Eamonn shook his head ruefully. "The mood of the people is restless. The other Princes write to tell me of the same in their own kingdoms, but it seems to have taken root here deeper than in other places."

"That is true," Josiah said with a nod. "I read a few of their signs."

"Josiah, listen to me. History validates the wisdom of the tech laws. In the Last Age, technology was used to deceive, subjugate, and isolate man. Corrupt governments and corporations controlled the minds, the very thoughts of men. They did it through guile and subterfuge, trickery. They corrupted and manipulated the people, agitating them into the final rebellion. In the end, the technology they wielded grew into an evil all its own and overtook them."

Eamonn held his son's troubled eyes. "Son, we must do everything we can to protect our kingdom and prepare for what is coming, even if they do not understand it, even if they disagree. Lucifer will not be bound forever, Josiah, and how much easier will it be for him if he has the technology at his fingertips to lead the world astray again?"

Josiah stared at Eamonn's signet ring and asked quietly, "Do you believe that? You really believe there was a Devil?"

Eamonn started a bit. "Of course, I do. Scripture is clear on that point."

"I think a lot of people don't believe that anymore. They say it's just old stories, legends, designed to scare people." Josiah looked up. "No one has seen the Iron King in two hundred years, Father. They don't believe in him anymore."

Eamonn nodded. "And therein lies the problem, Josiah. The want of technology is a symptom of a far greater disease."

He laid his hand on his son's shoulder and said, "So, now you understand why we must lead, despite popular opinion because popular opinion is often wrong. We, you and I specifically, are honor bound to rule Alanthia in righteous obedience. If we falter, then we are no better than those foolish rebels who shake their fists to Heaven and curse the Iron King. If we fail, we risk more than ourselves, we endanger the lives and souls of every Alanthian citizen."

Josiah slumped, and Eamonn recognized the burden on his young shoulders. "In the end, you must do what is right, and if you do not know, then err on the side of caution. Seek the Iron King, Josiah. He will guide you and show you what is right."

Josiah folded his hands in his lap and murmured, "That's where I am struggling, Father, because the laws restricting technology were made by man not the Iron King."

He rose from the settee without a word and left Eamonn contemplating the same thing.

May 2, 985 ME (The Beginning of the Rebellion)

Passages - Peter and Josiah

He was not supposed to be in the passageways, but seven-year-old Prince Peter ben Korah never did anything anyone told him. Well, almost anyone, but his father did not know about these places, and Peter was never going to tell him. His mother knew, but she kept it a secret.

So, it was risky, showing Josiah, but he thought about it for a long time, and decided it was the right thing to do. He crept through the narrow dark spaces, wearing his pajamas, off to what he dubbed their first Prince's Counsel.

It was late, and the Palace was in mourning, as everyone kept reminding him for two days. Mourning… everyone in black, weeping. It was terrible. He was sad Uncle Eamonn died, but the biggest impact on him seemed to be that it made everyone mean. Even the servants, who normally thought he was delightful, told him to be quiet. They refused to smile when he tried to charm them, and no one laughed at his jokes.

His nanny, Auntie G., even swatted his butt when he re-fused to wear that hideous court costume with the itchy lace cuffs. "You do not have a choice. It is required," she croaked and started sobbing again.

She stuffed him in that hot velvet suit and plunked him into a receiving line, which were the dumbest things ever, and being royal, Peter was forced to stand in all the time. It was torture, being still for hours, bowing every ten seconds until he was dizzy. Receiving lines were full of old people with bad breath, who said things like they were going to put a brick on his head because he was growing too fast. That was stupid. Even Peter knew a brick would not stop him from growing.

He bet most of those people in that receiving line did not even know Uncle Eamonn, they were just making a big deal about it. To his way of thinking, the only person who had a right to be upset was Josiah. His father died.

Peter's father pretended to be sad, but Peter could tell he was faking it. Mother said he pretended a lot, and she was right.

Peter felt a little guilty that he was not crying and carrying on like everybody else. In truth, he did not really know his uncle. Ruling Princes are busy, and Uncle Eamonn did not have time for little boys. His father certainly did not, but that was not necessarily a bad thing.

Josiah did not have time for him either, even though Peter tried really hard to get his attention. Though, Josiah was not around much anymore. He went off to the Royal Military Academy and left Peter alone with Mr. ben Merriweather. Secretly, he idolized Josiah, who at fifteen was already taller than everybody else in the family. Standing in that dreadful line today with nothing else to do, Peter noticed Josiah had grown whiskers, just like a man.

Josiah was also much better at being a royal than Peter, a good thing because Josiah was now the Ruling Prince, something Peter never wanted to be. Josiah understood all the rules of royal protocol, the etiquette, and which of the twelve forks he was supposed to eat with. But hardest of all, Josiah could use court speech.

Peter could not keep it straight and was hopeless at court language, which was even more ridiculous than receiving lines. Why they used 'thee and thou' sometimes and not others baffled him. Whenever he tried, he mixed it up and had no idea when he was supposed to add 'th' to the end of words. "It maketh absolutelyth no senseth." He giggled at his own joke.

However, his failure to grasp it was not funny. It made his father furious, but everything about him seemed to make his father mad, at least when they were alone. So, Peter did his best to avoid him.

Sometimes, like on holidays when it was just family, his cousin would spend time with him. But Josiah was older and got to do things Peter was too little for. He hated when adults said that. It was not fair. However, tonight he had a secret, and it was a big one. He thought if he shared it, maybe Josiah would hang out with him more.

When he reached the entrance to Josiah's chamber, he pressed his ear against the wainscoting to make sure his cousin was alone. Hearing nothing, he eased the panel open. Josiah did not notice him because he was perched on the edge of a window seat glaring outside. Peter could tell he was angry and almost lost his nerve, but Josiah was not nearly as scary as his father, so he brazened it out. "I can take you to see your father if you want me to. I know a secret way."

Josiah startled, going for the knife hidden on his hip. He froze when he saw Peter. "Jupiter's moon, Prince d'Or, don't sneak up on people like that!" Then in the universal manner of boys, brandished his new weapon, showing off. "I could have killed you."

"That is your father's dagger." Peter's eyes widened, hero-worship going full throttle at the sight of the gleaming blade. "Let me hold it."

Josiah gave him a reproving look and fingered the jeweled hilt. "No, you are too little."

Peter scowled. "I am not, and besides, if you want me to show you how to get to your father, you will let me see it."

Ten minutes later, Josiah reevaluated his opinion of his cousin. The sly little rascal showed him a secret passageway and led him through a labyrinth of tunnels without pausing. Peter seemed to know where he was going, while Josiah was hopelessly turned around. "Where are we?"

Peter whirled on him. "Be quiet, if my father finds out." The sentence hung as Peter shuddered. "Come on," he said and disappeared around a tight corner.

Peter's reaction gave Josiah pause. Peter was normally fearless. He would hop on a half-broken stallion without a second thought. He thrived on mischief, always trying to re-cruit Josiah into some hairbrained scheme they both knew would get them in trouble, but Peter never seemed to care.

Grief had fine-tuned his senses, and he became aware of not only what people were saying, but how they said it; more importantly, what they meant. His last couple of visits home, Josiah felt uneasy around his uncle who seemed to carry a vague aura of menace. Something lurked behind Uncle Korah's eyes that did not smile with the rest of his face, and Peter's fear of him was blatant. He filed the thought away.

The house slept, and in the dark passage only their steps disturbed the silence. His shoulders kept brushing the walls, and he had to duck several times. The narrow space made him claustrophobic, but it did not seem to bother Peter, so he kept his mouth shut. ·

He focused on the little candle Peter carried and kept walking, not sure what he was going to find. He had never seen a dead body before and was afraid it would look like the skeletons in the comics his friend at the Academy read. If it did, he was leaving.

Peter stopped outside a wooden panel that looked identi-cal to the dozen others they already passed. "This is it."

"How do you know?" Josiah asked, sharper than he in-tended.

"I am in here all the time. I know every inch of this place."

"You're weird," Josiah said and slid the panel open.

The moment he stepped inside he was hit with the strong smell of frankincense. Silver filigree incense urns fashioned after the Alanthian crown sat in the corners, pearling gray smoke, and giving the disconcerting impression that the crown was on fire. Josiah shivered.

Funeral arrangements of white lilies and roses lined the walls. The cloying scent made him gag. Oil lamps, mounted on silver sconces, sputtered and hissed. Their blue globes cast the room in winter hues of cold mist. Gooseflesh broke out on Josiah's arms, as the frigid tile chilled him through his bedroom slippers.

Peter stepped inside, and Josiah braced himself, looking toward his father's body. Lying in a gilded mahogany casket, lined with green silk, his father looked peaceful, merely asleep. Josiah experienced a rush of relief. He was not a skeleton.

But the scene, the man, the reality, felt unreal.

His mind rebelled. This could not be happening.

"Father," his voice cracked, and he glanced over his shoulder. Peter ignored him, walking to the door to keep watch. Josiah closed his eyes against the burning tears, took a shuddering, deep breath, and approached the body.

Standing at the coffin, he whispered, "I'm so scared." Then, he felt ashamed for voicing those words. His father would expect better of him. So, he started again.

"I promise, I will make you proud. I remember everything you taught me, everything: honor, duty, and sacrifice for my kingdom." He sniffed, fighting a rush of grief. He had to say this, had to get it out. "Above all, I will be obedient to the Iron King. I will do it, everything, I promise. I will put what I want, what I desire aside, and rule like you. I vow it, Father."

Silently sobbing, Josiah picked up Eamonn's hand. The weight of the kingdom rested on his young shoulders, and the greatest man he had ever known was dead. Harsh tears burned his eyes, and he let his father wipe them away, one last time.

At first, he thought the sputtering lamps were casting a blue shadow, but closer inspection turned his blood as cold as the hand he held. The long lace cuffs of his father's regal attire fell backward, revealing injuries. Flesh-colored paint rubbed off on his fingers. Josiah squinted in the dimly lit tomb. This was no shadow. A vivid band of bruising marred Eamonn's strong wrists, marks of restraint and struggle.

This was why they barred him from seeing the body, why they kept him away. His father had not died in a riding accident.

This was murder.

Blood rushed up his neck, cauterizing the grief. "Who did this to you?" Josiah croaked.

He squeezed his father's fingers, then dropped them in horror as he felt the skin begin to slip away from the body. He stumbled backward and fell into Peter.

"Someone's coming!" Peter hissed.

With a strength born of terror, Peter dragged Josiah through the hidden entrance a scant second before the door opened.

Separated from the tomb by a thin panel, they dared not move. Their single candle sputtered, and Peter prayed the sound was blending with the oil lamps inside. He cupped the open flame, afraid it might cast a shadow through the pinprick hole in the oak panel, but he could not risk the telltale smell of an extinguished wick. He turned to Josiah, wordlessly begging him to be quiet.

Ominous footsteps paced the stone tile, echoing like a death march. Peter crouched, ready to run, certain the panel would fly open any second. They were going to get caught. Josiah was feeling it. His fists were balled, and he shook all over.

Korah's low voice snaked through the panel. "Brother."

Peter closed his eyes, thinking "No, not him. Anybody but him." When he hazarded a glance at Josiah, he knew the terror he was feeling was written across his face.

"You know you deserved it, after what you did." Korah stopped pacing and waited.

Then in a voice that made Peter's stomach hurt, he screamed, "And did you think I would not find out?"

Peter jumped, hot wax dripping over his hand. He stifled a cry, sucking the burn. Josiah's face contorted into a black scowl.

"My perfect brother, Eamonn," a lifetime of envy dripped from Korah's lips, "you have no idea how tiresome that always was."

The young Princes exchanged a look of surprise. While the brothers had often disagreed, everyone thought they were close.

"You are not a saint. It is a farce, a pretext. I should know." A smile lurked behind his words, an odd pride. "But I am far better at it than you.

"I will say, you fooled everyone. Yet, I saw through you. The difference is you never saw through me. I did not let you," his voice sounded like a lover's caress, "not until the end."

Peter wanted to cover his ears, to stop the words. He did not want to hear this.

"I am done trying to be something I'm not. I am who I am, Eamonn, and I do not care who likes it. I will no longer make excuses to you, or Mother, or Alexa."

The tomb was silent for a count of three, then Korah snorted, "Ugh, don't look at me that way. I don't answer to you anymore."

The boys stiffened as Korah's insanity seeped through the wall.

"You are always so sure you're right, that you know what's best, for me and everyone else in this kingdom." Korah's words cracked like lightning. "But you know nothing!"

Peter heard him gasping, taking deep gulps of frankincense perfumed air.

Then, Korah gathered himself, his voice booming like a prosecutor in court. "You refused to reclaim what is ours, by birth, by blood, by land. Our prisons bulge with inventors and visionaries, and you put them there! You stripped the kingdom of the most brilliant minds of our age and stifled the genius that could resurrect our greatness. We were once the most industrious, powerful kingdom on Earth. It is all still here, Eamonn, buried beneath the rubble. I have seen it; I know. They bring me treasures all the time because they recognize that I am the visionary, a friend. You threw my friends in jail!"

A ragged cry ripped from Korah's chest. "You left me no choice. You should have listened to me. Why didn't you listen to me?"

Peter jumped as a sobbing Korah pounded his fist on the casket. It sounded like thunder.

"It does not matter now. Do you hear me? It does not matter." He cleared his throat, and the tears seemed to dry up.

"I will be the great emancipator. I will set the captives free and usher in a new age." His voice rang with vehement pride. "I have big plans and thanks to your," he scoffed, "sacrifice, I now have access to power greater than you ever dreamed. I will use that power, Brother, and restore Alanthia to its former glory. It is our duty; one you failed to understand or were too much of a coward to embrace. You were paralyzed."

The tomb grew quiet, only the convulsive clearing of Korah's throat indicated he was still with the body.

"I did what had to be done." He laughed, a breathless sound, without humor. "Honestly, I always have. You were just too stupid to see."

The taunt crawled over Josiah's skin like a spider. Peter covered his eyes, tears streaming down his cheeks.

"You think not?" Korah made a sound of disgust. "I took care of your wife." He spat the word like a hateful epithet. "Margaret—so young, so beautiful—so dead. Do you really think that was an accident?"

Peter smothered Josiah's outraged gasp, digging stubby fingers into his face. His mother! Korah was talking about his mother! *What?* Josiah's knuckles turned white. At some point during his uncle's diatribe, he unsheathed the knife.

He wanted to bust into the room and start slashing, but the abject terror emanating from Peter kept him still, kept him silent.

"I regret that I did not do it sooner; before she was bred and birthed. No matter, I shall take care of him as well," Korah said.

The callous words rang with such promise they chilled Josiah to the bone. The implications were horrifying.

"It is only fair," Korah added with a desolate note. The restless pacing stopped, and they heard Korah weeping. The sound was old and hollow, as if it came out of the darkest part of hell.

"I wish it didn't have to be this way." Footsteps moved toward the door as Korah delivered a tearful private farewell. "Goodbye, Brother. I love you, and I am sorry."

The door closed with a quiet click.

Josiah squeezed the knife, cursing himself as a coward, shaking with rage.

Peter threw the candle aside and climbed him like a monkey. Gripping the sides of his face, he brought them nose to nose. "If you want to live another day, follow me."

It took everything inside Peter not to run, not to pound through the passageways heedless of the noise. He knew what his father was capable of. His mother tried to hide it from him, but Peter knew. He had seen it, and now, he had heard it.

As they raced through the passageway, part of Josiah refused to believe what he had heard. He could not process it. His uncle was a maniac. He was behind his mother and father's murders. And if it were just Korah, he would fight, but there had to be other people involved. He obviously had help. He could not have staged his father's death alone. Someone put makeup on his father's wrists. Someone put his body in that field. Josiah knew Korah was with Aunt Alexa when they found the body, and he knew she was not involved, knew it. But who did this?

Josiah had no idea.

In the darkness, Josiah came to the stark realization that he could not trust anyone. If he picked the wrong person, he was as good as dead, like his mother, and now his father. His father, the bravest, smartest man he ever knew, had fallen to this conspiracy. Josiah did not doubt that he faced the same deadly fate. So, he ran. He ran after the bouncing candle his little cousin carried and prayed for wisdom.

As he ducked around the last corner, he knew there was only one place to go. There was only one who was incorruptible, only one who would avenge his father's death—the Iron King.

Alexa often awoke with her son crawling into her bed no matter how many nights she admonished him to stay in his own. She secretly cherished his evening visits, not minding that he took up the entire bed or that he kicked, thrashed, and slept sideways. She was neither startled nor surprised to hear the panel open but sat straight up when she heard the panic in his voice.

"Mother, wake up! Father is going to kill Josiah."

Her head jerked around, scanning the room, bracing herself, prepared for attack. "Where is he?" Whether she referred to Josiah or Korah, it did not matter. She feared this day was coming, and Princess Alexa ben Seamus was no fool. She was prepared.

Peter's urgent whisper cut through the night air; his face illuminated like a death mask above the candle. "I do not know where Father is, but Josiah is here." He jerked his cousin forward. "We must help him!"

Alexa rolled out of bed and hissed, "Peter, wake Auntie G. just like we practiced. Go!"

Spring 985 ME (The Rebellion Begins)

Death of a Prince - Korah

Perpetuated by the scandal papers, wild rumors began to circulate about the mysterious disappearance of Prince Josiah on the eve of Prince Eamonn's funeral. Anonymous Palace sources claimed the young Prince was a spoiled tyrant whose moods vacillated between morose withdrawal to fits of rage. Purported to be a violent, disturbed young man, born of privilege, and pampered by an indulgent father, the picture that emerged was damning.

The public started wondering if Eamonn's death was an accident. Vocal critics of the royal family and gossip mongers openly speculated that Josiah was the culprit. They put forth the theory that he snapped during a psychotic episode and killed his father.

Two weeks after Eamonn's funeral, Korah condescended to an interview with well-respected journalist, Ebenezer ben James.

Ushered into the Prince's study by a whey-faced servant, Ebenezer felt a somber heaviness come over him. It shrouded the Palace and hung in the air, which felt unnaturally cold, even menacing. Prince Korah sat in a chenille armchair, dressed in mourning, a black armband on his right sleeve. His normally handsome face bore signs of strain, and dark circles shadowed his eyes.

Ebenezer bowed to the Prince and said, "Good morning, my Esteemed. Thank you for agreeing to speak with me today."

"Of course, Ebenezer." Korah gestured to a matching armchair, inviting Ebenezer to sit. "You and I have always enjoyed an excellent relationship. So, if I was going to speak with the press, I wanted it to be you."

Ebenezer felt a flush of pleasure at the words. Looking down at his notes, he mentally shifted from combative to conciliatory. After all, the Prince had just buried his brother and was obviously in deep mourning.

At the end of the heart wrenching interview, Ebenezer had a new respect for Prince Korah and the scoop of a lifetime. He could hardly believe the story he just heard, too terrible, too tragic.

Though it clearly pained the Prince, Korah revealed the royal family's darkest secret. The rumors were partially true. Josiah had indeed been a deeply troubled young man, but he had not killed his father. The evidence was clear, Eamonn died in a riding accident. But the sad fact was, Josiah, distraught over the loss of his father and overwhelmed by the responsibilities thrust upon him, took his own life.

That was when Korah broke down, his red-rimmed eyes swimming with unshed tears. "We tried to help him, we truly did. Eamonn would not permit doctors to examine him, fearing it would taint Josiah's ability to rule one day. So, he let him suffer. He let us all suffer as we watched Josiah go deeper and deeper into depression. When Eamonn died, Josiah just broke. It was the final blow."

"Perhaps he ran away? What makes you suspect suicide?"

Korah looked away, covering his eyes with a shaky hand. "We found a note, Ebenezer. He left us a suicide note." Korah cleared his throat and added, "The Bureau has it."

As Ebenezer departed, Korah said, "On the heels of Eamonn's tragic accident, please ask Alanthians to bear with us," he faltered, and choked out the last, "as we grieve."

Ebenezer rode straight to Bureau Director Nabal's office. After presenting his credentials and a note signed by Prince Korah himself, they ushered him inside.

"Our office is, of course, conducting a thorough investigation." Director Nabal looked grave. "But I fear, as with Prince Eamonn's death, this is pretty cut and dried. Handwriting experts have confirmed, the suicide note is Prince Josiah's."

"But there is no body," Ebenezer pressed, desperate to get this story to print but cautious to gather all the facts.

"True." Director Nabal pressed his lips into a firm line

and looked down, deep furrows of regret etched on his thin face. "Unfortunately, there is overwhelming evidence that supports our suspicions."

Nabal passed a thick folder across his desk. "Some of that is off the record," he said and rubbed his forehead wearily. "Let us try to preserve a bit of the young Prince's dignity. I would hate to have this used as fodder in the press."

Nabal knew damn well Ebenezer was going to publish every salacious bit of information contained in that report. And he did.

The revelation rocked the kingdom.

There were naysayers. Conspiracy theories popped up like toadstools, many focused on the question, where was the dog? Why would a young man, intent on suicide, take his dog?

The official explanation was that the Prince had been a disturbed young man who carried his dog with him when he leapt to his death from the Golden Gate Bridge reconstruction site. Ebenezer ben James uncovered two witnesses who confirmed they had seen a teenage boy matching Prince Josiah's description with a dog near the bridge that fateful night.

No one noticed Mr. ben Merriweather had also disappeared, except Peter.

Autumn 985 ME (Four months into Rebellion)

The Great Persuader - Korah

Four months after Eamonn's funeral, a court declared Prince Josiah ben Eamonn dead, and Prince Korah ben Adam the rightful heir to the Alanthian throne. The evidence and bad publicity surrounding the young Prince's death ensured the public had no appetite to continue investigating the matter. They were content to let Eamonn's line rest in peace.

In celebration, Korah embarked on a grand tour. Fair of face, elegant of dress, and oh, so dashing, he charmed his way into the hearts and minds of the kingdom. Alanthians turned out by the thousands to hear him speak and catch a glimpse of the new royal family.

They loved Princess Alexa, who personified loveliness and grace. Always dressed at the height of fashion, she exuded class. Soft-spoken and demure, the elegant Princess became a source of national pride. Her pale complexion was flawless, her makeup perfect. Several weeks before Korah's formal coronation, she shocked the world by cutting off her glorious mane of red hair. A master stylist created a thoroughly modern style, and the shoulder length layered cut became all the rage. Thousands of Alanthian women showed up at their salons demanding 'Alexa Hair.'

Young Peter, they adored. A tad irreverent, with a smile that lit up the sky, the rascal became everyone's favorite royal. Even at seven, he exuded his father's quick wit and charm. Thousands of little girls fell hopelessly in love with him, imagining that one day they would grow up and marry the handsome Prince.

Prince Korah doted on them, in public.

A gifted orator, he mesmerized the frenzied crowds. "Look at this image, ladies and gentlemen," he said, gesturing to a huge backdrop of a happy family, driving a 1950s style car. "What can be wrong with that?"

The crowd shouted back, "Nothing."

Korah smiled and met the eyes of an eager young man. "The laws prohibiting that are archaic, written by men weary of war who lost their faith in men's ability to govern themselves. I ask you, are we like those people in the Last Age?"

"No!" roared the crowd.

He opened his arms. "Alanthians are good, honorable people. For almost one thousand years, we have proven that. We do not seek rebellion; we seek freedom!"

"Freedom, freedom, freedom," chanted the crowd.

"But there are those who are against us, who see dark clouds on the horizon. These self-proclaimed doomsday prophets say we are bringing about the end of the world."

He pointed his thumb over his shoulder to the wholesome family. "Yeah, they're scary. I'm afraid. How about you?"

The crowd laughed.

"We have a choice, Alanthia, and we have a chance. We can prove to the world that times have changed, that men can wield technology for the good of all. I ask you, how is that rebellion? How are dreams rebellion?"

Loud grumbles came from the crowd.

"I say to you this day, it is not. No, it's not!"

"No, it's not. No, it's not." They echoed back at him.

Behind the podium, unseen by human eyes, an evil entity smiled.

October 1, 985 ME (Six Months into Rebellion)

Silly Monkey

"Would you like to go for a walk?" Alexa asked from Peter's doorway.

He looked up from his schoolbook with such profound relief that she pressed a fist over her mouth to keep from laughing. "Yes," he said with a decisive slam of the text.

She held out her hand, and when he stood, she realized he was going through another growth spurt. The top of his head almost reached her shoulder. He would be taller than her before she knew it.

The Palace was quiet. Korah was away, giving a speech in Los Angeles, and would not be back for a couple of days. As they moved through the gleaming hallways with their perfect plasterwork, tasteful decor, and modern art, she felt a pang of discontent, which was ironic because she was the decorator. She was also the one who instigated the move to the New City Palace and pushed Korah to relocate. Drawn by the modern conveniences and easy access to the city, she brought them here.

But she missed Gilead, the ancient Palace of the Princes. It was where Peter was born, where she and Korah had lived, before everything fell apart.

Gilead had a solidness about it, a soul, and a history. Its chipped plasterwork told a thousand stories. The ancient weapons hanging on the walls were handled by the noble Princes of old. Faded rugs were gifts from faraway lands, brought by ships, sent by friends from long ago. The rooms knew generations of love, witnessed births and deaths of the Alanthian royal family. The ballroom hosted hundreds of parties, and she imagined the faint echo of banter and laughter still rang inside the gilded walls.

The New City Palace, well, it had none of that charm and had seen more heartache than laughter. The shell was truly ancient, a sprawling manor from the Last Age, but the royal family abandoned it in 90 ME when construction on Gilead was complete. It had fallen into complete ruin until the mid-970s when Eamonn began renovations. During its reconstruction, large sections were sealed off, buried underground. The renovations had the effect of creating a new space, and no sense of history remained in these gleaming hallways. Though, she thought with some asperity, the spirit of the Last Age lingered here.

Perhaps she was simply melancholy. The walls felt like they were closing in, which prompted her to seek out Peter.

"Where are we going?" Peter asked as they stepped outside.

The corner of her lip lifted. "The gardens or the stables?"

He grinned, looking just like her. "You like the gardens."

"Perhaps we will do both." She ruffled his hair. It needed to be cut. It hung over his collar and covered his ears, thick and a bit unruly, like Korah's.

"We can visit the gardens, Mother."

She tilted her head, studying him. "That's nice of you."

He shrugged. "Anything to get me out of memorizing my multiplication tables."

She swung his hand as they walked and said softly, "You'll get them. It will come."

He looked up at her, crossed his eyes, and stuck out his tongue.

Alexa giggled. "Silly monkey."

He made the face again.

So, she tickled his ribs, making monkey sounds.

He shrieked and tickled her back.

She twisted away, her yellow skirt flashing around her ankles. Their light-hearted laughter echoed across the vast lawn as she scampered away. "You can't catch me!"

"Oh, yes I can!"

And he did. It was the first time he beat her in a foot race.

Winded, she sat down on the stone bench at the center of the garden. "It's these shoes." She held up her pale-yellow silk flats. "Nobody can run in these."

"Girl shoes," he said succinctly and plopped down beside her. His face was slightly flushed, but he was not nearly as out of breath as she was. His feet swung off the bench, but they would not for long.

The grand fountain came on. One of the servants must have seen them enter the garden.

"Speaking of girls." She gave him a teasing look. "I saw the steward today. He told me that more than a hundred letters have arrived for you, just this week."

Peter grimaced. "Mother..."

She bumped his shoulder. "They are all in love with you."

"They send me letters with hearts and all sorts of mushy stuff." He made a face. "That is weird."

"Little girls are like that. They like boys long before boys like them." Alexa smiled wistfully, staring at the Prussian blue sky.

"Like you and Father?" Peter gave her a sidelong glance.

A hollow laugh came out her nose. "Yes, I suppose so. However, relationships between boys and girls can vary. For instance, between you and me, things are different, aren't they?"

He narrowed his brows and looked up at her considering, then broke into a grin. His seven-year-old teeth were slightly too big for his face, but the smile had the potential to become a devastating weapon one day. "I suppose so."

"That is my number one job, to be your mommy." She needed to make sure he understood this. She needed to tell him. "To love you, to be there for you, to keep you safe."

He groaned and rolled his eyes. "Now you are getting all mushy. Girls are weird."

But he let her hug him, and she knew he heard her. Boys...

October 23, 985 ME (Six Months into Rebellion)

Monsters Under My Bed - Alexa

The evening of the Coronation Ball, Princess Alexa lay still and quiet in her room, exhausted after endless hours of being on display. The ball was a resounding success, a triumph. The crush of the party and the long day made her body flutter with the queer combination of too little food, and too much red wine and stress. The relentless firing of adrenaline refused to abate, even though it was over. The farce was complete. Korah was officially on the throne.

She smiled through it all, and it was not entirely fake. A part of her was so proud of Korah, the other part, utterly repelled. She loved him, and she despised him. He drew her in, and then he destroyed her. Yet she stayed, she tried, and she hoped.

Tonight, for a few moments, the scales fell away, the malignant madness lifted, and there he was—her Korah. He looked at her with clear hazel eyes, so beautiful, so smart. And she saw the real him, her husband, witty, funny, and vulnerable; precious Korah.

To open the ball, he chose a sad and haunting tune. As they began to dance, the world fell away. It was just them; Korah and Alexa in each other's arms.

"I do love you, Alexa," he whispered as the first notes of the violin played.

They performed in front of the Kingdom, swirling on the parquet floor. As they danced, nothing else seemed to matter because he was there. Those glimmers, those brief seconds, they held her heart, tied her to his side. She did love him, heaven help her.

Lost in the memory of the dance, lost in his clear hazel eyes, she hoped he would come, the man she loved. She felt a presence in her room, but it was not her husband.

"Mother?" Peter scrambled into bed, burrowing under the covers with jerky little movements.

She tried to suppress her disappointment; it had been so long. She made a soft drowsy sound, feigning sleep, avoiding talk.

He cupped his hands around her ear and whispered, "I think there is a monster in the house. It smells like rotten eggs, and it is hunting."

His words acted like a jet of water, obliterating the tender web of fantasy she had been spinning, a fragile fairytale, a lie. Because, as handsome as the Prince might be, he was no hero. He had made a deal with a devil and invited him in. She knew it, and now, so did her son.

God help them.

May 16, 986 ME (One Year into the Rebellion)

You Don't Sound Like a Pilgrim to Me - Macedonia - Josiah

Appearances were deceiving. A cheery blue farmhouse and a young man traveling with a dog, neither were what they appeared to be on the surface. The farmhouse was a prison, and the young man was not an ordinary pilgrim. Josiah cursed himself for his stupidity, cursed his tongue for speaking an injudicious word, and cursed the hard-core revolutionary, who drugged him, and threw him in a locked room.

Ransom, he was being held for ransom. However, Josiah refused to tell Yane ben Sandanski his name, so the maniac had no idea where to send the demand. A ransom note would get him killed. If word reached his uncle that he was still alive, it was tantamount to a death sentence, which was why he wrote that fake suicide note before he escaped.

For two days, he steadfastly repeated the cover story he used since he left the Palace. "My name is Einar ben Galah. I am an orphan on pilgrimage. Our community in the Alanthian south was devastated by drought, so I left with my people. We were separated a week ago when brigands attacked our party. I escaped and am making my way back to the pilgrim road where I hope to rejoin them and continue my journey."

The story worked for over a year, bought him aid and succor, earned him sympathy, and a warm place to sleep when the weather became inclement, but it had not worked on the fire-breathing revolutionary holding him prisoner.

He should have never come to this place, should have run the moment he saw the odd gleam in Yane ben Sandanski's eyes. But he had become arrogant in his cover story, comfortable in the subterfuge, and did not recognize the danger.

"My people," came the gravelly voice outside the sturdy door. "I can always spot one of you. That stinking royal blood makes you move in a certain way; makes you speak with a forked tongue. I know you are lying to me. Only a royal would refer to his fellow travelers as 'my people', and only a snot-nosed royal says brigands. Besides, this dog ain't no ordinary mutt."

"Give me my dog!" Josiah demanded.

"You ain't in no position to be issuing orders," Sandanski barked. "I'll keep him alive, but you gotta tell me who you are."

Josiah repeated his story.

"You are a liar. You know how else I know? This dagger." Blood rushed to Josiah's face, imagining the man handling his father's weapon. "It's ancient, and I have a hard time believing that a farm kid would have such a thing."

Josiah heard the legs of the wooden chair scrape across the floor as the man settled in.

"Let me tell you why I hate the royals, so you might begin to understand. I will never let you go, not until you tell me who you are, boy."

Josiah groaned. When the man started ranting, he never shut up. Fifty days shy of completing his journey to the Golden City, he was trapped. Laying on a narrow cot, he covered his head with a pillow and tried to drown out his captor's voice that droned on long into the night.

November 6, 986 ME (Twenty Months into Rebellion)

Fallout - Korah and Alexa

Less than a year after Korah took the throne, he won. The ban was lifted, the tech laws repealed. Korah organized a rally for his supporters and declared a national holiday. Millions across the kingdom joined in the festivities.

However, there was a price to pay.

Not everyone was onboard. Anti-technology terrorists and religious zealots exploded bombs inside and out of the capitol building the night the ban was lifted. Fire and rubble rained down on the New City streets. Hundreds were killed in the week of rioting that rocked the kingdom.

Even after the police put down the violence, tensions mounted. Citizens argued in their houses, their churches, and favorite bars. The old versus the young, the faithful against the faithless, battle lines were drawn across Alanthia.

"Did you see this?" Alexa threw a paper across the breakfast table at Korah. The headline read:

'Storm Clouds Gather - No Rain'

"That article says rainfall is down over one hundred inches in the last year and a half." Alexa gave Korah a pointed look and shook her head. "The south is drying up. People are beginning to starve, most of them are leaving. Korah, you know this is a judgment. You know this is punishment."

Korah pushed the paper back at her. "Let them go. Most of them are against what we are trying to do, anyway."

"No! These are good, honest, hardworking people. They see what is happening." She pointed to the figures. A startling number of refugees were taking to the pilgrim roads, fleeing Alanthia on their way to the Golden Kingdom.

He gave it a cursory glance and continued eating his breakfast.

"We are not much better off here. Have you looked outside?"

Korah slammed his orange juice glass down, making her jump. "Let the Iron King try. It won't work on us." He gave a rueful shake of his head. "One decent thing my father did was prepare for such a contingency. Do you think that desalination project he contracted to Lenox was for cattle?" He shot her a scornful look. "As we speak, they are firing it up. I am not stupid, Alexa. I knew this might happen."

"You are treading a dangerous path, Korah. By ignoring the Princes' Council and severing diplomatic ties with the Golden Kingdom, you have put Alanthia on a collision course."

"Pft." Korah rose from the table and straightened his jacket. "Publicly the Princes might be saying that, but mark my words, privately they feel differently. They are watching, hedging their position. Alanthians are not the only ones who want the freedom to pursue a revitalized new world. We get letters every day from across the globe. People want this. I just happen to be the only Ruling Prince, smart enough and audacious enough, to go after it.

"For every one of them," he jabbed his finger on the newspaper story, "two are immigrating. The press is calling them

New City pilgrims." He glared down at her with a haughty expression. "I know what I'm doing, Alexa."

"What you are doing is divisive. There is a crack right down the center of Alanthia. I get letters, too. This will not end well."

Two days later, on the evening of November 8, 986 ME, anti-technology terrorists breached the Palace walls and launched an attack.

When the smoke cleared, a maidservant discovered Princess Alexa, beaten to death in her bedchamber.

November 12, 986 ME

Spinning - New City, Alanthia - Peter

Peter sat in his bedroom, alone. He was still dressed in his funeral suit, still wore the lace cuffs, still had the red sash draped across his chest. He could not move. He could not breathe. She was gone.

His mother was dead.

Like they had done to Josiah, they kept him from the body. However, he did not want to see her. He knew what she looked like. He had seen it happen.

There was no need to sneak through the passageways. There was no place in this house he wanted to go, and now, no place to hide. If he used the passageways, he would reveal that he knew about them, and one day he might need them.

He should have shown her. He should have made her explore with him. He should have protected her, but he had not, and it was too late. It was too late to insist they leave. It was too late to escape. They had given their escape to Josiah and now… she was dead.

He endured the funeral today without saying much, accepting condolences with his head bowed. No one forced him to talk. Even his father left him alone.

After the first hymn, before they began their speeches, he surprised everyone when he left the front pew and walked to her casket. He knew they were watching him, but he did not care. The casket was closed. The white wood felt cold under his hand, smooth, and so final. A spray of yellow roses lay on the lid. She liked yellow flowers. He planted some when he was little, right outside her window.

He did not speak the words aloud. She could not hear him in that thing. "I love you. You were a good mother. I am so sorry. I should have stopped him. I should have done something."

He closed his eyes and leaned his head back. They thought he was praying. He was not. "I promise, he will pay for what he did to you."

He waited. He waited for the Iron King to speak. He waited for a booming voice to come from the sky and condemn his father.

He waited.

Under the watchful eyes of the entire kingdom, he waited.

He blinked at the paintings of the Iron King on the ceiling. "Where are you? Why are you silent? She is dead! Why?"

Nothing happened. No one made a sound.

Standing at the front of the cathedral, with his hand resting on his mother's casket, the answer became clear. Like the Prince of Egypt, his father had been rejected, judged, and with him the entire kingdom. As Korah's son, he was abandoned, rejected, damned.

When he opened his eyes, the look that passed between father and son cemented the course of their relationship ever after.

Peter walked back to the pew with his head held high, meeting the pitying looks of the mourners. He memorized their faces. He memorized the moment and scanned the crowd. If the Iron King was not coming, perhaps there was another, one last hope.

He waited for Josiah.

He watched for him. Prayed that the doors to the church were going to burst open. He listened for the declaration that would name his father a murderer and Josiah the rightful ruler.

He waited for someone. Anyone.

He waited for deliverance—that did not come.

Josiah was not here. He was probably dead, buried in some unmarked grave between here and the Golden Kingdom. He had not escaped. Sitting on that hard pew, with hot tears burning his eyes, Peter suspected he would not either.

Speaker after speaker talked about his mother, but they talked about a stranger. They talked about her as a young girl or as the Princess. He did not know that person. She was Mommy, and she was gone.

He wanted to wail, but Princes did not cry in public, so he sat there, choking on the gurgling knot lodged in his throat. And later, he hated himself because on the way to the cemetery, when it was just him and his father in the state carriage, the knot broke free, and he cried. Worse than the tears, Korah hugged him, and they wept together. He clung to his father in devastated desperation, drowning in pain. Grief engulfed them. It was more horrible than the funeral, because Korah genuinely wept, too.

Alone in his room, full of self-loathing, and hurting so bad he wanted to die, he picked at the lace cuff.

"Poor, sad, little Prince," said a guttural voice out of the ether.

Abject terror animated Peter's limbs. He scrambled and dove, hiding under his bed. "Go away!"

An evil laugh filled his bedroom, reverberating with wickedness beyond the ages, a sound straight out of Hell. Every hair on his body stood on end, and electric jolts of fear shot down his spine.

"I'm not going anywhere, Peter. I am an invited guest. I have a right to be here."

"Leave me alone!" Peter pressed his fist to his mouth, trying not to whimper.

"Leave you alone? Oh, no, Peter, you belong to me now," it growled.

Peter wanted to scream, but fear strangled his vocal cords, and all he managed was a squeaky, "Help."

"No one is going to help you. Alexa is gone. You need to accept this is the way things are. You will learn." He laughed, low and diabolically evil. "We can be friends. Then you will love me. You will call me Master, young Prince."

A snake of cold terror slithered down Peter's spine, and he buried his face in his hands, shaking uncontrollably.

"I have great plans for you. Now, come out, so we can begin."

An invisible force dragged Peter, kicking and squirming from beneath his bed. The wool carpet peeled away the royal sash. "No!" he shouted, clawing at the carpet, trying to escape, but his dress shoes found no purchase, and his suit coat twisted around his torso, restricting his arms.

"Stop!"

Peter felt invisible bands lash his body. He lay frozen on the floor, trussed up like a mummy.

"How about a little game, Prince?" the evil entity taunted. "Would you like to go for a spin?"

Peter squeezed his eyes shut and tried not to cry. He tried not to show the monster he was afraid.

"Little boys like to play with tops, don't they? Would you like to *be* a top, Peter?"

His feet lifted into the air. They rose until he hung suspended upside down with his hair brushing the rug.

Then, he spun.

He spun until he vomited. He spun until he had an accident in his suit. He spun until the monster got tired of spinning him and threw him up against the wall. In a puddle of stinking urine and puke, he closed his eyes and covered his head, but that made the dizziness worse. The room kept revolving like everything was caught in a tornado. Peter could not stop spinning.

A dark shadow fell over him, blotting out all the light. The horrible rotten egg smell choked him. His legs and thighs burned with the acid of his own body. He cracked his head when it hit the wall and felt a trickle of blood running down his neck. Out of the black mist, the monster showed itself, and then Peter knew he was going to die.

March 987 ME (Two Years into Rebellion)

A New King

Princess Alexa's murder sparked a powder keg. Two weeks after she died, the kingdom exploded into civil war. It was short, bloody, and devastating. The rebels were crushed with brutal efficiency, thousands died. From the government's perspective, the war accomplished its goal. It purged the kingdom of naysayers.

Glorying in their triumph, a movement was born, Alanthians called for a new king and a disbanding of the outdated federal legislature. Under mounting public pressure, Korah accepted the elevated title, heretofore reserved for one. It was the severing blow, solidifying Alanthia's rebellion. They were on their own, charting their future without the Iron King.

In his new role, King Korah beat back the opponents of progress, annihilated the religious zealots, and silenced anyone who dared stand against him. A self-styled champion of the oppressed, he became the oppressor. He exerted immense control over the press. And just as his critics predicted, launched kingdom wide surveillance to ferret out dissidents. Those who spoke out quietly disappeared.

Across the vast kingdom, Alanthians reaped the harvest planted in rebellion. Animals began to hunt and kill, reverting to the curse. Crops failed, as farmers faced a new reality, battling weather, weed, and pestilence. Violent altercations sprang up between neighbors and villages. Murder, rape, and violent crime skyrocketed.

The justice system was overrun, becoming incompetent and callous. The accused and victims alike suffered from corruption and injustice.

Sickness returned. Hospital wards were full of mothers fretting over their children, and families grieved the bitter tears of lives cut short.

For one thousand years, Alanthians lived in paradise, heaven on Earth, but in rebellion everything changed.

Guided by an unseen hand, Korah directed crews to excavate the treasure trove of ruins buried in the Last Age. Wondrous new discoveries filled the daily papers. Public and private money poured into development and revitalization. People got rich.

As time wore on, Alanthia took on shocking similarities to America in the Last Days. And on the surface, they became the envy of the world—again.

May 20, 988 ME (Three Years into Rebellion)

Mad Dash - New City, Alanthia - Peter

"*Dio mio!*" Peter's nanny, Genevieve ben Willard, exclaimed when she found him lying on the library floor. "*Il mio piccolino*, what has happened to you?"

Peter cracked a swollen eye. He must look bad if she was speaking Italian. She only did that when she was really upset. "I got my report card."

"That filthy cock-sucking son of a whore!"

His lip was split, but he laughed anyway. "Sorry, Auntie G., that is funny."

"Look at you!" She got down on her knees but did not touch him. Her hands fluttered over his various injuries as if she did not know where to start. She settled on his face, wiping the blood from his nose.

Her gentle touch felt nice. He closed his eyes and hugged his left arm gingerly to his chest. "I should have studied harder. They are never going to let me in the Royal Military Academy with my grades."

"You are eleven-years-old and at least three years away from the RMA," she protested. "Besides, they have to let you in." He could tell she was furious, but she tried to keep her voice calm, soothing. "Don't think about that right now. Tell me, where are you hurt?"

Her voice shook, but thankfully she did not stop stroking him. It had been a long time since anyone touched him in anything other than anger. He did not want her to stop. "Auntie, I think my arm is broken. I fell."

"He hit you."

Peter cleared the blood pooling in the back of his throat. Usually he could hide the injuries, usually no one knew. "Yeah," he confessed thickly and was mortified to feel tears rolling down his cheeks.

Auntie G. took him to the hospital. She did not call the Palace doctors like she was supposed to. A week later, Korah dismissed her.

Lieutenant - The Great Pilgrim Road, Greece - Josiah

"Lui!" Sergeant Reuben ben Judah, of the Iron King's Army, shouted over his shoulder to the newly minted First Lieutenant Einar ben Yane. "We got another one, over here."

"Alive?" answered Josiah.

"Yes, I believe this is true." Reuben pressed his ear to the boy's chest. "Yes, there is a heartbeat."

Josiah abandoned the corpse of the young woman he had been examining, no hope for her. Scooping up his field medical bag, he ran across the smoldering pilgrim camp.

"Loosen his collar. Bloody hell, he is choking." Josiah dug his finger in the boy's slack mouth, feeling for an obstruction—nothing. He was young, no more than seven or eight, small boned. Josiah pulled him onto his lap and pounded his back hard with the flat of his hand. One. Two. Three.

Breathe, dammit. Four. Five.

Life—sputtering, gasping—life.

The child coughed and spit. His small hands went to his throat by reflex, then he vomited what looked like stew all over Josiah's lap. Josiah gently eased him into a sitting position, speaking in low, reassuring tones.

"Choking? He was choking? How did you know this?" Sergeant ben Judah asked with an incredulous edge to his voice.

"He turned blue," Josiah answered simply, checking the boy's pupils for signs of brain damage.

"But the whole camp, this was the work of bandits." He gestured around the pillaged ruins. Then he furrowed his brows, studying Josiah, truly looking at him for the first time.

"I just knew." Josiah shrugged, satisfied the boy was okay. But then he noticed the boy's horrified expression. He knew that look. He knew the feeling behind that look. Glancing over his shoulder, he saw the body. "Your father?"

The little boy nodded mutely.

Josiah moistened his lips and stared up at the Sergeant. Until that moment, Reuben ben Judah had dismissed him, thinking him another young officer in his way, a hindrance rather than a help. Officers came and went from this small platoon. The work here was not glamorous. They patrolled the bandit infested pilgrim roads running through Greece.

Josiah watched the Sergeant reevaluate him. Good. He should, because First Lieutenant Einar ben Yane of the Iron King's Fourth Dragoons was nothing like he first appeared.

Sergeant ben Judah glanced around at the scattered bodies. His face darkened. As they held each other's eyes, an understanding passed between them, a vow.

Josiah rose, lifting the boy in his arms, carrying him away from the sight of his murdered father. "We will find who did this, son. Sergeant Reuben ben Judah and I will find them, and when we do, we are going to kill them.

Part 2 - The Princes

January 6, 997 ME (Eleven Years into Rebellion)

The Contract – New City, Alanthia – Peter

Peter did not bother to hide the revulsion on his face as he slid the contract across Korah's desk. "You are delusional if you think I am signing that."

Korah raised a cool eyebrow. "You have no choice."

"About the woman I marry?" Peter laughed in scornful dismissal. "Oh, happy nineteenth birthday, Peter."

"Did I forget? Sorry. Happy birthday."

"I am not marrying her."

"Now which of us is delusional? Did you honestly think you were going to be allowed to choose your bride for love? That is not the way things are done. Do you think my parents loved each other?" Korah scoffed. "Do you think I chose your mother or Eamonn chose Margaret? Do not be ridiculous." He pushed the betrothal contract back across the desk. "Sign it. It has been negotiated."

"Have you met her?" Peter was aghast. Even for Korah, this was over the top.

Korah rolled his eyes, conveying how stupid he thought the question was. "Yes, of course. Why do you think I have taken two trips to Cairo in the last six months?"

"She is abominable."

"I think she is delightful."

"Then you marry her," Peter retorted.

"Impudent." Korah smashed his fist on the desk and rose in a temper. "There is a price to pay, Peter, for your fancy cars, and your clothes, and your money. There is a cost," he screamed.

Usually, there would be fists. Usually this type of outburst would be accompanied by a beating, but the Royal Military Academy had taught him more than military strategy. Prince Peter ben Korah was done being beaten, and he was done living under the thumb of this madman. "Oh, and what might that cost be, Father?"

"I will have your obedience, in this, and all matters." Korah said with deadly menace. Gone was the charming monarch, gone was the veneer of bored cynicism. The beast manifested in plain sight.

Peter blinked, refusing to back down. "I will not. I will not sign that contract. I will not marry that bitch. I do not care what you say, or what you do."

"Full of yourself, aren't you?" Korah spoke each word softly. "Do you honestly think I cannot break you?"

A cold chill came over the room. The putrid smell of sulfur filled his nose. He moistened his lips and tried to stand his ground, but his knees began to shake. He felt the evil presence behind him. "Damn you."

The corner of Korah's mouth lifted as he watched his son bound and dragged away.

June 30, 997 ME (Twelve Years into the Rebellion)

The Dungeon - New City, Alanthia - Peter

The black silk robe puddled around his elbow as Peter pressed a series of figures on a carved door, disengaging the lock. The irony that the most technically advanced house on the planet had a door locked with a medieval mechanism did not escape him, but it was appropriate for what lay behind it. The heavy wooden door swung open on well-oiled hinges, bringing the smell of fear, blood, and sulfur. His stomach flipped, and he shuddered in familiar horror. He cleared his throat convulsively and descended the steps into the bowels of hell.

They summoned him, and six months ago they taught him the dire and degrading consequences of ignoring such a missive. Down there, there was no choice, no hope, no escape. He lived the life of a royal prisoner, trapped. He pretended they broke him, pretended to be compliant. Now, he played a dangerous game, biding his time, acting a role.

After years of covert searching, he finally had confirmation; Josiah was still alive. He had survived. Both Princes had survived, and this fact changed everything.

Now, there was hope.

Now, there was a chance.

Now, there was a plan.

He had signed that damned contract. It bound him, at least on paper, to Princess Keyseelough ben Mubarak of Egypt. The day they announced it, bells rang throughout the kingdom. The Palace organized a week of festivities to mark the auspicious occasion. They spared no expense. Not since Korah's coronation had the New City Palace celebrated with such vigor, hosting dignitaries by day, and black mass by night.

Which was where Peter was headed, ordered to participate in the vile rituals his father and his betrothed thrived upon. They did it to appease the evil entity that stalked the Palace halls, the Dark Master, they called him. Peter simply referred to him as the monster.

They were searching for something. He did not know what. He did not care. He tried to dissociate when he was down here, to separate mind from body, to hide. Prince Peter ben Korah knew how to play their game, knew how to protect himself. They thought the drugs they pumped into him were enslaving him, they were wrong. In the mist, he was free.

He heard her voice, Keyseelough, the Hell Bitch. She was as wicked as Korah. Outwardly, she was beautiful, a sultry eyed Princess, robed in exotic silks, bedecked in jewels. Haughty and serene, the press waxed poetic about her honey-eyed voice and mysterious aura. However, appearances were deceiving. She was a witch, a spoiled, evil tempered, feces eating, horse-fucking, succubus. He never imagined he could despise anyone more than his father. He was wrong.

Loud chants echoed up the stairwell. He shook his head in resignation. It sounded like a good crowd tonight… great.

Volunteer - Northern Turkey - Josiah

Josiah was not supposed to be here. He was going to get his ass chewed out when he got back to the hospital, but nothing was keeping him out of this fight. He crouched around the corner of a mud hut, keeping low. To his right, his fellow soldiers moved into position.

Everything slowed down. His pounding heart calmed. He could hear his shallow breath and noted with almost canine clarity the pungent tang of unwashed male bodies wafting out of the hut's open windows. They were talking, normal conversation.

At the signal, they began to creep forward, but his friend, his comrade, his reason for being in this remote village, broke cover. With the cry of an avenging angel, Reuben ben Judah stormed the hut, his weapon raining fire.

Josiah swore. The temporary slow-motion shattered.

Reuben disappeared into a firestorm. Josiah barreled after him, his boots pounding the cracked dirt. The ratta-tat-tat of weapons continued unabated. Josiah felt a bullet whiz past him, a disconcerting sound, that had it been three inches closer, would have heralded his last moment on Earth.

He rushed into the hut with three of his men. Two shots were fired. Then everything grew still. The acrid stench of gunpowder and blood assailed his nose. Three bodies were sprawled on the floor like sorted laundry amid broken dishes and splintered furniture. A meager fire crackled in the adobe fireplace with the spilled contents of a cooking pot bubbling into blackened goo.

Reuben, his face streaked with grease paint and gunpowder, strolled out of one of the back bedrooms. His muscles bulged, and Josiah could see his carotid artery pulsing. Reuben raised his rifle and pumped it. "They are dead."

"What the bloody hell were you thinking?" Josiah bellowed.

"I made sure the last face these swine saw was that of a Reubenite. They knew who killed them and why," Reuben said through gritted teeth.

"You stupid, hot-headed fool! You almost got yourself killed, and you endangered the lives of every man in this platoon!"

Reuben snarled and gave him a mocking salute. "Captain."

Josiah wanted to throttle him. "Sergeant!"

Reuben drew himself up, unrepentant and stubborn. This had been personal.

Josiah noticed a crimson stain on Reuben's calf. "You're hit."

Reuben glanced down, disinterested. "I do not feel it. It does not matter."

Josiah narrowed his brows, shaking his head. Further rebuke died on his tongue as he watched Reuben's color drain. "Isaac, catch him. He's going down."

He ran to his fallen comrade and lifted his trouser leg. He screamed over his shoulder, "Bring my bag! They've hit an artery. Move!"

September 13, 998 ME (Thirteen Years into Rebellion)

Key to the Snare - New City, Alanthia - Peter

"Falcon," Alaina ben Thomas said over the phone, sounding breathless and excited, "we might have found a key to your snare. Pick me up at the Coffee Beanery off Chesterfield in thirty minutes."

Peter tried and missed the button to disconnect the call. Fumbling, he managed on the third try, though she had already hung up. He turned a jaundiced eye to one of the triplets and slurred, "I am sorry, love, but I have to go."

His announcement was met with pouty protests and lithe, slithering bodies that begged him to stay. He sat back on the sofa in the private room of his favorite dance club and let them try their best to convince him. The deep bass of the music pumped through his body, and one of the triplets ran her hand up his thigh. Peter returned the favor. They all wanted Prince d'Or in their beds, and he was happy to oblige. But duty, and whatever the hell that cryptic message was about, called.

They hung by his side as he maneuvered through the crowded club. "Sorry, ladies." He kissed each of them in turn and let Agent Nathan ben Henry, his head of security, usher him into his waiting car.

Twenty minutes later, two black SUV's pulled up to the coffee shop. One of his assets jumped in the back seat. Her leg came first, long, tan, and shapely. Alaina ben Thomas was stunning. She was also one of the most talented computer geniuses in the kingdom, a committed revolutionary, and when she was not yelling at him, his friend.

She coughed and waved away a cloud of cigarette smoke. "Mercy! What are you smoking, two at a time? Crack a window."

He looked particularly reprobate wearing lipstick stains and a bleary expression, completely plastered. He took a deep drag and blew the smoke at her. "I happened to be in the middle of a rather engaging evening, before I was so rudely interrupted."

She made a disgusted sound and cracked her window. "You reek."

"The identical triplets did not seem to mind, or perhaps they were twins." He shrugged. "I saw three, but there could have been two." With a lecherous grin, he added, "Though, you could make it up to me."

"Yeah, right." She flashed a two-carat diamond in his face. "How much have you had to drink?"

He lit another cigarette off the burning end of the butt. "What day is it?"

She raised her lip at him. "It's Monday."

Peter leaned his head back on the leather seat, contemplating. "Well, I started on Thursday."

"Just alcohol?" she asked in that suspicious tone.

He shot her a deadly glare and took another drag off his cigarette, not answering her question.

"You're a mess."

Peter snorted and idly blew a series of smoke rings. "The Hell Bitch is coming to town."

"Ah," she nodded. "Still, I am starting to worry about you."

"Oh, I am fine," he said, rubbing his bloodshot eyes.

"Okay, I suppose I will get to the point of this little *tête-à-tête*."

His head lolled to the side. "The triplets had some nice *tête-à-têtes*."

Despite herself, she laughed. "*Mon Dieu*, I should have brought you some coffee."

"Hmm, I like coffee." He smacked his lips, considering, then rolled down the partition. "Turn around, I need coffee, espresso, make it a triple, one sugar. Do you want coffee?" he asked Alaina.

"No. I'd like to sleep tonight," Alaina said, and he felt her growing impatience. She got feisty at him when he was wasted.

"Just me, Nathan. Miss Grumpy Pants back here wants to sleep." He raised the partition and grinned. "I've got better things on my mind than sleep. You sure? It could be fun."

"Tempting, but no," Alaina retorted sarcastically. "I prefer my men sober and disease free."

Peter put a hand over his heart. "You wound me to the core, Miss Pink." He called her by her code name. He was Falcon. She was Miss Pink. "Why do you call yourself that anyway? What's pink, Alaina?" He waggled his eyebrows at her.

She covered her eyes and chuckled. "It was my mother's nickname. She loved pink, wore it all the time."

He stubbed out his cigarette. The thought made him sad. Sometimes it hit him like that, seemingly out of nowhere. "My mother did not wear pink. It looks terrible on redheads." He downed another shot of rum. "So does red... black... blue." He slid down in his seat, his enjoyment of the evening evaporating.

"Maybe we should do this tomorrow," Alaina offered.

From behind closed eyes, he whispered, "It won't matter. Nothing will change. Tomorrow it will be the same." He gave her a profoundly weary sigh. "Go ahead. Tell me why you called. I am listening, just resting my eyes."

"All right," she said with more enthusiasm. "The plane carrying Princess Keyseelough made an emergency landing in Houston tonight."

He cracked an eye open, a smile hovering. "Did it crash?"

"No, nearly. It was out of flight plan, flying too high, and the cabin lost pressure."

"Hypoxia?" He chuckled malevolently. "Oh, that is brutal."

"How do you know about hypoxia?" Alaina seemed surprised.

He opened his arms wide. "Prince d'Or knows how to fly. I am a world-renowned playboy with my own planes, several helicopters, too. You forget who you are talking to." His hands collapsed. He was tired, and she was not going to have sex with him, so he stopped flirting with her. "Now tell me about the hypoxia Hell Bitch."

Alaina handed him her phone. "Check it out."

Peter blinked, trying to focus, then gasped. It was a picture of the witch who ruled the dungeon with his father. She had taken an interest in Keyseelough and was training her. Though it appeared by the picture of the two of them *in flagrante delicoto*, their interest in each other ran a bit deeper. Keyseelough's face was obscured, but he saw the pentagram tattoo on the inside of her thigh. It was her. He turned his head away in disgust. The old bitch had saggy tits. "Oh, I cannot unsee that!"

A second later, the ramifications of that photo hit him. He roared with laughter, curling his knees up to his chest and snorting. "Mistress Cunt and the Hell Bitch together?"

His laughter seemed to be contagious. She started giggling and the disapproving pique she brought with her disappeared.

Peter picked up the phone and squinted at the picture again, hysterical. "Oh, that is priceless. Did you put this up?" He pointed to the website address.

Alaina nodded.

Peter slid to the floorboard, laughing. "My father is going to have a conniption fit. One of his ministers, caught like that, with her? Bloody Hell, I cannot go back to the Palace tonight. He is going to be in a rage." He wheezed, coughing and laughing. "This is a scandal of epic proportions."

The car came to a stop. Moments later, Nathan presented his espresso. Alaina accepted it on his behalf because he was still laughing.

He just might get out of that damned contract after all.

March 6, 999 ME (Fourteen Years Into Rebellion)

Dark Rider - Macedonian Border - Prince Josiah

A duskiness hung over the barren fields. The whole region was deserted, but Josiah pressed onward. Clad in black leather, the clothes molded to his muscular frame like well-worn armor, but they were hot, ill-suited for the terrain. His stomach growled, but with a soldier's discipline, he ignored it and kept riding.

Despite his discomfort, honor demanded the odious task be seen through to its end. He would either kill the old bastard or forgive him; the outcome of the pending confrontation he knew not. The only thing Josiah knew was he could move neither forward nor backward until it was done.

He scanned the arid field. A few anemic plants struggled toward the leaden sky, yellow stalks stretched thin and viney among the cracks. He turned away, remembering the land as it once was, lush, alive, bursting with endless bounty.

A movement caught his eye, a black squirrel munching on an onion. So, some root vegetables remained in this godforsaken patch of dirt. He eyed the squirrel, sizing it up as a potential lunch. But squirrels were greasy, and he did not eat onions in any form, vile things. So, he pressed on.

As Josiah rounded the last corner, the place of his nightmares came into sight.

A farmhouse.

Once a deceptively cheery blue with white trim, the paint had faded to gray. The roof pitched at a drunken angle, and a briar climbed the warped siding like a black hand reclaiming the place to hell. A coil of dread curled in his stomach.

As he passed the barn, he noticed the door hung askew, its wooden edge buried deep in the dirt, long abandoned to time and the scorching east wind. Staring at the house, he detected no light or movement behind the dusty windows, no signs of life.

Part of him did not want to do this, but he was not turning back. This confrontation was a decade in the making, and Yane ben Sandanski would answer for his crimes, voluntarily or at the point of a dagger, it mattered little to Josiah. This place and this man sealed his downfall.

The day of reckoning was here.

Lashing his horse to the leaning porch railing, Josiah paused on the stoop, wondering if he should knock. He turned the knob, and finding it locked felt along the top of the door frame for the spare key. By reflex and muscle memory, he caught the door before it slammed. The hinges squeaked long and high, announcing his presence. He muttered an oath and felt the short hairs on the back of his neck prickle. The house smelled familiar, old man and stale tobacco, but another aroma wafted out of the kitchen, incongruent and shocking. Food.

"Sandanski?" he called into the gloom as his feet disturbed a thick coat of dust, which shimmered gold through a shaft of light.

"Prince Josiah ben Eamonn, of the royal house of Alanthia, you have come," a woman said from the back of the house. "Welcome, I have made for you supper."

The use of his name shot a flare up his spine. He had not used it in fourteen years. If they knew who he was, if they were waiting for him, he had walked into a trap. He pulled his dagger. "Show yourself."

In response, a flash of brilliant white light pulsed from the back room, blinding him. He shielded his eyes and stumbled, not losing control of his wits or his knife. "Who are you?"

"I am me. You are you." She waved a hand dismissively. "But the man you seek is not here."

His eyes adjusted to the light, and he beheld a creature of incredible beauty. She bowed and said, "I am Jelena."

Josiah's nose flared with a shuddering exhale as he turned away. He knew what she was, and he knew who sent her. A spike of fear jolted him.

The wooden floor creaked as she approached. By reflex, he squeezed the hilt of his dagger, but weapons were useless on one such as she.

With a long delicate finger, she lifted his chin, bringing him face to face with her. He blinked in fear and wonder. Shimmering with white light, she was glorious in contrast to the dilapidated shack. Her sapphire eyes sparkled with knowledge and a hint of mischief. Raven hair cascaded around her shoulders, flowing down her back like black water. The delicate scent of her skin evoked comforting memories of Auntie G.'s cinnamon apple cake.

By contrast, he was filthy and unshaven, leather and fear, giving him a feral stench. He stepped back, turning away.

She beamed with supernatural splendor and said, "Fear not."

To his shock, his hammering heart calmed.

"I bring you a message."

"I am your servant, madam."

She nodded, looking solemn. "The Millennium is drawing to a close, the time of paradise is threatened. Great evil struggles to pierce the gossamer veil and return to their former domain. These supernatural beings were the gods of the Last Age, the fallen elohim, Lucifer's army. They have been held in bondage, kept off Millennial Earth, as has the Great Serpent. If they are freed, they will foment war, bringing destruction and death. But worse, they are deceivers, with lying tongues and false promises, they will seduce mankind and steal the souls of the last generation, dragging them to their doom in the Lake of Fire."

Josiah swallowed, speechless.

Her blue eyes bore into his. "Your father's murder marked

the beginning of Alanthia's rebellion. So vile was the act that it rent the veil, and one of their kind broke free. He is an ancient evil and has aligned with Korah. He seeks the Black Key to unleash hell on Earth.

"Your exile is over, Prince Josiah. Seek restoration of what your uncle stole. Present yourself to the Iron King in your true name. He will instruct you on what you must do."

Jelena leaned in and brushed a kiss by his ear. Her soft breath sent chills down his spine. "Perilous times lie ahead, Josiah, and you were born to fulfill a destiny."

He started to speak, but she pressed her delicate fingers over his lips. "Enjoy your supper."

And in the twinkling of an eye, she vanished.

Prince d'Or - New City, Alanthia - Peter

Twenty-one-year-old Prince Peter ben Korah awoke to a tickle on his naked stomach. He opened a wine reddened eye and discovered the source, long sandy hair. Flashing the woman a lecherous grin, he laced his fingers behind his head and surrendered to her ministrations. He watched with distracted interest as she performed. She was not bad, just predictable, gorgeous, and rather boring.

Someone knocked on his bedroom door. He ignored it, until he finished.

With the breathless beauty still hovering above him, Peter bade the servant enter. Jarrod ben Adriel, his valet, came through, pushing a cart that bore a carafe of coffee and a single cup and saucer.

With imperturbable manners, Jarrod addressed the scrambling woman. "Prince Peter thanks you for your company, madam, and bids you adieu, with compliments." He presented her with a small box wrapped in gold paper.

A maid appeared at Jarrod's elbow, female garments gathered from the floor and a dressing robe in hand. She hustled the naked woman out the door before she could utter a coherent word, which was well enough, she had not been there for conversation.

Peter quirked a golden eyebrow and asked, "Perfume?"

"Of course, my Esteemed."

Peter stretched his neck and scrubbed his face with both hands before accepting the coffee, the woman already forgotten. He inhaled, anticipating the sugared, creamed elixir of life. He drained it in a single gulp and let Jarrod take the cup without replacing it on the saucer. He fell back on the pillows with a groan, as Jarrod prepared his second, more leisurely cup.

Jarrod motioned toward the hallway. Three maids rushed into the gilded chamber, opening blinds, dumping overflowing ashtrays, and gathering empty wine bottles. Using the service cart, they cleared away the dishes of leftover caviar, smoked salmon, and broken bits of cheese.

The youngest maid curtsied to Peter, removing the remnants of strawberries and Swiss ganache from a silver dish by his bed, tactfully ignoring a strawberry stain on the sheets. He winked at her with exaggerated roguishness, and she blushed. Another maid retrieved his discarded clothes. She did not flinch, but he knew they stank of cigarettes and alcohol. Hell, he stank of cigarettes and alcohol, and sex, plenty of sex. He experienced a sense of relief when he heard someone start his bath. He had a rotten headache. Stupid, to get that trashed.

In keeping with their custom, Jarrod began the day by reading his agenda. "Your father is scheduled to return from Cairo. He will be in residence this evening, my Esteemed."

Peter squeezed the bridge of his nose and made a low sound of disgust. "Alone, I hope."

Jarrod nodded. "We have had no instructions to prepare for the arrival of your betrothed, my Esteemed."

"Small mercies," Peter said, taking a sip of coffee. "It would be just like him to spring the Hell Bitch on me. How many times has he pulled that in the last three years? Make sure she is not coming."

"I shall inquire." Jarrod did not bat an eye at Peter's characterization of his betrothed.

"Please do so."

Taking his cue, Jarrod continued with Peter's schedule. "This morning at 9:00 am and 10:00 am, you have your fencing and Krav Maga instructors, respectively." He paused and referred to his list. "Your luncheon engagement, at 12:30 pm, is in the solarium with the Board of Trustees for the Street Kids of Alanthia. At 3:45 pm, you are ribbon cutting in Midtown, followed by a charity auction at the Royal Museum of Art at 8:30 pm."

Jarrod stowed the agenda in his breast pocket and asked, "Given the location of the latter two appointments, shall I assume you will dress at the penthouse this evening?"

"Just handle it," Peter said, squeezing his throbbing temples.

"Certainly." Jarrod poured him a glass of water and placed two headache pills on the bedside table, not quite disguising his concern over last night's drunken debauchery. But he held his tongue and did not nag. Retreating on silent feet, he disappeared into the dressing room to assemble the five changes of clothes required for the day.

Peter popped the pills in a single gulp and rolled over to replace the water goblet. His hand arrested midair. The temperature in the room plummeted. Frost formed on the glass, freezing his fingers to the crystal. He flung it away, but it tumbled in slow motion, landing soundlessly on the thick rug.

The monster lurked.

Peter felt a sharp pain between his eyes. His skull throbbed like it was being cleaved in half. He pressed his palms over his temples and squeezed. In a low growl, he whispered, "Go away, damn you."

There was no sound, no tangible movement, but a shadow fell over his bed. The gagging stench of sulfur surrounded him, and he willed himself not to vomit.

Jarrod emerged from the dressing room and announced, "My Esteemed, your bath is prepared."

At his valet's words, the maids and the evil presence departed.

Peter blew out a shaky breath and threw off the silk coverlet. He stalked across the room, heedless of his naked body, which had grown long and lean. "Attend me," he ordered in a surly royal tone.

Jarrod nodded, executing a slight bow. "Yes, of course, my Esteemed."

Lowering himself into the steaming water, he inhaled the peppermint bath salts, letting them banish the stench of rotten eggs. Safe, for the moment, he sighed in relief. Resting his head against the bath pillow, he waited for the pills to work and fought down the nausea. He attempted to recapture this morning's pleasant awakening but found he could not remember if the woman was a brunette or a blonde, ruling out redheads, because he never slept with redheads. He submerged, and in the silence, decided she had been a brunette.

Ribbon Cutting – New City, Alanthia - Peter

It was all pomp, but it served a purpose. Simple in practice, show up with great fanfare, stand around, look regal, which Prince Peter ben Korah could do dressed in overalls. He smiled, nodded at the right moments, and appeared perfectly innocuous, nothing but the golden boy, Prince d'Or.

It was all they required of him, all they expected. He surmised it was because he was blond, the universal hair color of morons. Consequently, people saw what they wanted, and he did not disabuse them, rather he played the role. He was born to it, and his survival in Korah's household depended on it.

He pretended to be harmless; he was not.

Prince d'Or was a persona, a useless royal figurehead, sent across the kingdom from factory opening to factory opening, cutting ribbons. Dead for a thousand years, industrial Alanthia roared back to life with a vengeance. The outside world looked on with envy while Prince d'Or smiled pretty for the cameras and broke ground with gold plated shovels.

The press adored him; they always had. He was dashing and gave them enough 'bad boy' fodder that they lapped him up like lobster bisque. He sold papers. The people could not get enough of him, his clothes, his girlfriends (even though he was betrothed), his stable of horses, his cars, his parties. His father thought he was a farce, but even Korah could not deny—the PR was good.

Today, he toured a microprocessor factory, enduring a sophomoric, no, elementary explanation about what they did. He stifled the desire to roll his eyes, as if he did not know what a microprocessor did.

"Through there," the overstuffed sycophant gestured, "is our research and development lab, top secret, of course." Peter looked suitably disappointed, so the eager executive added, "Would you like to see it?"

Peter checked his watch and turned to Jarrod. "Do we have time?"

Jarrod nodded, playing his part. "My Esteemed, you have a massage booked this afternoon. Shall I cancel?"

Peter appeared to consider, noting the executive's eyes held that peculiar mix of disdain and obsequiousness. "Yes, please do. I shall accompany Mr. ben Harris. After all, my father is most interested in this factory. Please, Mr. ben Harris, lead the way."

Peter knew the use of their names always charmed them. He flashed his famous smile and walked through the sealed doors. People loved hearing him say their names, and they loved telling him their secrets.

It was all part of the plan.

March 18, 999 ME

Endings and Beginnings - The Golden City - Josiah

Two weeks after he encountered Jelena on Sandanski's farm and fourteen years into his exile, Josiah waited in line to gain entrance into the Golden City. A thousand-year-old olive tree shaded the Semitic gatekeeper who stared up at him in disbelief. Josiah resisted the urge to sneer and repeated, "I am Prince Josiah ben Eamonn, of the royal house of Alanthia."

The gatekeeper stretched his neck forward like an ancient turtle coming out of his shell and narrowed his large penetrating eyes, studying Josiah.

Parched and in a foul mood after standing in line for three hours, Josiah drew himself up to his full height of 6'3" and managed to look regal despite his dusty clothes and the crevices of dirt ringing his neck.

The brackets around the gatekeeper's mouth deepened, and he asked in a sarcastic tone, "Back from the dead?"

"In a manner, I was summoned by a messenger of the Iron King with instructions to present myself."

The old man's bushy eyebrows came to a point over his hawk nose. "You are not the first to appear at this gate, trying to claim that name."

Josiah did not offer an explanation. He simply met the old man's eyes and laid a hand on his jeweled dagger.

The gatekeeper did not flinch under the intimidating glare, but his eyes fixed on the dagger, noting the crown on the hilt, the sapphire in the center. "Imposters are always ready with their stories, but none of them looked like your father, nu?" He shrugged, recorded Josiah's name, and motioned him through. "Welcome to the Golden City, my Esteemed. Enjoy your stay."

Josiah walked through the Lion's Gate into paradise.

No drought touched this lush land. No ill wind blew away

feeble crops. Starving beggars did not swarm him for alms. The Golden City bustled with life and prosperity. Gone were the pinched, worried looks, and haggard faces he became accustomed to as he traveled through Greece. Everything and everyone brimmed with health and vigor in the city of the Iron King.

Heavy laden fruit trees lined the streets, their bounty free to all. Every flower known to man, and some with no names, burst forth in a profusion of color, overflowing from burnished pots and stone lined beds. Languages of every sort created a confused babble, like the distant chatter of a zoo. There was a bustle of brightly colored kaftans, floral dresses, and jeweled turbans. Incongruent and conspicuous, Alanthian pilgrims were easy to spot in their jeans and printed T-shirts. A lively band played on the corner, entertaining a sizable crowd who threw shekels into their overflowing tip basket. Crowds ebbed and flowed into shops, sampled food from the open-air stalls, and gloried in the gold-paved streets.

Above it all, the city's crowned jewel drew even the most jaded traveler's eye to Ezekiel's Temple. The vast complex loomed on a hill, elevated above the bustle. From his vantage point, Josiah could not see the temple proper, only the outer court. Singers, in shimmering white robes, waved palm branches and twirled in worshipful celebration. Hundreds of miles above the temple complex, the dazzling city of New Jerusalem orbited, emitting the golden light whereby the kingdom derived its name.

A floral scented wind ruffled his hair, and Josiah raised his face to the sky, basking in a moment of peace. A low insistent growl of his stomach and the aroma coming from a street vendor's kebab cart reminded him how long he had been without a decent meal. He ignored his stomach to attend the more pressing matters of water and a bath. Cupping his hands, he drank deeply from King David's Fountain. The huge granite edifice greeted scores of pilgrims as they poured into the city, shouting in triumph, joyous at their journeys' end.

Josiah left the fountain and the kebabs behind, winding his way through the crowd toward the public baths. Protocol dictated that upon entry, new arrivals wash away the dust of their journey, and with it, the burdens they carried. Symbolically and physically clean, they were fit to explore the wonders of the Golden City. After two weeks of travel, Josiah needed no further encouragement to enter the ancient bathhouse.

He checked his personal arsenal and saddle bags with the steward, a wizened old man who eyed him with the same scrutiny as the gatekeeper but thankfully asked no questions. He offered Josiah a robe and two white towels. Josiah raised a brow, noting other travelers were not afforded the same luxury.

Sinking into the steaming water, he breathed a long sigh of relief. Across the marble pool, a half dozen other travelers chatted amiably, but his well-practiced menace and intimidating size discouraged idle conversation, so they left him in peace.

High walls surrounded the men's bath, flanked by enormous jujube trees. A plethora of brightly colored birds chirped and cavorted among the branches, feasting on the glossy red fruit. One intrepid explorer swooped down, staring at Josiah with curious black eyes. Josiah mimicked the head tilt of the rainbow festooned little fellow. They held each other's gaze for a moment, but at the sound of approaching feet the bee-eater decided he had pressing matters elsewhere and flew off.

Josiah sank deeper into the water, contemplating the pumps of soap and shampoo near where the other men congregated. He did not want to speak, even to say, excuse me. It seemed like too much of an effort. Never one for idle chatter, his conflicting thoughts made him less inclined than normal.

He built a life in exile, one he loved. But the moment he uttered his name outside the city gate, the wheels were set into motion. As surely as the night he went into exile, the exchange with the gatekeeper irrevocably changed the future. His old life was over.

After he escaped Yane ben Sandanski's farm, he joined the Iron King's army, using the alias Einar ben Yane. Einar because it meant lone warrior, and Yane to remind him, so he would never forget. His lack of papers, dubious background, or the fact that he was not a Golden Kingdom citizen were brushed aside, and he was fast-tracked into officers training. It was likely the Iron King's doing.

As a First Lieutenant, they gave him command of a platoon patrolling the pilgrim roads inside Greece. He earned a reputation as a fierce warrior and a persistent foe of the bandits who preyed on the innocent travelers.

During his deployment, a natural talent emerged, that of a healer. Among the troops and pilgrims, he discovered he had an innate sense for how to treat wounds and care for the sick. At nineteen, he was recruited into the medical corps. His royal education, quick intelligence, and driving ambition propelled him through the program. He became a surgeon in the Iron King's Army at twenty-five.

But now, his future was uncertain. He might succeed in wresting his throne from his uncle, but the action would likely result in untold bloodshed. The thought sickened him. He was, himself, prepared to pay the ultimate price, but the looming specter of grieving widows and orphans haunted him. Thousands were sure to die when he marched on Alanthia, and he was no closer today, than he had been the day he rode away from Sandanski's farm to reconciling it in his mind.

As he contemplated these weighty issues, he saw them coming. It had begun.

Through hooded eyes, he silently acknowledged the squadron of servants, bearing unsolicited silver trays. Each murmured, "My Esteemed," before presenting their offerings and retreating. Their gazes lingered just long enough to describe him later.

The trays were heavy laden with pastries, fruit, cheese, and meat. Josiah skimmed over the food and selected a finely milled bar of alabaster soap. He lifted it to his nose and nodded his approval to the eager attendant who was observing from a discreet distance.

The luxurious lather carried away weeks' worth of grime. His skin pebbled in pleasure, drinking in the rich moisture. It felt good to be clean. Josiah popped a grape in his mouth, then submerged, rinsing shampoo from his jet-black hair. Half the dust of Greece floated away in the steaming water.

When he surfaced, a uniformed courtier hurried toward him. Josiah scowled. They were not even going to let him finish bathing.

Unthwarted by his glower, the Palace servant bowed. "My Esteemed, welcome to the Golden City. Prince Yehonathan ben Hezekiah requests the honor of thy presence. Thy arrival has been anticipated, and he eagerly awaits thy attendance."

Josiah blinked his spikey wet lashes, eyeing the courtier. "I am bathing at present."

The courtier bowed again, backing away. "Of course, my Esteemed, I shall await thy convenience."

Josiah relaxed against the marble bench, resigned. He hoped to have the afternoon to wander around and gather his thoughts, but it was not to be. His old life was over, and with it, anonymity. He sighed and said, "I shall require clothing."

Dinner Amongst "Friends" - The Golden City - Josiah

Prince Josiah regarded his bejeweled dinner companions through a thin veil of contempt. The heads of the Golden Kingdom's twelve houses hastily assembled at Prince Yehonathan's table for an impromptu dinner in his honor.

It had been half a lifetime since he attended such an affair, but he decided little had changed. Well-dressed servants presented platters of gourmet food, to spectacularly dressed guests seated at a table laid with crystal glasses and a dozen pieces of cutlery, the use of which required he plumb the depths of his memory. The unfamiliar ring of court speech sounded like a foreign language he used to know. His terse answers were due in part to the fact he had to mentally translate common speech into court language before he spoke, but only in part.

He listened to the dinner conversations and could not believe how out of touch these people were. They prattled about looming global rebellion and the collapse of decency and morality. They complained about the huge influx of refugees into the Golden City. They lamented about housing shortages and the strain the new arrivals put on public services. In unctuous tones, they extolled their own virtues, condemned everyone outside the Golden Kingdom, making particular reference to Alanthia, present company excluded, or so they said. They praised the Iron King's decision to withhold rain from vast portions of Earth, pontificating that harmony would soon return. They assured each other that everything would soon return to the way it used to be.

Hidden just beneath their high-minded discourse and flowery speeches, Josiah knew the real reason they were here. Gossip. News of the resurrected Alanthian Prince spread like wildfire. They jostled to the front of the line, the first to gawk at him, to see for themselves that he was not dead. They squirmed in their chairs and tried to suppress their ghoulish curiosity.

Had he killed his father? Was he crazy?

They studied him, trying to recall exactly what his father looked like. A few of the older women had known his mother. They compared their mental notes and tried to confirm if he was who he claimed to be.

The scandal and his story were too delicious to ignore, spice for their mundane, leisure-dominated lives. They licked their chops in eager anticipation, hungry for morsels they could feed their envious friends tomorrow. Josiah deflected their coy questions with vague non-answers and felt their frustration rising. They wanted to know.

At length, the most pompous of all, Eli ben Dan, hefted his bulk forward with throat clearing, attention drawing, self-importance. "It might be presumptuous, but I think I speak for us all, Prince Josiah. We received the news of thy return with great relief." General agreement echoed across the dining room, several raised wine goblets in toast. "However, we must know, where hast thou been, and why hast thou hidden thyself?"

Josiah composed his face, sitting impassive, letting the old windbag speak. He knew men like Eli ben Dan. They would talk over anyone who tried to speak until they made their points. So, he sat there, still, and silent. If Eli had been a bandit along the pilgrim road, he would have recognized the stare Josiah gave him, but he did not.

"We wonder, what sort of man thou hast become?" Eli's chins wobbled as he built up steam. "Certainly, honor should have bound thee to thy duty, which thou hast neglected these many years."

Josiah put his fork down and folded his hands in his lap, no expression on his handsome, square-jawed face.

"Twould have saved us all an enormous disturbance if thou had not shirked thy responsibilities." He looked around, gathering support. "Before all is said and done, the whole world followeth Korah to ruin." Eli gestured with his pudgy arms and moved in for the kill. "I say, if I were thee, I would have dispatched that villain from my house long since."

Eli's accusations were met with uncomfortable silence from the women. Several men signaled their agreement, though none mustered the courage to look at the end of the table where Josiah sat on display.

Josiah dabbed the corner of his mouth with his napkin and said quietly, "Forsooth, Eli, hast thou confronted *King* Korah?" His uncle's name tasted bitter on his tongue. There was only one King. "What hast thou done?"

Eli shifted his bulk, stunned at the turn of the conversation.

"Nothing?" Josiah narrowed his eyes, focused on his accuser. "I think thou art content to write him letters of condemnation whilst sitting at fine tables, making grand speeches from behind turkey legs."

Eli turned crimson, the bones of one such leg sitting on the plate in front of him.

"Disturbance?" Josiah tilted his head and mocked, "Ye refer to the brewing crisis we face as a disturbance?" His heart began to pound, and he struggled to keep his temper in check. His stress was compounded by the difficulty of maintaining court language in a fury.

"From whence I have come and how I abided in exile, I owe neither explanation, nor justification to ye." Josiah swept them all with a look of disdain. "To the King alone, do I owe an account, and give an account I will, but not before he giveth an account to me."

There was a collective intake of breath. The tinkling of fine silver on bone china ceased.

"Oh, does that offend ye? Then I ask, who among ye can lay a single grievance at the Iron King's feet?" He looked from face to face. All turned away. "Not one of ye?" His laughter rang hollow, as bitter as his indictment. "It may be truly spoken, that I alone can do so in righteousness for the unpunished injustice that hast befallen my kingdom and my family."

He rose to his imposing height, braced his hands on the table, and leaned in with a savage expression on his face. "Why has he delayed judgment? Where has he been?"

Silence.

Josiah shook with old anger. "Have any of ye had thy house, and thy place stolen? Were ye cast out, thy name scorned and besmirched? Is thy father's blood unavenged? Who among ye waited in vain for justice from our righteous King for years?"

The air crackled with tension. "None?"

He waited for the space of three heart beats, then exploded, "So, ye dare not stand with false boasting of what ye would have done!"

An elderly lady spilled a wine goblet. No servant moved to clean it up.

"Where were ye when thousands of Alanthians took up arms to fight Korah? Didst ye send provisions, weaponry, or troops?" Josiah slammed his fist on the table, making the cutlery jump. "Nay, ye did not!

"What of the innocents caught up in rebellion, that ye are so sure, if ye were I, ye would have put down? What do ye suggest I do with them? Do ye even spare a thought to the innocent blood that might be spilled?"

The middle-aged Reubenite to his left pressed her fingers to her temple, hiding. The Benjamite with gravy on his tie pinched the bridge of his nose. No one answered Josiah. No one had the answers.

"Can ye make it rain?" he scoffed. "How many of ye have prayed, nay, begged for rain that refuses to fall? Have ye watched thy farms wither and die, blown away by the east wind? What do ye know of the hardship that drive desperate men from their land into rebellion? They blame their plight on an uncaring and distant King.

"Do ye understand why youth seeketh the promise of technology and the wonders of the Last Age? Do ye know anything at all?" Josiah's pulse beat in the cords of his muscular neck. "Did I not know the foul wickedness that arises in the west firsthand, I might be wont to join myself."

A collective gasp issued among the guests.

He whirled on them anew, in mocking ferocity. "Oh, ye, who sit at fine tables, wearing linen and rubies, who have never known a moment of hunger or oppressive thirst, burst with condemnation. Thy pugnacious superiority is anathema to me. I dare say, ye do not know a single thing of true meaning that transpires beyond the walls of thy well-watered flower gardens."

He shook his head ruefully, his anger spent. "That I even deigned to enter these gates must mean I am the basest of beasts, the foulest cur, sniffing at the Iron King's table, waiting for a crumb to fall, and holding myself thankful for even that. Yet, here I find myself." Josiah closed his eyes. "The most forsaken of Princes, seeking what scrap of justice I might find, and what succor and resources I might gather from ye. Because I do go." His nose flared, and he inhaled an unsteady breath. "I will go to do this thing ye deign I should have accomplished as an outcast boy of fifteen with no resources or aid from the likes of ye."

They turned away from him in shame.

"I will put down that vile usurper and try to bring my kingdom back into fellowship with our good King, not for myself, for I have long since given up hope of that. I do so, to honor the memory of my father, the noble and faithful Prince Eamonn ben Adam of Alanthia."

Josiah stiffened, scanning the downcast faces of his dinner companions. "I bid ye, good eve."

He left with his head held high like the proud and fallen Prince that he was.

The Golden City Palace was the home of Prince Yehonathan ben Hezekiah, who was the second highest ranking royal official in the world. He answered directly and only to the Iron King. The Prince of the Golden Kingdom served as a liaison between the Iron King and the nine other Ruling Princes. By birthright, Josiah was one of the nine, but legally he was dead, and dead men ruled no kingdoms.

Yehonathan found Josiah brooding outside the main drawing room, staring at the azure river flowing along the back of the Palace property. The riverbank was flanked with fruit trees, which bore a different crop every month. This month it was mango. Heavy green and pink orbs dotted the lush trees, bending the branches low with their hanging bounty.

In his mid-sixties, Yehonathan still retained the vigor of his youth, though his hair had turned gray and deep lines creased his forehead. His voice was gravelly, rough, and accustomed to command. He moved beside Josiah and said, "Quite a performance, Prince."

Josiah made a rueful growl. "Aye, it was. I must beg thy pardon. 'Twas ill-mannered and a discourteous act of temper, a poor way to repay thy hospitality."

"Indeed," Yehonathan agreed but added with a quiet touch of humor, "but no more than those indolent gossips deserved. Thou gave them a bit of truth to consider."

The corner of Josiah's mouth twitched.

Yehonathan clapped him on the back. "Difficult on the digestion, though. I find I am a bit dyspeptic. Wilt thou join me?" He motioned to a servant, who stepped forward with a selection of wine glasses.

Josiah kept his face impassive. "I must respectfully decline. I do not partake of spirits."

Yehonathan shrugged and took a crystal glass. "Alas, a modern-day Samson."

"Lest, I might find myself seduced by Delila, captured, and blinded by my enemies, I find it a prudent course of action."

"Well, we must all be thankful there was not the jawbone of an ass at my dinner table this eve."

The corner of Josiah's mouth twitched again.

The two men stood in silence, contemplating the serene gardens. Below, a groundskeeper cut a chessboard pattern in the lawn, sending the clean smell of fresh grass up to the balcony. The rhythmic clicking of the mower blades melded with the lapping river and the rustle of wind through the trees, hypnotic and relaxing. After the spent strong emotions and a long journey, Josiah steeled himself, gathering his wits for the courtier's games to come. He was in the Golden City, and tonight was half a lifetime in the making.

"I sense in thee, Prince Josiah, a forward speaking man of plain words, as was thy father before thee. If it so pleases, we shall speak frankly at thy leave." Yehonathan gestured to a well-appointed sitting area further down the veranda.

Josiah's future, his kingdom's future, and perhaps the peace of the entire world hung in the balance. Everything hinged on this negotiation.

Let the royal games begin.

March 20, 999 ME

Jihadists - New City, Alanthia - Peter

On the New City Palace grounds, Peter flattened himself against the saddle, evading a scimitar that sliced through the air, hissing like a viper. Their mounts came within a hair's breadth of colliding, and the cloak of the rider slapped his face. The black wool stank, sour and smokey. He thought, "Bloody hell, why do these guys wear this stuff? They all look like demented villains out of a comic book."

He stayed low, his heart pounding in time with the horse's hooves. Great clods of dirt exploded in their wake as he evaded his attackers. Peter shouted a command, loosened the reins a fraction, and gave the stallion his head. They surged forward, twelve hundred pounds of hammering thunder, under his control, responding to a mere shift of his thigh, a light pressure of his hand.

Unified perfection.

Three assassins, sent to kill him, and not for the first time, which was why he trained daily and was always armed, even out for a casual ride on the Palace grounds. Two black-clad riders charged from the front, and he sensed the scimitar wielding lunatic coming up fast. Peter raised his sword, blocking another vicious slash to his back. He squeezed his thighs and leaned back. The stallion reared and kicked the second attacker square in the face, snapping his neck. Peter kept his seat and with a howl of rage stabbed the rear attacker through the gut. The horse lunged forward with a bloodcurdling war cry of its own, allowing Peter to jerk his blade free.

They galloped after the last attacker, who was wisely attempting to flee. Battle surged through his body, the sword, the horse, the man became one berserk vengeance. He struck the lethal blow from behind, reveling in the crunch of bone and sinew. Bloodlust made him want to bathe in the arterial spray that exploded from the man's severed head.

Wheeling the stallion around, wrath pounded in Peter's ears, blocking out all sounds save his own harsh breathing. The horse's ribs bellowed under his thighs. They were both bathed in sweat.

Nothing moved.

He scanned the trees, hoping there were more, wanting more. He would kill them all. Surrounded by corpses, he roared to the sky, to the monster, to his father, "Is that all you have got?"

The manicured grounds were silent, the vast acreage deceptively peaceful. He envisioned riding through the Palace, into his father's office, and driving a sword through Korah's black heart. Then he would be free, his nightmare over.

But cold reason crept in, cooling his wrath. The monster could not be killed with a sword, of that, he was certain.

According to his intelligence, Josiah was in the Golden City. They were almost ready; the time was coming.

Peter just needed to stay alive until it did.

Part 3 - Camp Eiran

November 7, 998 ME

Desert - Southern Greece - Davianna

Heat rolled off the barren Greek landscape in waves, distorting the horizon, confusing and full of deception. Davianna ben David stumbled under the weight of her pack and went down on one knee. The impact cracked the thin crust of earth like a pane of glass, which shattered into a starburst, strange and lovely. She stared at it in dazed fascination until the pointed toe of a pink boot obliterated the delicate pattern.

Unencumbered, Zanah ben Joseph put her hands on her slender hips and glowered down at her daughter. "Don't dawdle," she said, her voice raw with thirst. "I won't wait if you fall behind."

Davianna raised her dirt-smudged face, her eyes fatigued and crusty with dried tears. She scanned their surroundings. The parched hills were devoid of life and color, holding no trace of civilization. A gust of wind blasted her skin. She turned into it, trying to detect the scent of cook fires or horses, any clue they were traveling in the right direction, but the cruel wind carried only desert heat and dust. Pulling a scarf over her sunburned nose, she turned away. When the stinging onslaught abated, she looked up at her mother and said, "You don't know where you are going."

"I'll do well enough," Zanah snarled, "without you or your father."

Davianna struggled to her feet, too exhausted to resume the battle that raged between them. With a groaning heave, she resettled her double pack and sidestepped under the weight. Her muscles seized as every cell in her body screamed for water. Her lower lip cracked, and she tasted blood, copper and slick, oddly comforting.

An uneasy foreboding swept over her, and she turned. But she saw nothing but miles of empty desert. Something was out there. She sensed it pursuing them, hunting. If she did not find Camp Eiran today, her father would not be the only one who died in this desert.

February 14, 999 ME

Pilgrim Camp – Davianna and Astrid

It was perhaps the worst play ever produced, truly wretched, just as they predicted. For ten days, two reluctant audience members concocted a series of outlandish excuses for why they missed it, each excuse becoming more implausible than the last. The cockamamie stories and the hilarity they produced were infinitely more entertaining than the play. The evening of the performance, no plausible explanation manifested, so they fidgeted on hard benches and wished it would hurry up and end.

"You know she has a mustache, right?" Davianna ben David whispered out of the side of her mouth, referring to Portia, the self-absorbed lead actress and creator of this monstrosity.

Her companion, Astrid ben Agnor, made an involuntary snort and gave her a sidelong glance. "Shh, don't start."

But the corners of Astrid's mouth were trembling, so in a voice cracking whisper, Davianna added, "And a bit of a beard, too."

Astrid began to giggle.

Davianna put a fist to her mouth and deliberately turned away, focusing on the scuffed boot of the boy beside her. She felt it building, the laughter, and this was no place for it, which made it worse.

On the open-air stage, the lead actor continued his inane monologue, "My love, the fairest of all pilgrims, you are a Princess among peasants. Your courage and beauty are beyond compare, your brown locks shimmer like light from the Golden City."

Davianna feigned a gagging noise.

Astrid bowed her head and muttered, "Those brown locks hanging from your chin."

Davianna squeezed her eyes and curled into herself, trying not to laugh.

Down the row, a girl glared at them through mean piggy eyes. "Be quiet."

Davianna covered her face with both hands, shoulders shaking.

Astrid snorted at the mean girl.

That was their undoing. They fell into each other, wracked with giggles that burst free in gasps and spurts.

Thirty feet away, yon bearded and mustached, Portia was overacting opposite the piggy-eyed girl's equally porcine brother in the melodramatic climax of the play. Heads turned, and a chorus of, "Shh," came at them from all directions.

Astrid made the first move, grabbing Davianna's arm. They stumbled out of their seats, bent over with bottled laughter. Clearing the meeting hall, they rocketed away, ran fifty yards, and collapsed, uproarious.

To the passersby, Davianna and Astrid hanging on each other, locked in hysterical laughter was nothing unusual.

One was rarely seen without the other in their temporary home of Camp Eiran.

The camp was in southern Greece, thousands of miles from their Alanthian homeland, a stop along the pilgrim road. By decree, all able-bodied adults were commanded, once in their lives, to travel to the world's capital, the Golden City, to pay homage to the Iron King. For a thousand years, pilgrims undertook the journey. Once a blessing, over the last decade, it became fraught with hardship and peril. Nowhere did the journey become more treacherous than Greece, which is where the girls found themselves—stranded.

Davianna and her mother, Zanah, stumbled into Camp Eiran a week after her father's death. Sick from dehydration and grief, Davianna refused to leave their tent. This infuriated Zanah, who reviled camp life and was impatient for Davianna to resume her chores. But a few days after they arrived, Zanah noticed Astrid hauling water from the river, deduced that the girls were about the same age, and convinced the spunky redhead to introduce herself.

"Hi, I'm Astrid. Would you like to come listen to some music?" The sparkle in Astrid's blue eyes gave Davianna the courage to try.

Weeks later, around the community campfire, Astrid told their friends, "You should have seen her. She knocked me down escaping that tent."

"I did not," Davianna protested. "You jerked me by the arm and drug me across the camp."

Whichever version of events was true, the girls were now inseparable. Uprooted from their Alanthian homeland, two-and-a-half years into their pilgrimage, their friendship formed an oasis in the Greek desert.

Outside the meeting hall, with the play wrapping up, Astrid bumped Davianna's shoulder. "Look, there he is." She pointed to a blond in his early twenties leaning against a tree. "See, I told you he'd be here."

Davianna sighed in dreamy appreciation. "He is pristine."

Astrid raised a tweezed auburn eyebrow, admiring the young man's handsome face and cool swagger. "Priss-teen!"

"You know?" Davianna rubbed her chin, her big brown eyes telegraphing the zinger. "I think Portia has a better beard."

The two girls staggered away in peals of laughter, weaving their way between the dust covered tents.

"Come on," Davianna wheezed, tucking a lock of chestnut hair behind her ear. "My place, I've got something to show you."

Davianna steered Astrid through the flap. The dark interior smelled of Zanah's spicy perfume and stale canvas. Davianna put a finger to her lips as they tiptoed inside. Lighting the small oil lamp and securing the tent flaps, she dove for her pack, producing a small black box.

Astrid gasped, taking an involuntary step back. "Where did you get that?" She glanced around, then reached out a tentative hand, whispering, "Have you opened it?"

"Without you?" Davianna snorted and shifted her weight. "No, I was scared."

Astrid grimaced and withdrew her hand, but her eyes remained transfixed on the black box. "Pandora, who gave you that?"

March 6, 999 ME

Illicit Interludes

Along the river embankment, a quarter mile from the main camp, a giant oak marked a hiding place. The soil underneath the tree fell away with the drought, and its gnarled roots curled overhead, forming an enclosure that smelled of old earth and dried acorns. Pine boughs strategically hid the entrance, and inside, two hearts pounded with the disquiet of illicit adventure.

Today was supposed to be the day of discovery, which

was the plan yesterday and the day before that. For three weeks, they giggled, whispered, and snuck away, intending to uncover the forbidden mysteries of the black box. Every day, Davianna backed out with a promised that tomorrow they would open it. Astrid always relented with a great show of eye rolling bravado and blustering impatience.

The sun hung low in the sky, and at this distance the bustle of the camp was a mere rumble. They were well hidden and alone.

Astrid nodded with firm resolve, ready to begin. "All right, Davi, tell me about the man who gave this to you."

Davianna held the box on her lap, her brown eyes warming in remembrance. "He seemed gentle, and he had a kind voice."

They both relaxed with the retelling.

"I was walking back from our grain apple tree, when he was just there, beside me. He called my name and said it in a way that reminded me of Daddy. The way he used to say it before… well, before." She pushed down the memory, lest she start crying.

"I wasn't nervous, strange because I didn't know him. He is not a pilgrim or anyone I've ever seen. Do you think he was royalty or something?"

Astrid shook her head. "The only royal in Greece is Antiochus, and he is a wicked man, which is why we are stranded in this drought. He is being punished by the Iron King. You said the man who gave this to you was nice, so it can't be him."

"You're right, sorry." Davianna frowned, trying to recapture that moment. "We were walking in golden light, not the hot sun, more like light from New Jerusalem, warm and soft. It made everything beautiful, the greens vivid, the sky blue. It was cool, as if the drought disappeared, and the world looked like it used to when we were little. Do you remember?"

"I remember." Astrid closed her eyes, picturing it clearly, paradise.

Davianna continued, "I had two grain apples, and for some reason, I had to give them to him. I'd just picked them off the forest floor, probably a month old, but I could not help myself. He was so," she paused, searching, "thankful, isn't the right word... gracious. That's it. He was gracious and accepted them like they were a treasure."

Feeling self-conscious, Davianna ran her fingers through her brown hair, separating a tangle from the long ends. "I don't know what I was thinking, giving him overripe fruit." She gazed off into space until Astrid elbowed her.

She shook herself back into the story. "Sorry. What was I saying? Yeah, right. Okay, fruit. I gave him the fruit, and he smiled. I don't know, I can't explain it, but his eyes were so kind and warm. I just wanted to fall at his feet and cry, but I didn't." Davianna paused and narrowed her brows, remembering. "You know, Tridi, I think he held my elbow."

Astrid pursed her lips. "You haven't mentioned that before. Keep going and try to remember it all."

Davianna concentrated, but the encounter was fleeting, more impression than substance, like a dream. If not for the black box, she would be inclined to believe it had been a dream. "He said the time was drawing closer, and he was giving me something to guard, to keep safe. It was in my pocket. I reached in, and there it was. When I looked up, he was gone." She lifted her palms in a helpless gesture.

Astrid set her shoulders and bobbed her head, ready for the recap. "So, when he held your elbow that is when he put it in your pocket, right?"

"I guess so."

Astrid bit her thumbnail, thinking. "He did not say you could not use it, right? He said it was yours."

Davianna demurred. "Well, he said he was giving it to me."

Astrid reached for the box. "Then I say we open it."

Davianna stayed her hand. "Tridi, he told me I was supposed to keep it safe. He did not say I could use it." She gave Astrid a pointed look then scrambled over to the entrance to ensure they were not being spied on. "If this is an artifact from the Last Age, even having it is against the law here, let alone using it. If we get caught, we'll be arrested, or worse, cast out. These things, these technologies, my daddy said they played a role in the downfall of the people before the Great Judgment. Since they lifted the ban in Alanthia, everything went bad. That's why we all left."

Astrid stroked the box. "Then why give it to you if you aren't supposed to use it?"

It was a rabbit trail, covered countless times, and still they had no clear answers. "I have no idea, but it's getting dark. I don't think today is a good day." Davianna wrapped the box in a silk scarf she'd taken from her mother's things and slipped it in her pocket.

Astrid narrowed her blue cat eyes, teasing, "You are such a chicken. Come on. Guan should be back soon and promised to bring me a rabbit for dinner."

Davianna groaned, "Pristine rabbit?"

"Priss-teen, indeed," Astrid called over her shoulder and scampered up the bank.

Davianna emerged at a more sedate pace, grumbling, "More like piss-tine."

Camp Eiran hummed with activity as dinner preparation began in earnest. Davianna was frustrated, but not surprised, to find her tent empty. Zanah, never much of a homemaker before her father died, was even less of one now. Davianna stared at her own rumpled cot, her mother's untouched for more than a week.

Three tents down, the sweet-faced toddler Nico fussed and fretted as his young mother tried to make dinner. Davianna retrieved a cup of rice and beans from their meager supply. These, in exchange for entertaining Nico, might earn her dinner from Mrs. ben Gingle, again.

After supper, Davianna snuggled with Nico on her lap

and made up a new installment of Sammy the Bad Frog from Lily Pad Lane. When the story ended, she got a sloppy good-night kiss from Nico and handed the sleepy boy to his father.

As she took her leave, Mrs. ben Gingle stood up, wiping her hands nervously on her apron. "Davianna?"

"Yes, ma'am?" Davianna heard the music coming from the campfire and was eager to join her friends.

Mrs. ben Gingle had an odd look in her eyes, like she wanted to say something but was not quite sure how to go about it. "Nico liked your story tonight. You are good with him."

Davianna shrugged. "My daddy used to make up stories like that. He invented the character, so I like telling them." She looked down at her scuffed boot and kicked the dust.

"It's a shame about your dad." Mrs. ben Gingle glanced over her shoulder, back in the tent. "I've talked to Hosea, and we think you are a nice girl, Davianna." Color flooded her face. "Well, it's just that—"

"I have to go," Davianna said with a forced smile. "Thanks, thanks for everything." She rushed away before Mrs. ben Gingle could say anything more.

Whatever it was, it had not been good.

She wove through the dusty paths to the community fire, past families cleaning up supper dishes, and mothers wrangling overtired children. She ignored the careworn old woman who eyed her suspiciously and whispered in disapproving tones as she walked by. She avoided the bachelor's tents, though she thought with some asperity, her mother did not.

She reached the fire and composed herself, smiling despite her angst. 'Always smile when you enter a room, Dee-dee.' Her daddy's voice came clear in her mind. 'It's no use going through life wearing your troubles on your face.'

Her current trouble was that dinners at Mrs. ben Gingle's were likely a thing of the past, and her mother was nowhere to be found.

In the firelight, she saw Astrid sitting on Guan's lap, toying with his hair. Davianna nodded to everyone and took her customary spot beside Astrid. Around the fire people were listening with varying degrees of attention to Portia who was performing a scene from the wretched play for what felt like the hundredth time. Davianna figured it was better than being alone in her empty tent, but not much.

She pretended to tie the frayed lace on her boot, avoiding the eyes of Portia's hulking brother, George. He was the one who found them in the desert the day she and her mother arrived at Camp Eiran. They were out of water and delirious. Zanah had collapsed and was in and out of consciousness. Davianna was panicked, unsure of what to do. When she spotted him, it felt like the Savior himself had shown up. He hefted Zanah over his shoulder and carried their packs into camp. He undoubtedly saved their lives, but since, he always seemed to be hanging around, watching her. He never said a word, never did anything untoward, but all that blank staring unnerved her.

Astrid and Guan completely ignored Portia, whispering and kissing. Davianna glanced at them, and Guan caught her eye. He moved to kiss Astrid's ear, but it was a pretext. Hidden from the others, he shot Davianna a lecherous grin and blew her a kiss.

Davianna felt her cheeks flame. He kept doing things like that, sending her secret glances, touching her a little too friendly, whispering veiled innuendos. Davianna tried to ignore it, tried to pretend it was her overactive imagination. Tonight, staring into the fire, she had not mistaken that blown kiss and knew this was going to cause big trouble.

Portia, peeved that she was being ignored, said in a high-pitched voice, "Oh, Astrid. Oh, Guan." Punctuating her taunt with theatrical kissing noises, she regained her audience's attention, "Guan, you are so handsome. I love your hair. It's as pretty as a girl's."

Good natured laughter and teasing erupted around the

fire. Guan's face turned red, and he pushed Astrid away, harder than was strictly necessary. She made a game of it, renewing her ardor with comic exaggeration, to the delight of all, except Guan and Davianna.

A bell rang, and a collective groan rose from the young people. It was the call to nightly meeting. Davianna stood and smoothed her dress, feeling the weight of the box in her left pocket.

Portia flounced over, pulling George behind her. "Come on, Davianna, walk with George and me."

There was no diplomatic way to refuse.

Astrid and Guan walked side by side, their hands slung low around each other's waists. As they moved off, he slid his hand down, copping a cheap feel. Davianna looked away and caught the interplay between Astrid's mother and stepfather. Emaline elbowed Frank, drawing his attention to the pair, and neither of her parents looked pleased.

Astrid was in no hurry. Meeting was the same every night. Somebody prayed. Somebody read a verse. They asked for blessing and safe passage on their pilgrimage to the Golden City, and since coming to Greece, for rain.

Pilgrim camps varied in age and accommodation, but the meeting space was one feature they all had in common. Astrid liked this one, with the sky overhead and the river nearby. The musicians were not bad either. For Astrid, music was the only redeeming thing about meeting. She hated this place, hated this pilgrimage, would rather be anywhere else in the world but here.

She stopped at the back row, which was where they sat every night because it was easier to sneak out if the speakers got long winded. Davianna extricated herself from George and Portia, hurrying over and rolling her eyes. She feigned a creepy shiver and sidled down the long bench, ahead of Astrid and Guan.

The meeting filled up quickly. Davianna stood atop the

bench, scanning the crowd. When the last of the stragglers came through the arches, she sat down with an aggravated sigh.

Zanah's prolonged absence was a source of anxiety for them both. Any day, rain might return. When that happened, her Stepfather Frank would make them leave, and if they left, what would happen to Davianna? Astrid squeezed her knee and tried to sound reassuring. "I am sure your mother will be back tomorrow."

Davianna forced a smile but did not say what they both feared; Zanah was never coming back.

The musicians began. The guitarist played low and soft. Portia's father came in on the violin. The song was haunting and sad. Everyone bowed their heads, singing or praying quietly.

Astrid pretended to pray, but Guan kept trying to slip a hand inside her dress. She nudged him away with a giggle and slapped at his hand.

When he did it a second time, she gave him a warning growl, "Stop it."

He did not.

The third time, her temper flared, and she pinched his arm, hard.

He withdrew with a hiss. "Whatever," he said with an angry pout and left.

Astrid raised her lip, annoyed, and glad to be rid of him. She did not appreciate being pawed.

Davianna sent her a questioning glance, having missed the interplay in her silent prayers.

Astrid shrugged, then waved a dismissive hand after him. "He's mad, but I don't care. He's been weird all night."

Davianna bit her bottom lip and glanced over her shoulder. "You're right. He is weird."

Thankfully, meeting did not last long. Nobody got carried away, which was fine with Astrid. She came alive when the sun went down. As an unapologetic night person, she was ready to have a little fun. "Come on, there's Mom."

Emaline chatted with a group of friends, but when the girls walked up, the mothers kept talking. Astrid tried half a dozen times to get Emaline's attention, but no amount of deep sighing, impatient body language, or the beginnings of, "Mom—" stopped Emaline once she got on a roll.

Finally, the other ladies excused themselves.

Astrid attempted to keep the annoyance out of her voice, but she did not quite succeed. "Mom, is it okay if I sleep at Davianna's tonight?"

Emaline sent a wordless glance toward Frank. "No, honey, not tonight."

Astrid shot a look at Frank. "Why, because he says so?"

The tilt of Emaline's head gave a clear warning. "Watch your tone, young lady. The answer is no, not tonight."

"Thanks, Mom," Astrid said with deep sarcasm and stalked off, bristling with fury.

They walked in silence with Emaline and Frank close behind. When they reached Astrid's tent, she lingered for a moment. Hugging Davianna, she said, "Sorry. Maybe tomorrow," then added in a fierce whisper, "I really hate him."

"It's okay, Tridi. I'll see you in the morning."

Astrid watched Davianna walk away, puzzled by the flash of fear she saw cross her friend's face.

Davianna plucked her way through the tents, thinking Mrs. ben Gingle might not be the only one placing distance between her family and Davianna. If Emaline and Frank began keeping Astrid away, she would be in real trouble. She heard the whispers, knew where they came from. Her mother had not made a particularly good impression on anyone other than the bachelors in camp. It was why, in the end, they traveled alone, which was fine when her daddy was alive, disastrous after he was gone.

Davianna was furious with her mother and more than a little afraid. "Where are you?" She muttered in the darkness. "You've been gone for more than a week, Mother. You can't just leave me alone in the middle of Greece with no money."

"Hey," said a voice from the shadows.

Davianna startled, as Guan materialized and joined her on the dark pathway. "Oh, hi."

"I thought Astrid was staying at your place tonight?"

Davianna put as much distance between them as possible without making it obvious. "No. Though, knowing Astrid, she might convince her mother and be around shortly. You never can tell."

"Hmm, I suppose she could surprise you." His tone was companionable, his eyes calculating. "I surprised Astrid with a rabbit. Did you see it?"

Davianna raised a brow at him. He was such a liar. "No, I didn't."

Sly and suggestive, he ran his hand over the front of his pants. "It was big."

She flinched and kept walking, faster now. Rounding the corner, her tent was dark. At the edge of the camp, they were alone. Adopting a breezy tone, she said, "Well, okay, good night."

He moved in front of her, stinking of sour wine. "What's the hurry? Your mom's not back."

Her forehead crinkled in annoyance. "You are Astrid's boyfriend. Now let me by." She tried to push past him.

He countered, blocking her way. "No, I don't think I will."

Davianna's eyes darted, looking for anyone. "What are you playing at?" she hissed.

With an indolent shrug, he leered at her breasts and raised a questioning eyebrow.

Davianna scoffed, and with bravery she did not feel, said, "Yeah, right."

Guan's pale gray eyes darkened. "I see the looks you've been giving me. The way you flip your hair." He touched a chestnut curl. "You are pretty, and that ass, oh my goodness, that sweet ass. Don't be a tease, Davianna. Everyone knows you're like your mother."

Her mouth fell open in outrage.

Without warning, he pinned her hands behind her back and swooped in, delivering a punishing, slobbery kiss. He stank of alcohol and bad teeth. While not a big man, he was stronger than she imagined.

"Get off me!" Davianna struggled, trying to pull away.

His hand squeezed her wrists, and he thrust his hips against hers, grinding. "I'm going to get off all right."

She felt his repulsive hard member against her belly and panicked. He made an animal growl and backed her to the entrance of the tent.

This was no stolen kiss, no slimy flirtation, if he got her inside… She fought.

But his hands were everywhere, and he was strong. He lifted her off the ground, moving fast, her feet kicking dust and dirt. The tent flap was secured, he could not simply barge in. He put a hand over her mouth, covering her scream. His eyes turned black, lust crazed. He jerked her pelvis against his, pounding hard.

Davianna went wild, fighting with all her might. He pulled the tent flap open.

Then it stopped.

She pushed off, but the scream died in her throat.

"What's this, Davianna?" Guan held the box from her pocket.

"Give that back!" she croaked and lunged at him.

Guan stiff armed her, keeping her at bay, staring at the box. The wrapping fell away, and a wicked grin split his face.

"Give it to me." Davianna reached for it again.

He tapped the top and shook his head. "Somebody has been a very bad girl."

"Shut up, it's—"

A hand coalesced out of the darkness. She heard his grunt of pain, and before the scene registered, Guan was hoisted into the air by his collar, gagging and writhing like a worm on a hook. Davianna stumbled backward and tripped over a stake, landing on her rump with a whoosh.

She could just make out George's face, holding a squirming Guan suspended in midair. His expression was unperturbed as he uttered the first words Davianna ever heard him speak, "Don't touch Davianna."

Guan choked out a reply, which George seemed to interpret as assent. He dropped him. Guan's legs buckled, and he fell forward, coughing. He caught himself, face to face with her, his pupils dilated black against demon red cheeks. He scrambled to his feet, and whirled, ready to fight.

George stood silent, watching.

Guan jerked his collar, still gasping, with spit dribbled on his chin. He glared at George but seemed to think better of fighting a man twice his size. Glowering at Davianna sprawled in the dirt, he spat, "Wait until I tell Astrid what a dirty little whore you are." Then he pointed and said, "Fuck you, George. She was coming on to me."

Davianna sat frozen in outraged panic as Guan stalked off. She pulled at her hair, terrified and furious, but she did not say a word, did not dare make a ruckus.

With slow deliberate movements, George retrieved the box Guan had dropped during the fight. "You're safe now," he croaked and hauled her up as if she weighed little more than a feather.

She tried to thank him, but nothing came out. Her hands shook so badly she could not get the box into her pocket. She gave up, whimpering in frustration.

Holding open the tent flap, George gently guided her through. "I'll watch. You sleep."

Davianna nodded convulsively and ducked under his arm.

Inside, she dove for her pack and hid the cursed box. She could not bear to touch it. Frantic, she scrubbed her mouth, still tasting sour wine and Guan's rancid breath. Upending the canteen, she tried to wash it away. A cut on the inside of her cheek burned. Her upper lip throbbed. Dabbing at it gingerly, she winced at the swelling. A pink stain of blood and water came away on her finger. The tent filled with the desperate pants of a hunted animal, and she vaguely realized the sounds were coming from her.

She threw the canteen aside and ripped the blankets off her mother's undisturbed bed. "Where are you?"

The sheet caught on a sharp corner. Davianna jerked it free, then tore it in half. "If you aren't going to sleep in this bed, you won't have one!" She took out her anger, her fear, her frustration on Zanah's cot.

When the tumult subsided, she collapsed cross legged in the dirt, amid the remnants of sheets, blankets, and feathers.

Damn, she knew something like this was going to happen, knew it.

She fell over sideways and curled into a ball. Her eyes rested on her pack, where the hidden box seemed to mock her. That thing was dangerous. They would probably expel her from camp, or worse, put her out in the desert by herself. She almost died out there.

Daddy had.

She had no money, no connections, and no one to turn to, except Astrid, but after tonight, even that was threatened. If Guan painted a picture, if he told Astrid she tried to seduce him, she might believe him. Everyone might believe him. Half of them already believed she was a slut, despite evidence to the contrary. She would be shunned, alone.

Davianna covered her injured face with a blanket and let the tears flow, weeping long into the night.

March 7, 999 ME

Letters

Davianna woke the following morning, her eyes crusted shut, her body aching. Rolling over with a groan, she realized she had slept on the ground in a dirty nest. She pulled a feather out of her hair, a straggler from her mother's destroyed pillow. One had found purchase in the tent flap and fluttered in the draft. She ran a finger over her upper lip, still tender, but the swelling had gone down.

She pushed to her feet, surveying the wreckage. In the light she saw her dress was torn, the left pocket ripped, hanging upside down, pulled away from the seam. She was filthy. Smacking her lips, she realized she was also parched. The canteen she slung across the tent was empty.

Pulling her dusty dress over her head, it joined the blankets and tattered sheet. "That was dumb," she said into the silence. "Now you've got to wash all this mess." Aggravated at her own stupidity, she knew she would have to hide the evidence of her tantrum. Zanah, if she ever came back, would be furious. She never let Davianna touch any of her things, let alone rip them to shreds.

Exhibiting a defiance that surprised even herself, she threw open the lid of her mother's trunk. They abandoned most of their possessions, and Zanah's trunk had been the last thing they left behind. A week after they arrived at Camp Eiran, Zanah cajoled a man to retrieve it with his wagon. But Davianna's things were buried under the shifting sands, like her father.

The most telling sign that Zanah was not coming back was this trunk. She had not shared it with Astrid, but all her mother's nice clothes were gone. Davianna extracted a black silk dressing robe, embroidered with white flowers. Zanah owned it for as long as Davianna could remember. The embroidery frayed in places, the threads of one flower completely undone. "No wonder she left this behind."

She stared into the depths of the nearly empty trunk, the familiar spicy scent of her mother's perfume escaped, mingling with the smells of dusty canvas and morning cook fires. Davianna lifted out a blue dress. Her daddy bought this one, and Davianna had been with him. She could not remember if it was a birthday present or some other special occasion, but she remembered thinking it was the prettiest blue she had ever seen. To her knowledge, Zanah had never worn it.

Davianna held it up to her chest and looked down. "It's probably going to be loose there." It might be impractical for camp, too pretty, too short. It would hit her mid-calf, but her boots would cover that. It might be tight in the arms, but it was clean. As she slipped it on, she felt like she declared to the world, "I was his daughter, not just hers."

Leaving the chaos of feathers behind, she trudged to the river, to bathe and do laundry. Dread followed her.

There was a women's section around the river bend, hidden from the camp. She nodded a silent greeting to the dozen women and girls already there. Dropping the heavy laundry bag, she stretched her aching back.

While she bathed, she kept glancing over her shoulder, certain she would see a red-faced Astrid storming toward her. No one came.

Bathed and dressed, she brushed her teeth, trying to avoid the small cuts inside her mouth. Preoccupied, she yelped and nearly toppled in fully clothed at a loud, "Boo!"

Astrid fell on the bank, laughing.

Davianna turned with her hands on her hips. She hated being scared. Glancing around, she realized they were alone. The rest of the bathers were back at camp, preparing breakfast.

"Good morning!" Astrid chirped and tossed Davianna a pear as a peace offering.

Davianna curled her lip in a sneer and flinched when it stung. "What are you so chipper about?" She took a bite of the pear, surmising Guan had not told Astrid anything, yet.

Astrid batted her long lashes and replied in a sing-song voice, "Oh, nothing."

"Yeah, right." Davianna dropped her toothbrush in her small toiletry basket. Astrid was obviously dying to tell her something and judging by her expression it was good news.

Astrid widened her blue eyes and pulled a paper from her pocket. "I got a letter from Daddy."

Davianna brightened and sat down beside her. "Let's see then."

Astrid clutched it to her heart. "He's in the New City, Davi!"

"Truly?" Davianna held out her hand.

The letter was short, written in small script.

Dear Astrid,

I've finally moved to the New City and cannot believe I waited this long to do it. What a place it is! The New City is wondrous and beautiful, just like you.

There is an energy here, full of opportunities, a perfect place for a man like me. I bought a nice, big car and am making a small fortune in the computer business. I can't tell you the details, but a friend of mine got me in on the deal of a lifetime. Great things are getting ready to happen for your daddy.

Obey your mother. I'll write again soon.
Love,
Daddy

Astrid squealed, "Isn't it amazing?"

"Computers, wow." Davianna glanced around to make sure they were not being overheard since talk of technology was frowned upon in pilgrim camps.

Lost in a daydream, Astrid stared across the river. "Imagine how much faster we could travel if we had a car?"

Davianna thought of the wagon and her little filly they had to sell in France. A long stretch of desert stood between them and the seaport that would take them to the Golden Kingdom. "I think I would like a car, though I would probably be scared."

"I wouldn't, and those folks in the New City aren't." Astrid nodded with certainty. "Wondrous and beautiful, oh I want to go."

"My mother always wanted to, but Daddy was against it."

"I saw a drawing once when we were in Spain. The buildings reached to the sky." Astrid threw up her hands and laid back on the riverbank. "I am sure he has a great house, probably with a big deck for entertaining. He is so much fun, Davi, and always threw the best parties."

Astrid launched into a story about an innocent, happy time, before the divorce, before Frank, or the pilgrimage. Memories poured out of her, and with Davianna she was free to share them. In her family tent, she was not.

As Astrid's story ended, Davianna whispered, "Did you tell your mother about the letter?"

"Pfft, she knows." Astrid rolled her eyes. "She and Frank were eating breakfast when it came. I didn't read it in front of them. I came looking for you."

Davianna's tremulous smile hid her growing anxiety. She hoped Astrid still felt that way tonight because Guan was lurking at the edge of the camp, watching them.

Driftwood

At the nightly fire, Astrid fidgeted in her chair, uncomfortable as the wooden staves dug into the back of her legs, and the flames burned her cheeks. Twisting around, she searched the shadows. The conversation tonight felt stilted, lacking its normal relaxed banter. Something was going on, and she had a sneaking suspicion Guan's absence had something to do with it.

She caught Davianna's attention, gesturing to Guan's empty chair. Davianna shrugged and looked away. Before Astrid could say anything, Emaline passed Davianna a cup of water.

Astrid narrowed her eyes, resenting her mother's presence at the fire. Several of the older folks had joined them tonight, which was unusual. They did it under the pretext that Wallace, Portia's father, was going to play his violin, but the violin stayed in its case, and Wallace was talking to Frank and George.

The bell for meeting might ring at any moment, and still there was no sign of Guan, hadn't been all day. Her mother was firm in her stance that the bachelors' quarters were off limits, so he had to come to her. She had pinched him last night, so he might still be pouting. Adopting a casualness she did not feel, she asked, "Where's Guan?"

All talk stopped. Davianna froze with her cup halfway to her mouth.

Astrid looked around. "What?" No one would meet her eyes.

Frank leaned forward and took a stick, poking the red coals, making the already roaring fire hotter. He gestured with his chin toward the east, adopting the dismissive, unconcerned attitude she hated. "He left this morning."

"He left, where?" She looked around reflexively, as if he were sitting at the fire, and she missed him. Still, no one would look at her.

A log popped, and Davianna jumped, spilling water in her lap. No one moved; no one spoke.

And then she knew.

In a voice that contained every ounce of contempt burning in her gut, she looked at Frank and hissed, "What did you do?"

Frank sat back, giving her a level gaze. "I told him to get the hell outta here."

Astrid erupted from her chair. "Why?"

Frank made a dismissive shrug, and then he did what he always did, he judged, summing up a person with a few caustic words. "He was a bad seed."

"Says you?" Astrid shook her fist and screamed, "You have no right, not after what you did!"

Emaline stepped forward. "Astrid, come with me."

Astrid whirled on her. "No! I will not listen to you defend him, not tonight, not after this!" She pointed a shaking finger at Frank, enunciating clearly, quietly. "I hate you." Then, turning on her heel, she stormed off.

Davianna wished the ground would swallow her up.

The men exchanged looks, but everyone remained silent. Frank met her eyes, unperturbed by Astrid's outburst. "Davianna," he gave her a pointed nod and said quietly, "go on after her."

Davianna scrambled out of her chair, escaping their knowing looks. She plunged into the darkness, calling, "Tridi, wait."

Astrid did not stop.

When Davianna caught up, Astrid was raging and spewing incoherent curses. She jerked her arm away and sprinted, making a dash toward the river.

"I hate him!" Her cry echoed over the water. "He brought us here. I did not want to come. I never wanted to come. He ruins everything!"

"I know, Tridi. I know."

At length, the anger burned itself out, and Astrid sagged. "He's the reason, you know, the reason he is gone."

Davianna understood she was not talking about Guan. "I'm sorry."

The desolation on her face went beyond her years. "Davi," she said, as her face contorted into a sob.

Davianna felt it, the pain of losing her own daddy. She held it at bay, banked it by necessity, to get on with it, to get through it. But standing on the riverbank, so far from home, everyone and everything seemed lost. She felt like she was drowning. She opened her arms, crying.

Astrid rushed forward, pulling her tight, squeezing with all her might.

They clung together with their tears mingling. Their friendship felt like a piece of driftwood that floated by after a shipwreck. They held on for dear life as the tempest around them raged.

March 27, 999 ME

Openings

Three weeks after Astrid received her father's letter, Davianna received a letter of her own. It arrived on pink paper, smelling of her mother's perfume. She stared down at the elaborate script with its exaggerated curlicues. 'Get ready. We leave tomorrow.'

Four months since they stumbled into Camp Eiran, they were abandoning their pilgrimage. They were not going to the Golden City like her father wanted. They were moving back to Alanthia because Zanah had met a rich man. They were going to the New City.

The poison letter fell in the dust.

"Tomorrow," she whispered.

When she thought about it later, she never knew how long she sat there, staring at her father's battered backpack. She decided the weight in her pocket shifted against her thigh, spurring her into action.

She bolted from the tent, the letter forgotten, abandoned where it lay.

Three rows over and five tents down, she ran. Throwing open the flap, she fell on top of Astrid, shaking her. "Get up."

Astrid buried her head under the pillow and croaked, "Go away."

"No. Come on. It's time."

The urgency in Davianna's voice penetrated Astrid's stupor. She lifted a corner of her pillow, one cat blue eye squinting against the light. "It's time?"

Davianna sat back on her heels and nodded.

Astrid fortified herself with a deep sigh. "Well, get off me."

Davianna hooted and started to extricate herself, tickling Astrid's ribs. "Get up, get up! Rise and shine, shine and rise," her teasing became a ghostly echo of her father's morning ritual.

Astrid squealed, squirmed, and tickled back.

They lay in a heap of twisted blankets, gasping and giggling.

Emaline entered the tent and chuckled, "You girls."

Davianna refused to say a word as she dragged Astrid through the camp to their hiding place. She walked in a dissociative-like state, as if tomorrow would not come. She could not, would not think of it. They were together, right now, and it was happening. They were going to open the box.

Davianna did not care about the consequences, if they threw her out of camp, it no longer mattered. The worst was already happening. They were taking her away from Astrid.

Later, she would tell Astrid about the letter, about leaving, but not now. Right now, they were having a last adventure, one last thing, one last day. She vowed it was going to be fun. Like it used to be, before Daddy died, before everything fell apart.

Under the oak tree, there was no preamble, no story review. Story time was over.

Brimming with excitement, Davianna fumbled with the seal and removed the lid. Inside sat a slender rectangle of mirrored onyx, forbidden and seductive.

"We were right, Davi. It is ancient." Astrid took the empty lid and read the label. "Prototype 1.C, NSA - Project Rusor."

"NSA?" Davianna breathed.

"Oh, shit," Astrid swore quietly.

They knew their history. At the end of the Last Age, the entire world was monitored and controlled by a single, powerful organization. No aspect of human life was beyond its purview. It had, in many ways, become a god.

Davianna squeezed her eyes shut. She was not going to chicken out, not this time. With a surprisingly steady hand, she lifted the device from the box. It felt solid, smooth, and sleek. Her flushed face reflected on the surface. "Now what?"

"Are there any instructions in there?" Astrid took the empty box and checked under the insert.

Nothing.

"Push the button?" Astrid's finger hovered over a tiny switch on the side, then pulled away as if she had been shocked.

Davianna paled.

Astrid narrowed her eyes, truly looking at Davianna. "What are you not telling me?"

Davianna blinked and glanced away, chewing on her bottom lip. "Nothing. Are we going to do this?"

"All right." Astrid scooted closer. "Give it to me. I'll do it."

Davianna's eyes grew huge in the dark space. Astrid could not distinguish between the dark brown irises and her pupils. "You're sure?"

Astrid nodded. "Yes."

Davianna pressed her lips into a grim line and handed it over.

Astrid pushed the button.

The screen lit up. Davianna jumped. Astrid dropped the device. Neither expected anything to happen.

They started giggling.

With the utmost care, as if it might explode, Astrid picked it back up. Illuminated on the jet-black background was a white apple with a bite out of it. It was the most enticing thing she ever saw.

"Oh, that's creepy." Davianna swallowed audibly.

"Hush," Astrid said, staring at it transfixed.

When the apple faded away, they gasped.

"Is that it?" Astrid's breathless question filled the empty hideaway.

"It can't be." Davianna shook her head and pointed to the button again.

Astrid closed her eyes and pressed.

The apple reappeared, but this time a deep, disembodied voice said, "Welcome."

Davianna shrieked, and Astrid threw the device across

the hideout. It landed in the dirt, the screen still lit, glowing in the darkness.

Astrid's breath was coming fast as they watched the flickering screen. "It talks."

Davianna licked her lips, her mouth dry, her palms sweating. "I can't believe it."

"That's one hell of a battery," Astrid said, scooting backwards.

Davianna made a snorting laugh through her teeth, on the edge of nervous hysteria. Scrambling across the floor, she retrieved it. "If you are going to do something. Do it right."

The screen showed a thumbprint, 'Place thumb here'.

Davianna's hand shook as she followed the instruction.

Three more taps and the screen flashed. "Set up the second user."

Davianna handed it to Astrid. "You do it, too." She wanted Astrid's fingerprint with her when she left.

They shared a look, if Astrid did this, she would be irrevocably tied to this device, casting her lot with Davianna.

Astrid opened her palm. "Hand it over."

Sixty seconds later, their thumbprints were recorded.

The device made several loud pinging noises, flashing strange images and symbols that they could not truly see. It vibrated and buzzed in Davianna's hand. She resisted the urge to throw it.

"Project Rusor launched," came the disembodied voice again. "Would you like to listen to some music while you wait?"

A large white square appeared on the screen, an eighth note, written in tiny letters underneath, the magic word, *music*.

"While we wait for what?" Davianna choked. Music from the Last Age was absolutely forbidden in pilgrim camps.

"Oh, no. I think this is bad." Astrid gulped.

Davianna wanted to let go, wanted to put it down, but her hand stuck to the device, as if held by a magnetic force.

"May I suggest," the voice sounded less disembodied, more sinister. A cartoon tongue and lips filled the screen. Electric energy pulsed through the artifact, up Davianna's arm. Her jaw dropped. The title chilled her to the bone as she breathed, "Sympathy for the Devil?" She tossed it away and covered her mouth with both hands, stifling a scream.

"Oh, shit!" Astrid leapt on the device. "Turn it off! Turn it off!"

"I don't know how!" Davianna panicked.

"Play a song, girls," said the voice.

The terrified looks they exchanged would have been comical if evil had not snaked its way into their hiding place.

Without them trying, without them touching it, strange bongos began to play.

Davianna jerked the device out of Astrid's hands and hit the button, holding it with all her might.

It went dead... the music stopped.

"Oh, no!" Davianna held it in a death grip, her knuckles white, her hands shaking.

"What the hell is that thing?" Astrid demanded.

"I don't know. I don't know."

Astrid crawled to the entrance, sure the elders would be bearing down on them, certain the music had reached the camp. It had been loud. "We've got to get out of here."

Davianna nodded convulsively. "Go. I'll put this thing back in the box. I'll hide it."

Astrid stared at the sky, no thunder, no lightning. They were not dead. Yet.

Migraine

An hour later, Astrid wanted to die as she vomited the remainder of last night's dinner into the basin her mother held under her chin. Blinded with pain, the migraine pierced her left temple. She whimpered, as practiced hands eased her down on the cot and placed a cool cloth over her eyes, shrouding her in gray darkness.

Her tea steeped, its familiar smell suffusing the air, calm and panic mingled in a ceramic pot. Bile rose in the back of her throat. She retched again.

She tried not to move, tried not to think, tried to be nothing. Her neck was in a vise, locked in screaming agony. As the pounding pressure built, Astrid pressed her palm into her eye as every heartbeat drove the stiletto deeper into her brain. The pain was so intense, so magnificent, there should be blood, but there wasn't.

She tried to hold it at arm's length, but it pulled her under. Her breathing turned to pants, rapid and shallow. Emaline's voice penetrated the agony, soothing, offering tea. Blindly, Astrid inhaled the pungent brew. Her stomach flipped, and she began to gag. With an economy of motion, the teacup was replaced with the basin, and she retched. They had done this before.

The headache struck like lightning. Had it been those drums or those odd flashing pictures? Had that done it? Had the device sent a horrible signal into her brain?

Her rational mind rejected the notion.

Afterward, standing on the edge of the riverbank, shaking and sweating, Davianna told her the truth. Why she had gotten up the courage today, why what they did ultimately did not matter. Astrid did not have to be afraid they would kick her out of camp because Davianna was leaving. Tomorrow.

The pain intensified, building to such a crashing crescendo she thought her head might explode. Davianna was leaving, and Astrid wanted to die.

A lifetime of dreadful memories beat inside her skull, reverberating like a big bass drum. Months spent in her sickbed, solitary, darkness: boom! Laying in silence, wracked with pain with no respite or relief: boom! No friends, no light, nothing: boom! Tomorrow, tomorrow her best friend was leaving: boom!

She tried not to cry. It hurt to cry, but it hurt not to cry. Tears leaked out of the corners of her eyes, pooling in her ears, giving her the disconcerting feeling that she was underwater, drowning. This could not be happening, not again.

No one understood her, except Davianna. No one needed her, but Davianna did. If Davianna left, there would be no one to laugh with, no one to be silly with, no one to simply be herself with.

Astrid knew who she was, and so did Davianna, but without her friend, would she morph into the hot-tempered redhead everyone expected her to be? It was a caricature, not who she truly was.

She was Davianna ben David's best friend, the second half of a whole. Among the dusty tents of Camp Eiran, they were each other's shelter from the storm, safety in a world gone mad, laughter through tears. They were more than just friends, they were connected on a soul level, sisters of the heart. Astrid did not love anyone like she loved Davianna, not since Daddy left.

The headache exacted its revenge, forcing her to disengage, to step outside her body. She imagined that she floated in the air, looking down on herself, perfectly still. She watched her skin alternately pale and flush. The warm cloth formed a blindfold, blocking oamut everything.

A small clock ticked on her mother's side table, each metallic sound bringing her inexorably closer to goodbye. Laying in the dark, with the stench of vomit on her dress, she heard her heart break. The pain in her head felt insignificant by comparison.

Cockamamie Scheme

For six hours, Davianna kept a stubborn vigil. Emaline tried to shoo her off, but the girl showed more grit than Emaline witnessed from her thus far. Emaline pitied her, poor little thing, abandoned in this camp, her mother run off to heaven knew where, and her father dead. Moreover, she had grown fond of Davianna and was thankful for the happiness she brought Astrid.

Seeing Davianna was not going to be deterred, Emaline pressed a bar of unscented soap into her hand, "Go bathe, brush your teeth, and don't eat anything." At Davianna's quizzical look, she explained in her Mississippi twang, "Astrid's migraines leave her with a heightened sense of smell. A well-meaning bouquet or a neighbor cooking sausage will send her spiraling right back down. This was a bad one. So tonight, while everyone is at evening meeting, we'll move our tent to the outer perimeter."

"You don't need to do that." The expression on Davianna's face was a mixture of gloom and excitement.

Emaline could only imagine the cockamamie scheme coming next. "Is that so?"

"Yes, ma'am. You see, I am leaving tomorrow. I should have been packing. My mother is coming." She sagged in defeat. "But I didn't want to leave Astrid. This was our last day."

Emaline now understood the headache.

"Instead of packing this very fine campsite," Davianna gestured with her hand, as if the cordoned off space was a glorious manor. "I already have to pack mine." She looked up with pleading eyes. "Astrid can stay with me. Then at least, we can have one last night together." Emaline started to shake her head, but Davianna cut her off. "I promise it will be okay. I promise." She leaned forward and whispered, "We have a secret hiding spot, no flowers or cook fires."

Emaline gave Davianna a dubious look.

Beginning to panic, Davianna plead her case. "Oh, please, Mrs. Emaline, please." With tears glistening in the late afternoon light, she sniffed and said, "Astrid is my best friend. The person I love most in this world. They... they are m-m-making me leave her."

Emaline pulled Davianna into her arms and held her as she cried, her own heart breaking with each ragged sob.

"We only have tonight. I will never see her again. Please?"

Instinct told her no, but the desperate girl was impossible to ignore. It was a lot to pack. Frank would be back shortly, and there was nothing ready for supper. After hunting all day, he would not be happy about moving. That would probably spark an argument between him and Astrid, the first of many more to come. Without Davianna, Astrid would be a handful.

Tapping the end of her nose, she considered Davianna's idea. Emaline was highly attuned to the growing dangers of camp life. Human predators were everywhere. They avoided a catastrophe with that little pissant Guan, who she was leery of from the start; she never liked the look in his eyes. But the thought of Guan brought her around to George. She knew George secretly guarded Davianna. He had for months, keeping stray men from wandering into her tent and taking advantage of a young girl alone. She would set him as guard. No harm would befall the girls this night.

Hiding place, indeed.

The Riverside

Darkness so thick it held substance blanketed the land. Tucked away and hiding from a world that no longer made sense, the two girls snuggled into their bedrolls.

Davianna was exhausted after a frenzied evening of packing. She pushed herself at a frantic pace, fearing if she did not hurry, Emaline would change her mind. A well-worn dusty pack at her feet held her meager possessions which included an old shirt of her daddy's and a small miniature of him at twenty, on his wedding day. She left her mother's remaining items and all their household goods in the care of Mrs. ben Gingle. Nico cried when she told him she was leaving.

Everything was ready to go, and time was moving too fast.

Astrid fluffed her lavender scented headache pillow and sighed.

"Would you like tea?" Davianna yawned and gestured to the small tea chest Emaline had sent with Astrid.

"No, it keeps me awake." Astrid sat up and retrieved her extra set of clothes. Emaline had sent those too in case she vomited. She tucked them under her arm, cushioning the hard ground.

"I'm sorry your head hurts."

"It's okay. It will be better in the morning."

"Do you think turning that thing on caused it, Tridi?"

Astrid closed her eyes, too tired to think. "I don't see how."

Davianna felt a hot tear leak out of her eye. "You're the best friend I ever had."

Astrid sniffed and said in a small voice, "Me, too."

Without another word, they clasped hands, dreading the morning and the pain. Heartbroken beyond speaking, the song of the crickets and the lazy lapping of the river lulled them into a deep sleep.

Nightmares crept into their hideaway. The earth shook, the sky roared with thunder. Terrified screams and shouting filled the air, mingling with the stench of fire and blood. Astrid clutched her head and moaned. Davianna burrowed against her, crying softly. They clung to each other. When the nightmare ended, they both fell into dreamless sleep.

Part 4 - The Hunt

March 27, 999 ME

Dungeons and Dragons - New City - Korah

King Korah sat on his throne, not the ancestral throne where he smiled and wore the face of the benevolent ruler, neither his father nor his brother sat in this seat. No, tonight he sat on a throne bought with blood, paid for with his soul. Korah presided over the dungeon where his reign was born.

He did not delude himself. He was not the king here, simply a conduit, the voice the Dark Master spoke through if he chose. However, being the voice of power had its perks, and its costs, but he focused on neither.

Tonight, he was being obedient, if not a tad bored. Another ritual, another ceremony, another sacrifice, it had grown tiresome, though he kept that thought out of his head. Otherwise, he would pay for it.

For weeks, the Dark Master had been in a frenzy, calling them forth, proclaiming they were at the cusp of discovery. They went through the motions, performed the rituals, and waited. Nothing. Korah had a kingdom to run, and these middle of the night forays were becoming tedious.

Ba'alat Ob, the Mistress who speaks to the dead, or the new bitch, as Korah privately referred to her, put on quite a show. He gave her credit. She threw herself into the role, trying to prove she was worthy of the name. He watched with detached interest. There was an insanity about her that was intriguing, yet she lacked the calculated cruelty and cunning that had been the hallmark of her predecessor. She was prone to histrionics and flashes of rage, utterly unpredictable. He wondered how long the Dark Master would allow her to stay in her current position. He doubted long. However, she had stamina. Night after night, she left nothing on the table.

Then something changed. Korah leaned forward. He felt something shift. His hazel eyes grew alert. The hair on the back of his arms pricked under his silk robe. The air crackled, something pulsed, something fought for release.

The Dark Master howled. Korah channeled the shout, "It is found!"

The atmosphere in the chamber began to shimmer with black, throbbing energy. Korah leapt to his feet as the coven fell to their knees. The bitch ran up the steps to join him on the dais. He exchanged a look with her, and it felt eerily reminiscent of that day, so long ago, when he first brought forth the Dark Master. Korah's eyes darted toward the stone slab, half expecting to see his brother's corpse.

As it was that day, the smell of sulfur suffused the air, and a sense of doom, of awesome power, filled the underground cavern. For the first time in more than a decade, the Dark Master manifested. Several new members shrieked in terror. The elders began to weep. They remembered.

The great and powerful Dark Master stood in their midst.

Terror ripped through the chamber.

The sheer magnitude of him was overwhelming. Silhouetted against the torches, he stood thirty feet tall, wearing armor that looked like dragon's scales and absorbed all light that dared touch it. Atop his head sat a crown of many spires, each depicting men in the throes of gruesome death. Dreadlocks fell down his back, moving and coiling like venomous snakes. Powerful raven wings brushed the backs of his calves as he stood. Korah had seen them unfurl on the battlefield at the end of the Civil War, and they covered a line of mounted riders twenty strong. The Dark Master scanned the room with black and gold snake eyes that never blinked, settling on Korah. He did not appear pleased.

He snarled, bearing fangs set in a face of reptilian horror. "I think you have forgotten who you serve!"

Korah and the Mistress bowed low, dreading what was to come. If he was in a temper, it would not go well for them.

"I am Marduk," he thundered. "The Prince of Persia and Alanthia, your Master."

"All hail the Dark Master, wise warrior, your might and power are unparalleled."

"And who am I, to you?" he demanded.

"Thou art a god, ageless, timeless."

Korah hazarded a look, curious to see if he had aged. Marduk was an elohim, an angel in the simplest terms, albeit a fallen one. From what Korah could tell, he appeared unchanged, utterly magnificent, terrifying.

"Then why do you show no more reverence to me than you would a dog? Do you think I do not see?" He swept them with his penetrating eyes. No one lifted their heads. No one dared. "I have more intelligence in my fingernail," he flashed a razor-sharp talon, "than you paltry humans do collectively."

"Forgive us, Dark Master," they murmured.

"Who resurrected Alanthia out of the dark ages?"

"You did, Dark Master."

"Who unlocked the secrets of knowledge and power?"

"You did, Dark Master."

"Where would you be without me?" He did not wait for an answer, continuing his tirade. "Trapped in slavery, that is where! I have made you great. I made you wealthy. I gave you power beyond your wildest imagination, and you repay me by daydreaming?" The ground shook as he stalked over and screamed in Korah's face. "You of all men!"

"Forgive me, Dark Master. I am your humble and obedient servant."

"For one thousand years, man floundered under the tyranny of the Iron King, while my brethren and I, mankind's greatest allies and friends, were imprisoned. Our knowledge forbidden to you, but I came to save you, to set you free. Through my own will and cunning, I devised a plan to liberate myself, and have chosen you as my people. Yet you squander it all?" he bellowed.

Beside him, the bitch flinched. Marduk's breath was rancid.

"We have a choice. We have built the foundation. We can rule in the coming age or be squashed like bugs."

"We choose you and victory, my Lord," Korah ventured.

Marduk whipped his head around, the dreadlocks animating into vipers. "Do you have the fortitude, Korah ben Adam?"

Korah wisely went down to one knee, genuflecting. "With your help, Dark Master, we can accomplish anything. What would you have me do?"

"Find the Black Key."

Korah looked up in surprise. "You have detected it, my lord?"

"What in the hell do you think we have been doing?"

"Forgive my impertinence."

Marduk flicked his hand, and Korah flew across the chamber, crashing into his throne with a bruising thud. He lay on the ground, gasping, but did not rise. He knew doing so would provoke Marduk's wrath. Not terribly hurt, he feigned greater injury than he sustained.

Satisfied, Marduk turned to the bitch. "Ba'alat Ob, go to the adherents. Find out if they detected the disturbance. Attend me before dawn."

With an explosion of black smoke, he disappeared.

Marduk hid his excitement from those idiots, but he felt it. He knew. The key had been found, at last!

He flew to the highest peak in the New City, where he could survey his kingdom. Standing atop the San Benito Mountains, he calculated his next move.

"Where is it?" His guttural voice carried away on the evening wind.

The Millennium was ending and before it did, he had to find the Black Key. He had to take possession of it, before others broke free, before he had to contend with more of his own kind. If he freed them, they might rally to his side. If he had control, they might stand a chance.

He ruled the humans easily enough. Few understood his race or his abilities. They never had, which was a weapon he used to ruthless advantage. He was not a disembodied spirit; he was not a demon. Men used the terms fallen angel and demon interchangeably, demonstrating their ignorance. As an elohim, Marduk would never lower himself to possess the body of a human, not when his own form was so vastly superior. He might invade a human's mind or influence their actions, but he would not possess them. Demons, with no bodies of their own, had no choice.

While different in form, the fallen elohim and demons shared the same fate during the Millennium. For a thousand years, they were imprisoned, kept off the Earth by the Iron King.

However, that was about to change. The Black Key had been found, and the elohim were going to break free, just like he had. However, if he planned carefully, if he was cunning enough, he could rule them all.

He appraised the valley, flickering with electric lights and racing cars. While the rest of the world rusticated in darkness, technology reigned in Alanthia. Pride swelled his chest as he surveyed *his* work. They lived in a paradise of *his* making. They loved *him*, worshiped *him*, and chose *him* over the Iron King. They always did when given the right enticement.

Marduk had no doubt Alanthia, *his* new kingdom, would gain control of the Black Key, and with it, he would rule.

Hours later, Ba'alat Ob materialized out of the mist. He did not change his appearance. He knew it scared her, even if she would not admit it.

"My lord," she knelt at his feet.

"Ba'alat Ob, you are tardy." She was not, but he accused her anyway.

"Forgive me, Dark Master. I was detained." She offered no excuses, but it took time to check in with the covens positioned across the globe.

"What tidings do you bring?"

"Your infinite wisdom was again demonstrated, my lord. As you suspected, there was a deep disturbance in the spirit realm today, a rumbling, an awakening."

A wicked grin split his black face. "Where?"

"The most violent reading happened in Cairo, my lord. Princess Keyseelough reported an attack on her kingdom. The enemy responded to her worship of you with fire and brimstone"

Marduk made a low suspicious growl.

The witch groveled. "However, it may have come from Greece. We cannot be sure. Antiochus is unresponsive. I was unable to confirm whether he conducted the ritual as you commanded."

Envy - Athens, Greece - Antiochus

In a marble Palace, forty miles from Camp Eiran, Monarch Antiochus of Greece, hurled a jeweled goblet across his library. 'Alanthia sent a satellite signal today.' Antiochus read the missive again and fumed. "Marduk lives in Korah's house. Korah gets away with murder, and the Iron King does nothing!"

Antiochus paced his library, grumbling. "Meanwhile, we have no rain, and everything I do, every small thing, is severely punished." He stared at the world map on his wall. Greece bordered the Golden Kingdom, as such, the Iron King rendered swift and sure judgment, sending troops to patrol inside Greece. And any effort Antiochus made toward modernization and technology was quashed. Meanwhile, Korah, in faraway Alanthia, openly flaunted his rebellion and went unpunished. The two kingdoms and monarchs were not held to the same standards. The disparity infuriated Antiochus.

Greece was spiraling beyond his control. His son, heir, and greatest weapon was gone. His power was slipping, his people fleeing, and with them, tax revenues. His coffers and land were drying up. A constant parade of beggars arrived at his gate, demanding action. "Peasants," he spat, staring at their campfires.

Yet, he faced bigger problems than a bunch of beggars. Marduk was going to be furious because he disregarded the latest high-handed command, threw it in the fire, and burned it. It was a waste of time, fruitless. He was done following orders. His circumstances were worse now than before he threw his lot in with them. He should have known better. Marduk was Korah's man, that much was certain. There was no help coming from that quarter.

Antiochus ran his finger over the shelves loaded with scrolls and writings, some ancient, some modern, most prophecies. He was convinced his library of ancient books, magical knowledge, and archaic rituals held the answers. He extracted one, leaned his bald head over the parchment, and read aloud, "The strongest of all, from Olympus he ruled. Call him forth to gain favor. Find the Key. Open the door." Antiochus sat back with a grunt of frustration.

The butler came in and announced, "My Esteemed, your dinner guests have begun to arrive, but Captain Orion ben Drachmas begs an audience."

Antiochus bade him enter.

The Captain of the Guard kissed his ring, bowing low. "My Esteemed, we have detained a migrant from Camp Eiran who claims he has seen the artifact we have been searching for."

"The Black Key?" Antiochus controlled a burst of excitement and said in a bored tone, "Many have claimed so in the past. Why do you bring this to me now? I have a houseful of guests that have begun to arrive, as you just heard."

Orion's smile dripped with sly satisfaction. "Because, my Esteemed, this one appeared to be new, untouched in a box, and borne by a maiden just as yon prophecy foretold." He nodded toward a scroll spread on Antiochus' desk.

Antiochus leaned forward, rubbing his hands. "Bring him in."

Orion nodded and ushered a slender youth of about twenty into the study.

Antiochus smiled, pleasantly surprised by the youth's handsome face, shimmering blond hair, and cool gray eyes. "Good evening, son. Thank you for coming."

He stared at Antiochus with such eagerness that Antiochus squirmed in his seat, heat rushing to his loins. The young man's Adam's Apple bobbed as he swallowed. It was erotic, full of promise. The boy wore the clothes of a pilgrim but lacked the pious milk-faced countenance of those fools. He had an aura of darkness that spoke to Antiochus and set him aflame. "Please, come in. Can I offer you some refreshments? Perhaps some wine?"

Orion stilled.

Antiochus cut him a deadly glare. "Leave us, Captain. See that we are not disturbed."

Without a word or a backward glance, Captain Orion left Guan ben Sheldon to his fate.

He did not go far. It would not take long.

It did not.

Twenty minutes later, the youth scurried out of the monarch's study, red-faced and sweating. "That was fucked up!" he snarled at Orion.

Orion scoffed at the ill choice of words. "Indeed. He is Greek. What did you expect?"

Guan balled his fists at his sides, shaking with rage. "I expect that reward."

"You will get it, if the information you provided is true." Shooing him away, he said, "Go wait where I showed you."

"Son of a bitch," the boy muttered and limped down the hall.

"You are not dead. Suck it up." Orion laughed and waited for his orders.

The taunting laughter of the guard echoed down the ornate hall, chasing Guan around the corner. Rounding it in a blind rage, he ran headlong into two people.

He felt something hit him, felt it come over him, and darkness enter his soul. His body contorted and spasmed. He convulsed, tangling his hand into several strands of the woman's long necklace. He jerked as another spasm rocked him, his fist tightening on the beads. He stumbled and tried to steady himself. The necklace broke. Silver beads exploded in a spectacular shower, scattering over the ground, rolling into the corners, bouncing everywhere. Guan slipped and stumbled, holding on to the woman, who was shrieking now.

He froze. He knew that voice, recognized that face.

"Ow!" she complained in a high-pitched girly voice. "My necklace!"

This was too much of a coincidence. Guan pushed past her, ducking his head and muttering. "Sorry, excuse me."

What was she doing here?

Zanah ben Joseph's outrage carried down the corridor, "Marco, did you see that? He broke my pretty necklace."

Her companion writhed on the ground, coughing and sputtering. Guan picked up his pace.

"Do something!" Zanah demanded, then stomped her high heel and turned to Guan. "You there, come back."

Guan rounded the corner, glancing backward. The man on his knees gasped, ignoring the rolling beads. "*Cazzo!*"

Guan broke into a run. This was a sign. A bad omen. Bad luck. He got the hell out of there.

March 28, 999 ME

Late Risers - Eiran, Greece - Davianna and Astrid

The pain in Astrid's left temple was still there, a ghost from the brain rape yesterday. She did not dare open her eyes until she went through the ritual. Pins and needles in her toes and fingers? No. Bile and vomit? A little but manageable. Neck stiff or locked in place? She moved left and right. Stiff, not locked, good. Now the head… yes, she was right, just the ghost, not the beast.

She had to pee, and Davianna had her leg thrown over her, squishing her bladder. Astrid did not move, instead she grunted. The leg did not budge. Astrid growled, louder this time. Still nothing. She would have to speak, but she hated speaking in the morning. "Davi, move your leg."

Blessed relief, as Davianna rolled away with a grunt of her own.

It was quiet out, eerily quiet, no birds sang. "Hmm," she thought absently. She hated freaking birds anyway. Despite her bladder, she fell back to sleep, not in a hurry to face the day.

Later, Davianna stretched and yawned.

Through the haze, Astrid realized they slept a long time. "What time is it?" she asked without opening her eyes.

Davianna stretched and yawned again, gauging the light outside, but it was impossible to tell. She sat up and rummaged through her sack. Rubbing the sleep from her eyes, she said, "Tridi, it's 2:08 pm."

"What?"

Davianna handed her the watch.

Astrid squinted at it, her face registered disbelief, then alarm. "Why didn't anybody wake us up? I told my mother where we were."

Davianna bit her bottom lip. "My mother was to be here at eleven."

Blue eyes met brown, wide and full of fear.

"Something's wrong," they said in unison.

"I have to pee," Astrid whispered.

"As do I."

"Well, come on then." Astrid peeked through the pine boughs. "There's nobody out here."

The first thing they noticed was the trampled grass.

They found George's body twenty yards from their hiding spot, his great skull caved in.

Astrid covered Davianna's scream, pulling her down behind a scraggly bush. "Shut up," she hissed, averting her eyes from the corpse. "Look!"

Wisps of smoke rose over the campground, nothing stirred. They listened. No voices, no pots and pans, no children crying, no human sounds came from the bustling camp they left the night before. Tents were scattered among cooking utensils and clothing. A terrible odor wafted on the breeze.

"Oh, God," Davianna breathed, in prayer or petition, she did not know.

Then their minds processed the charred lumps, bodies.

"Mother!" Astrid cried and would have run into the carnage if Davianna had not tackled her to the ground, covering her mouth and stifling her sobs.

"Stop," Davianna ordered, tears rolling down her face. "They might still be there. We have to go. We have to run!

Part 5 - Prince Josiah

April 9, 999 ME

Coroner - Eiran, Greece - Josiah

Rumors of the Camp Eiran massacre spread like wild-fire, hundreds, maybe thousands dead. Josiah raced down the dusty roads, scattering terrified travelers in his wake. They gave him a wide berth, scurrying into the woods ahead of his wagon and thundering horses.

He left behind the identity of Prince Josiah, resuming the name of the exile, Captain Einar ben Yane. While in the Golden City, Yehonathan negotiated with the Iron King on Josiah's behalf, and they reached a deal. Josiah would undertake one last mission, and upon its successful completion, he would have the full might and power of the Iron King's army at his disposal. From there he would march against Korah, avenge his father, and take back Alanthia.

The mission appeared deceptively simple, retrieve a girl from Eiran Pilgrim Camp and escort her to the Golden City.

With the four gray geldings hidden down river, he prowled the perimeter of the camp. It was still, except for a tattered remnant of a tent fluttering in the breeze. He did not approach until he was certain it was deserted.

The stench was ominous.

At full light, the carnage came into gruesome clarity. Josiah kicked the charred remains of a cook pot. Burning with fury and frustration, he growled to the sky, "Nothing is ever easy with you is it?"

After a cursory investigation, he realized it would take several days to determine if Davianna ben David was among the dead. A grisly task, but in the process, he would document the evidence and identify the remains, if he could. Their families deserved answers, and the perpetrators deserved consequences.

As he suspected, there were no survivors. The grim work put him in a foul mood. Prowling from tent to tent, he compared the dead faces to the sketch Yehonathan had given him. Most were too burned for easy identification. With each set of bodies, each family, he got madder. He stomped through the campground snarling and cursing like a Tasmanian devil.

Among the ruins sat a festive tent, decorated with fanciful scenes of a pilgrimage that would never be completed. He pushed back the colorful tent flap and froze.

A low, menacing growl came from the interior. Josiah unsheathed his dagger and crouched, ready for attack. The tent grew quiet. He waited, heard a slight rustling, another growl. It sounded like a single animal. Cautiously, he stepped inside.

The tent erupted with deep throated barking. A dark shadow burst from a nest of blankets and made a tentative charge. Josiah prepared to strike, but the short-legged body retreated, yapping like mad. He sheathed his weapon and cast a baleful eye at his would-be assailant.

A dog.

He looked heavenward and sighed. "Your idea of a joke?"

When the barking stopped, Josiah dropped to his haunches and held out a hand. "Hey, boy, what are you doing here?" Wary brown dachshund eyes stared back, a low rumble in his little chest. "Come here. I won't hurt you."

At length, the dog limped forward. He was just a baby, and he was hurt. His long nose was dry and cracked, his stubby back leg burned. Every step the wounded puppy took was an indictment against the men who led this slaughter. Every painful whimper seared the anger burning in Josiah's heart. The little animal represented everything that had gone wrong here, everything wrong with the world.

The dog made a tentative sniff at Josiah's outstretched palm. Josiah allowed it to lick him, then lay a gentle hand on its sleek head. A long tail began to wag, and the puppy rolled over for a belly scratch. Josiah realized he would save at least one patient today. What it was going to cost him, he did not know.

Stubborn Dog

It was the most stubborn animal Josiah ever encountered, demanding as well. He bandaged its leg, fed it, made sure it was hydrated, then put it down on its nest and tried to go back to work. The dog was having none of it. It howled, barked, and refused to stay wherever he left it, even chewing off its bandage. He found a piece of rope and tethered it. An hour later, the barking was driving him mad. He yelled at it, which made it cower. That made Josiah feel like a heel, so he petted it again, reluctantly.

He conceived a solution, though he was loath to employ it. He searched for an alternative, determined there was none, and scowled. Adoring eyes looked up at him from the sling he wore across his chest, a smile on its long-nosed face. It tried to kiss him! Ick!

But at least it stopped barking.

As the day dragged on, he found himself talking to it. Its comical tan brows and oversized ears raised and lowered with intelligence. The grisliness of the task seemed to be blunted by the tail that beat against his side whenever he spoke.

Josiah refused to confer a name on it. If you named a dog, it became yours. After the heartbreak and grief over his beloved Rex, he swore that he would never have another dog. No, he decided, as soon as he finished here, he would find it a family and a good home. Until then, he was stuck with it.

That night, laying in his bedroll, he could hear it inching toward him. He resolutely put it in its own bed, four times. It had been a tiresome, interminable day, but the persistent little devil would not stay put.

Josiah, Prince of Alanthia, did not sleep with dogs, ever. When he escaped from the Palace, he and Rex spent over a year on the road. Rex never slept with him. This whimsical fellow with his ridiculous short legs was barely in the same species as Rex. Yet, here he came with a subservient whine. Back again. Stubborn!

With a sigh of exasperation, Josiah relented and lifted the covers. "Come on."

The animal burrowed down the bedroll with wiggling excitement, curling at his feet with a contented sigh. "You stay down there," Josiah ordered, but as he fell asleep, he had the passing thought that it was not so bad. The dog was warm, and his fur was soft.

Josiah rolled over the next morning and found the dog's head on the pillow, gazing at him with the lazy smile of a sated lover.

April 10-16, 999 ME

Three Hundred Twenty-One

Josiah moved from tent to tent, documenting contents and bodies. If possible, he established their identities with papers, miniatures, or possessions. He gathered and cataloged the evidence. He did autopsies.

In one tent, he found the family papers for David ben

Jesse, Zanah ben Joseph, and Davianna ben David. His heart thundered as he carefully examined the bodies, but there was no young girl among the dead and most of the family belongings were of a family named Gingle.

He meticulously searched the chest that held Davianna's family papers and surmised the clothing belonged to the mother. He contemplated a winter cap with a few strands of long brown hair. It was girlish, incongruent among the other items in the trunk, so he was fairly certain it belonged to Davianna.

That was when the rascal made himself useful. He scampered over and dropped his nose in Josiah's lap. On a whim, Josiah let him smell the hat.

"Go find the girl! Go get her."

The dog wagged his tail and barked.

Josiah gave him the scent again. "Get her."

Low to the ground, with a keen sense of smell, the dachshund took off.

He surmised it was a wild goose chase, but worth a try.

Ten minutes later, the puppy barked and sat down under a large tree by the riverbank. Pine boughs were scattered hither and yon, but the nearest pine was twenty yards away. There was an enclave, and closer inspection revealed evidence of a campsite, evacuated in a hurry. Relief flooded through him. She had escaped.

Over the next few days, the dachshund earned Josiah's admiration and made himself indispensable. He bore up under his injury, going to work sniffing out remains. He also did not chatter or make significant demands, unless Josiah counted the sleeping arrangements, and even those were not so bad. Each night, he burned the bodies, gruesome, soul sucking work. He realized he was grateful for the company of the dog. The little guy turned into quite a soldier.

By the evening of the fifth day, he was confident they discovered them all, all three hundred twenty-one men, women, and children.

Leaving camp the next morning, Benjamin, Benny for short, sat beside Josiah. Exuberant barks echoed Josiah's excitement to be underway. He had a girl to find, and thanks to an old winter hat, Benny had a scent. They would be back to the Golden City within the week

Part 6 - Playing with Fire

April 9, 999 ME

Hungry, Cold, and Tired - Davianna and Astrid

Davianna and Astrid traveled on foot, carrying the few items they stashed in their riverbank shelter the day they escaped. They hid from everyone. Moving in stealth and silence, survival instinct took over. The first few days they barely spoke.

But as time passed, Astrid muttered little more than a cursory yes or no. Overwhelmed with grief, she felt like she was suffocating. An invisible steel band tightened around her chest, making every breath a struggle. Copious tears leaked from her eyes, unheeded and unnoticed. Snot clogged her nose, and her mind stayed foggy. Anger bubbled to the surface, bursting out of her in scowls and grunts as they trekked across the barren countryside. Davianna exacerbated it by the constant checking and rechecking of her left pocket. Astrid knew that device had something to do with her mother's death. She wanted to hurl it from a steep ravine they navigated the day before, yet she did not. Something stopped her. Something kept her from pouncing on Davianna and beating her for bringing that thing into the camp.

Her head hurt, not a puking migraine, she could not function with one of those. No, this was the dull pounding, never ending kind that plagued her since she was eight. The sole respite in her life had been her five-month friendship with Davianna. Now the headaches were back, and her mother was gone.

Her stomach growled. Davianna's answered in kind. And for the first time in a week, Astrid managed a smile.

Water was a constant concern, but each day they found enough. Venturing west, a forbidding mountain range peeked over the horizon. The next day, it came into full view. The peaks loomed like an impenetrable wall, abating neither north nor south.

On the tenth day, they arrived at the base of the mountain they agreed was the smallest. Gazing up, they could not imagine how they ever perceived this mountain small. Its cloud obscured zenith seemed insurmountable. A solitary goats' footpath marked the way up.

However, they were ecstatic to discover a stream pooling at the base, so they made camp and bathed. That evening, they munched on the berries they had become adept at finding and waited with mouthwatering anticipation for the fish to cook.

Astrid seemed inordinately pleased with her catch. She even told Davianna a story about the time her daddy taught her to fish. It was a crack in the armor, one Davianna had been waiting for. Except the moment was fleeting. As they finished dinner and settled in, the familiar uneasiness returned. They lay silent save for the tears Astrid shed at night when she thought Davianna was asleep.

Desperate, Davianna whispered, "Are you ever going to forgive me, Tridi?"

Astrid was quiet for a moment, then she rolled away and answered in the flat tone that Davianna was so weary of, "Go to sleep, Davianna. You didn't do anything wrong."

But it felt like she had, and the wall between them seemed as high as the mountain.

The next morning, Astrid woke to find Davianna sitting on a log, staring at her with watery eyes.

"I understand why you hate me now. Do you want me to leave?" Davianna's voice cracked as she plunged ahead with what was certainly a prepared speech. "It might be safer for you, anyway. I think those men back at the camp… I think they were looking for me," she touched her left pocket, "for this."

Astrid sat up, stiff from the hard ground. For two weeks, she thought, but never spoke the words.

Davianna looked away. "I'm not stupid, you know. I know what it feels like when one person does not want to be with another. I know what it looks like." Her voice trailed off, and her dress swung around her ankles as she rose. Pointing to a neat bundle at Astrid's feet, she said, "I've left you half our things."

Astrid whispered, "Where will you go?"

"My father wanted to go to the Golden City. I think that's my best chance."

Astrid could not speak. Weeks of anger and grief tied her tongue. She had stopped talking, and now words strangled her, so she said nothing.

Davianna's chin began to quiver, but she tried to school her features. "You take this pass, Tridi. I still think it's a good one. Go find your daddy." She closed her eyes and swallowed. "I love you." Then without looking at Astrid, she turned and walked away.

Astrid watched her go. She noticed a slight limp, saw how ragged the pretty blue dress had become, the rip at the hem frayed all the way around. Her hair was tangled and needed to be cut. She saw Davianna's shoulders convulse, but she made no sound. She waited for her to turn around. There was no way she was leaving, but she kept walking.

This is what they had dreaded, what they had cried about, what they feared, and Astrid was watching her go. If she let her leave, she would never have to think about that damn device again. She would not look at her and remember Camp Eiran. She would not keep seeing George's caved in skull or keep imagining her mother as a charred body, smoldering in the dust. She could just let her walk away—into the desert—by herself.

"Wait."

The words hung in the charged air. Davianna turned, her face resolute, her big brown eyes swimming. "What?"

"You can't fish," Astrid choked.

One corner of Davianna's mouth trembled. "And you'll get lost."

"I'm sorry I missed the play, I was angry."

Davianna clamped a hand over her mouth, then said, "I'm sorry I missed the play. I'm just so sorry."

Astrid scrambled to her feet. They ran to each other, sobbing. When they hugged, the piece of driftwood righted itself on the stormy sea.

April 10, 999 ME

Fraidy Cat - Davianna and Astrid

At midday, the girls found a flat clearing and collapsed. Davianna figured they were halfway up the mountain, but it was hard to gauge.

They ate fish again. Not as delicious as the night before, but still better than berries.

"Would you have actually left today?" Astrid asked, studying Davianna's face, watching her reaction.

Davianna grew sheepish. "Yes, no, I don't know."

"Ha!" Astrid declared with triumph. "I didn't think so, fraidy cat."

Davianna stuck her tongue out. "I'm not a fraidy cat. Okay, I am kind of, but I had a plan."

Astrid snorted. "What sort of plan?"

"I was going to just follow you until you got lost or had some sort of jam. Then I would help, and you would stop being so mad at me." Davianna blushed.

"You were going to rescue me?"

Shrugging, she said, "Well, it was all I could think of at the time. It seemed like a good idea last night, you know? Why do plans always sound good in the dark, then in the light of day seem crazy?"

"I don't know, but that one is a doozy." Astrid sniffed and then added with a teasing glint in her eye, "Davianna saves the day!"

Davianna drew herself up, lips pressed together in a suppressed smile. "Hey, you never know. I could be brave."

Astrid dropped her chin and teased, "Then why would you need me?"

Davianna chuckled. "Because you are my best friend, and nobody else laughs with me the way you do."

"That is true." Astrid wiped her hands on a leaf and kept her voice light. "Do you really think that thing brought the murderers?"

Davianna touched her left pocket. "I don't know."

Astrid gathered her gear. "Well, come on then. We've got a long way to go before we clear this mountain."

Unlikely Pilgrim - Olympus - Antiochus

Dressed in the rags of a pilgrim, Antiochus climbed his kingdom's sacred mountain, Olympus. Slung across his back, he carried dark writings of the ancients of Sparta and Athens. They dated back to the First Age, the greatest of his kingdom. He thought one of the scrolls may have been penned by Alexander himself. That was the key, the final piece of the puzzle he had been missing. He was certain the great conqueror had harnessed the power that ruled from Olympus. Tonight, Antiochus would do the same.

Captain Orion ben Drachmas and his men returned from that filthy pilgrim camp without the Black Key. It was a crushing disappointment that sent Antiochus into a rage. However, his wrath was assuaged when, instead of the artifact, Orion presented him with the small scroll that made everything clear.

As he climbed this mountain, he knew he had no other choice. He knew his history, forty-three years he had ruled Greece, and he had not gone to the Golden City in thirty-nine. The Prince of Egypt had been killed forty years into his rebellion. Time was running out. He had one chance to stop his destruction.

As he climbed, he mentally prepared himself for the task at hand, to sacrifice his soul in worship to the gods of Greece. He would call them from the abyss, bind them to himself, and rule without the looming threat of destruction.

The lone trek remained. By nightfall, it would be done.

Mountain Climbing – Serbia- Davianna and Astrid

Hundreds of miles away, Davianna and Astrid trekked up their own mountain. The narrow passes were steep but manageable. At dusk, they found a campsite and fell to the rocky ground, exhausted. Staring up into the night sky, they lay quietly, their breathing labored from the steep climb and the thin air.

Davianna rallied and managed a small fire. They munched on berries and nearly inedible fish. As the sun set, they snuggled into their bedrolls. It was cold up on the mountain. Small animals rustled in the dried leaves, but otherwise, the night was still.

Davianna hoped they would not fall back into the strained silence. She prayed the night would not bring the pain of Emaline's death or fresh tears of grief. Astrid's tears always carried anger, and there was nowhere else for that anger to go except at her, and Davianna was tired. She was also scared.

Astrid was not the only one grieving a parent, though Davianna did not say it aloud. She would not do that to Astrid. She would not seek to minimize her pain.

Shortly after her father died, someone said, "I know how you feel." Davianna wanted to scream, "No you don't! No, you cannot possibly know how I feel! You cannot know what I lost. You cannot know who he was or what he meant to me. You cannot know what he left behind. You do not know how I feel!" But she had not said any of those things. She nodded and walked away.

It was one reason she did not speak of her father. To do so, opened the wound. It made her vulnerable and weak, but worse, it might spark questions. Astrid might ask how he died, and Davianna never talked about that—ever.

"I'm sorry I missed the play, but my feet hurt," Astrid said.

Davianna chuckled. "I'm sorry I missed the play. I twisted my ankle on a loose rock today."

"I'm sorry I missed the play. I've got a terrible case of chapped lips."

Davianna coughed and rolled over to take a drink from her canteen, feeling better than she had in weeks. "Better than a chapped bum."

Astrid laughed.

They fell into companionable silence.

"I was curious about that device, too," Astrid confessed.

Davianna rolled over, shocked.

Astrid snickered at Davianna's thunderstruck expression. "It wasn't just you. We both wanted to see it. I played a role."

Davianna breathed a sigh of relief, unsure what to say.

Astrid rested her cheek on her outstretched arm, staring into their small campfire. "Sometimes, I want to look at it again. I don't know why."

Davianna did too, but she would have never said it. "What do you think it is?"

"I don't know. Maybe we were just scared. Maybe that's

just how stuff from the Last Age worked, and it was just weird to us."

"Do you think?" Davianna had wondered the same thing. Her hand moved to her left pocket by rote.

They shared a look across the flames.

Astrid narrowed her cat blue eyes and grinned. "Do you want to look again?"

To Rule - Olympus - Antiochus

On the lonely peek of Olympus, Antiochus completed the ancient ritual. The last of his blood drained away, running in rivulets off the stone altar. He smelled it, copper and death. He fell, exsanguinating under the altar.

Nothing happened.

The ritual failed like all the others he had been doing for months: trying, seeking, conjuring. He had been rejected, but this time, it was worse. By his own foolish hand, he sacrificed his soul and his life, for nothing.

Failure tasted as bitter as the bile choking him. He gagged and sputtered, as great shudders wracked his body. The death rattles began. It was an ignominious end to his great rule, the death of a monarch, a Prince, on a lonely mountain. His blood shed for his kingdom… for nothing.

A song blew on the wind, haunting, sinister. Antiochus knew it was a fitting end. He felt the flames engulfing his body, his fate was sealed. Hell awaited.

The altar above him cracked. Blood dripped into his eyes, blinding him. It filled his mouth, drowning him. The moon faded to a tiny spot as his life ebbed away.

In the final seconds before the flames engulfed him, a pulse of energy erupted from the earth. It tore through his body with great and terrible power. Lifted twenty feet in the air, he levitated, screaming in agony. He was surrounded by fire, and he felt like he was being incinerated, yet he lived.

Olympus began to rumble and groan. The tectonic plates,

stable for one thousand years, shifted as an earthquake shook the Millennium. Sulfurous gas escaped the Earth's fiery core, rushing up through the dormant mountain and blowing the ancient peak to smithereens. Olympus belched a great cloud of ash. Volcanic rock bombed the surrounding countryside, incinerating everything in its path. Lava exploded into the night sky, creating the abominable shape of a horrible winged dragon. It moved, animated, and a beast roared with hellish fury, triumph, and release.

The sound sent terror ripping through the souls of men as a prisoner broke his fetters and escaped. The legendary Prince of Greece, Baal, Jupiter, an elohim with too many names to count, Zeus was loosed.

Antiochus landed one hundred feet from the altar, covered in ash and singed, but very much alive. He rolled to his knees, bowing in worship, glorying in his triumph.

Across the globe in Alanthia, Marduk howled in outrage.

From Camp Eiran, Josiah looked up at the distant sky in horror.

Peter, alone in the back of his limousine, vomited.

All around the world, the faithful fell to their knees.

In Heaven, the Archangel Michael mustered his brethren and prepared for war.

The Golden Dome - Davianna and Astrid

When the earthquake struck, Davianna and Astrid panicked. Clinging to each other in terror, small rocks began to pelt them. Stuck on a precarious ledge, they had nowhere to run, no escape. They were trapped.

"Yeshua, please help us!" Davianna screamed.

Astrid pushed Davianna to the ground and fell on top of her, shielding her from the falling rocks.

A malevolent roar rent the night air, assaulting their minds and spirits. They shrieked.

Astrid lay on top of her, cursing and grunting each time a rock hit her.

When the earthquake started, Astrid dropped the device. Instinct warned Davianna to hide that thing, it was playing the most terrible song she had ever heard. But Astrid was squishing her, and she could not reach it. She shouted, but her voice was lost in the tumult. Davianna clawed at the dirt and managed to grab it. Holding the button with all her might, she turned it off. But it was too late, the earthquake did not stop. With a desperate shove, she got it in her pocket.

A geyser of light burst from their campfire. There was no heat, yet it came from the fire. It sounded like a rushing wind, but there was no breeze. It settled around them like twinkling stars falling from the sky, forming a diaphanous golden dome.

Inside, everything went silent.

Astrid looked up, her left temple bleeding. "Davi," she whispered, awestruck, her voice echoing back at her.

They were surrounded, protected by a shimmering bubble. The maelstrom continued outside, but no rock invaded their shelter, no sound penetrated their haven. Beneath their prostrate bodies, the ground was solid, steady.

Davianna lifted her chin from the dirt, her eyes darting. With the wind knocked out of her, she croaked, "Get your fat ass off me."

It was such a strange thing to say, given the circumstances, and said in such a comical voice that Astrid started to laugh.

Davianna turned on her, incredulous.

Her outraged expression made Astrid laugh even harder.

Davianna stood slack jawed. Despite herself, she began to chuckle. "Jupiter's moon, Tridi, we made an earthquake!"

They dissolved in hysterics; their laughing faces illuminated by the magnificent light.

Gasping, Davianna begged, "Stop laughing. This isn't funny."

Astrid wiped away a mixture of tears and blood from her cheek and protested, "I do not have a fat ass."

The uncontrollable laughter began anew.

Davianna dabbed at her chin and saw blood. "You broke my face."

"You broke the Earth!" Astrid countered, and they kept on.

As their laughter subsided, so did the rumbling and shaking. The dome dissolved into golden sparks that floated into the air like embers from the campfire from whence it sprang.

A woman stepped out of the shadows, her face hidden. She was statuesque, a slender arm cocked on her hip. Davianna jumped when she spoke. "Are you two done laughing about breaking the Earth?" The stunned girls exchanged a glance, the stranger did not wait for an answer. "You come with me before you cause more trouble."

Astrid gave a shrug that signaled, "Why not." She figured tonight, or her life, could not get any weirder, they just had a gold dome over them. What could possibly happen?

April 11, 999 ME

Serbian's Cottage

They climbed for an hour in the dark up the steep mountain, following a woman who called herself Jelena. She held a glowing torch aloft, lighting the path, dispelling the shadows. Her arm never wavered, and she did not tire, unlike the girls. They trudged after her, exhausted. Their feet burned and the blisters opened anew, making each step painful.

Jelena pestered, taunted, and pushed. She never stopped scolding them, half the time it was in a language neither understood. She reminded Davianna of a demented Russian gymnastics coach she had when she was eight. However, the accent was not quite the same.

At one point, Astrid surreptitiously pointed and whispered, "Do you believe this woman?"

Davianna laughed between gasps for air.

Jelena turned. "You two, quit that laughing. What do

you have to laugh about, Earthquake Girls? You are lucky Jelena comes to find you."

Chastised, they kept following.

Finally, they reached a gray stone cottage with an impossibly angled roof. Davianna stared at it, utterly drained, and thought idly that the roof was thatch. Upon closer inspection she realized it was constructed of rows of close-fitting staves of wood arranged in tiers.

Jelena flicked the torch over her head, extinguishing it like a match. The girls exchanged a speculative glance. That was weird. Neither said a word.

Jelena shooed them inside like they were chickens, "Put your things in the corner and sit down."

They obliged, it was impossible not to, the woman was a whirlwind of commanding efficiency and demanding hospitality. The interior was cozy with stone and wood walls, red curtains, and overstuffed furniture. A huge kitchen dominated the space, and their hostess busied herself dishing up aromatic food. When Jelena turned with two heaping plates, both girls were struck dumb.

She was exquisite, beauty beyond this realm, regal and tall, with long straight limbs, powerful and perfect. Her alabaster skin glowed with an iridescent shimmer. Her intelligent eyes flashed like royal sapphires, and her hair was an indescribable jet that moved like dancing smoke.

A Gune!

Davianna ducked her head, looking away.

Astrid sat frozen.

Jelena looked at them in exasperation. "You just now see I am Gune?" She pronounced the Greek word, GOO-nay, which meant bride.

She set the plates down with a clatter and threw up her hands. "Stupid girls, we have been together all night and only now you see? Oh, there is much work to do." She raised her eyes heavenward. The girls did not move, she made a long-suffering sound. "Eat!"

The command snapped them out of their trance, and they began to eat, neither looking up from their plates as they devoured every morsel of chicken and potatoes. It was their first decent meal in weeks.

Much restored, they dared a glance up. To Davianna's shock, Jelena winked. It was such a human thing to do for a Gune, who at one point *had* been human, but it still unnerved her.

Davianna understood what Jelena was. Many believed they were just legends, but her daddy had taught her the truth. They were powerful beings from the Last Age, who aligned with the will of the Iron King, and operated in his full authority. Cherished and adored, Yeshua bestowed upon them his own power and honored them above all others. They were elevated higher than the angels, the church, the Bride of the Last Age.

The last of them disappeared off the Earth en masse. Those were the only Gune who ever appeared on Earth, the Raptured ones. Their appearances were rare and always heralded times of great trouble. Jelena's presence, in this place, at this time, felt ominous.

Jelena's dark brows drew down to a point over her fine nose as she studied Davianna. "You look like her."

Davianna cleared her throat before asking in a squeaky voice, "Like who?"

Jelena's blue eyes sparkled. "Like your aunt many times over. She is esteemed among our people."

Davianna leaned forward. "My aunt is a Gune?"

"Yes," Jelena laughed, the sound deep and throaty. "She was my boss, my favorite boss, ever. Do not tell her I said that. She keeps telling me, 'Jelena, I have not been your boss for over a thousand years.'" She shrugged. "But she is the boss, whether she likes it or not. She is also my best friend."

Astrid sputtered, "Gune have best friends?"

"Of course, we do. You have best friends here. We have best friends there. Everything you have, we have better."

"So," Davianna began tentatively, "my great-great-great, however many times, great-aunt sent you, from Heaven?" Her voice climbed on the last word.

Jelena nodded, answering as if Davianna was slow. "Well, that is where Gune live."

"But," Astrid said in the same incredulous tone, "Gune are just legend."

"Do I look like legend?"

They shook their heads emphatically. Indeed, this one looked quite real. Davianna's head began to swim, and she ran her fingers through her hair. It puffed up around her like a lion's mane.

Jelena chuckled. "She did that, too." She smiled at the memory. "Come, you are tired. It is safe here. Those that seek you are occupied tonight. You rest." She pointed to the open stairway to the right.

As the girls were heading up, Jelena called, "Davianna?"

She turned. "Yes, ma'am?"

"Leave me the device. You two caused enough trouble for one night."

The next morning the girls woke to the smell of fresh bread, eggs, and coffee. After breakfast, Jelena offered them use of the bathroom. Astrid nearly wept. It was utopia after weeks on the run and years in camp. They luxuriated in hot water, making liberal use of lotions, shampoos, and hair products.

Davianna grimaced at her reflection, her hair was huge. Astrid agreed to give her a haircut if there was time. Neither knew how long they would be here. For the moment, it felt divine just to be clean.

As they showered, Astrid lamented about putting back on their filthy clothes. Since they had no others, they were resigned. To their immense pleasure, clean clothes waited for them.

"What is this?" Davianna held up the black tunic Jelena laid out on the twin bed.

"I don't know, but I have one too." Astrid said, holding hers up to demonstrate.

Davianna stroked the lightweight fabric. "It's so soft. I've never felt anything like it." She pulled it over her head. It was double layered, so there was no need for undergarments. The inner layer molded to her skin; the outer hung loose past her hips.

Astrid jumped into matching black leggings. "Oh, these feel good."

Davianna laughed. "You don't have to worry about showing your panties if you fall down."

The corner of Astrid's lip quivered in a suppressed smile. "Cause I ain't wearing any."

"I don't think my mother ever did," Davianna said drolly.

"Are you coming, or are you dawdling all day?" Jelena called from downstairs. "Move."

They exchanged identical looks of contrition and exasperation. They finished dressing, pulling on tall socks that had them oohing and ahhing in relief as the unique fabric cradled their blisters and sore feet. They left their new black boots in the corner and headed downstairs.

Jelena waited for them, sitting on an overstuffed red chair. She gestured to the sofa and waited for them to settle. She placed the device on the table. It looked like an ominous centerpiece.

Davianna and Astrid huddled together, their heads bowed in shame.

"Do you know what this is?" Jelena asked.

"It plays music," Astrid answered, looking down and cleaning a speck of dirt under her fingernail.

"I did not ask what it did. I asked if you knew what it was. Do you?" Jelena's blue eyes narrowed.

Davianna bit her bottom lip and looked away.

To her utter shock, Astrid replied, "It's an Apple iPhone. Though, I think it's been modified." Davianna's mouth fell open, but Astrid shrugged. "I read about them a long time ago. My daddy had a book on ancient tech."

"Modified?" Jelena snorted, then gave Astrid a speculative look. "And did this book tell you the consequences of these devices?"

"Well, no. It was more about what they did. The last half of the book talked about why we should be allowed to have these things now." Astrid gave Jelena a hard look of defiance. "They've used phones in the New City for years."

Jelena's black eyebrows lifted. "A rebel."

The corners of Astrid's mouth turned down in a brief frown, then she lifted her shoulder in a slight shrug. "Just not anti-tech." The baleful look Jelena gave Astrid made her feisty. "Did you have a phone, Jelena?"

Jelena dismissed the question with a flick of her hand.

Astrid sat back, satisfied, her point made.

Jelena tapped her long finger on the device. "I did not have a satanic phone."

Davianna's eyes bulged.

"Well, neither do I," Astrid declared and crossed her arms, determined to win the argument.

"Hey," Davianna cried foul. "You pushed the button!"

Jelena held up her hand, ignoring Davianna. "I did not leave the throne room of the Most High to banter with you, Astrid ben Agnor and Emaline of Ireland."

"Ireland?" Astrid scoffed. "I am not from Ireland but Alanthia. Texas to be more precise."

Jelena looked her up and down. "Red hair, blue eyes, pale complexion, and a fiery temper? Do not be a fool, Ireland." She rolled her eyes, dismissing Astrid as ridiculous. "I know your lineage back to Adam. I am Gune."

Game, set, match to Jelena.

Davianna chuckled and asked, "How about me? My daddy was born and raised in Britain. Mom is from Georgia."

Jelena gave a half smile, "We are all daughters of Eve, are we not?"

Her eyes held a wealth of secret knowledge. Davianna stared into their sapphire depths and saw unfathomable wisdom and understanding, like a vast blue ocean that stretched beyond the horizon toward infinity. She longed to step into that sea, to float upon its waters, to go into the deep, and let the waves wash over her. She felt it calling to her, and she experienced a spirit of well-being, smiling in dreamy relaxation.

Jelena reached out her hand and took Davianna's. "He is with you."

Davianna felt a rush of sudden tears, her daddy brought suddenly and vividly to mind. She turned away as a jolt of grief hit her.

Jelena brought her back to the calamity at hand. "This is no ordinary device. It carries a great curse."

Astrid read Davianna's distress and pulled her tight. They stared at the phone in silent trepidation.

"You are right to be afraid. There are many who seek it and its power. You must not ever use it again," Jelena warned.

"We agreed on that last night," Davianna offered, "before we looked at it. If anything bad happened—"

"Like an earthquake," Astrid chimed in.

"That we wouldn't ever do it again," Davianna finished with solemn gravity.

Jelena nodded, pleased. "Good. Then we do not waste time on that. I will tell you it's story, so you understand why you must never give in to temptation again."

She templed her fingers and leaned forward. "As the Last Age drew to a close, the Iron King's victory was imminent. Man's rebellion, led by Lucifer and his ruling elohim, had failed. It was their second great defeat. The consequences of the first were they were cast out of Heaven onto Earth. When they failed to wrest the Earth away from the Iron King during the Great Judgment, they faced the Lake of Fire."

The girls looked at her wide-eyed.

"The fallen elohim are powerful and wicked creatures, equal in strength and might to the holy angels. For more than six thousand years, they ruled the nations with brutal oppression and great injustice. But the day of their defeat was upon them, and they blamed their leader, Lucifer.

"Faced with a mutiny and the coming of the Iron King, Lucifer conceived a plan. He made a pact with his elohim."

The air crackled with anticipation. Both girls leaned forward.

"They had no other choice, so they accepted his plan."

"What was it?" Astrid gripped Davianna's knee.

"He promised to hide them from the coming destruction and face defeat alone. He would take the punishment, to be bound in chains and thrown into the bottomless pit for one thousand years, the sentence to be carried out by his greatest enemy, the Archangel Michael." Jelena smiled and added, "Who is marvelous and majestic, by the way."

Davianna's mouth fell open.

Jelena continued, "Then Lucifer promised, at the appointed time, they would be released to once again rise and make war against the Iron King."

Davianna and Astrid's eyes widened, enthralled by the story.

"For once, in his existence Lucifer did not lie. He traveled with each elohim to their kingdoms and hid them, until the time of the end, until now. He used powerful magic from his own time, his own kingdom, of his own making."

They paled.

"He sealed and locked them in," she tapped the artifact on the table, "with a key."

Two thundering hearts pounded in the silence.

Jelena leaned forward, her voice low and fierce. "So, can you guess what you two have done by turning on this particular device?"

"Why can't we destroy it?" Davianna asked an hour later.

Jelena shrugged. "Go ahead, try again."

Davianna swung the hammer, again. It bounced off, again. Astrid picked it up and threw it against the wall. Nothing.

Fire did not burn it; water did not drown it. They tried

in vain to destroy it. Astrid accidentally pushed the button, and it sprang to life, its power source beyond battery and electricity. They retreated from it in horror, but Jelena waved a hand, and it ceased.

Inspiration struck Davianna, and she put it in Jelena's hands. "You do it."

Jelena gave a rueful smile. "It was given to you, to keep safe." Jelena took the device and lifted Davianna's tunic.

Davianna looked down.

"On the inside of your tunic, there is a pocket." Jelena slipped the device inside.

Davianna felt the familiar weight against her left hip. She sighed, turning away. "I don't want this. There has been a mistake. I am the last person who should be given something like this, something to protect."

Visions of Guan's assault, of George's caved in skull, of the smoking tents, came to mind. "Why was I given this?" She whirled, looking for an answer, but Jelena had vanished.

Astrid glanced around the room. "Faith and begorrah."

Who Else Knows?

"You are not Irish. Quit with the lilt,"

"Ayr, but I am lassie," Astrid countered.

Davianna put her hand on her hip. "Now, you sound like a pirate." She paced. "I have to think."

"Aye, but it's ha-a-h-h-r-r-d." Astrid embraced her inner pirate with gusto.

Davianna threw a grape at her.

Astrid opened her mouth. "It will keep me from gettin' the scurvy. Throw me another, ye wench."

By the time the cluster was picked clean, they'd each caught two. The rest were scattered across the floor.

"You are picking them up." Davianna tiptoed into the kitchen, squishing a grape. "I'll cook dinner."

Astrid gathered the grapes. "As much as I would like to hang out here, I mean, just for the bathroom alone. I think you are right. We have to go."

Davianna looked up from her chopping. "Last night, Jelena said, 'Those that seek you are occupied tonight.' So, we are being hunted."

Astrid dumped the grapes into a bowl and washed them. "How do they know? Did you show anybody else?"

Davianna blushed.

"What, who else?" Astrid demanded.

Davianna cursed her expressive face. "A couple people saw it."

Grapes and water exploded out of the sink. Davianna jumped.

"That thing got my mother killed. Who'd you tell?" Texas fury pulsed off Astrid.

"I didn't tell anybody. They saw it, or took it, I didn't mean it. He grabbed me. It was dark. I tried to scream, but he had his hand over my mouth, and I couldn't. I fought him, but he was so strong." The knife clattered and spun on the cutting board as she fled the kitchen.

Astrid stared after her in horror. A snake of dread slithered down her spine and coiled in her gut. In Belgium, one of the girls in camp had been raped. Her mother nursed the physical injuries, but Astrid remembered the haunted look of the girl. Davianna just had the same expression.

Astrid went after her.

She found her curled in the bed, facing the wall, sniffling. Astrid sat down and rested a gentle hand on Davianna's shoulder. "Why didn't you tell me?"

Davianna sniffed and said miserably, "I was ashamed. I thought you wouldn't believe me." Then she added with bitterness, "He said I teased him, which I didn't. He called me a whore, just like my mother."

"I'm so sorry. Are you okay?" A horrifying thought occurred to her. "You aren't pregnant, are you?"

"No!" Davianna's head snapped around, "No, it didn't go that far, but he pulled that cursed thing out of my pocket. He knew what it was. Then, George was there, and he ran away."

"Who was it?" Astrid crooned, stroking Davianna's head.

Davianna relaxed under the soothing touch and closed her eyes. "It doesn't matter."

Astrid nodded. "Yeah, they are all gone."

But Davianna knew one who was not.

Boys - Serbia

They spent hours discussing disguises. The realities of the road and the need to travel quickly eliminated their more elaborate ideas. They ruled out aging themselves, too much time, too much makeup. Astrid suggested coloring their hair, but hair grew, and roots were noticeable.

"You should have asked her," Astrid lamented in frustration. "Why didn't we ask her?"

Davianna studied her reflection. Her long brown hair laying in heaps at her feet. Astrid's red curls were already discarded in the waste bin. "I don't think she was supposed to tell us what to do, otherwise she would have."

Astrid eyed a stray piece and snipped. "Well, we should have asked."

"We don't have a choice, do we?" Davianna said logically. "We know they are hunting us in Greece, so we can't go back that way. Our route to the Golden City is cut off, at least from where we are now."

Astrid nodded. "We know my daddy is in the New City, and your mother was headed there."

Davianna looked grave. "They are the only family we have left. Based on what you have told me, your daddy is our best chance. As a tech investor, he will probably know somebody that can destroy this thing."

Astrid sighed. "And in the process—"

"Don't say it." She did not want to consider all the obstacles standing between them and the New City. Davianna scrunched up her face, scowling, trying to look masculine. "Do I look like a boy?"

"You'd better, or we're both dead." Astrid examined her

own face. "I think we need dirt. It will cover the fact that we don't have whiskers."

"I am more worried about my bum than my whiskers," Davianna said, looking over her shoulder. "Portia would not have had that problem."

Astrid snorted, but it was not as funny now.

In the end, the extraordinary clothing Jelena gave them made up their minds. The hooded black tunics, leggings, and lace-up boots fit them perfectly. The material was light and flexible and the longer they wore it they realized it shifted and changed color in the light. The tight double layer tunic flattened their chests.

But the biggest surprise of all were the knee-high boots. Concealed slots inside the shanks held gold coins, more wealth than either pilgrim girl had ever seen. Black travel bags constructed of the same material as their tunics, yielded more surprises, some known, some unknown.

With dirt-smudged faces, they burned their old clothes, the box the device came in, and the hair they sacrificed on the bathroom floor. The ashes of their old lives floated on a warm spring wind. Davianna and Astrid left the Serbian cottage and disappeared.

April 12, 999 ME

King Korah's Report - New City, Alanthia

Korah knew the price of power. He knew the ephemeral nature of it, too. He harbored no delusions that the power he served felt any loyalty to him. Marduk could turn on him in an instant. So, Korah was careful. He was smart, and he never lost sight of the fine line he walked. The price he paid was high, the sacrifices beyond imagining. But King Korah ben Adam was the most powerful man on the planet, and he planned to stay that way.

Feeling Marduk's presence enter the room, he motioned

for the Minister of Technology and Security, Stephen ben McSwilley, to enter. After the formalities were dispensed with, he accepted the report, reviewing it with a frown. Korah laid it on his desk and leveled Stephen a black glare. "If I interpret this report correctly, you do not know where the device is?"

Stephen cleared the phlegm from his throat. "My Esteemed, as you know, our technology is being used further and further afield, albeit illegally outside Alanthia. Thus, detecting and triangulating a single device is extremely difficult. Globally, the receiver stations and network capabilities are not there."

Korah's eyes narrowed, and Stephen began to sweat. "I can say, under your astute direction, one of our engineers used the previous artifact you provided to build a model that targets devices of ancient origin."

Korah tented his fingers, listening. "So, you can find it?"

Stephen wiped his brow. "If it is turned on and connected to a network, we will pinpoint its location, my Esteemed."

"Just not now," Korah taunted, his voice light and menacing.

"The device is not on, my Esteemed. However, I assure you the moment it is, we will find it."

What went without saying is that Stephen ben McSwilley better not fail.

Marduk seethed. Their failure to locate the Black Key infuriated him. He patrolled the Earth for the last two weeks and detected nothing. He had a sneaking suspicion that it was being protected, and that protection was not the work of man.

He would find it. He had to find it. It was imperative. There was no other way. He had not ruled Alanthia for fourteen years to sit back and do nothing. And now he had Zeus to contend with. One of his greatest rivals was free. If he had his choice, Zeus would have never seen the light of day.

He stalked Korah's study, waiting for the quivering little technocrat to leave. McSwilley exaggerated their ability to find the Black Key. If it was in Greece, there was not a single functioning tower to triangulate a signal.

When the door shut, he spoke into Korah's brain. They did not converse aloud. Servants were everywhere. "I do not care what it takes, Korah. Find it."

Korah stilled but did not look up from the report he was reviewing. "I am sure we will. I am sending physical assets, the best."

"Perhaps take their wives and children hostage until they find it," Marduk said with relish.

"As you wish, Dark Master." Korah folded his hands, his expression bland. "Though, as we discovered before the war, Alanthians tend to become uneasy about such tactics."

"Squeamish, sniveling, cowards," Marduk growled.

"They are simply different from the men you ruled in the Last Age, Dark Master." Korah sat back and sighed.

"True," Marduk agreed, then added to torment Korah. "Though, I still have my contingent of wild men. Don't I, Korah?"

Korah's lips pressed into a thin line. Korah hated the jihadists. Hated them, but he did not flash that though. He knew Marduk would read it. It was a game they played.

He rose from behind his desk and poured a brandy, asking aloud, "What are your plans?"

Marduk answered telepathically, "I am going to Greece."

Old Rivals – Athens, Greece

"I see you are back." Marduk landed with a thud on the roof of Antiochus' Palace.

Zeus scowled, then gave a throaty laugh. "Oh, it's you. I had hoped for someone a bit more entertaining."

Marduk sneered. "Sorry to disappoint you."

"You are as hideous as ever." Zeus unfurled his wings with a flourish and struck a coquettish pose. "How do I look?"

It was an act, designed to provoke Marduk, who was not

fooled. Zeus was not a vapid, harmless queen, but it did irritate him. "You look the same."

"Thank you," Zeus said, batting his eyelashes and blowing a kiss.

Marduk scoffed. Zeus did look well, but he should not. Marduk had been violently ill when he broke out. He suspected his counter-magic had not melded well with Lucifer's. Even now, he did not feel as strong as he had before their imprisonment, though he would never admit it.

Zeus grinned at Marduk's brooding silence, baiting him. "I feel marvelous." He preened. "I suppose emerging through blood will do that."

Marduk controlled his features. "Through blood?" Blood would bestow enormous power on his rival.

Zeus flicked his forked tongue, tasting Marduk's anger. "At the exact moment I broke bonds." He brushed his flowing blonde hair over his shoulder and grinned.

The primary reason Marduk found Zeus so insufferable was his vanity. He managed to retain a measure of his former beauty. They all lost it after the first war, except Zeus. He still looked like a holy angel, from the neck up. From the neck down, he was covered in scaly armor like the rest of them, though Zeus managed to carry off the lizard green. Marduk did not bear the slightest resemblance to who he had been before, though he could transform himself if he chose. He never looked in a mirror. He had fallen far, and the price was written on his face.

"Still jealous?" Zeus asked innocently, but beneath the smooth taunt lay an undertone of menace.

Marduk drew himself up, his hair animating into vipers. He may not be beautiful, but he was fearsome. "Of you, the original Sodomite?"

Zeus shrugged. "Pussy is overrated."

Marduk grinned malevolently. Zeus had no idea what Marduk had been up to, had no idea what he had done in Greece while his rival was bound. "That is a matter of opinion."

Zeus narrowed his eyes. Marduk could feel him try to push in on his thoughts, trying to discern the reason for the self-satisfied grin. Marduk swatted him away effortlessly.

Zeus put his hands on his hips, adopting a petulant tone. "So, tell me, how did the Prince of *Persia* find his way to America?"

"It is called Alanthia now, and I chose to be there."

Zeus held out his hand, admiring his razor-sharp talons. "Do not be coy. You are out of your place, and from what I gather, you have been there quite some time. I know you. How did you come out so early?"

Marduk narrowed his eyes and said, "After the last disaster, I was not going to blindly follow Lucifer again." The vipers hissing on his head coiled and settled. "You're free, apparently you had the same idea."

Zeus shrugged. "Hmm, perhaps that is why the two of us never got along. We are too much alike."

Marduk circled, his hand on his sword. "We are nothing alike."

"Calm down." Zeus rolled his eyes in an exaggerated fashion, though his hand was at his sword. "I merely convinced him to put me first on the list. But you? Go ahead, tell me. I do want to know how you did it. What does it matter now?"

Marduk walked to the edge of the Palace roof, staring off into the distance. Every word he said to Zeus would eventually make it back to Lucifer, but he was bursting with pride and needed to tell someone. For fourteen years, he had not had a conversation with another of his kind. As much as he hated Zeus, he seemed better than nothing. "I suspected a ruse. You know how Lucifer can be."

Zeus snorted. "I am well acquainted with his ways.".

"I've read the unholy book. In the end, only he and Gog are specifically mentioned as being released. I suspected a trick, or even worse, the Most High."

A string of blasphemies issued from Zeus' corner of the rooftop. Marduk gave him a mocking bow, appreciating the creativity. "I did not trust him, so I set up a counter curse. If at any time during the thousand years someone tried to call him forth, I would be released."

Zeus placed a hand over his black heart and said, *"Touché."*

"I knew there was a chance none of us would be freed in the end. But I also knew, he would not leave anything to chance. He planned to ensure his freedom, but I knew he would not be released through a song." He sneered. "He always underestimates the enemy. There is no way he is getting out before Michael releases him."

"Michael," Zeus growled. "That—"

"I knew Lucifer would plant devices all over the planet, with instructions on how to call him forth, while all ours might be on a single device lost to history and eternity." He grinned with wicked pride. "My plan paid off."

"So how long have you been free?" Zeus asked with an edge in his voice.

"Fourteen years."

"They summoned you from there?" Zeus laughed at the irony. "Your biggest adversary in the Last Age, America, calls forth Marduk, the Prince of Iran? Oh, she is going to be furious."

Marduk smirked.

"And your strongman?"

Marduk puffed up with pride, Zeus needed to understand that he was firmly in charge. "Korah? While he is no Nebuchadnezzar, he is deliciously devious. Under my guidance, he has become the most powerful ruler in the world, and he's not afraid of a little fun, killed his brother when he called me forth and took the throne. I could have done worse."

Zeus seethed. Antiochus was all too ready to report on the injustice perpetrated against Greece by Marduk and this Korah. "What song did Lucifer choose?"

Marduk scoffed. "Oh, please, do you have to ask?"

"Do not tell me, he was not so trite as to pick that one?"

"Ever the vain pompous ass." The comment was a dou-

ble-edged dig, spoken as Marduk glared directly into Zeus'
bloodshot eyes. As he flew away, Marduk sang a stanza, in a
perfect imitation of the long-dead Mick Jagger.

Part 7 - Convergence

April - November 999 ME

The Secret to Hiding - Astrid and Davianna

The secret to hiding was not doing it. Astrid and Davianna learned nothing aroused suspicion quicker than acting furtive. If spotted, they acted natural. These days, young people traveling alone did not rouse suspicion, so they blended into the crowds. They posed as brother and sister, especially when one needed a haircut. Often, they were two boys, but they were never two young ladies, and they were never Davianna and Astrid.

They learned to walk like boys, talk like boys, and scratched themselves, a lot. They pretended to be shy, so they did not have to speak. They listened, and they learned. Pilgrim campfires and coffee houses became their classrooms. They absorbed stories about far-off places. Picking up details about peoples' lives, they built their disguises, their backstories, and disappeared behind a web of tales.

Astrid emerged as the people person. She became an expert in interpreting body language, expressions, and tones of voice. She determined who they traded with and where they stayed. No one took advantage of them, no one fooled her. But her greatest talent, Astrid sensed danger, and in the running, she became fierce.

Davianna's natural talent for details, trivial facts, and accents became vital. Practicing when they were alone, she grew into an accomplished mimic. When they did speak to strangers, Davianna did the talking, employing accents she picked up. She had an ear for cadence and dialect, and no one questioned their cover stories. Davianna also possessed a brilliant sense of direction, so she plotted their circuitous route out of Greece and across Europe.

Fighting the instinct to run in a straight, logical line, they meandered, doubled back, and detoured. They hopped on and off boats in Italy, traveling the Po river across the country. They walked, especially at the beginning. Through the dense forests of Slovenia, they rode horseback. In Vesoul, they bought bikes and pedaled across France. In Belgium, they bought a small cart and a fine jackass they called Dudley. They evaded and escaped. They were hunted, and they knew it.

They purchased weapons and armed themselves. Instead of fleeing when fights broke out among the travelers, they pulled back, watching from the shadows, learning. In Ljubljana, Astrid took a self-defense class and taught Davianna. When they were alone, they practiced.

At first, they expected to be captured at any moment. Real and imagined dangers lurked under every rock, around every corner. When they set out, the plan was to avoid populated areas and travel in the wilderness, but one night in early May, a menacing growl from the shadows convinced them that a bedroll on the ground was no safer than a hotel room in the city. Across the globe, animals turned back into predators. They, too, began to hunt.

Moving among people was nerve wracking. Neither knew who Jelena meant when she said, 'Those who pursue you,' so they assumed everyone posed a threat. But as time wore on, their confidence grew. Hiding their faces kept them from seeing who was around, which made them vulnerable, blind. Hyper-aware, they studied everyone. Anyone spotted in more than one location, that was a hunter.

They identified three dogged pursuers. A stocky, acne-scarred Greek, who almost caught them in Bologna. A black-haired, handsome man, they nicknamed the Dark Prince, because despite his military bearing, he had an air about him that was distinctly above the fray. He almost caught them several times, coming close in Belgrade, then again in Geneva, and Orleans. There was a dead-eyed Egyptian, who frightened Davianna the most. In Lyon, she literally ran into him as she was leaving a shop. To her immense relief, he had not recognized her. They evacuated twenty minutes later.

There were more. They knew it.

Sometimes they were tipped off by an odd accent, phrase, or word, perhaps a furtive glance, a duck into a shop, or a newspaper raised as they scanned a palazzo or park. They were not always sure, but if they detected anything, they took off. They were pursued, day and night, with never a respite, never a rest. They slept lightly, moved quickly, and never, ever, let their guard down.

Early on, they slipped up. They made a mistake. In Zagreb, Davianna called Astrid by name, in English, in her own accent, in her own voice. Astrid answered. They were overheard. Alanthians this time, unremarkable men who wore casual clothes with dress shoes. An hour later, their hotel was surrounded.

Panicking, they dug into the Gune gear bags. Much of the contents at that point remained a mystery. Astrid fumbled with a rectangular device with five red prongs sprouting from the top. "I have no idea what this is." She pointed it out the window and pushed the button. Davianna rummaged through her bag, looking for anything. Astrid squealed with delight. "Look, Davi!"

Davianna ran to the window and saw a half a dozen men on their knees, clutching their heads.

Astrid grabbed her by the arm, and they bolted. Davianna tossed a coin to the startled cook as they barreled through his hotel kitchen. "You did not see us!"

Jumping down the steps, they landed in a service alley and ran. Their feet echoed against the damp stone walls, as they listened for the sound of pursuit. They cleared the alley and slipped into a bustling street market. They picked the hotel for exactly this reason, and it paid off.

On the other side of the market, and ten minutes into the twisting old city section, they stopped, bent over and gasping, but safe. Davianna raised her chin and said, "What was that thing? I did not hear anything when you pressed the button."

Astrid covered her nose; somebody was cooking cabbage, and it stank. "I think it hit their earpieces. I saw their faces when I did it. It must have screeched."

Davianna smirked. "Good. I hope it addled their brains."

Astrid crossed her eyes and rotated her fingers in a circle around her temples. "Duh!"

Giggling, Davianna scanned their location. "Come on. Let's get out of here."

Later that afternoon, Astrid saw a pair of them still searching. She pulled Davianna down and peered over the rail of the wagon. They were hidden among a large group of pilgrims, going back where they came from. As they passed, Astrid studied them and decided it was their hair cuts. They cut hair just a wee bit different in Alanthia.

They never forgot the lessons they learned in Zagreb.

Danger lurked everywhere, and they encountered all sorts of unsavory characters. Astrid kneed a drunken man in Liege, who cornered her as she was coming out of a pub bathroom. Davianna encountered a street gang in Calais, who saw her pay for supplies with a gold coin. They chased her through dark and twisting streets, intent on robbery, rape, or murder. Perhaps all three, she did not know. All Davianna ben David knew was that night she thought she was going to die.

An unusually hot summer scorched Europe. The oppressive heat amplified the angry, dangerous mood growing among the people. Violent fights broke out. Theft, rape, and even murder became commonplace in the pilgrim's camps, which had been safe for a thousand years. By late August, they avoided the camps altogether and stuck to the cities.

They tricked their pursuers, huddling together in hotel rooms and on hard ground. They cried bitter tears of grief and laughed uproariously because that is who they were. Davianna and Astrid survived, slipped into the shadows, and blew away with the wind.

When they arrived in London on November 10, 999 ME, they had been running for two hundred and twenty-seven days. A year to the day, when Astrid came to Davianna's tent and asked, "Would you like to come listen to some music?" Everything had changed.

November 11, 999 ME

Quandary – Windsor - Prince Josiah

Sipping Earl Grey, Josiah studied the stocky man through the grimy cafe window. The girls were here, in Windsor, holed up in a hotel across the street. Unfortunately, so was the Greek. He was hunting the girls; Josiah was certain. He spotted him four times in the last six months.

In Bologna, he discovered the man's identity, Captain Orion ben Drachmas, Antiochus' man. His gut told him Antiochus played a role in the Camp Eiran Massacre, and perhaps this man had, too.

In Milan, he turned the meticulously gathered evidence from the camp over to Mossad. Thus far, no charges had been brought against anyone. But years in the army and in exile taught him, everything took time.

A well-placed knife in the Greek's kidney would drop him. Josiah would not lose a moment's sleep killing the man in battle or in defense of the girls, but he could not countenance cold blooded murder, nor could he leave to find Mossad, not with Drachmas lurking outside the girl's hotel. He could not go to the local police because there was the inconvenient matter of his own resurrection to consider. The girls were not the only ones being hunted.

Over the last six months, he developed a begrudging admiration for Davianna ben David and Astrid ben Agnor. In Italy, he stopped underestimating them. They led him on a wild chase across the continent, slipping through his fingers time and again. He lost their trail for days, sometimes weeks, but he had them now. Unfortunately, so did Captain ben Drachmas, and Josiah feared others were not far behind.

London, Then - Davianna and Astrid

"That freaking Greek is out front," Astrid hissed as she peeked through the curtains.

Davianna leapt across the room, coming to her side. "That arrogant swine, does he think we cannot see him?"

Agitated, Astrid opened and closed her Italian stiletto. "The Greeks killed my mother."

By rote, Davianna checked the knife at her belt, the two strapped in her wrist guards, and the cursed device in her left pocket. "He knows we're in here."

"Yeah, he doesn't look like a tourist, does he?"

The Greek appeared to be admiring a leaning shop, but his eyes kept cutting toward their hotel.

Davianna moved away from the window. "You think the Dark Prince is out there, too?"

"Yep. He's in the bakery, drinking tea." Astrid lowered her spy glasses and stowed them in her Gune bag.

"And the Egyptian, we haven't seen him yet?" Davianna shivered.

Astrid shook her head. "He's not here. I think we lost him before Calais."

Davianna scanned the room, searching for listening devices. "What about the techies? Any sign of those bloodless bastards?"

Astrid looked up and down the street. "No, but I guarantee they will be along." As a precaution, she made sure the noise canceling device was turned on.

The day had dawned bright and clear, perfect for sightseeing. "Darn it! I wanted to take a tour of Windsor Castle. My daddy used to tell me about it. You know he was born about fifty miles from here." Her voice trailed off as she moved away from the window.

"We could still go." Astrid shrugged, knowing they wouldn't.

Davianna snorted. "We could pull a Bologna?"

Astrid considered and played along. "Geneva."

Davianna shook her head. "Chambery could work, but we need to stay in London." She called over her shoulder, checking the hall through the peephole. "Why not Bologna?"

"Because I want the Greek gone, not arrested." There was cold certainty in Astrid's voice.

Hunted for months, in London, they planned to turn the tables.

Davianna nodded once, resolute. "London, then." She spread out the detailed map and got to work.

Astrid never took her eyes off the street. "London."

Greek Drawing - Josiah

Outside the Windsor Castle Hotel, Captain Orion ben Drachmas could barely contain his excitement. He had them, room 105, trapped. He would do it tonight, while they were sleeping.

Distracted by a dark fantasy, they almost slipped past him. It was a laugh that caught his attention, the wave of a hand, and the gleam of red hair that gave her away. Perhaps it would not be tonight. They were his, at last.

The teacup clattered in the saucer when Josiah saw them exit the hotel. They never dressed as girls, not both of them, not simultaneously. They wore no hoods, employed no disguises. It was the first time he had ever seen them as they truly were. Something was wrong.

He slipped out of the shop, growing trepidation and urgency propelled him forward. He suppressed the urge to shout, to flag them down. In the bright sun, Astrid's ginger hair acted like a beacon. His blood ran cold when he realized what they were doing. They were drawing the Greek. No evasive movements, no attempts to hide, they were leading him into a narrow alley.

He swore and broke into a run. Turning into the alley, he saw the Greek fall to his knees and a pair of skirts disappear around the corner.

Josiah sprinted forward, Orion held out a bloody hand staring at it, astonished. The girls vanished. Josiah eased the man to the uneven cobblestones, applying pressure to the wound.

"Those wicked little cunts," Orion swore.

Josiah glared down at him. If he took the pressure off the chest wound, the bastard would bleed out. "I think you are getting what you deserve, Greek."

A young blond man called from the other end of the alley, "What's happening, mate?"

Josiah looked up. "Wounded man. Call for emergency services."

Orion's voice was garbled and gasping as blood filled his lungs.

Josiah continued applying pressure, deciding to keep the man alive because he did not want the police hunting his two girls. Damn them.

Covent Garden - Davianna

Later that evening, Davianna sunk into a luxurious bubble bath by degrees, moaning with pleasure at each interval.

The marble tub and flickering jasmine candles created an oasis of peace in the ancient One Aldwych Hotel.

Astrid was resting, amid their numerous shopping bags. They spent all but one drachma today on hotels, clothes, and delicious food. But more importantly, they had first-class tickets to the New City. Neither fretted about the funds. There would be money in the boots tomorrow. Every shekel they spent was replaced while they slept. It was a daily miracle.

The hotels they chose ran the social strata between mega luxury to the meanest poverty. They thought it was safer to hide in luxury. No one searched for running pilgrim girls in hotels like this, and the bathtubs were better.

They changed identities, disguises, and locations, sometimes by the hour. Like today, the two girls who fled the alley were not the two boys who boarded the tourist ferry in Windsor. Nor were they the brother and sister who disembarked near Waterloo Bridge and checked into the hotel.

Regardless, they never dropped their guard. Even floating in a luxurious marble tub, Davianna's favorite blade and Gune gear were at hand, ever present, indispensable.

She rinsed her hair, which needed to be cut again. She hated that part of running, the loss of being who she was. Astrid missed her pretty fingernails. Davianna missed her hair.

With the scene from the alley running through her mind, she closed her eyes and tried to relax. A fierce longing rose out of the jasmine scented water. She missed the way things used to be, when people were not trying to kill her, before every stranger on the street was a potential assassin. She was tired of looking over her shoulder, sick of being scared.

And tonight, she missed her father.

She ached to hear his voice, to see his smile. She wanted to rest her head on his shoulder and know everything was all right because Daddy was here. The world was safe with him in it; *she* was safe.

When was the last time she truly felt that?

She closed her eyes, trying to remember. Then it came to her, further back than she imagined, a time before drought, rebellion, and financial ruin, at the house in Taylorsville, the nice one, with the big porch and backyard swing.

She was little, too young to recognize the battles raging between her parents, or the rebellion about to infect her kingdom. Prince Eamonn was still on the throne.

She saw her father's face, his warm brown eyes, the wrinkles in the corners when he smiled. She heard his voice and his laugh. They were playing in that magical backyard.

"Push me higher, Daddy."

"Higher? Like this?" He gave her a mighty push.

She felt her long hair flying behind her, the rush of air in her ears. He pushed her again, and she soared. Leaning back, parallel to the ground, flying higher and faster, she felt like her toes could touch the sky.

"Pump your legs!" he encouraged and stepped out of the way.

She tried it, exhilarated that she could keep going without him pushing her. On the fifth pass, she jumped out of the seat at the swing's highest arc. She landed on her feet and threw up her arms like she had seen the big girls do in gymnastics class. "Did you see me?"

"I did, you were flying."

Mom leaned out the backdoor. "You are going to break your leg, Davianna. David, don't push her so hard."

Daddy waved at Mom and said, "Okay." Then he turned to her with a smile and gestured to the balance beam he had made for her. "Show me what you've learned his week, Dee-dee."

She smiled at the nickname, the only one she ever had, Davianna ben David was Dee-dee to her daddy.

The beam was low to the ground and not as big as the one they had in class, but she could practice. She scampered over to it. At five-years-old, and only three months into her lessons, she could do little more than walk without falling off, but she performed a dip walk with the aplomb of an Olympian. He applauded when she finished her first pass, so she did it again. Emboldened, she tried walking on her tiptoes. She fell off but climbed back up and finished.

"I think you can jump."

Her eyes grew huge, and she looked at the beam. She could jump off a swing but the beam? She might miss. She might slip and twist her ankle. She might get hurt. "Do you think?"

He nodded.

She bounced on her toes, but her feet did not leave the beam. She tried again, merely lifting her chest. Her feet stayed put. His brown eyes sparkled with laughter. Davianna gave him a sheepish giggle and tried again. She jumped. Her arms wind milled, but she managed to stay on the beam. "I did it, Daddy!"

He grinned. "Of course, you did. You have been practicing." He picked her up and kissed the top of her head, carrying her into the house for lunch. "Remember that. You only fail if you stop trying, if you quit, or if you try to do things outside the Iron King's will for your life."

"What's his will for my life?" She looked up at him, expecting a clear answer.

"He shows us, Dee-dee, and if you don't know, then you pray and ask him. You read the Bible and do what it says. If you do those things, you won't go wrong."

Mom snorted as she handed her the jelly sandwich and left the room.

Daddy watched her leave and sat down at the kitchen table. "Sometimes, if we are blessed, the things we want are his will for our lives." He hung his head and said quietly, "But sometimes we make mistakes."

She took a bite. Grape. Her favorite. "I don't want to make mistakes, Daddy."

He smiled at her. "You will. It is part of life. If you surround yourself with good people, they will help you, but you must listen to good advice because others might see things you cannot. And if you want something bad enough, you might make excuses, then you will make a mistake. Remember that. Sometimes we want something so much that we ignore what is right." He cast a mournful eye into the living room and added. "And that, dear daughter, will cause a lifetime of grief."

Thousands of miles from Taylorsville and more than a decade since their conversation, Davianna whispered, "What is his will for my life, Daddy?"

Grief struck like heat lightning, unbidden and violent.

"Daddy, what am I supposed to do?"

Only silence met her plaintive cry. Daddy was gone, buried beneath the shifting sands of the Greek desert.

She curled into herself, shaking in pain, suffocated by grief. She gulped the jasmine scented air; it was an ugly cry. "I miss you." Cradling her head on her arms, she leaned against the edge of the tub. "Why did you have to die? Why did you leave me? I can't... I can't do this without you."

Whether it was her imagination, a memory, or a true presence she did not know, but she heard his voice. "Shh, Dee-dee, don't cry."

"Daddy." The single word held all the love and longing of her heart. "I'm so sorry. I should not have opened that box. You taught me better. I was outside his will. I think—I knew it. I was mad at Mom, and now, everything is a mess." She hiccupped and gasped.

"And today, in that alley?" Hugging her knees to her chest, she sobbed. She cried in the silence of the bathroom until the tears ran dry.

Pulling the drain on the tub, she imagined her pain swirling into the murky depths of the Thames. Grief was a luxury. She needed to pull it together.

Emerging from the bathroom, puffy eyed and spent, she was not surprised to see Astrid sleeping. Her crying jag had not been silent. Astrid would have checked on her if she heard. They did that for each other. On Emaline's birthday, Astrid claimed she had a headache and stayed in bed, but Davianna knew the truth.

Tonight, Astrid really did have a headache. She had not complained, but Davianna recognized the pinched expression, and the fitful movements coming from her side of the room confirmed it. A headache stalked her.

A migraine could be a disaster. The entire reason they were in London, the whole trek across Europe had led to this. By international treaty, there were two flights operating in and out of Europe, one functioning airport: London. One flight went to Alanthia, one to the Golden Kingdom. Davianna and Astrid had a choice, east or west. The available tickets made the choice for them. They had seats on the Alanthian flight, tomorrow. Tel Aviv tickets were booked out for a month.

Astrid was just going to have to force herself to do it, migraine or not. They had to be on that plane. They could not stay in London, not after the events in the alley. Not only were the hunters after them now, the police would be looking for them.

Davianna's hands felt clammy, and she had the restless unease that sometimes overtook her. She ran to the window and looked out, picturing police moving in to arrest them. Scanning the narrow streets, she saw nothing. However, her view was partially obscured by a tree, and she could not see the other side of the hotel from her room. If the police were coming, they might not approach from this side. She ran her fingers through her damp hair and wondered if she was just being paranoid. Pacing in the semi-darkness, she contemplated going to bed, but sleep would be impossible. She needed to make sure they were safe. She needed to get out.

Dressing in her Gune Black, she armed herself. The familiar clothing made her feel powerful. The tunic and leggings never got dirty. They never stank, tore, or showed signs of wear. The material blended into the background like a cuttlefish in a reef. She strapped on her knives, taking Astrid's stiletto for good measure. On silent feet, she slipped into the hallway and disappeared.

Errand Boy – London - Josiah

As Josiah left the Windsor Police Station, he was vexed, exceedingly vexed. Bureaucratic red tape always frustrated him. But worse, he was being followed. He spent the evening evading his pursuers, lost them in Slough, then doubled back to Windsor to pick up Benny, and took off. The girls might disappear into the tangle of metro-London, but so could he.

His Feltham hotel was dingy, old, and too small for his large frame. After three millennia, London was still cramped. He collapsed onto the bed, petting Benny, who snuggled beside him.

"I saw her today, boy. The little minx slipped through my hands again."

The dachshund did not seem to mind, splayed on his back, tongue lolling in ecstasy, enjoying his belly rub.

A sharp rap at the door transformed them both. They were alert, ready to fight.

"Captain," an urgent whisper came from the hall, "it is Reuben ben Judah. Come with me."

His gear bag sat open. Josiah clicked his cheek, and Benny jumped in. They were gone from the room in seconds. The two men exchanged a silent greeting and disappeared into the cold night.

Josiah raised an eyebrow when he saw their means of transport but recognized the expediency of a bicycle and hopped on. Exhausted after his long day, he would have preferred a horse. Pedaling down Uxbridge Road, he might have even gotten in a car. They were rare, but a recent international treaty lifted the ban on Alanthian exports, and they were pouring into Europe. Still, Reuben's choice did not raise any speculative glances as they rode into the city.

They left their bicycles in a public rack and jogged into

Kensington Park. When they reached St. Govor's Well, Josiah watched in amazement as Reuben pressed the cobblestones in a pattern. With a scraping of old stones, the well opened, revealing a hidden passageway.

They descended the spiral staircase, emerging onto a narrow walkway that skirted the edge of an underground river. Torches lit the way. They were expected.

They embraced, brief and rough.

Josiah smiled into his friend's face. "Good to see you, man. How is the leg?"

After the mud hut incident, Reuben faced disciplinary action. They offered him a deal, a dishonorable discharge or Mossad. Reuben readily agreed to Mossad. The covert organization fit his personality, talents, and unconventional style. He distinguished himself as an exceptional operative. Josiah had not seen him since he became Agent Reuben ben Judah.

Reuben grinned and stretched his calf. "My leg, it is still there, thanks to you."

"Well enough." Josiah nodded. "Where are we going?"

"The Embassy. Prince Yehonathan is waiting."

Benny's long nose poked through the zipper, impatient to be free. Josiah let him loose, much to Reuben's amusement. "Captain, I do not say this to cause offense, but this is a ridiculous looking dog."

Josiah rose from his haunches. "Do not let his size fool you. He has the heart of a lion."

Benjamin sniffed Reuben's leg and sat at his feet, wagging his tail, and quizzing up at him with intelligent brown eyes. Reuben grinned. "I would not expect you to travel with a dog."

Josiah scoffed. "He has no idea he's a dog, trust me." He clicked his tongue, and Benny went ahead of them with his nose to the ground. "Good tracker, does not complain."

Reuben fell into step. "Which I know you appreciate. Anyone that served with you will attest, you do not tolerate *kvetching*."

Josiah shrugged. "Waste of energy. Bad for morale."

"Aye, this is true." Their footsteps were amplified in the cavern's depths. Reuben raised an eyebrow at Josiah and asked, "At some point, were you planning to tell me you were a Prince?"

Josiah looked a bit sheepish. "Sorry about that."

Reuben snorted. "I should have known."

"Glad you didn't."

Reuben paused and put a hand on Josiah's shoulder. "If you need my help, if you need anything, I will be there for you."

"Thank you," Josiah said, deeply touched. "I do not have many friends, none as Prince Josiah ben Eamonn. It is nice to know, I have at least one."

"You do indeed, my Esteemed."

Josiah closed his eyes and nodded.

Twenty minutes later, he entrusted Benny to Reuben's care and settled into an overstuffed chair in front of a softly crackling fire. He flexed his ankle, relieving a cramp in his calf. A servant brought a tray of cinnamon spiced cider and scones, inquired after his needs, and departed. Josiah savored the warm food and the fire. Easing back in the comfortable chair, he relaxed. Soldiers, doctors, and Princes in exile learned to capture moments of peace when they came.

He dozed off.

He awoke to find Yehonathan sitting in the wingback chair beside him. In the manner of a doctor, he came instantly awake, rising and offering his hand. "Please, pardon me."

Yehonathan shook Josiah's hand, a touch of amusement in his eye. "Welcome to London, Prince."

They sat in companionable silence, staring into the dancing flames. Josiah waited. He had been summoned, let Yehonathan tell him why.

"We are delivering thy evidence against Captain Orion ben Drachmas to Prince Edward. 'Twas good work thou did in Greece."

Josiah tapped his toe unconsciously and looked at the ceiling. "Yet Antiochus' reign of terror continues."

"Aye, but I surmise 'twill not much longer. The Iron King's patience is not infinite in the matter of rebellious Princes."

Josiah did not suppress the small snort of impatience.

"Korah's time cometh, as will thine." Yehonathan shrugged a shoulder as if the matter was of little importance to him, then said, "Davianna ben David is here."

Josiah gave him a sharp look. "In the Embassy?"

Yehonathan shook his head. "Nay, in Covent Garden. She and her companion are at the One Aldwych Hotel."

Josiah's dark brow lifted in speculation. "I see."

Yehonathan raised his hands in a manner that told Josiah it was not his choice. "The King commanded that we guard her only."

"How long have you known her whereabouts?" Josiah asked with deep suspicion.

"For some time." Yehonathan, again, shrugged his innocence.

Josiah exploded from the chair, snarling, "You knew where she was and sent me across this continent on a folly, as a foolish errand boy?"

Yehonathan met his eyes. "The King confideth not in me the reasons for his commands, and I do not question."

Josiah stalked away, vibrating with anger. "Naturally."

"He hath guarded thee, Prince." Yehonathan's voice was stern. "As thou knowest well."

Josiah recognized the truth in Yehonathan's words. The most recent example was two nights ago. Outnumbered ten to one, he watched a gang of thugs closing in on Davianna. From nowhere, several fighters joined his side, then quickly disappeared into the night. "Calais?"

Yehonathan deliberately crossed an ankle over one knee and sat back. "And Geneva and Orleans."

"Geneva? Orleans?" Josiah's whole body tightened in anger. "You intervened then, which allowed her to escape—two times!" He paced in front of the fireplace, absolutely furious.

"The King's will." Yehonathan gestured with open palms. "But that is not why I summoned thee." He dropped his hands to the armrests and leaned forward, an unmistakable command in his voice. "Sit down, cease thy prowling, and listen."

Josiah threw himself into the chair.

"Korah has found thee."

This was not news to Josiah, who remained silent, his veiled eyes glowing with fury and contempt.

"He has ordered thy murder. Madness over taketh him; thou art in mortal peril."

Josiah scoffed, "With Korah as my uncle, I have been in mortal peril since the day I was born."

"True, yet thou remaineth alive. Thy steps are ordered, thy path guarded, and thy purpose?"

Josiah sighed in resignation, repeating the oath of the Iron King's Army. "My purpose is to serve the King."

"Aye." Satisfied with the answer, Yehonathan adjusted the signet ring on his right hand and said, "He wishes thee to convey a message to thy intrepid maiden."

That surprised Josiah. "A message? Not ferry her back to the Golden City as he commanded?"

Yehonathan shook his head. "Nay, not at present, but she will go when the time cometh."

"And when might that be?" Josiah asked, his voice dripping with sarcasm.

Yehonathan shrugged. "When the King has destined."

"Destiny." Josiah lifted his lip at the irony, remembering the Gune's words to him at Sandanski's farm. "We are mere puppets in his game."

"Thou hast free will. There are no locks on thy doors, no chains that bind thee to him. He has never done so with man."

Josiah nodded. He knew it was true. Resigned to do another futile errand, he asked, "How shall I deliver any message without her disappearing again?"

Prince Yehonathan rang a small bell on the table beside him. A servant entered, bearing a silver tray. "Present her this, from the King, she will listen."

Josiah was skeptical but pocketed the item, then left the Embassy to find the girl.

Waterloo Bridge - Davianna and Josiah

Davianna prowled Covent Garden, but detected no pursuers, saw no signs of danger. Feeling melancholy after her bout of grief, she was drawn to view London from the ancient Waterloo Bridge. She felt certain that her father had adored the sight. They always talked about coming here, but the boat they caught on pilgrimage took them to Spain first, and they had not gotten the chance. She imagined him beside her, spinning tales, pointing out landmarks, and laughing. Under normal circumstances, she would have never ventured onto a bridge at night, alone. Tonight, she felt strangely compelled to be here, at peace. She had a vague expectation of finding Jelena, but it was not the Gune who came to her in the night.

The Dark Prince approached with purpose, but without menace. Some strange compulsion seized her, and she did not run. It was reckless, like in the alley, however, she was bone weary and sick of running, sick of hiding. In London, they were confronting. She was going to find out what he wanted.

She leaned her elbows against the railing and waited, watching out of the corner of her eye. He was bigger up close, tall, and heavily muscled. A shadow of a beard darkened his handsome face. His hair ruffled in the breeze, inky-black and wavy, longer than the last time she saw him. He stopped two yards from where she stood. Turning to face him, her heart beat a rhythm, an ancient, primal response to a very handsome man. She was not afraid of him, not like the others who hunted her.

Standing so close to her, Josiah wondered how she ever

passed for a boy. No boy alive ever sported such an exquisite ass. She was petite, not spare. He could see the muscles in her legs through her black leggings. To his mind, her rich brown hair looked like a pixie's, not a lad's. Without a word, he palmed the pomegranate Yehonathan had given him, offering it to her.

One corner of her mouth lifted, and she chuckled. "Fruit? You bring me fruit? If I had known that is why you were chasing me across Europe, perhaps I would have let you catch me. I adore grain apples."

Her voice surprised him, deeper than he expected, not girlish at all. Her accent was a complete shock, but he knew she was a talented mimic, so it might not be authentic. He blinked and cleared his throat. "The Iron King sends his regards, and bids me to deliver a message."

She eyed him speculatively, staring at the fruit. He was intrigued by the quick progression of thoughts that crossed her oval face: consideration, surprise, comprehension. She closed the distance between them. In the breeze, he could smell jasmine. She took the grain apple and held it between them, staring into his eyes.

"The King gave you this and told you to give it to me with a message?" At his nod, she said quietly, "The King... I suspected as much."

Josiah fought the urge to grab her around the waist and haul her from this bridge. For six months, he had pursued her. She was his mission, his goal, the key to getting back his kingdom. Now, she stood before him like Eve offering an apple to a besotted Adam. Staring into her dark brown eyes, he was enchanted. Disguising the rush of heat, he executed a formal bow and said, "May I beg the lady's presence while we stroll? I fear 'tis a bitter night."

"May I know your name, kind sir, for I am not in the habit of walking out with strangers."

He smiled, showing straight white teeth. "Doctor Einar ben Yane, retired Captain of the King's Army, Surgeon, Fourth Dragoons, at your service, my lady."

"Doctor?" she asked, surprised, and took his proffered arm. "I did not imagine you as a doctor."

Next to him, she was tiny, her head barely reaching his shoulder. Yet as they walked, he realized she fit perfectly against him. He shortened his stride to accommodate her. He felt the leather sheath on her forearm, the knife at her side, as her hip bumped into him. It sent a jolt of fire down his leg.

They walked in silence as a gray fog rose from the river. Neither knew what to say.

Davianna held his arm, warm and heavy. His leather jacket felt soft, supple with age. He smelled like the night air and clean sweat, from exercise, rather than labor. He also carried a faint undertone of antiseptic, which convinced her he was a doctor, more than his words. She realized the elusive peace she came searching for was upon her. It felt vaguely reminiscent of that day she walked with the stranger outside Camp Eiran. No, she mentally corrected, *The King*. Yet the tenor of *that* meeting had been peace and light; this was heat.

"You are in grave danger, Davianna ben David." The rich timbre of his voice reverberated through his chest. She tightened her grip on his arm, and he patted her hand. "Not from me. You have never been in danger from me."

Davianna peered up at him, reviewing their mad flight across the continent. A long silence passed between them, full of narrow escapes, glimpses of one another, and looming danger. "You were in Calais." It was a statement, not a question.

He gave a brief nod and was shocked when she turned into his arms, hugging him hard. "Thank you," she whispered.

Her fierce reaction conveyed her fear. After months of chasing the little minx, he failed to recognize that she might be afraid, just canny, and infuriatingly sly. He cursed himself for a fool. Of course, she was frightened. He knew who and what chased her.

"And were you in Dunkirk?" She raised her head, trying to hide the fear in her eyes. "Did you stop the Egyptian?"

He felt her trembling, from cold or fright he could not tell. He resisted the insane urge to kiss the top of her head. "He will not trouble you again."

She sagged in relief, and he held her in the silence.

As they began to walk again, she bowed her head and said, "But there will be more. I am beset upon by the whole world."

He knew what that felt like. "Yet, thou art not alone." He lifted her chin and stared into her big brown eyes. "That was the message I was sent to deliver."

"That's it?" An incredulous laugh bubbled to the surface. "With the hounds of hell upon me, the message is, thou art not alone?" Davianna drew her brows down in amused sarcasm. "Oh, that's helpful."

He felt a sudden rush of empathy. "I am familiar with his ways in these matters."

"And did he send you as protection, that I might not be alone?" Wariness mixed with a touch of hope crossed her face.

Again, he wanted to take her by the hand and run. Instead, he said, "No. I fear that I am more sought after than thee." He saw the hope drain out of her.

"Truly? Who would hunt thee?"

"Do not allow it to trouble thee. Thou hast enough to consider without giving over to worry about me."

She shrugged. "I find it eases the burden, the consideration of others."

Josiah admired that quality in her, had seen evidence that she spoke the truth. They left a trail of clothing at pilgrim camps across the continent. It was one of the ways he tracked her. "Where is thy companion? I have brought her medicine, for her headaches."

Her eyes brightened as she pocketed the medicine. "How didst thou know about her headaches?"

He was utterly enchanted, surmising that she could blend in at court, quite an actress. He switched back to common speech to see if she would too. "I have followed you two for six months. Did you imagine that a lass, or a lad," he raised a sardonic eyebrow at her, "struck blind with migraine would go unremarked upon?"

Several times, Astrid had been debilitated. Davianna was frantic in Venice and again in Liege when the pain seized Astrid, and the tea chest was empty. The implications of his statement dawned on her. "Have you tracked us through tea?"

Her indignation beguiled him. "I used the tea, among other methods, but you have proven yourself quite intrepid."

She gave a little shake of her shoulders and flashed him an impish grin. "I do my best. The tea though, that was an error."

Josiah shrugged. "Perhaps." He paused, weighing his next words. "But it might prove useful. If you need to find me, if you need my help, there is a way to convey a message."

She wrinkled her forehead, looking at him with deep suspicion.

"The blend is specific, and I do not believe anyone else has put it together. I have given you enough medicine, so you don't have to take chances. But if you need me, if you are in trouble, find a tea shop run by citizens of the Golden Kingdom and order the tea Astrid uses. They will get the message to me. I'll come."

"A tea network?" she asked with deep skepticism.

"I have not served in the Iron King's army for more than a decade without learning a few secrets."

She looked up at him through her long black lashes. "How do I know that's not a trap?"

He lowered his head and said softly, "I suppose you don't, but honestly have you ever felt threatened by me?"

The corner of her mouth twitched, and she said in a deep southern accent, "Well, you were hoppin' mad in Geneva."

She did it on purpose, to charm him, and it worked, until he remembered how angry he *had* been in Geneva.

"Don't flare your nose at me." She smiled up at him with beguiling innocence. "I have good reasons to be running, and you know it. If you are not arresting me, and you aren't coming with me, then tell me how else you were tracking us. I don't want to keep making the same mistakes and have some other fool find us."

"Fool?" He chuckled and relaxed, thoroughly entertained.

"You know what I meant." She bumped her hip against his playfully. "How else?"

A cold wind stung his eyes as he looked at the dark silhouettes of London. A dense fog crept in, surrounding them in silence, concealing them. He decided to tell her. She was right. She needed to know. Yet he feared it would make her even more elusive. "The clothes you two leave behind, the tea, and Astrid's remarkable red hair." He did not add her amazing derriere, which always elicited comments from the men he questioned. There was nothing she could do about that, and he was loath to mention it.

"The hair," she groaned, "I was afraid of that."

They were alone this late in the evening, but as they descended the Riverside Terrace steps, she became wary.

He sensed the change. "Mossad surrounds us, my lady. We are safe at present."

"Mossad, again?"

Josiah raised a brow at her in speculation.

Davianna shrugged. "I've caught sight of them now and then, just like I have you." She strongly suspected he was Mossad with his dark hair and olive skin. However, his nose was not right, and his accent was decidedly not Golden Kingdom. It was a peculiar mix of upper class Alanthian and somewhere else she could not identify, perhaps Greece, but she could not be sure..

Josiah ran his tongue over his upper teeth, trying to control the flare of temper. The errand boy mission still infuriated him. "I suspect they have been guarding you two since Greece."

That surprised her. The first time she had seen them was in Italy. She sighed in weary resignation and repeated his words back to him, "Thou art not alone."

"Indeed," he nodded, and looked over his shoulder, searching the shadows.

"So, no more messages from the King? No cryptic instructions about where we are supposed to go?" Davianna hoped for an answer. The New City seemed the most dangerous place on Earth, even if it was their best hope of destroying the device.

"I do not know, and it is not safe for you to tell me." Josiah's strange undertone caught her attention. "Because, if I do not know, I cannot be compelled, or otherwise persuaded, to divulge that information."

Dreadful understanding dawned. "They are hunting you, too."

He nodded. "Aye."

She rubbed her temple. "But you are an officer in the King's army."

Her naivete' both charmed and alarmed him. "We are not as we all may appear, Davianna."

She pulled away, eyeing him suspiciously. "I weary of deceptions, Doctor."

He held her eyes for a second, an infinity.

She blinked, breaking the spell, and slipped into the mist.

Josiah watched her go, feeling strangely bereft, as if when she left, she took something from him. On his ride back to the Embassy, he wondered whether she had taken it, or had she filled a space he never knew was empty.

Lime and Water - New York - Peter

There was a party at Prince d'Or's New York penthouse, full of beautiful people, wretchedly, vapidly, beautiful people. Peter ran a gauntlet of pouty-lipped stunners, purring for his attention, tossing their long hair, and offering him a view of their long legs and expensive heels. He moved among them with indolent grace, comfortable in their society, the ruler of their set. He strolled to a window, perusing his guests with an imperious air, completely bored.

Ice clinked in his glass and a servant hurried over with a refill. A statuesque brunette in a pink gossamer dress caught his eye. She beckoned him with a long, pink fingernail.

He flashed her a lecherous grin and signaled her to join him… in his bedroom. Strolling down the hall, his hand rested on her back, just below the friend zone.

His dimly lit bedroom was decorated in sleek masculine furnishings of gray and silver. The balcony afforded a breathtaking view of the city. As they entered, she resolutely lifted his hand off her waist and looked around. "Prince d'Or's lair. Nice."

He flashed her a grin, his dimple adding to his exaggerated roguishness.

"What are you drinking?"

He toasted her with the crystal glass. "Water with lime. Do you want to test it?"

"I might." Alaina ben Thomas raised a brown penciled eyebrow at him, clearly conveying that she would.

"It was never the alcohol, Alaina." Peter turned away. "You know that."

"I know that any intoxication is dangerous, Peter."

He held up a hand for her to stop. "Hence, the water with lime."

"You're still clean?" Alaina asked, dead serious.

She had a right to be concerned. Their lives depended on his ability to stay clear headed, strong, and sober. They were in the final phases of a plan born after he emerged from the dungeon and forty-five days of drug induced torture.

More than two-and-a-half years later, he still battled the dark demon of addiction acquired in the pit. He floated in and out of hell. He binged, then spent months sober. It fooled him, gave him the illusion of control. He thought he could stop whenever he wanted, until he could not. But like everything else in his life, he kept it secret, kept it hidden, but Alaina saw the truth.

She was his most regular outside contact in The Resistance, the organization they formed to overthrow Korah and install his cousin on the throne. Jarrod, who was also involved, saw him every day, but his relationship with his valet and the lines between them, prevented Jarrod from confronting him. He and Alaina had no such boundaries. She confronted him.

In late December last year, she called an emergency meeting. He showed up wasted, again.

"I am not going to keep hiding this! You either get some help, clean yourself up, or I am telling the others. There is too much at stake. People are risking their lives for you, for this plan." She grabbed his arm. "I have lost too many friends to drugs."

He jerked away from her. "I'll stop."

"No, you won't. Dammit, Peter, why are you doing this to yourself?"

He turned on her and snapped. "I did not do this to myself! They did it to me. He did it to me. Bloody hell, Alaina, do you think I woke up one morning and decided to become a drug addict? Do you?"

If she would have yelled at him, he would have fought. However, she did the one thing he had no weapon against, she cried. "I know what they did to you, Peter. The question is, when are you going to stop letting them do it?"

He checked himself into a private clinic the next day. He had been clean since, except for one night. He had gotten completely trashed at the club, not drugs, alcohol. He woke up with a woman he still had no clear recollection of. "I have been sober since March. I swear." He raised his glass and drank.

He saw the ghost of a smile cross her face. "Good." She

sighed and opened her clutch. "Here. And by the way, you don't pay me enough."

He chuckled, taking the papers from her. "I do not pay you anything."

"Like I said, not enough. This wig is abominable." She pointed to the absurd brunette coiffure. "I'm dressed like a prostitute, and these tacky shoes are killing me."

He leaned forward and kissed her cheek. "Poor, Alaina. I am beastly."

"Perfectly," she retorted and collapsed into a low-backed chair, shucking her pink heels. "But no one recognized me, so I will give you props on the disguise."

"I thought about a maid's costume, only fair, after all, but I do not sleep with maids."

She snickered, remembering how he dressed the first time they met and surmised he probably slept with half the servants in the Palace.

He flipped through the pictures in rapid succession. "Where were these taken?"

"Outside London, today."

He contemplated them with a deep frown. "Today? Why is he at a police station?"

She motioned to the report that he did not bother to read. "It's in the report."

"Humor me," he said, giving her a warning look.

Alaina tucked an impossibly long leg under her and settled in. "He told the police he has been tracking a fugitive across Europe for six months. There was a massacre in some pilgrim camp in Greece earlier this year. He claims Orion ben Drachmas led it."

"Greece?" Peter shook his head; Greece was a mess. "What name did he use?"

"Doctor Einar ben Yane, Captain of the King's Army, Surgeon… and apparent bounty hunter."

"My cousin, the saint," Peter dead panned,

"That is not the half of it. It seems Doctor ben Yane not

only did the autopsies of the massacred victims, he tracked and apprehended the suspect, who was in the act of accosting two young boys. They fled the scene, but the Greek was stabbed during the scuffle."

Peter groaned. "Oh, do not tell me."

Her mouth trembled with amusement. "Then the hero saved the villain's life, right there on the street."

Peter closed his eyes and groaned cynically. "Saint, indeed."

Alaina made a jaw cracking yawn. "The rest is in the report."

He collapsed into the chair beside her, holding up his hand for her to stop. "Much as you might complain, you love this. Tell me the rest." He looked weary, but tilted his head, giving her a charming smile. "Besides, if you leave too soon, you will ruin my reputation."

She rolled her eyes, but he was correct, as usual. "This arrest is big. I did some research on the case. Greece has been trying to cover it up, unsuccessfully. The massacre has been swirling around Antiochus for months, and he is under fire in the international community over it. I found a report where Mossad alleges that the orders for the attack came straight from Antiochus and that Captain Orion ben Drachmas led it. The Palace will know tomorrow that Prince Josiah is in London."

Peter massaged his left temple. "Do we know where he is?"

Alaina shook her head. "No. He disappeared after he left the police station. London does not have surveillance cameras everywhere like we do."

"A blessing and a curse, I suppose." Peter shrugged. "He has stayed alive this long. I just wonder what he is up to. I thought after he presented himself at Yehonathan's court last spring, we would already be underway. Instead, before I can get a message to him, he bloody disappears for six months, then turns up at a police station?"

Alaina shrugged. "Your guess is as good as mine. One thing is clear, he is not using his real name, and from what we can tell, he has not made a single move to contact either Monarch Antiochus or Prince Edward."

"He would not go near Antiochus, who is as bad, or worse, than Korah." Peter continued massaging his temple. "Yet, he presented himself to Yehonathan, and that tells me something. That tells me he has a plan."

"What?"

"I have no idea. And if you are correct, and Korah's forces are hot on his tail, we cannot risk a message." Peter stared down at the fuzzy photographs. "It feels like I have been waiting on him my whole life." He swallowed and took another drink. "Thank you, Alaina. Let me know what else you find, normal channels."

She unfolded from her chair and adjusted the glam wig, staring at his reflection in the mirror as she did. His face was half in shadow. He had a strong jaw, and those eyes, all emerald green and tortured. He was one of those men who was hard to look at because he was so heart-wrenchingly beautiful. A bad boy with a troubled spirit. But more than that, he was a Prince with a light of mischief in his smile that drove women wild. They wanted to touch him, fix him, heal him. They tried. He let them try. Over the years, she watched a parade of them try. He never kept them around, and he never healed.

"Take care." Alaina smiled.

"Goodnight, Alaina."

She slipped out the door, feeling his melancholy follow her. She wove her way through the party where his guests seemed to be enjoying themselves, despite their host's absence. Waiting for the elevator, she hoped he would be all right. He seemed tired, slightly off tonight, and she worried about him.

They had a complex relationship. He was complex. Sometimes they were completely professional, other times friendly. Peter was normally charming and could be an outrageous flirt. If he felt peeved or did not want to talk about a subject, he could be cutting. In the familiarity, sometimes she forgot he was royalty, and sometimes he reminded her. But no matter how friendly they became, he kept part of himself aloof, separate. Whether it was his royal blood, because he was royalty down to his last atom, or for security reasons, she was not sure. But he isolated himself. He had to if he wanted to stay alive, if they all wanted to stay alive. He played the role of Prince d'Or in public and in the Palace. Tonight, his drooping shoulders and tired eyes conveyed the toll it took on him.

But treason was difficult and dangerous business.

She hailed a cab, feeling disconcerted, uneasy. She suspected he walked through life that way, though he did not complain. When she opened the cab door, the memory of her own troubled man waited for her. New Orleans jazz greeted her as she slipped into the backseat, and the soulful clarinet made her want to weep.

Peter slumped in his chair, studying the pictures. He wondered why Josiah was really in London, and if he had any idea of the hell Korah planned to unleash on him. Peter shuddered. He knew it all too well.

Forcing himself out of his seat, he walked to the wall safe. He stowed the pictures and slammed the door, harder than he intended.

Then he staggered.

"Bloody hell?"

Black spots burst in front of his eyes, and he caught himself against the dresser. His hand slipped, scattering his watch and cufflinks onto the carpet. He rested his head on the hard, wooden surface and tried to catch his breath. "What?" he said into the hollow of his arms.

Noises became distorted. The party in the living room grew distant. He had the sensation of careening headlong down a deep well. His knees gave way, and he cracked his chin as he fell. "Oh, son of a bitch." The room spun crazily, and his body pulsed with that peculiar sensation of alternating hot and cold. Vomit rose up his throat.

He had been drugged.

Cold terror swamped him. They were coming. Evil was coming. He could feel it. He put his hands over his face and whispered, "Oh God, I cannot take this anymore."

The party outside grew quiet. They had been dismissed. Evil did not operate with an audience.

The door squeaked as it opened, and he cursed himself as an idiot for ditching his security. He knew he would be meeting Alaina tonight, and they could not risk even his trusted guards seeing her again. Now… he was going to pay.

"Did you enjoy your whore tonight?"

Despite the drugs, despite being on the floor, he opened his eyes and shot Keyseelough a look of such abject hatred, she should have run. She would have if she had not paid someone to spike his drink.

"Get the fuck out of my house." Peter struggled to his feet. He was not going to stay on his knees, not in front of her.

"I'm not leaving." She looked around contemptuously, crossed her arms, and said, "I am taking inventory for when I redecorate."

He took three steps forward, intending to seize her and throw her out, but the world tilted, and he stopped. "What did you give me?"

She made a dismissive snort and moved deeper into the room, out of his reach. "What do you care? You have spent our entire betrothal on drugs and in whores' beds."

"Can you blame me when the alternative is being in yours?" His tongue felt thick in his mouth, and he thought he slurred the last word, but he was not sure. "I would rather eat shit. Oh, but you do that, do you not?"

Keyseelough turned, ignoring the jibe, her haughty eyes

full of offended royal pride. "You ignore me, disregard me, and shame me in front of the whole world by lying with the scum of the earth."

"At least it is just women I sleep with, but I suppose we have that in common." He wished for a wall or a piece of furniture he could lean against. He was an island surrounded by a sea of nothingness. "Furthermore, I limit my sexual partners to those of my own species."

She flicked a hand of dismissal. "That was nothing."

He wanted to throw up as the memory crashed in on him. He squeezed the bridge of his nose and tried to control his breathing. "Just go."

"No, Peter ben Korah, I no longer care what you want. I am tired of waiting. We are both tired of waiting. Tonight, the Dark Master and I will teach you the way it is to be."

"You will have to… kill me first." As he said it, the drugs overcame his iron will, and he collapsed.

He did not know how long he was out, a minute, a week? He had not known the first time, and he did not know now. He smelled something, incense, he thought. He tried to roll over and realized he was restrained. "You fucking bitch."

"Ah, you are now awake." She bent over him and kissed him full on the lips. Her black hair was loose, falling over his face, surrounding him, smothering him.

He realized she was naked. And so was he.

"Get off me," he growled.

In answer, she began to stroke his cock. He realized he was not smelling incense, it was oil. He was covered in it. Bile rose in his throat, and he gagged. He felt the evil in her, knew her intent. Even in the worst of the torture, they had not done this. Not this.

He could barely breathe. Her hair felt like a black shroud, wrapping him in death, suffocating the light, extinguishing hope.

The temperature plummeted. He knew who entered the

room. He wanted to scream. He wanted to cry out, but he stopped doing that long ago. No one would come.

"You are bound to me," Keyseelough said, digging her fingernails into his temples, "to us." Red fire shot through her fingertips and into his brain, savaging him. He tried to seize his head, but he could not. He panicked and thrashed. The electrical storm short circuited every synapse in his body, and he convulsed.

He heard the monster laugh as her tongue caressed him, stroking him, sucking him. He could not bear it, but his traitorous body had no such objections. It was violation beyond what he could endure.

He disassociated, searching for a place to hide. There it was—the safe place, glowing with warm light at the end of a dark hallway. If he could get there, it would be all right. He ran through a gauntlet of razor-sharp claws and fiery tongues.

"You are mine, Prince," the monster taunted. "I told you that a long time ago."

He imagined the sneering smile of his father, "It's time, Son. Submit."

"No!" he shouted, running in his mind, fleeing the terror that stalked him. He was naked, running in the passages, his mother screaming behind him. If he did not run, he would see her corpse, and he did not want to see her. He never wanted to see her, not like that. And he could not bear to let her see him, not like this.

Oil… Keyseelough was dripping oil on his body, rubbing him, and chanting. That horrible chanting. He could hear the drums. They pounded in his head. She would take him and pull him down in that dungeon. He would be the sacrifice.

He fought. He fought her. He fought the drugs. He fought the monster. Peter fought himself. He had to make it. The door to the safe place was closing, just a crack of light visible now. He was going to die. He dove. It slammed behind him just as the Hell Bitch mounted him. And for a little while, Peter ben Korah disappeared.

Gimme Shelter - Peter

When he woke, she was gone. She had the decency to un-tie him. He was thankful for that. Thankful he would not be found naked, bound, and shamed. He did not think he could muster the elan to joke his way out of it. The very thought made him sick. He stumbled to the bathroom and puked: hard, chest heaving, commode echoing, vomit.

The drugs clawed at him. "Give me more. I need more."

He collapsed onto the cold tile floor, freezing. His mouth tasted foul with sickness and the lingering taste of her. His body was sticky, covered in that cursed oil, and her. She was all over him. Just as she would be... for the rest of his life.

He was never going to escape.

He was never going to get out.

He was what he always was, a prisoner, a pawn.

Nothing.

Worse than nothing, a junkie.

It did not matter what he did; they would always drag him back. They would control him.

"I need it," his body screamed. "Call your dealer. It will make the pain stop."

It had to stop. He had to make it stop.

They were never going to stop. They would find him. He could not go far enough. He could not run fast enough.

They would win. They always won.

He was fooling himself if he thought otherwise.

It was stupid. He was stupid.

When had he forgotten that? When had he convinced himself that he could fight them and actually win?

When had he ever won?

He crawled on his hands and knees: naked, raped, vio-lated.

He reached the nightstand and pulled out the gun.

The Unseen - London

Great and powerful elohim, the archangels, guarded London that night. Straddling one end of Waterloo Bridge, stood the Captain of the Guard, Gabriel. His golden wings, each twenty feet long, were taut, ready for flight. Prince Michael, bedecked in royal purple, held his fearsome black sword, and watched from atop the King's Embassy. Raphael, with his beautiful countenance of legend and Renaissance Art, stood atop the One Aldwych Hotel, his sword drawn, itching for battle. Uriel, who stood guard over Eden, posted atop Big Ben, and scanned the horizon with the golden eyes of a falcon. Two of their ancient foes roamed the Earth. Tonight, the four Archangels were on a mission, to ensure the meeting taking place below proceeded uninterrupted by any malicious character, human or angelic.

As Davianna ben David slipped through the entrance of the hotel, Gabriel joined Raphael on the roof. London was quiet.

"The foul dogs did not dare to show their faces." Raphael brandished his sword, royal-blue fire shot from the end in a glittering display of sapphire light. "I hoped to dispatch Zeus straight to the Lake of Fire."

Gabriel empathized, "We must be patient, my friend."

Raphael roared with laughter. "You speak to me of patience? There has been no one in Heaven or Earth spoiling for a fight more than you, Captain. Every one of these 4947 days you have stomped about, indignant over Marduk's early escape."

Gabriel sent him a sidelong glare. "I have not fought. You speak the truth, but he has seen my sword in the sky. He knows I await."

"Not planning another twenty-one-day fight then?" Raphael goaded.

Gabriel sent him a glare. The Most High recorded the battle between Gabriel and Marduk in the book of Daniel, and ever after, Gabriel's pride was held in check. "Marduk has always been a mighty fighter. Your nemesis is a woman," Gabriel taunted. "No, he is worse than a woman, Zeus the Prince of Greece."

Uriel left his post on Big Ben, shooting through the sky like a gyrfalcon and landing beside them. "There is no sign of them."

Raphael looked toward the Embassy. "Prince Michael is restless."

Gabriel nodded in agreement. "He is called to the pit in fifty-two days."

As if summoned, Michael shot into the sky like a blazing rocket, corkscrewing his mighty sword before him. The Prince of Hosts had style. He landed among his brethren and asked, "Gabriel, the discourse between the humans, did it go as planned?"

Gabriel confirmed, "Aye, my Prince, everything proceeded accordingly."

Michael nodded his approval, then smiled. "Brothers, the Most High has lifted the ban. We are no longer restrained."

Gabriel roared with pleasure and shot into the sky like a comet. His battle cry echoed over London, "Marduk!" His long wait was over, at last.

Uriel joined him in celebration, declaring to the heavens. "Hear ye, oh sons of god, ye fallen elohim, the time of thy wickedness draws nigh. Prepare to meet your doom in the Lake of Fire!"

Raphael looked to the east. For the entire age of man, he had battled Zeus, who like Marduk, maneuvered an early release. The enmity between them stretched back eons, for other than Lucifer, Raphael and Zeus were the most beautiful beings the Most High ever created.

Michael pointed toward Athens. "Zeus, the Prince of Greece has been stealthy. I anticipated he and Marduk would battle, but they have been remarkably quiet."

Raphael nodded. "Aye, my Prince. Other than the parlay,

I have detected no activity between them."

Gabriel landed with a thud. His eyes blazed with righteous purpose, and Michael could tell he was waiting for orders, ready for action. "Brother, the Most High orders you to assail Marduk, the Prince of Persia. His sins against Alanthia have come to an end. He is in New York. Uriel, go as well, that Egyptian whore is with him."

Gabriel and Uriel roared and shot off like heat-seeking missiles locked in on their targets.

Michael saw Raphael's eager expression. "Go, remind Zeus of thy presence."

Raphael bowed, unsheathed his sword, and went to pick a fight.

As Michael stood watch over London, he knew his own fight would happen soon enough, and he was ready.

Psalm 82- New York City, Alanthia - Keyseelough

Keyseelough stood on the rooftop of the penthouse, confident she had finally brought Peter to heel. The Dark Master's presence at her side proved she had found favor. Thus, she felt brazen, bold in her victory. She pointed across the Hudson River and asked, "Is that a statue to Mother Isis? Some say it is, but others say it is not."

Marduk shrugged and stared at the vile thing. "She would tell you it was, but it is not. She did not rule here."

"Why did you allow it to be erected?"

"You have to ask?" Marduk turned away from the hideous image. "Any idol worship pulls them away, especially when they do not recognize it. Besides, as much as I hated the fucking bitch, she was a goddess, and it irks our enemy."

For Alanthians, the monument was enormously popular, and its reestablishment caused nationalistic fervor throughout the land. While it served Marduk's purpose in drawing them away from the Iron King, it niggled at him, provoking a jealous rage. So, he ordered the reconstruction of his grand obelisk, destroyed during the last war, and placed it across the harbor from the statue.

"Do you think we will find it, this Black Key? I would like to meet Mother Isis."

Marduk narrowed his eyes, jealous. "Do you find me lacking?"

She fell to her knees. "I meant no disrespect, Dark Master. No, that is not what I meant. It is only that you have spoken of her to me."

Not placated so easily, he bellowed, "You presume upon me. You are not Ba'alat Ob. You were defeated, rightfully so. Do not—"

His tirade was cut short. His chastisement of one of his high-ranking witches died on his tongue. Without warning, the Hosts of Heaven fell upon him.

Gabriel's golden sword flashed.

Marduk took a vicious blow to the shoulder, stumbling backward, howling in pain and outrage.

Uriel fell upon Keyseelough. She pulled a poison dagger, but he turned it on her; and she slashed herself, a vicious cut running the length of her left arm. She struck out again, enraged. Uriel grabbed her by the hair and flew off. Her hellish shrieks of agony echoed into the night.

Marduk caught himself against the balcony, pulling his sword. But his wound gushed black blood, and his arm hung at an odd angle.

Gabriel backed away, flabbergasted, staring at the severed tendons. Then a grin broke across his face. His voice was quiet. Gabriel, the messenger of God, did not speak idle words. If he would have shouted it, Marduk would have reacted in fury. Instead the softly spoken words chilled him to the bone.

"You are elohim, Marduk, son of the Most High, nevertheless, like a man you shall die, and fall like any Prince." Gabriel advanced, with his golden sword glowing. "And do you know what that means, lizard? Thou art mortal."

It was a judgment, passed down eons ago at the Divine Council, a sentence handed down to him and all his brethren by the Most High.

Marduk howled, and their swords clashed.

The Sins of Adam – New York - Peter

There was a ruckus outside that Peter did not bother to investigate. His eyes burned with desolate tears; the metallic taste of the gun felt strangely comforting, powerful. He was in control, time to end the pain.

Instead of the lingering stench of oil and sex, a new smell filled the room, the origins of which hid in the recesses of his mind, but he could not place it. Regardless, he was thankful that in his last moments he was not gagging with the stink of sulfur.

Through the crack in the balcony door, another scent blew in, fresh hay, stables... his horses.

He dropped the gun and began to cry. It was a dry, ragged sound.

The horses... and the people who loved them... they were the only things... the only times... They would not understand. He scrambled across the bed and grabbed his phone. "Please pick up. Please pick up..."

Silence.

He threw the phone across the room and grabbed the weapon again, his hand shaking so hard he could barely get his finger around the trigger. "You're a good shot, Prince d'Or. Don't fuck this up," he said in the silence and raised the weapon.

"Peter, beloved son, put down the gun."

The gun lowered, but not by his own hand.

He kept his eyes closed, too afraid to see who had come into the room. He shook, cold to the center of his soul, full of self-loathing, and pain. Oh, the pain. "Please make it stop, please?"

"I have heard thy prayers."

Peter shook his head, hot tears running down his face. "Do not look at me. I am filthy."

"Fear not, for I know the end from the beginning. I know thy heart, Peter ben Korah. It was given unto me when thou were a small child, and thou hast never turned."

He suspected he was hallucinating, so he answered, "Perhaps, it was just to spite them."

"No, for if thy heart had been hardened, it would have turned long since. Thou art faithful and loved, Peter."

Peter buried his face in his lap, pulling the sheet over his head. He could not believe it. He could not bear it. "No. You cannot say that after what I have done... what I have seen?"

"Repent, for the sins of thy own heart. I will cleanse thee and clothe thee in my righteousness. Put thy faith and trust in Me. I will order thy steps and guard thee every day of thy life."

"You will?" Peter pulled the sheet tight, overcome.

"Yes."

"I thought you did not care, because I was his son. So, I thought that maybe... maybe if I helped put Josiah back on the throne..."

"I saw."

Snot clogged his nose, and the plaintive cry ripped from his soul. "Then why did you not stop it? Any of it? Why?" He felt a tender touch on his shoulder when he did not think he could bear to let anyone touch him ever again.

"Alas, Earth, even Millennial Earth is not Heaven, and the sins of Adam are visited on the generations. The harvest of which, thou hast reaped tonight, but it is over. They shall not touch thee again."

Peter wept.

"But as in Adam all die, so in Me, all will be made alive. Peter, thou art alive, dwell in Me."

Shaken to the bone, he was indeed alive.

"For I know the plans I have for thee, plans for thy welfare and not for evil, to give thee a future and a hope."

"Hope?" his voice cracked.

"Those who hope in Me shall renew their strength. They shall soar on wings like eagles; they shall run and not grow weary; they shall walk and not be faint. Remember that, Peter."

Peter hazarded a look up and met the kindest eyes he had ever seen. There was no deception in their hazel depths, no avarice, or malice, or deceit, only love.

"Rest now, my child."

Peace saturated his battered soul, and he fell into a deep, restful sleep, under the watchful eye of the Lord.

The Fall of Greece - Athens - Antiochus

Wrath infected Antiochus' brain, as he felt the small bones crack under his squeezing fingers. Light faded from the squirming minister's eyes, his life's energy surging into Antiochus. It gave him ultimate power. The room was silent save for the man in his death throes, his final seconds, gurgling, thrashing, then nothing. Antiochus released his grip with a flourish, and set Duke Alexander, the Minister of Finance, upright in his chair. The room stank of sulfur and excrement.

Unseen by human eyes, an evil beyond imagination hovered behind Antiochus, cackling with delight. Zeus loved watching men die.

In a macabre gesture, Antiochus put the pen back in the dead man's limp hand. Turning to the table, he asked, "Would anyone else like to comment on the state of the treasury?"

The ministers shook their heads in mute terror.

"No? Then shall we proceed?"

Zeus stalked his next victim, a pretty man, wearing a dapper gray suit and a red tie. Laying a scaly green claw on his shoulder, he hissed, "Would you like to dance with me?" The man shuddered, and Zeus laughed.

Antiochus was proving to be a pliable strongman, though

not worthy of his name. There was much work to do before this Antiochus surpassed his namesake. Zeus sighed. Those were heady days indeed, glorious, when Greece ruled the world, and he was the greatest among the elohim. Soon, it would rise from the ashes, and he would rule once again. But they had a long way to go.

Zeus was furious over Marduk's treachery. Fourteen years early? It was an outrage, and he would be punished for escaping his territorial boundary and invading another's, Alanthia or America or whatever rubbish they called that cursed place these days, was not Marduk's. He would not be allowed to keep it. Foolish for him to build it up for another. Zeus hated those people, reviled their ambition, industriousness, and greed. The damned protestant work ethic seemed to be hard coded in their DNA.

His own Spartan warriors were long dead, replaced with these women lovers. They disgusted him. But that was about to change, even if he had to kill every one of these useless ministers to do it. They were nothing to him. So, he screamed a jealous tirade in Antiochus' ear, who spit out the invectives with perfect submission.

"Why does Alanthia thrive, and you cursed dogs flounder? I have ordered a modern state, and you bring me a third-rate hovel?"

While Antiochus berated his ministers, Zeus leaned against the portico, watching. Something was brewing among them, an undercurrent, an excitement. They were ready to explode. Passing secret glances, they were waiting, urging the others to be the one to act. Zeus grinned. This smelled like a *coup d'état*.

Perhaps he had misjudged them.

Zeus' money was on the sweaty one with the paunchy jowls. He bounced in his seat, fidgeting, and fingering a sheaf of papers. As Antiochus yelled, the man's face grew crimson. He looked like he was about to have a stroke. Which one was he? Oh, yes, Konstantinos ben Apostolakis, the Minister of

Agriculture. "This atrocity you have committed before us, cannot pass," Konstantinos shouted, erupting from his chair.

Zeus almost laughed when a gun appeared in his hand. It shook so hard he was likely to blow out a window rather than kill anyone.

Three of the ministers rose and joined their comrade.

"Duke Alexander was an honorable man; he was our friend. You, Antiochus, are no friend to Greece, not since Philomela died."

Antiochus bared his teeth and snarled, "Do not speak her name in this house!"

"It must be said!" Konstantinos bellowed. "It was her son, the raising of him…"

"Do not speak to me of my dead son!" Antiochus screeched.

"He was a monster!" Konstantinos grabbed the large stack of papers and shook them at Antiochus. "And we have the proof. These were obtained in Captain Orion ben Drachmas' quarters. Do you know what they are?"

Antiochus advanced on Konstantinos but stopped when the minister cocked the weapon. His hand had grown steady.

"These papers document the abomination of him, from the time he was born. You enabled his wickedness and brought evil to our land."

Zeus growled and started to end this charade, but stopped cold as the minister screamed, "He was the very spawn of the devil, a horrible creature, a predator. You allowed him to terrorize our kingdom, to kill the poor, and the pilgrims traversing Greece. He was not human, Antiochus!"

Not human? Zeus froze.

With the corpse of their friend staring out at them, the Minister of Defense opened a folder of photographs. "Orion ben Drachmas cataloged everything." The pictures were gory: desecrated bodies, scattered limbs, severed heads. "Captain ben Drachmas notated each photo with names and dates. The trail of blood leads straight back to you!" Konstantinos pushed them across the table, "This is what you have done."

The last photo, too horrible to look upon, remained face down, hidden. Konstantinos reached down with his free hand and flipped it over.

Antiochus' son.

Zeus' howl of outrage shook the Palace. It was a war cry, and the Greeks responded to its bloody siren's song. They fell upon their monarch like ravenous beasts, attacking with hands and claws, feet, and teeth. They tore him apart until he resembled nothing more than the blood-spattered pictures.

The animal frenzy that possessed them infected Greece years before. And the man who brought it, who welcomed it into the kingdom, and used it for his own brutal means, reaped his deadly reward. For Antiochus failed to understand that he could not invite evil in and then ask it to behave.

War in Heaven

The moment Zeus cleared the Palace, he met an enemy even greater than Marduk—Raphael.

"Misbegotten, son of a whore! I wondered when you would show your ugly face." Zeus flew at him.

Raphael countered, throwing Zeus backward. "Ugly? Have you looked in the mirror, reptile?"

This enraged Zeus because it was the truth. He seized Raphael with the intent to bite his face off, but a blow to the solar plexus caved in his chest. He gasped, recoiling under the force. Brandishing his sword, a look of confused panic crossed his face.

Raphael circled, puzzled by the reaction. He had hit him hard to be sure, but not that hard. "You have grown soft."

Zeus shook himself and charged.

Their swords clashed, blue on black, the sound echoing off the distant mountains. Raphael spun and his blade found purchase, buried deep in Zeus' thigh.

Zeus bellowed in pain and shot higher into the sky, barely avoiding the killing blow Raphael aimed at his head.

Wounded. He was wounded.

Raphael gave chase.

Zeus fought a desperate retreat, feeling blood gushing from his wound, weakening him by the second.

The sounds of another battle came from a distance, he hazarded a glance over his shoulder. Two fighters were streaking toward them, Gabriel and Marduk, locked in mortal combat. Zeus saw to his horror that while Gabriel was hale and hearty, Marduk was also wounded.

Gabriel raised his sword, sure and lethal. It was a kill strike.

Zeus hated Marduk, but he hated Gabriel more. He hit Gabriel midair, interrupting the blow, and scattering the four angels like a cue ball breaking a rack on a billiard table.

Zeus swooped in, taking a position at Marduk's back with Gabriel and Raphael circling them.

"You asshole," Zeus cursed Marduk. "You bring him to my doorstep?"

"Not on purpose," Marduk lied and heard how winded he sounded. His bad arm hung useless at his side. He had no other choice, and his gamble paid off. Zeus had saved his life. "It's the curse... Psalm 82."

"Fuck."

"Now what?" Marduk asked.

"Olympus for me. I have to tend this wound." Zeus whispered, eyeing Raphael who was in conversation with Gabriel.

They were in a face off.

"Son of a bitch, that's Babylon for me." Marduk growled.

Both were referring to the hiding places where they spent their captivity, the one place on Earth where there was a chance they might still hold dominion. If the ban was lifted, if the Hosts of Heaven were free to attack, they were outnumbered, and worse, they were injured. Retreat was the only option, the only avenue of survival.

Zeus could not resist the dig. "Guess you left your heart in San Francisco."

"Shut up," Marduk said, glaring at Gabriel, comprehending the complete ruination of his plans, his work, and his aspirations. It would all be for naught if he returned to Babylon and abandoned Alanthia.

"I know what you did in my territory. Don't think this makes us friends," Zeus growled.

Gabriel circled Marduk like a thug on a street corner. "How is your arm, lefty?"

Marduk sneered and brandished his sword, black fangs dripping slime.

"You both look terrible," Raphael mocked with bored amusement, studying his fingernails as if he had just gotten a manicure. Then sniffing the air, he said, "And you smell like… death."

Marduk cursed them both in an abominable foul tongue, the language of Hell.

Gabriel's eyes blazed fire, and he dropped the casual taunting. "I could kill you right now, Marduk, Prince of Persia, like a man," he gloated. "But I find I am rather enjoying watching you suffer, though it is nothing when compared to burning for eternity. You will pay for your sins, and no one will hear you scream in the Lake of Fire."

Marduk's black heart burned with unquenchable hatred… and fear.

Gabriel read it all in Marduk's dragon eyes. "Would you like to see your comrades? Uriel will be here soon. He holds the key. Would you like to hear them screaming? The Watchers are still screaming, Marduk… after all these centuries… they are still burning. You have committed the same sins, so you will share their fate, but the Most High has reserved a special punishment for you because your wickedness is rivaled only by Satan's."

Terror invaded Marduk's black soul, but he drew himself up with as much dignity as he could muster and said, "I will meet you in Persia, and we will see who dies."

"I think tonight, it is Zeus," Raphael said.

As he spoke, Zeus made a strangled gurgle.

While Gabriel and Marduk sparred, Raphael had been watching the blood gush from Zeus' thigh. He had been on enough of men's battlefields to recognize a mortal wound.

Zeus' wings collapsed, and he plummeted to the ground.

"Oh, how the mighty have fallen." Raphael's voice shook as he watched his rival's spiraling descent.

Marduk looked on in horror, for an instant unable to comprehend what he witnessed, the true death of an elohim, an immortal dying right before his eyes. It was the fulfillment of a prophecy, the carrying out of a death sentence.

Alone, wounded, and surrounded by his enemies, Marduk realized he was seconds away from the same fate. He shot off like a strike of lightning. Gabriel's mocking laugh followed him.

Part 8 - Alanthia

November 12, 999 ME

The Evening News - Davianna and Astrid

Disguised as a middle-aged woman in sensible shoes and a salt and pepper wig, Davianna sat on an uncomfortable chair at New Alanthia Airport in New York City, watching her first newscast. She did not recognize the country she left behind a scant three years ago—television. Astrid was dressed as her purple haired, sulking teenage son, slumped beside her, pretending to be bored.

"Good evening, I'm Sondra ben Pierson, filling in for the vacationing Ebenezer ben James.

"Our top story tonight is the assassination of Monarch Antiochus of Greece. Last night, Republican activists, disgruntled with the slow pace of Greece's technological overhaul, stormed the Palace, and murdered the monarch during a ministers' meeting. In an act of heroism and self-sacrifice, Duke Alexander of Sparta, the Minister of Finance, was killed trying to save the monarch from the attackers.

"While the suspects remain at large. Greece is responding with overwhelming force against dissident groups across the country.

"This story comes on the heels of the mysterious arrest of Captain Orion ben Drachmas near London yesterday. According to sources, Drachmas is a member of the Greek secret police and is accused of leading the massacre of the Eiran Pilgrim Camp last spring. He was injured during the arrest but is in stable condition."

Astrid hissed an invective under her breath. Davianna stared out the window, pretending to be oblivious.

"In another terror attack, jihadist militants stormed the headquarters of Facetec Industries just before noon yesterday. The terrorists killed several key executives before private security fought them off. Facetec, creators of facial recognition software, opened with much fanfare earlier this year. Their revolutionary product is touted by many to be the next weapon in our ongoing war on terrorism. Sadly, this marks the tenth anti-technology terror attack of the year.

"Police say, the same group taking credit for Facetec was responsible for the March 20th assassination attempt on Prince Peter."

Pictures of police cars surrounding the Palace lit up the screen.

"Our cameras caught up with the Prince near his exclusive penthouse in New York. He expressed his sympathy for the victims' families but would not comment on his long-awaited wedding to Princess Keyseelough of Egypt, or her purported support of the jihadists.

"The Prince has much sympathy among his hordes of supporters, who see the wedding as an archaic relic of the past. Betrothed two-and-a-half years ago, the couple are rarely seen together."

"Clearly, this is a forced marriage," said noted body language expert, Scott ben John. "Look at the tilt of his head here as he greets her at the art festival in Milan last year. He despises her."

The golden-haired Adonis was shown sitting beside the sultry beauty, neither looked happy.

"Speaking of Princes," the beautiful reporter continued, "these fuzzy pictures taken in a London police station yesterday have sent the conspiracy crowd into a frenzy of speculation. They claim this figure is none other than long dead, Prince Josiah ben Eamonn."

The camera zoomed in briefly, then a painting of young Josiah, done in honor of his bar mitzvah, flashed on the screen.

Davianna gripped Astrid's knee so hard she yelped. Astrid, ever alert to danger, cut her eyes to Davianna.

"The Dark Prince," Davianna mouthed and motioned to the screen.

Astrid, lost in thought over the survival of the Greek Captain, missed the latter part of the newscast and signaled she did not follow.

Davianna controlled her frustration, it would have to wait, they could not speak of such things in public, but she was reeling at the revelation and the ramifications. She turned her attention back to the newscast.

"Windsor police deny the photo is of the Prince, and the Palace press office released the following statement, 'For many years, imposters have tried to present themselves as our dearly departed Prince. The untimely death of Prince Josiah was a tragedy and is still an open wound for the royal family. We ask the public to respect our grief and let the Prince's memory rest in peace.'"

The camera panned to the anchor, who looked suitably grave. "In other news, residents in three cities, Athens, London, and New York reported an unusual sky show last evening. Amateur video from London and New York seems to show two comets streaking across the night sky. Witnesses in Athens say they saw multiple comets, but no video of that event has surfaced.

"Scientists say the atmospheric readings over the cities remained normal and that the video from London was likely fireworks. The one taken over New York has been dismissed as lightning from the sudden and violent storm that set off alarms across the city."

Two planes and sixteen hours later, two young boys exited Korah International Airport and took their first taxi ride, into the New City. Three hours and four disguises later, a teenage girl and her elderly grandfather checked into a hotel in the ancient section of town. The weary travelers barely spoke as they fell into bed, exhausted.

November 19, 999 ME

Where to Look? - Davianna and Astrid

A week after they arrived in the New City, Astrid refolded her daddy's letter, grown soft with handling, its creases embedded with the dust of Europe. She bit her thumbnail, and for the millionth time, wished for a return address or a clue where they might begin to search. She knew he was an investor. Alas, this was not a lead. The New City was full of tech companies. She could not just call them all and ask if her daddy was there.

Agnor was a salesman when she was growing up, selling everything from plows to paper. He traveled most of the time, but all her great childhood memories were with him. Flush with cash and presents, fine food, and parties, life was good when Daddy came home.

When he was gone things got tough. They moved to San Antonio when she was eight, but she never dwelt on the two years they spent in that small apartment. It had been a miserable time. But he came back when she was ten, showing up with a big surprise.

Daddy bought a new house in Houston. It was the nicest place they ever lived. Astrid got her own room, and he let her paint it pale yellow. They had a pool in the neighborhood, and he bought her a blue metallic bike that he said was the color of her eyes.

But he left six months after they moved in.

She was twelve the last time she saw him, the day her life changed forever. The haunting memory would play when she least expected it. It came to visit now.

Riding her bike home from school, she saw his rig in front of the house. She dropped the bike in the yard and ran through the backdoor.

Her exuberant greeting died on her tongue, and she froze in the small mudroom off the kitchen.

They were fighting, not just arguing, fighting.

She could still hear the screaming, the dishes crashing, and her mother crying. Frank and Daddy were hitting each other. Daddy reared back to bash Frank in the face. Blood flew off his fist, spattering her drawing hanging on the refrigerator. Frank ducked and tackled Daddy, throwing him into the kitchen table. It crashed under their weight. Chairs fell all over, and the big bowl Momma used to make biscuits cracked in two. Momma screamed, and for a minute, Astrid thought she was upset about her bowl. But Daddy got to his feet and said a very bad word to Frank.

She could still remember his face, so angry.

Then he looked at Momma, and for a second Astrid thought he was going to hit her. Frank scrambled to his feet, stepping in front of Momma. Daddy looked between them, and without a word he stormed out.

The slamming door sucked all the air out of the house. She ran outside, to catch him, to talk to him, but he did not look like Daddy. He was covered in blood and mad. Astrid hid around the corner of the house and watched him leave. She thought, "I'll just talk to him later."

But he never came back. He left her behind. Forever.

She turned away, pretending she had something in her eye. They were dead, Momma, Frank... only Daddy was left. She had to find him. He would help them, and everything would be okay.

One Step Ahead - Peter

In a seedy hotel on the outskirts of the city, Alaina and Peter were wrapping up a previously scheduled briefing, but Peter could tell Alaina had other news she seemed eager to share. "What else?"

"You remember the mysterious Greek Captain and your cousin?" Alaina asked.

"Yes." He glanced off to the side. He needed no help remembering that day.

"Well, we've been watching that one. Since Antiochus' assassination, Captain Orion ben Drachmas is ready to tell where the bodies are buried, in exchange for a plea."

Peter sat back, considering. "That pilgrim camp massacre?"

"You got it." She set her jaw in a grim line and said, "The Greeks were searching for an artifact, a device."

Peter swore under his breath and felt dizzy for a moment. He knew who else was searching for an artifact.

"We have picked up intelligence chatter from several sources, including Korah's. Everybody believes it's in the hands of a pair of girls." Alaina gestured to her laptop screen where two crude sketches appeared. "These two were in that camp. They escaped and have been running since the end of March."

Peter was impressed. "Through Greece?" He shook his head. "That place has been a mess for years, quite dangerous."

"It is. Unfortunately, it takes off about four months on pilgrimage and folks still try it."

Peter was quiet for a moment, staring at the sketches, thinking. "Alaina?"

She knew that tone. Despite the persona, Prince d'Or was not an empty-headed playboy. "What?"

He rubbed a knuckle over his bottom lip, his brows narrowed. "What if my cousin was not actually tracking the Greek across the continent but those girls? What if he is also looking for that artifact?"

Her jaw dropped. "Of course! Him being a bounty hunter never made sense."

He stroked his chin, deep in thought. "Which might mean those girls were in London." He nodded toward the screen. "Find out if there is any footage from Windsor, and if so, it might not have been two boys the Greek attacked. That could have been a cover story"

"You might be right." She mentally reviewed the facts of the case. Her fingers froze over the keyboard.

"What?" Peter asked, leaning in to look at her screen. It showed him nothing but a bunch of jumbled letters and numbers, hacker language.

Her voice was quiet, and she spoke very slowly. "What if it was one of the girls who stabbed that Greek Captain?"

Peter drew his brows down as he considered the possibility, then chuckled, "If that is the case, my cousin faced a hell of a choice, did he not? Save the villain or catch the two girls he had been tracking for six months?" He shook his head, in admiration and irony. "Saint, indeed."

November 20, 999 ME

Video - Peter

The following day, Alaina worked her magic and sent Peter a video from Windsor. He watched it in the privacy of his office. The Greek Captain held a map, staring at a crooked building. Davianna and Astrid emerged from the hotel and walked in front of him. The Greek ignored them, but the one on the left drew his attention.

It bothered him, that one on the left, why did she do that? They were unnoticed. He watched it again, irrationally hoping she would just walk by this time, and became irritated when she did not. It was stupid and reckless. Did she not understand what men like him did to girls like her?

He studied the report on the screen. The evidence against this guy was damning. With all the sordid revelations coming out, Peter realized Korah was not the only crazy monarch on the loose. In some ways, Antiochus made Korah look like a school-boy. Though, Peter suspected he did not know half of what Korah did, the half he knew was bad enough.

Regardless, Alaina was right, with Antiochus dead, the cockroaches were coming out of the woodwork. All the misdeeds seemed to run through Captain Orion ben Drachmas' secret guard. Mossad had credible evidence the guy led the Camp Eiran massacre, and he was chasing those girls. Peter was certain.

He hated bullies. He hated bullies that preyed on innocents even more.

He watched the video again, and again, and again.

Then he realized the draw, why he kept looking at the girl. He figured out why he wanted to scream every time she drew that dangerous man's attention. He pinched the bridge of his nose, then lit a cigarette. It was crazy, but he was a bit crazy, had been for weeks.

He could not even put a name on that night in his penthouse, tried not to think about it, any of it. But he fled New York the day after, running like they were going to invade his bedroom at any moment. He was back in the New City, for one reason and one reason only, to finish it, to complete the plan. His network was here. His people were here. Everything was here, everything he worked for, and he would not let the Hell Bitch, or one more night of the monster's fun and games, derail it all.

However, this video was a complication. These two girls had something. They had that artifact. They had what the monster, his father, and the Hell Bitch were looking for, and if they found it, they were going to release Hell on Earth.

At the moment, Peter could do nothing about the wicked trio, but he just might be able to do something about this scummy Greek. He would need to do it in secret. This sort of thing… well, he would not want anyone to know, but that was all right, there were tons of things no one knew about. Besides, he was Prince d'Or, no one would suspect a thing.

Jarrod entered the study, and Peter blanked the screen, adopting a bored expression. "Jarrod, I have been thinking things over, and I have decided that I do not want Greek for lunch. Please terminate that plan."

Jarrod narrowed his eyes, confused. Peter saw a flash of concern cross his face. He was clearly trying to ascertain if Peter was riding the white horse.

Peter quirked an eyebrow at his valet.

Jarrod studied him, but he remained silent. He understood that sometimes this Palace had ears.

"You know, the last time I was in England, I had the most delightful fish and chips. There was a shop in Windsor."

Jarrod blinked, thinking. Then Peter saw his message get through. "Certainly, my Esteemed." Jarrod nodded. "I will make the appropriate arrangements."

Peter gave him a diabolical half smile. "I would expect no less."

"Of course." Jarrod executed a formal bow and left the room.

The video played again.

Bubba

Astrid's father, Agnor ben Randall, was big, bold, and blusterous. Larger than life, everybody called him Bubba, and he liked it. Bubba claimed he came from Houston oil money and wore the cowboy hat to prove it. He drove giant cars, liked good BBQ, and loose women. Bubba lived the good life. Flashing gold rings and wads of cash, he knew everybody, and everybody loved Bubba. He was great fun at the bar and always had a hot investment tip. Bartenders, waitresses, and hotel maids gave him their life savings. Even after their money was gone, they still sort of liked him because he was a helluva nice fella.

On the morning of November 20th, Bubba woke up broke. It was not the first time, or if he was honest, the last. He rolled his considerable bulk off the lumpy mattress, belched, and cast a dubious eye at the dregs of whiskey in the glass beside his bed. He shrugged and drained it.

He was not at the 'skip town' point of being broke, so he was not packing, yet. Scrubbing his beefy hands over his face, he finally admitted to himself that going into business with that Italian had been a mistake, but Facetec should have been a sure bet. "That's what I get for trying to play it straight. The thing was supposed to be legitimate, even pretty boy, Prince d'Or opened their office." But Facetec was a con.

As the architect of a hundred such schemes, he could smell it. He would bet his last shekel that son of a bitch, Marco ben Massimo, was trying to screw him. Rumor was the Italian was cashing in insurance policies on his dead partners and closing shop, using the terrorist attack as a cover. If Facetec folded, Bubba's sizable investment was gone.

He got in the shower and determined he needed to pay a visit to that Italian, just to make sure he saw the error of his ways. Nobody screwed Bubba and got away with it. Nobody.

Zanah

Zanah ben Joseph pondered the contents of her bulging closet, trying to decide what to wear. Holding up a red silk dress, she turned, this way and that, admiring the way the color complimented her skin. At thirty-seven, she was still young and still beautiful. Most people said her dark brown eyes were her most arresting feature. She learned to bat her eyelashes when she was an infant, but did it again, just to make sure it was still as winsome as ever. It was.

She hung the red silk up and pulled out the purple halter. Now this one, she liked. Her long dark hair looked good with this color. She fluffed the layers, arranging them around her shoulders, and critically examining the growth of the highlights. It was time for a touch up.

No, the purple did not fit her mood. She had to rise on her tiptoes to hang it back up. She was petite, just a hair over five feet.

Most of the clothes in her closet had come from exclusive shops that catered to women like her, rich and skinny with big tits. Well, she was not rich, but Marco was, and he paid the bills.

She pulled down a cream-colored evening dress. Now, this one was divine. The neckline showed off her breasts, which she had earned. She laid the gown on the bed and strolled to her dressing table. Opening a small jar, she dabbed a bit of the expensive miracle cream onto her left breast. The saleslady promised it would get rid of the stretch mark, but the mark was old, and the cream might not work.

The stretch mark was Davianna's fault.

Pregnancy had wrecked her body. She had been a cheerleader, and before Davianna was born, she had been perfect. Afterward, she was ruined, and the stretch mark had been the least of it. She gained seventeen pounds and looked like a cow. Feeling ugly and unattractive, she insisted David do something about it. He should. He got her pregnant.

It was David's fault.

Zanah lifted her heavy breasts and smiled. She knew how to get what she wanted. She learned from the best, her own mother. So, she hounded David, employing pretty pouts and tears. When that did not work, she escalated to tantrums. She cried and carried on. Finally, she shunned his touch and refused to nurse their baby daughter. That did it.

Back then, he wanted to make her happy, so he stopped being selfish and used their savings to buy her the surgery. Of course, she did not tell anyone. To friends and relatives, she claimed her new voluptuous figure was a byproduct of pregnancy, no one other than her plastic surgeon and her husband knew the truth.

Zanah turned to the side, critically checking her profile. They still looked good. But staring in the mirror in her New City mansion bedroom, she had a moment of clarity. If she was honest with herself, the surgery should have made her happy. It did not.

With a flick of her hand, she dismissed the troubling thought. It was of course, not her fault, because her nose was still hideous, and Davianna made it worse. When she was two, she threw a tantrum over naptime. Zanah was not going to be bullied by the little brat, so she carried her upstairs kicking and squirming. Davianna arched her back when she tried to put her in the crib, and her head smashed Zanah, right in the nose.

She bled everywhere.

They were both screaming, and her busybody neighbor ran inside without knocking. Then the old witch had the audacity to yell at Zanah, who was clearly the injured party in the whole affair. She was the one dripping blood from a nose that swelled up like a manatee. She was the one with two black eyes. But all the other mothers on the street took the neighbor's side and were not nice to her after that, which was the bitch's fault.

Afterward, the hideous bump on Zanah's nose did not go away. David just did not understand, but he was an idiot. She did not believe for one minute that it was cute, that it gave her perfect face character. It was awful. When her usual methods of persuasion failed, she donned a veil and refused to take it off. She got her second surgery, which not only took out the hideous bump, but reshaped her nose into a cute turned up little thing.

Now, she was happy.

To celebrate, she went shopping. David was such a beast about that too. He did not understand that the new clothes made her feel good. He needed to make more money anyway, it was her way of telling him that was how they should live.

Staring into her closet, with its rainbow of silks, linens, and cashmeres, she grinned. She had everything she wanted now, no thanks to him.

Moving to the window, she did not bother with a dressing gown. Let them look. She was beautiful. She matched this house, which was a hell of a lot better than anything David ever gave her. And it was not like she had not encouraged him. She was always house hunting. She found the nicest homes, which he rejected, pleading poverty, saying they could not afford them. He was just so mean.

But there was one he liked, one they all liked in Taylorsville. She changed her tactics, becoming sweet, encouraging. She was a goddess in bed. He bought it for her.

A new business venture provided the capital. He was finally doing what he was supposed to do, giving her the life she deserved, but it was short-lived. He lost everything. He failed. And they had to leave that house, they had to leave town. It was that stupid investor's fault.

They did not have a lot of money, and instead of spending what they did have on her, David spoiled Davianna rotten. It cost money for all those gymnastics lessons and those loud toys he bought her. Davianna turned into such a brat, prancing around the house in her little gymnastics clothes, showing off for anyone who would watch. "Look at me, look at me! Did you see?" Zanah snorted at the memory. She hated the smell of that gym, and Davianna's stupid, fake British accent. She adopted it from David, just to be nasty.

Though, gymnastics had not been all bad. It got Davianna out of the house. If it had not been so expensive, Zanah would have been happy to let her live with her coaches to train. As it was, she only came home at night and always on some sort of training diet. That infuriated Zanah because she resented cooking in general and having to make two meals a night was ridiculous. So, she made David do it.

However, when Davianna got hurt and quit gymnastics, that is when the trouble started. That's when she started strutting around town like a little whore. Everyone noticed it. She pretended she was not doing anything, but Zanah saw it. She knew that power, she wielded it with greater skill than her fifteen-year-old daughter, so Davianna did not fool her, not for a minute.

It came to a head at the market. Zanah stopped to talk to Christopher, the handsome, twenty-two-year-old butcher. They were friendly. She had them around town, the men she liked, the ones who liked her. She liked to flirt, and men, all men, flirted back. It was harmless, and she enjoyed it. David did not flirt anymore, so she got it elsewhere.

She and Christopher were talking, and Davianna was hemming and hawing, ruining everything. "Fine, go shop. I'll be along in a minute."

Davianna rolled her eyes, literally, rolled her eyes. Zanah wanted to slap her. Then the little brat walked away, shaking her butt, on purpose!

Christopher followed her progress all the way down the aisle. "Where did Davianna get that sweet little ass?"

Zanah erupted and threw a pound of hamburger at him. She stormed off in feigned maternal outrage. However, she knew what he meant. The implication was clear. Davianna had not inherited her figure from her. Zanah was far too thin to have anything that could remotely be called a sweet little ass. Nice tits, yes. A sweet ass, no. And that was when she became very unhappy. It was Christopher's fault.

Zanah got up from her vanity and paced her room, re-membering how angry she had been. She turned in the full-length mirror and looked over her shoulder at her sweet little ass and decided for the one hundredth time, it had been worth it. Though, she never imagined the price. She pulled out a pair of black silk trousers and slid them over her hips, admiring her profile. Yes, it had been worth it.

She did not bother trying to convince David to let her have the procedure. After the fight they had when she told him about the grocery store, they were barely speaking. She knew he would never let her do it, but she also knew, if she did it, he would just have to live with it. So, she figured out a plan. She smiled in the mirror, still proud of how smart she had been.

She picked an emerald green blouse out of the closet and tried it on with the black silk pants.

Her new plastic surgeon worked with a credit agency. It had been as simple as filling out a one-page form. She timed it perfectly, David and Davianna were on some wretched church retreat. She sent them off with a smile, even kissed David goodbye.

When they returned, he was livid. It was the biggest fight of their marriage, and she had to admit, he scared her that night.

She had not looked at the interest rate or the monthly payment. Why should she? That was David's problem. He would just have to figure it out.

In the end, the credit company came after them. He threw it up in her face, complained all the time. He had to take a second job, but she did not care. Why would she care? He was supposed to provide for her. He was supposed to make her happy.

Then he did it, the worst thing in their marriage, the severing blow.

He came home with a wagon. She had a tantrum. She knew what that damn wagon meant. Those religious zealots at that church he attended every Sunday were always talking about it, always preaching about it. He came inside and announced that he had sold everything to pay off their debts. They were leaving—on fucking pilgrimage.

Zanah punished David for that little stunt. She used her sexy figure and southern charm to seduce a dozen men. He deserved every damn cuckold she threw in his face. Yet, even then, he would not let her go home. He would not turn around and take them back. He kept pushing onward.

So, to get her way, she spent all their money and stranded them three times, reasoning he would have to stop then. The stubborn bastard had shown more initiative than he had when they were home and connived to get enough money to keep going. She hated him, and every mile they traveled, she grew to hate Davianna, too. Her daughter always stuck up for her miserable father. They made her life hell, the two of them with their heads together laughing, like there was anything remotely funny about being on pilgrimage.

She had not shed a tear when he died, repulsed by him in death as in life. She could still see his dead bulging eyes, disgusting. Served him right for bringing her into that god-forsaken desert. It took six weeks before her skin returned to normal.

She found a hot spring about two miles from Camp Eiran and began a rigorous personal care regime to rehabilitate herself. The desert almost killed her, and she looked like hell when they stumbled into that camp. But she finally got Davianna to stop crying and do her chores. Zanah was not lugging water. She was not.

It was at the hot springs, where she met Marco ben Massimo. He had come upon her when she was bathing, seduced her in the soft grass. It was erotic, with the steam rising all around them, his smooth Italian skin glistening with dew. He was insatiable, driving her to heights of ecstasy she had never known. The force of his passion consumed her, made her reckless with abandon, and she left Camp Eiran without a backward glance.

She knew he was a bad boy, but after being married to a monk, she figured she deserved a change of pace. She earned it. And it was so good. Those first few weeks… absolute heaven. Rescued from desolation and penury, he treated her like a queen. They stayed in breathtaking hotels. He gave her expensive gifts, took her to the finest restaurants, and at night drove her wild. She thought her dreams were coming true. He swept her off her feet and rescued her from a life of drudgery. Those blissful weeks, she lived the dream. Lavished in luxury, she even dined with royalty. Then it was over.

It was Davianna's fault.

Marco insisted they bring her with them to the New City. From the moment they left Antiochus' mansion, he changed.

He was furious when they discovered the camp destroyed and realized Davianna was gone. He withdrew, became brooding and cruel. But he was beautiful, and he had money, so she stayed.

When they arrived in the New City, she realized her dream had a nightmare side to it. There was a cost. If she wanted to keep her fine clothes, if she wanted to live in this beautiful house, and walk in the gardens (which had a gardener), she had to earn it.

The way she earned it was on her back. She was a present for his business associates, to seal the deal, or soothe anxious nerves. She did not appreciate that, not at all. It made her mad.

It was Marco's fault.

At first, when he told her, she flat out rejected it, but then she saw behind the charming facade. He was a rattlesnake, and rattlesnakes were lethal. She sometimes wondered if that is why he was so angry when they discovered Davianna was dead. Had he planned to have her perform the same services? Perhaps, but Zanah did not give it more than a passing thought, because she rarely, if ever, thought about Davianna.

She was dead. Oh, fucking well.

Zanah slipped on the gold earrings with the small emeralds that went with the green blouse. That looked good. She sat down at her vanity to refresh her makeup. They were having a party tonight, and Marco told her to dress nice. Zanah applied another coat of black mascara to her long lashes.

A part of her knew she should be mourning her daughter, not blaming her for dying and ruining her relationship with Marco. She sat back admiring herself and decided it did not change the way she felt. They were never close.

"Look at me now, David," she snarled the name of her dead husband into the dressing mirror. Just the thought of him made her scowl. Why she ever married him, she could not recall, let alone stay with him. Bastard.

She noticed a thin line over the bridge of her nose and

hastily smoothed a dab of moisturizer into it. She was still beautiful and planned to keep it that way. It was her ticket out of here.

A knock sounded at the door. She fluffed her hair and plastered a fake smile on her face. She learned to be nice, Marco ben Massimo knew how to hurt a girl, bad.

The door opened, and a huge man with red hair and sun spotted skin ambled in.

"Howdy, ma'am," he drawled. "My name's Bubba."

November 22, 999 ME

Desk Job - Guan

Desk jobs were dangerous. Guan ben Sheldon survived a journey halfway around the world, only to be nearly cut in half by a scimitar wielding asshole while he was sitting at his desk eating a burrito. "It was just his luck," Guan thought, "he did not have any."

The job at Facetec seemed like a sign that was over. They hired him without any actual computer skills, set him up with an easy job, and paid him more money than he ever earned in his life. Now the company looked like it was going under, and he would be back to square one.

He was not the only one pissed off about it. The big Texan was back again, red-faced and raising hell in Massimo's office, carrying on about his investment. Guan's ears perked up. He might not know anything about computers, but he could spot an opportunity, and that dude had money.

The office was packing up for the night. When the big dude stormed out, Guan waited for him. "Hey, Mister, you got a minute?"

Guan and Bubba went for a beer. Bubba bought a few rounds, flashing gold rings and a big wad of cash. In the universal language of men, the conversation turned to sports.

"I'll tell you what, I've been a wrestling fan my whole life. I wrestled back in school." Bubba flexed a beefy arm. "I've got a wrestler I know, me and him go way back, and he got me box seats for the Extravaganza coming up. I'm hosting some big investors," he lowered his voice, "in this new tech venture I've got cooking."

Bubba started bragging about some skinny bitch with big tits he was banging, but Guan was only half listening. The guy was full of shit.

"I am telling you, boy, she is pristine!" Bubba said with a booming laugh.

"Pristine?" Guan kept his voice mild, studying the man closer.

Blue cat eyes sparkled back at him. "Priss-teen!"

He said it with just the right intonation, just the right accent, and just the right expression, blue eyes, red hair…

Guan ordered another round and offered a toast. "To your health, Bubba." They drank, and Guan asked, "Hey, Bubba ain't your real name, is it?"

Bubba wiped his mouth with the back of his sleeve. "Oh, hell no. Real name's Agnor, but it never stuck. I don't look like no Agnor, do I, boy?"

Ding-ding-ding…. Astrid ben *Agnor*… this yahoo was her precious daddy. He was all she ever talked about. When he was trying to get in her pants, he pretended to be interested. It was nauseating. But he knew her. After the massacre, the one person she would go looking for was her daddy.

He knew they escaped. He had hung around the outskirts of the Palace to claim his reward. For fuck's sake, he had earned it. He talked to one of the soldiers when they got back, the whole damn thing had gone sideways, and he got out of there. Served those religious pricks right. Heh.

Deciding Greece and those two girls had caused him enough trouble, he headed for the New City. Sitting in a smoky bar with this loudmouth asshole, he thought perhaps his luck had again changed. If that Greek was willing to pay for it, he reckoned there would be others. Sooner or later that girl, her friend, and that device were going to show up. All he had to do was wait. "Hey Bubba, maybe I can invest in that new tech. What do you say?"

Not Good Enough - Stephen

Stephen ben McSwilley, the Minister of Technology and Security, was one of the greatest technology pioneers in the world. He rose to his position, not because he was a politician, but because he was an extraordinary talent and came to Korah's attention early in his life. Stephen understood the entire field of computing, research, development, and networking at a level matched by few in the world. He was not the most talented in the individual fields, he hired people for those roles. He was a soft-spoken man, liked praise for a job well done, and loved his work with a passion that bordered on obsession. Alanthia's unsung hero in the technology explosion was the unassuming, slightly gawky, Stephen ben McSwilley.

Through his leadership, they harnessed technology and modernized the entire kingdom. Television, radio, internet, and mobile communications, his department revived all these things in thirteen short years. Yet, as he waited in the parlor outside King Korah's office, he knew nothing he accomplished would be on the discussion table. He was here to deliver his thirty-third weekly report on the search for the mystery device, Davianna ben David, and Astrid ben Agnor.

He and his team made Herculean efforts across the globe to accomplish what appeared to now be the king's sole objective. Stephen stopped sleeping months ago. His team was in no better shape. Projects of strategic importance were unattended. The entire focus of the ministry revolved around a single goal, and Stephen was failing, according to the King.

It was no matter that his team invented new surveillance programs and techniques that would benefit the kingdom for decades to come. It was inconsequential that they pinpointed and provided photographic evidence of the two exact locations and dates when the device was turned on. King Korah did not seem to care that they were days away from activating a one-thousand-year-old satellite network, which would give them visibility to sixty percent of the world's surface, in real time.

King Korah dismissed the fact that Stephen's team identified and surveilled every blood relative of both girls' families down to the fifth cousin. It was negligible that they discovered a covert tracking signal emanating from Tel Aviv, the technology zone in the Golden Kingdom. Through extraordinary correlation, computing, and detective work they determined the tracking signal was following the exact device they were searching for. To their frustration, before they could act on the information, the signal was terminated.

No, the only thing that mattered to King Korah was that he did not have what he wanted.

The incessant calls, messages, and meetings were destroying Stephen. The King vacillated between jovial encouragement and wrath. He insisted on details, then lambasted Stephen for being too technical. When Stephen tried to patiently explain, King Korah erupted, declaring he was not an imbecile. Korah demanded hourly updates then complained when the information changed or if it stayed the same.

Korah brought in outside consultants who sought to earn favor with him by criticizing Stephen's work. Korah put them on competing projects, built on the infrastructure and networks that Stephen and his team created. Then Korah allowed the outsiders to operate at their leisure, praising them for any insignificant nugget they brought to the investigation, most of which, Stephen's team had already ascertained and presented to the King. It was infuriating.

The most egregious of the contractors was Facetec founder, Marco ben Massimo, that charlatan poisoned Korah's mind with half-truths and promises that his miracle software would get the job done where Stephen's team could not. Stephen lost a friend in that Facetec massacre; he hated that slimy Italian bastard.

Stephen understood the situation had escalated to a point where he no longer enjoyed the confidence of the King, which was completely unjustified, undeserved, and unfair. However, he was loath to give up. To stop, meant failure, it meant Korah was right. Stephen ben McSwilley never failed. He was going to find those girls.

December 1, 999 ME

Bounty

"Good evening, I'm Sondra ben Pierson filling in once again for Ebenezer ben James. Our top story tonight is a bizarre tale of legend, murder, and international intrigue.

"We begin in an ancient New City research lab where scientists have discovered what they believe to be the final computing technology of the Last Age. According to newly discovered records, twelve highly advanced prototypes were produced before the research lab was buried by a massive earthquake. Three of the devices are purported to still be in existence. Unbelievably, two have been recovered in the last ten years but were so badly degraded they have not given over their secrets as researchers had hoped. The third has become something of a legend for tech enthusiasts and treasure hunters alike. Which is where our story moves from legend, to Greece, and on to London.

"In London, accused mass murderer Captain Orion ben Drachmas was found dead in his cell last night. Officials say the matter is under investigation, but it appears he succumbed to injuries sustained while assaulting two young boys. Captain ben Drachmas maintained his innocence and through defense counsel claimed his forces were searching for the lost artifact when they arrived at Camp Eiran on March 27th and found the camp already aflame.

"Officials in Athens confirm the account and claim that the massacre was an attempt to cover up the valuable theft. 'Ancient artifact thieves and smugglers have been using the camps for years,' said Prince Dimitri, the most likely ascendant to the Greek throne.

"When asked for comment, here at home, Alanthian Attorney General Nabal had this to say, "Unfortunately, it has become all too common for ancient artifacts of immense value to the public to be sold for personal profit. Alanthians know it is only through our common goal of sharing the rediscoveries of the past that we might embrace our future, which makes the theft and possession of ancient technology so egregious." His gray eyes stared into the camera, "Working with the global community, we must ensure this black market is terminated. Greek officials believe that the perfectly preserved device from the New City site has been stolen and is in the possession of a pair of artifact thieves disguised as young pilgrim girls."

Two crude sketches flashed up on the screen.

"Davianna ben David and Astrid ben Agnor, members of a brutal international smuggling ring, were last seen in Greece. They appear to be traveling together with the valuable artifact.

"King Korah, an ardent supporter of technological research and the public welfare, has offered a five-million-shekel reward for their arrest and safe delivery of the artifact. As an incentive, a one-million-shekel bonus will be paid if the dangerous criminals are apprehended and the device safely delivered to the Palace before New Year's Eve."

In a cramped hotel room, Davianna started to cry. Astrid did not seem to hear, she simply turned white.

Bubba and Zanah sat up in bed, saying in unison, "That's my daughter."

Guan sputtered beer all over the bartender and got himself thrown out of the pub for his trouble.

Prince Josiah ben Eamonn turned to Prince Yehonathan and said without preamble, "I'm going now."

Prince Peter froze. If Korah was offering that kind of reward, his suspicions were confirmed. Horrified realization dawned; the timing told him everything. He must find it and them first.

Every lowlife criminal, every government, every brutal despot with dreams of glory, and every anti-technology lunatic took notice. The entire world began to hunt Davianna ben David and Astrid ben Agnor.

December 3, 999 ME

Danish Wrestler - Josiah

Carsten ben Hansen, professional wrestler from Copenhagen, traveled to the New City to participate in the revived Worldwide Wrestling Extravaganza scheduled for December 28th at the new Korah Arena. Carsten ben Hansen was a flamboyant European Super-Star, dressed in the glittering red and white of the ancient Danish flag. The 6'3" hulk flexed his muscles for pictures, tossed his long blond hair, and signed autographs for adoring fans who followed his career for years, or so they claimed, because until twenty-four hours ago, Carsten ben Hansen had not existed.

The exiled Prince Josiah returned with flash, albeit in a wig that itched and a prosthetic nose and ears that were driving him mad. He flourished the glittering cape around his shoulders and got into a limousine, on his way to the Ritz. He settled into the backseat and sighed with relief. What a fiasco.

The partition rolled down and Agent Reuben ben Judah smirked, *"Vi er røde, vi er hvide!"* he taunted, quoting a Danish song sung during sporting events.

Josiah glared at him. "Shut up, Reuben, or I will break a chair over your back."

Reuben laughed.

Since the discovery of the old WWE wrestling archives and rebroadcast of them, the sport exploded into a mania that gripped the New City. It was a perfect disguise to smuggle Josiah into the country. Audacious, bold, and completely overlooked by anybody searching for a skulking exiled Prince. It also provided him a public platform, one he hoped Davianna would see and seek him out. Because thus far, nobody, not even Mossad, knew where she was hiding.

December 4, 999 ME

Unholy Connections - Guan

Guan glanced furtively over his shoulder as the office emptied for the night. Their last day at Facetec approached, and if he wanted that bounty, he had to act fast. He had been shadowing his colleagues, asking questions, learning. Tonight, he put that new knowledge to the test. He planned to find those girls.

He pulled up the sketches everyone was using and studied them. They were not quite right, Astrid's chin was more pronounced, though the sketch artist captured her cat eyes and high cheekbones. Something was off about the sketch of Davianna, her nose. It was not that wide, and her eyes were bigger and closer together. Guan opened the powerful Facetec software and began fiddling with the sketches. Tapping into his memories, he manipulated the images until two familiar faces coalesced on the screen.

"There you little bitches are."

He saved the images and opened a search titled, "Shoplifters". Nobody would care about shoplifters. The software whirled in the background, doing its thing. He minimized the screen and started a second project, the ace up his sleeve.

Agnor ben Randall a.k.a. Bubba.

Since starting at Facetec, he became attuned to the power

of photography. Facetec provided camera phones for all their employees and encouraged them to take pictures of everyone. He had several of Bubba. He picked one he knew the software would get the most data points from and uploaded it. He might not have known anything about computers a few months ago, but Guan ben Sheldon learned fast.

Ten minutes later the software hit paydirt. Guan discovered Bubba was wanted in six cities. He was a con, swindled people out of their dough. Guan shook his head. Good thing he did not expect to get his investment back, but this little nugget could be used. It made the fat bastard open to blackmail.

The software tracked Bubba across the city. Guan watched with detached interest and was not surprised to see the dude staying in a hotel sleazier than the one Guan lived in. What a piece of shit, pretending he was some big-time investor.

Then something caught his eye. He leaned forward studying the screen. Pausing the program, he backed up several frames. His eyes bulged in genuine disbelief. Davianna's whore of a mother sat in a restaurant with that big bastard.

What the hell was she doing here?

The last time he saw her was when he ran into her at Antiochus' palace. He was out of his head. Of course, he would have been. That was messed up.

He rolled the footage again. Son of a bitch, she was sitting beside his boss, Marco ben Massimo. That is where he had seen the guy before. It had been bugging the shit out of him for weeks. He could not remember. Now it all became clear.

He grinned. Not only did he know where Astrid's father was, he knew where Davianna's mother was, too. And with Facetec running his new data points, he would find those girls one way or the other. Guan laughed. He did not have an ace up his sleeve, he held a royal flush. That reward was as good as his.

December 5, 999 ME

Code Red - Peter

Peter's phone rang, and Alaina ben Thomas' sultry voice cooed, "Hello, lover."

His eyes widened for a moment, 'Hello, lover,' was the signal for Code Red. He schooled his features. "Well hello to you, sweetheart. Glad you called. Some friends and I are going to Danceria tonight. Perhaps you would like to join us?"

"Oh, Peter, that would be dreamy. Can you come by early? I'll show you my bikini wax."

He chuckled. "In that case, I will pick you up at your place. Shall we say 8:00 pm?"

"I'll be waiting."

Jarrod took the phone from his hand. "My Esteemed, will you be going out tonight?"

"Yes, Jarrod. Have my red Tsunami coupe brought up at 7:30 pm. I will not require a driver." Peter laid back on his lounge chair by the indoor pool and added, "Prepare an overnight bag, just in case."

"As you wish, my Esteemed. I will pack appropriately for a romantic interlude."

Peter's boyish grin signaled his pleasure.

Across the pool, unseen by human eyes Marduk lurked, eavesdropping on the exchange. He made a brief foray into the Palace, risked his life coming here, but he needed to know what was happening.

As he leaned against the corner, he seethed with hatred. He was injured. His arm would not stop bleeding. Peter's smug smile made him want to dig his claws into the little turd's brain and discover what he was planning. But he was weak, and every time he got near Peter, he felt worse.

It was a disaster. Keyseelough was poisoned, close to death back in Egypt, and Zeus? Marduk shuddered and refused to dwell on his rival's fate. The plan for New Year's Eve was crucial. Only Lucifer could save him now. He was dying. It was truly intolerable.

Peter rose and walked with that infuriating casualness close to where Marduk stood. He reached down and adjusted his sandal. When he did it, he brushed against him, which caused hellfire to shoot through his body. He screamed in outrage, but that was a mistake.

Gabriel must have been watching, he must have been listening, because he burst into the Palace and attacked.

Three hours later, when Marduk dove into his hidey-hole in Babylon, he decided it would be awhile before he left again. Because now, his right calf was bleeding.

At 8:15 pm, Peter arrived at Alaina ben Thomas' house. They embraced for the ever-present paparazzi, putting on a show. He kissed her on the front stoop and backed her in the door with a proprietary hand on her derriere. They never met at her house, ever. In the years they worked together, they were never publicly seen in each other's company.

This was Code Red protocol.

Like lovers, they ran up the steps to her bedroom aware that telephoto lenses were capturing their every movement. She made a show of closing her bedroom blinds, her stunning figure silhouetted for the photographers. Turning to face him, she held her finger over her lips and tiptoed to a stereo mounted in the wall. The sound of their voices filled the room, and she adjusted the volume on a pre-recorded audio track. If the press aimed high powered microphones at the windows, all they would hear was muffled love talk. It had taken them hours to record it, they kept bursting into hysterics. For two years, Alaina kept it, waiting for Code Red.

Inside her nightstand, a hidden button activated an access panel. The bookshelf emitted a faint click and a cold draft escaped from her secret computer lab. Alaina nearly pushed Peter through in her excitement. Her aquamarine eyes were blazing. "We've hit it big today."

He waved away the report she tried to give him and sat down in one of the small rolling chairs. The whirl of computers and servers made a pleasant buzzing noise, which covered his pounding heart. "What did you get?"

"Himari and I had a work session today."

Peter raised an eyebrow at her.

"It was fine. We made sure we were safe." She waved him away, eager to share what they had discovered.

"You are certain?"

"Yes, of course." The big-eyed look she gave him suggested she might explode if he did not let her talk.

He chuckled. "All right, go ahead."

She pointed at him and tilted her head, beaming. "Hacking the facial recognition software companies paid off. You were right, all of them are running programs nonstop to find those girls."

This was no surprise. Their own facial recognition programs were doing the same for weeks.

"We noticed something interesting on Facetec's server today. They uploaded several additional data points, different from the sketches."

Peter leaned forward. "Do they have a picture?"

"No, it doesn't appear so. None that we found, anyway. We got intelligence that Mossad knows what is going on, but we are relatively certain no one else has put Josiah and the girls together." Peter cleared his throat, an impatient gesture she recognized. "What got our attention is this upload." She brought up a picture of a big man at a bar.

"This guy is Agnor ben Randall, small time con artist wanted in numerous cities, and Astrid ben Agnor's father."

"Okay." Peter thought it was interesting, but not earth shattering. The guy looked nothing like his daughter. "Where is he?"

"Right here in New City, staying at some rundown hotel over in Simpson's Corners, but wait, it gets better."

Peter's emerald eyes darkened. "Go on."

Alaina grinned. She loved this work. "We reviewed the search and noticed the user zoomed in on her." An attractive dark-haired woman in her late 30s came up on the screen. "You are not going to believe this, but we figured out this is none other than Zanah ben Joseph, widowed wife of David, and mother of the other girl, Davianna."

"Impressive." Peter's cool demeanor gave away nothing.

"And if that wasn't exciting enough," Alaina preened, giving him a gorgeous smile. "Himari and I took the amended data points from the Facetec upload, ran matching software against the parents, and tightened up the search protocols we pulled from London."

Two new images lit up the screen.

"Here are your girls, Peter. I think we have the best images of them out there."

The face with cat eyes truly startled him. He had thought, had suspected, but to have it confirmed? It was like looking at a ghost. Despite his coursing adrenaline, he kept his face impassive, his voice bland. "Which one is which?"

Though he knew.

"Davianna ben David on the right, Astrid ben Agnor on the left."

He nodded. "Hits from the new data?"

Alaina smiled like a high stake's poker player laying down a winning hand. "We got them coming into Korah International."

His teeth clenched. "When?"

"November 13th."

He felt the blood leave his face. He had flown into Korah International on November 13th, the same day he fled New York. She was here. They were here, right in his father's clutches. His voice sounded strangled. "Anything since?"

"Strangely, no." Alaina tapped her lip in thought. "Although with these new data points, we will find them." She narrowed her brows and touched his shoulder. "Are you okay?"

Peter wrenched away and started pacing. "I am fine, Alaina. But I will not be, none of us will, if we do not find those girls. If we fail, all hell is going to break loose."

Frozen - Davianna and Astrid

"Twenty-seven days in this hotel room." Astrid complained. "We've never spent more than two days anywhere."

Davianna bit her bottom lip, as frustrated as Astrid. "I don't know what else to do."

"Me either." Astrid flopped on her bed with a huff and aimed the remote at the TV.

Eight years before, a tech investor, wealthy beyond his wildest imagination, conceived a plan that no one thought would work. He financed a multi-million-shekel excavation of Hollywood, and a team of archeologists unearthed two dozen vaults designed to survive a nuclear holocaust. Inside they found one hundred years of the Last Age's entertainment, perfectly preserved, and ready for re-release. The treasure trove was purported to be worth over three billion shekels.

Of course, the technology to play, view, and distribute the material had to be developed, sold and purchased, but the entrepreneurial Alanthian spirit was alive and well and by the late 90's, at least in the New City and New York, television and movies were as common as they were at the end of the Last Age. And as foreign as they had seemed to Davianna and Astrid when they first arrived, twenty-seven days later, they were normal.

"Find some cartoons or something," Davianna complained. "I hate the news, it's depressing, and I'm sick of seeing that sketch."

"Fine," Astrid grumbled and started flipping.

Neither paid much attention to the flickering screen. They tried to think.

Davianna gave up and peeked out the window, watching the street, alert for unusual activity and police. "The entire world is hunting us, and we are stuck in the middle of the most technologically advanced society on the planet."

"I just wish we could find Daddy."

Davianna shook her head. "Even if we could, which we haven't, we can't risk putting this thing in anybody's hands. It's too powerful, too dangerous, and now, worth way too much money."

"I am sure we could trust him. But you're right, he might not know how to destroy it, and we can't risk anybody else."

Davianna silently counted three cameras lining their street, and this was the ancient section of town. "We've got to figure a way past these cameras."

Astrid said, "A single photograph, that's all it would take. Wigs, makeup, disguises, accents fool people, not computers, Davianna. We need clay and latex to change our faces."

"We need to high tail it out of here."

But they were frozen.

December 10, 999 ME

Outrageous - Josiah

"No." Josiah held up a hand. "I will not do it. It is ridiculous."

Reuben nodded, smiling. "It is brilliant, yes?"

"It is lunacy. No!"

"We lost them. It is too risky to activate the tracking device inside this city. Korah's men caught the signal in September. If we activate the tracker and Korah's men are watching, it will lead them right to the girls before we can intervene. It would be like putting a target on them, but without the signal we have no way to track them." Reuben made a thoroughly Jewish shrug, throwing up his hands at the futility of it. "Mossad is working around the clock, but we've got nothing. They have disappeared, gone underground. I cannot think of another way to draw them out. Can you?"

Josiah tapped his toe, impatient with the conversation and this ludicrous idea. "It is one thing to walk through an airport or go to a nightclub dressed in that... that get up." He snarled with contempt. "To actually wrestle and throw pomegranates at my opponents as a shtick? You are insane."

Reuben chuckled, there were many inside Mossad who agreed with Josiah. "Wrestling is the rage. You get on TV, Davianna sees you, and we go. Trust me, I know this will work."

"There is also a chance that the wig or stupid prosthetics will come off in the ring and long dead, Prince Josiah becomes the Crown Prince of Alanthia during the Worldwide Wrestling Extravaganza. At which point, I would be murdered within the day."

"Yes, yes, there is that possibility." Reuben paused and with a sidelong glance, added, "You have to admit, it would make amazing TV, no?"

Josiah shot him a look and then laughed at the outright absurdity of it. "No!" The pomegranates were a good idea. TV was a good idea. Professional wrestling was a horrific idea, getting killed even worse. "We have to have another angle."

"Well, we've covered all the tea shops in the city, but so far we've turned up nothing." Reuben rubbed his jaw, thinking.

Josiah knew Davianna ben David. She would only send him a message if she were desperate, and she might not do it even then. If he could let her know he was here, there was a chance. "Do you still think they are hiding in the old part of the city?"

"Yes, yes, for sure." Reuben nodded. "I canvassed the area myself last week. If they are here that is where they are hiding. It's crowded. There are very few cameras, and it is the type of place where people do not ask questions."

Josiah knocked his forehead with his fist, thoroughly frustrated. "That part of town has been dangerous for decades.

That is why my father put the park there. They knocked down a ton of vacant buildings to give the kids a place to play, to revitalize the area."

Reuben stood up, stretching his calf. "The park is still there. From what I saw the businesses along the park are still open. So, I guess it worked. However, it is still not a nice neighborhood, and we will never find them in there. There are too many places to hide. Even if we could involve the local authorities, I did not see a single cop the afternoon I spent there. I saw many drug addicts, prostitutes, and anarchists though."

"Fantastic, that is just utterly fantastic. Davianna ben David is carrying the most dangerous artifact known to mankind, and she is likely hiding in one of the most dangerous sections of the kingdom. All the while, we do not have a clue how to find her." Josiah growled in frustration. "I should have never let her out of my sight. I should have told Yehonathan to go pound sand instead of letting him convince me to go into hiding when we were in London."

Reuben stopped stretching his calf and pointed a finger at Josiah. "No, you are wrong. We got intelligence, no fewer than fifty of Korah's agents were looking for you. You did the right thing."

Josiah sat down on the couch with a huff.

"What about Astrid ben Agnor's father? He is in the city. What if we have him pose as your manager? Get him on TV with you?" Reuben suggested.

"Are you still stuck on the wrestling? No, even if I agreed, I doubt Agnor would. You said he had a dozen outstanding warrants." Josiah drummed his fingers on his thigh. "What about the mother?"

"That shiksa?" Reuben waved the suggestion away. "I would not trust her. Neither of their parents are upstanding citizens, and they are tangled up with Marco ben Massimo. He is one bad character." Reuben rose and went to the kitchen, examining the refrigerator for something to eat.

Calling from the kitchen, he said, "They took the money we gave them quick enough, but I do not believe they understand the danger their daughters are in. They are supposed to call me if they hear from the girls, but Mossad does not pay as much as Korah, yes? I bet that reward is where both those alley cats are hoping to land."

"Then they are too risky. If we involve them, we run the risk of luring the girls into a trap baited with their parents." Josiah concluded, "Odds are, if we're thinking about using the parents, then so are others, including Marco ben Massimo."

December 11, 999 ME

My Guest - Bubba

For a big man, Bubba was not given to profuse perspiration, yet his forehead sported a distinctive sheen. Sitting across the breakfast table from Marco ben Massimo, he felt queasy, and his hand shook slightly as he sipped his coffee.

Massimo gave Bubba a reptilian smile and ate an orange segment. "So, my friend, Agnor, I trust that you find your new accommodations to your liking?"

Bubba cleared his throat. "Quite generous of you, Marco. The view of the garden is right pretty. Reminds me of my momma's house back in Houston."

"I am pleased to hear it. I enjoy having my uh, close business associates as guests in my home." He raised a thin flute of champagne in toast, then added, "I am sorry to say, that it hurt my heart to hear you tried to leave last night. I am a deeply disappointed that you have disrespected my hospitality."

Marco looked like a Renaissance painting of Lucifer, and that made Bubba nervous. "Well, Marco if I were you, I'd be saying the same thing. But I've got to tell you, appearances are not always the truth, right? I have an important meeting with several large investors, and I'm afraid I must be going."

Massimo pulled the napkin off his lap and ran it back and forth between his hands, shaping it into a long tube. "Agnor, I would not hear of you leaving, so soon." In a quick motion he snapped the napkins ends taut.

Simultaneously Massimo's goons held Bubba in his chair. One of them wrapped a similar napkin around his neck, squeezing like a python. They held him in his seat, the cloth crushing his windpipe. Struggling for air, his eyes bulged, his face turned crimson. Then it stopped. He bent forward, gagging and choking. Coffee spilled in his lap.

Massimo's light blue eyes were obscured by pleasure dilated pupils. "Take our guest to his room. See that he does not leave." He waved a dismissive hand, and Bubba was unceremoniously escorted out.

As he was being hauled away, he saw Zanah with her head bowed over her poached egg, untouched and staring at her like a watery all-seeing eye. She did not move.

December 21, 999 ME

Tea - Davianna and Astrid

The headache was not going away. Astrid refused the medicine Davianna got for her on Waterloo Bridge, threw it away before they left London. They were out of tea and out of choices, and Astrid was in no shape to continue arguing about it.

"It's time, past time. You need that tea, and I need to get a message to the Dark Prince. There is no other way."

"Just let me think," Astrid squeezed her temples.

Davianna ran her fingers through her hair in frustration. "We have nowhere else to turn. I'm taking the risk."

Throwing the door open, she skulked into the dark hallway and down the steps. The inaction was maddening, boredom and fear, their enemy. So Davianna committed to doing what must be done. She just prayed it would work.

She snuck out the service entrance door behind the hotel and sidled along the fence, deep in shadow. The cold air felt exhilarating, and her limbs rejoiced in movement that was not their small room.

Dusk fell, and the night people slithered out of their dens: prostitutes, junkies, and scariest of all, anarchists. Black-clad, pierced, and tattooed, the anarchists roamed the streets looking for trouble. Davianna, disguised as a boy, dressed in her Gune Black, tried to blend in with the crumbling buildings.

The mountains in the distance glimmered with lights, New City sprawl. Their once lush slopes reverted to the sandy brown hills they were in the Last Age. Only the Bay and the mighty Pacific kept the city in water. Yet, palm branches littered the avenues and skeletal remains of giant trees dotted the landscape. California reverted to desert before their eyes.

Tucked among old-fashioned stores, Davianna entered a spice and tea shop. The earthy scent was pleasant, and she breathed a sigh of relief. The Semitic woman behind the counter greeted her with a smile, her olive complexion smooth and ageless in the lantern light. "Shalom, how may I assist?"

Davianna shuffled her feet and stared at the floor. In a heavy French accent she said, *"Oui* Madame, my sister has a headache. You have tea, *s'il vous plaît?"*

Charmed, the woman bustled about. "Yes, yes I am sure. Is there a specific kind?"

Davianna scratched her arm and then dug in her pocket. *"Maman* wrote it." Davianna handed her the note. "You have?"

The shopkeeper studied the note then looked straight into Davianna's eyes. "This is unique. We have the individual teas. Shall I make you a blend?"

"Oui, merci." Davianna poked around the shop while the shopkeeper prepared the parcel. "Have you been in the New City long time?"

"Fifty years, but we will not stay much longer." Her voice became wistful. "I do not wish to be Lot's wife, nu?"

Davianna plunged ahead. "We are from Calais, but I like the New City very much, especially Prince Eamonn's Fountain. I go there to watch the sunset. Tomorrow it will be very early, due to... how you say, Solstice? Sometimes I meet friends there. It is beautiful, no?"

The shopkeeper smiled, and an understanding passed between them. The French 'boy' took the small parcel and left. The shopkeeper picked up the phone and made a call.

December 22, 999 ME

You Are Not Going - Davianna and Astrid

Astrid's face flamed red as she stepped in front of Davianna, blocking the door. "No, you cannot do this. It is crazy."

Davianna stood her ground. "I am not arguing with you anymore. Move." Dressed and ready, sunset would be in forty minutes.

"You do not know who will be waiting for you, Davianna." Astrid threw up her arms. "What are you thinking?"

"I think," Davianna's voice climbed, "that we cannot stay here any longer. We have to move."

"You don't get to decide, not alone!" Astrid insisted. "We do it together."

Davianna bit her bottom lip and looked down at her black boots. "No, I have to do this alone."

"The hell you say," Astrid snorted. "My picture is everywhere, too. Remember, we are international artifact thieves." She backed against the door. "Together."

"Tridi, they want this device. They don't want you. If they take me, they will have it, and you will be safe. If they take you," she paused, her nose flaring, "they will torture you. They will force you to tell them where I am, then they will kill you. If they take me, there is a chance we both come out alive."

Davianna said it so matter of fact, Astrid blinked in disbelief.

"You know I am right." Davianna took a step forward.

"I would never betray you!"

Davianna gave her a smile, sad and full of regret. "I know you would not want to, but you would, and at what cost?" Davianna rubbed the back of her neck. "Do you forget the key I hold? Do you forget the power that created it?"

Astrid pursed her lips. "I haven't forgotten."

Davianna shook her head in rueful resignation. "We've played this like a game, like some sort of adventure."

A broken cry ripped from Astrid's throat. "My mother died."

Davianna turned away, unable to bear the look on Astrid's face.

Dust motes floated through a shaft of evening light, shining through the dingy window. City sounds filtered through the walls, horns and cars, people talking; inside a stale hotel room, two hearts broke.

"And I won't let you die." Davianna moved Astrid away from the door, leaving before she lost her nerve.

Prince Eamonn's Fountain - Josiah and Davianna

Built during Prince Eamonn's reign and before the technology explosion, the park had no cameras, which made it a perfect meeting spot. Davianna idly pulled at the papery bark of a birch tree, watching the sunset through the fountain. Deep in the enormous complex, this time of the year, she thought she was alone. Though, she could not be sure. There were shadows everywhere, danger lurking behind every tree.

She wished for a moment of peace, longed for the calm she experienced on Waterloo Bridge. Yet it eluded her. Despite her bravado back in the room, she was scared. He might not come. It might not have even been him on TV. He might not even be in the New City. She might have mistaken the silent interplay between her and the shopkeeper. But they were out of options and out of time.

She scouted a half dozen escape routes. As the sun disappeared over the horizon, the park moved from twilight to full dark. Two more minutes, he had two more minutes.

Standing there, expecting to be captured any second, the folly of this plan became clear, like all their other harebrained schemes. And Astrid was worried, which was always a bad sign, but Astrid did not know everything, and Davianna could not make her understand why she trusted the Dark Prince. She could not explain it. She also did not divulge her suspicions about his true identity.

A Prince coming to her rescue.

To say it aloud sounded ridiculous, even to her own ears, especially considering the nickname they gave him. This was not a fairytale. It was a horror story, and she better remember it.

A twig snapped behind her. She waited, prepared for arms that might seize her, hands that might bind her. Her heart thundered, and her fists clenched. Months of hiding taught her not to run. Still she crouched, ready for flight. In the instant before she moved, she saw him.

He stood with his arms crossed and his legs braced. The fading light cast his face in a cold blue glow. "Thou art not alone."

Despite her trembling, Davianna's voice sounded deep and husky. "Tonight, I have been very much alone."

"He loved this park," Josiah murmured, staring across the bay, the wind blowing black curls away from his forehead. He shook away the memory and moved beside her. "Come, we will go. It is unsafe here."

His accent sounded different, flat and broad, New City, Alanthian. He seemed different, so she pulled away. "It's not safe anywhere, Doc." There was still enough light to see his face. She studied him, still handsome, but haunted, angry. There was no peace about him tonight.

"That's where you are wrong, girl. Stop being stubborn and come with me." Josiah was suddenly furious with her, for the worry, wondering whether she was alive or dead. He was home at last, and he wanted to get on with his life. He reached out to grab her arm.

Adrenaline roared up her spine. A mistake, he was a hunter, just like the rest. She cursed herself for a fool and blasted off. The Gune Black camouflaged her, making her invisible in the falling darkness. Only her footfalls sounded, pumping in a full out tear. Her legs were powerful, swift, and sure. Darting like a rabbit, she ran like the devil was after her.

His hand caught empty air. Josiah stood stunned for a split second. She was there, and then she bolted. He took off after her, his mind working as fast as his legs, and he thought, "She doesn't run like a girl. Holy shit, she is fast."

He lost her for a second, behind a corner, then power and fury surged through his body, and he caught her around the waist. Momentum took them down. He held her with one arm and broke their fall.

She squirmed under him, frantic, clawing at the dirt, at him, fighting like a wild cat.

"Stop it. I'm not going to hurt you!"

Davianna gasped. "Get off me!"

He froze and heard footsteps coming fast. "Kiss me." He flipped her over, unsheathing the knife at her belt.

She could not breathe. He was crushing her. He had her knife. He was going to stab her. He was going to rape her.

He nuzzled her ear, hissing, "Police. Kiss me!"

Then she understood, if she did not kiss him, they would think he was attacking her. They might try to arrest him; they would discover her. "Oh, God!" she prayed and kissed him.

He was so heavy, the frozen ground so hard. Her heart thundered. His lips covered hers... and she could not breathe. Spots darkened her vision. She tore her mouth away, gasping, "Can't breathe."

He scrambled up, drawling, "Come on, baby. Let's get on home. It's right cold out here."

A nanosecond before the police officer was upon them, the ruse registered. She needed to mimic his drawl, easy. "Well, help me up, Gilroy. You are bad. Tacklin' me out here, like you're still playin' football." He pulled her up, and she collapsed into him. In a gasping whisper that she prayed sounded sexy, added, "I've still got my cheerleadin' uniform."

The police officer's light shined on them, Davianna buried her face in Josiah's chest, turning away.

"Park's closing, folks. Please move along."

Josiah nuzzled her ear, keeping his face averted. "Yes sir, Officer. Good night." Shielding Davianna, he made a polite nod to the officer and led her away. "Come on, Tammy. Let's go play… football."

Just out of earshot, she gasped, and her knees buckled.

He caught her around the waist and moved his hand to her stomach. "Breathe, use your belly." He pushed gently. "In through your mouth, out through the belly, slow." He breathed with her several times and kept walking. "It's okay. You just got the wind knocked out of you." He hastened their steps, coaxing, "That's right, slow, doing good."

She stumbled, her face pale and sweaty. He practically carried her to a black sedan, their feet crunched gravel as they made their way to the solitary vehicle in the parking lot. Davianna's mind worked furiously. She could not run. She could barely breathe, and if that police officer was watching them, she had to get in the car. He opened the door and would have picked her up like a baby if she let him. She pushed his hands away and fell into the seat.

Fumbling inside her tunic, she placed a small device on the dash and flipped the switch. He raised a questioning brow. She shrugged. "Signal jamming." Then she held out her hand and said with a halting gasp, "Give me back my knife."

He pulled it from his pocket and offered it to her, palm up.

She sheathed it, giving him a sidelong look. "You know how to drive?"

The corner of his mouth twitched. "I learned a week ago."

"Don't kill us, Gilroy."

Josiah snorted, amused. "I'll try not to." Then he added with nose flaring irritation, "Although you nearly did back there."

"Me?" Although weak and quavering, her voice held an edge of indignation. "You tackled me."

"You ran," Josiah countered, though he still could not believe how fast.

"You grabbed me." Davianna crossed her arms and turned away. "It startled me. I hate being startled."

Josiah pressed his lips in a straight line. "Sorry."

She tilted her chin up, refusing to look at him, and gave him a harrumph. But she caught sight of something and twisted in her seat, pulling her hood over her head, and curling into a ball. "Avoid the traffic cameras, please."

He snorted and turned down a dark street.

She glared at him suspiciously. "Where are we going?"

"Sit up, your diaphragm needs space. I'm taking you to a safe house. Then we can get you out of the city."

"No, that's not the plan. I will not abandon Astrid, and with that bounty, there can be no 'we' in whatever we do." Groaning, she sat up. "Gosh, this hurts."

"Diaphragm spasms, it will pass."

"How much do you weigh? Gah, freaking squished me." She rubbed her shoulder grumpily.

He ignored her and kept driving.

"I am serious. I am not going anywhere without Astrid. Do not involve anyone else. It's too much money. My own mother would turn me in."

Josiah did not comment. She was likely right about her mother, but all his plans included Mossad. Being Hebrew, they alone were incorruptible, sealed by the Iron King. He recognized her stubborn streak and decided not to argue with her. "What do you propose?"

She was silent as the New City streets raced by. At length,

she whispered, "I did not steal that artifact or do any of the things they say."

He concentrated on the road. "I know." He heard her swallow and passed her a bottle of water.

She took a drink and said, "I'm in big trouble. The original plan was to get to the New City, find Astrid's father, and get his help. If he could not destroy this thing, then at least I could leave her with him, and she'd be safe." She pushed on her stomach, trying to relieve a cramp. "I can't do that now. That bounty is for her, too. If they find her… they will kill her, to get to me."

Josiah glanced over at her. It was time to tell her the truth, or at least part of it. "I've been following you on orders, which were to find you and safely escort you to the Golden City." He pulled into a dark parking lot.

"I am your orders?" At his nod, she asked, "Who gave them?"

"The King."

Her eyes narrowed. "Which one?"

"The only one."

"So, you've met him?" Davianna tilted her head, studying him, wishing she had Astrid's ability to interpret body language.

"No." His voice held a bitter edge. "I have tried. The orders came through Prince Yehonathan when I was in the Golden City."

Davianna's lips pressed flat. "When?"

"March of this year."

Davianna slumped down in her seat, running over in her mind all that had happened. "February would have been better."

Josiah spent a lifetime pondering those quagmires. She did not seem to expect an answer, and he did not have one to give her.

She sighed heavily and counted off on her fingers as she spoke, "There are three huge events coming up, wrestling,

New Year's, and the royal wedding. People are flooding into town. That is when we need to move, which is why we're still here. That and," she gave a self-deprecating snort, "we've been petrified."

Josiah, the soldier, recognized her look. He had seen it on his men's faces before battle. Dreaded anticipation, the sick desire to just get on with it, to fight. It warred with the instinct to run, to hide, and let the maelstrom pass by. He knew that fear, had lived it. It made him angry at himself and at her, so he barked, "That will get you killed."

She jumped in her seat. Then, without thinking, smacked him in the chest with her open palm. "Don't do that!"

Prince Josiah ben Eamonn, Commanding Officer and Surgeon of the King's Army, drew himself up with regal authority, thoroughly affronted. "I do not tolerate impertinence."

Davianna drew back, intimidated. He filled the entire space, sucking the air from her lungs again. Her hand flew to the door handle.

He saw the panic and grabbed her wrist. She was not one of his soldiers. She was a scared kid. So, he softened his tone, and said, "I know what I am doing, don't run."

She stilled, regarding him with a stony expression.

With utter clarity, he saw her mind working again. He did not force her, did not soothe, or cajole, did not bully. He let go of her wrist and said the one thing she needed to hear. "I will keep you both alive, and nobody will get their hands on what you carry."

She stared out the passenger window for a long time. Her voice when she spoke was completely deadpan. "I think Nacho Libre is going to kick Carsten ben Hansen's ass."

It knocked him awry, such an off the wall thing to say. He boomed with laughter.

She raised an impish brow and the tension between them evaporated.

Josiah drew himself up. "Nacho is *en snothvalp!*"

Davianna cracked up. "You threw a pomegranate at him!"
They dissolved in hilarity.

"That wig?" Davianna wiped tears from her cheeks. "Astrid kept playing it over and over again. She loves Nacho Libre."

That made him laugh even harder.

Fifteen Data Points - Prince Peter

Peter's head of security, Nathan ben Henry, searched the scantily clad Japanese woman before admitting her into Danceria's private suite. She strutted boldly over to Prince d'Or, put her hand on her hip, and appraised him with a possessive leer. Then without warning or regard, she straddled him.

He feigned approval of her salacious behavior. His hand signal stopped Nathan from pulling her off. The girls next to him were annoyed. The men thought it great fun.

Himari Nakamura, a.k.a. Sunflower532, was arguably the world's foremost hacker, who despised Korah with a visceral hatred and was one of a handful of people who knew of Peter's involvement in The Resistance. If he had not let her in, she likely would have hacked her way in. And if she was not his agent, he would have flung her to the bodyguards for straddling him.

Leaning forward, Himari cooed, "Dance with me, fine Prince."

His dimpled smile flashed pure lechery. "I am." He rose from the couch with her still clinging to him and walked to the dance floor.

Over the music, she whispered, "Fifteen data points. Two hits. Doc and Sparrow. Eamonn Park. Four hours ago."

A sudden hush fell over the crowd, but the music kept blasting. Alert to the change, Peter froze mid stride with Himari's tiny legs wrapped around his waist.

The Hell Bitch stormed in.

Princess Keyseelough reached him in three strides and

flung Himari off him like a piece of trash. She looked him up and down with a possessive leer, reeking of death. Stepping forward, she slithered down his body, as if she were trying to claim him. When her body touched his, she made an inhuman sound of pain.

His emerald eyes bore straight into hers with deadly rancor and abject loathing.

Panic crossed her face, and she recoiled. Then the witch gathered herself with regal poise and slunk out of the room.

Nathan lifted Himari off the floor. Peter turned to the room and gave a boyish shrug of innocent guilt.

The room erupted in roars of laughter.

The sound blistered Keyseelough's ears and ignited an unholy malevolence in her black soul.

As she rounded the corner, unseen by human eyes, the archangel Uriel subdued her. "I told you before, that you were never to touch him again. I curse you, Keyseelough, Princess of Egypt. If you ever return to this land, you will suffer a fate that will make you wish for death." He pressed her against the wall. "Go back to Cairo."

He read it in her eyes. She would leave, but she was coming back. He shook his head, leaving her to her fate, and his curse. The music resumed inside the club. Uriel took up his post, tapping his toe to the beat.

Tatbir - King Korah

Korah sat straight up in his bed, a nightmare seared into his brain. He had been in the dungeon, chained to the cold slab instead of his brother. Peter loomed above him with a knife, his executioner. He rubbed his eyes, trying to banish the memory, surprised when tears came away on his palms. A painful gripe seized his bowels, turning them watery and hot.

He climbed out of bed with the dream still with him. The tile under his bare feet felt disconcerting, like the stone slab. Chilled to the core, he poured a liberal glass of brandy and drained it, then another, until the third began to thaw the ice.

"Dark Master, please come to thy humble servant. I seek thy wisdom." Korah chanted, seeking a trance that did not come. "I praise the god of wisdom," he called, feeling weak and bereft.

For weeks, he had been alone.

Cold chills wracked his body. He fell on his face, crying out in the darkness. The presence, with him for almost fifteen years, was gone. He surmised he had done something to displease the master and groaned. Korah knew the personal cost it would take to satisfy the god he served. He knelt on the tile, waiting in vain. The pain in his knees signaled mere supplication would not suffice. After avoiding this for weeks, Korah knew what he had to do.

With slow deliberate movements, he went to the secret room behind his closet. As he opened the door, the stench of old blood rose like a specter. He stripped naked and removed a jewel handled leather whip from the altar. Kneeling in front of Marduk's edifice, he began the tatbir, a self-flagellation ritual, required to appease the fickle temper of his god.

Barton, Korah's valet, found him at dawn: whipped, bloody, and alone.

December 23, 999 ME

Kink in the Plans - Peter

The ashtray in Peter's New City penthouse overflowed. Gray smoke hung in cirrus clouds above the living room stirred only by his rapid pacing as he lit one cigarette off the butt of another. The stench of burnt coffee lingered just beneath the cigarette smoke. A pot in the kitchen burnt to sludge, simmering into black ash in the glass carafe.

He wore last night's rumpled clothes, and his usual perfect hair bore wide finger marks through the golden waves.

He looked like a cherub after a rough night.

A newspaper, with a full-color picture of him nose to nose with Keyseelough and Himari sprawling in the background, lay on the rustic coffee table. The Front-Page Headline read:

ROYAL WEDDING OFF?
Playboy Prince Goes TOO Far?

In a scene witnessed by dozens at Danceria, the soon to be wed royal couple, Prince Peter ben Korah and Princess Keyseelough ben Mubarak, had a public falling out. Sources say, immediately after the Princess and her entire delegation departed for Cairo. There has been no official comment from either the Palace or the Egyptian delegation, but royal watchers have long speculated the relationship between the two has been strained.

World leaders from across the globe have already begun arriving to attend the Palaces' New Year's Eve Gala. Formal wedding festivities are scheduled to kick off on New Year's Day and will culminate on January 10th with the wedding ceremony. The question remains, will Prince d'Or actually make it down the aisle?

Peter threw the newspaper down with disgust. Korah would be enraged. The betrothal, the contracts, the alliance, all of it gone, and with them three years' worth of negotiations. The wedding expenses, the planned parties, events, and ceremonies would all have to be canceled. It would be Alanthian humiliation on a global scale. Which was the plan, but it was supposed to happen after Peter was gone, not before.

He never had any intention of marrying the Hell Bitch, ever. Not for one minute did he ever consider the possibility. He despised her before, and he hated her now with a pathological violence that bordered on obsession. She was lucky he did not strangle her last night, damn lucky.

He heard she almost died. He prayed she would, actually prayed, but she had not. She looked like shit and smelled even worse. What was up with that awful scream when she touched him? Not that he minded. He thought he heard the monster scream like that a few weeks ago, but he could not be certain. That wicked bastard was keeping a low profile. However, Peter knew he was still lurking around somewhere.

According to the papers, Keyseelough was gone. At least for the moment.

Now, Peter needed to figure out how to stay alive long enough to escape. His father may well be a murderous madman, nevertheless he was methodical. Korah would not kill Peter—yet.

His best strategy was to stay in the public eye, be visible and charming. As a defense, it kept him alive. Korah could not afford the mysterious death of another Prince swirling around him and certainly not one as popular as Peter.

Not that it was ever a possibility, but Peter figured out a long time ago that if he married the Hell Bitch, he was dead. The list of potential assassins was long and convoluted. He suspected that was the motivation for the attack back in March. The anti-tech jihadists were crawling all over the Middle East, and in their eyes, he was irrevocably tied to Korah's tech. As such, he was number two on their hit list. Marrying their beloved Princess would propel him to head infidel.

At home, once married, he moved from presumed heir to the throne to potential rival, and dear old dad would never tolerate that. Peter was a dead man running or staying. He liked his chances better running.

But everything was threatened now.

No, that was not true, his escape plan was intact. Everything, down to the last-minute detail, was in order, ready to go. He could go now. He could disappear. He blew out a long cloud of smoke and said into the silence, "Prince d'Or, dead at last." Perhaps it would even cast suspicion on Korah, a delicious thought.

One thing stopped him, fifteen data points. They were

spotted. If he had them, his father did too. There would be no escape if more of those monsters were released, they would torment him forever.

Keyseelough was still alive. Josiah was still missing. The girls and that artifact were still nowhere to be found. The Monster was still roaming around. The drugs still called to him. Korah stilled ruled Alanthia. Nothing had changed.

No matter what his drug addled brain may have hallucinated last month. He knew the truth. He was overwrought. He was strung out. He imagined the whole encounter with Yeshua, and a part of him wanted to just take his chances and leave. Leave it all behind and be done: the kingdom, his cousin, everything. He questioned whether all these plans and work were even worth it. Was there any hope? Would they even want Josiah on the throne, or had the kingdom gone so deep into rebellion there was no Alanthia left for Josiah to take back? Was there even a semblance of the kingdom Prince Eamonn ruled? It seemed like a lost cause, and Peter was sick of fighting lost causes. He was also sick of being the one left behind.

He lit another cigarette and stared out at the gray sky.

Yet that girl, that reckless blue-eyed girl, tormented him. It was insanity. His life was on the line, and he was wasting energy on a runaway girl. With a reward that size, it was only a matter of time before Korah caught her. No doubt. That kind of money practically ensured it, and then Peter knew what would happen.

He took a deep drag... Fifteen data points... exhale... Fifteen data points... Josiah found them. Korah's men would be closing in, and he would kill them all. Fifteen data points... Korah would be unstoppable with more of those monsters and if those monsters were let loose, Peter would never be free.

He stubbed out his cigarette and got to work.

December 24, 999 ME

Time to Move - Davianna and Astrid

Forty-two days after they checked in, elderly Gavin ben Beauregard, and his shy devoted teenage granddaughter, Susan, of Lancaster England, checked out of the Lansford Hotel. Pulling away from the hotel, Josiah hazarded a glance at Astrid ben Agnor. She was dressed as a tiny old man, radiating hostility so palpable it was almost comical. Davianna wiggled under a pile of blankets in the back seat of the sedan, hiding.

Astrid huffed, "We are being followed."

Josiah checked the mirrors; he did not see anyone. "Where?"

Astrid stared straight ahead, not moving her lips as she said, "The cameras are following the car."

From the backseat, Josiah heard a stream of muttered cursing that sounded remarkably like the cartoon character Yosemite Sam.

"Plan B," he said firmly.

Astrid shot him a contemptuous look. "Your original plan then." The distrust in her eyes told him she suspected he never intended to go with Plan A, their plan. Plan B involved Mossad.

Three hours, four cars, and many disguises later, they arrived at the hotel safe house. They wheeled Davianna into the room hidden inside the laundry basket of a maid's trolley, Astrid under the tablecloth of a room service cart.

Josiah detected that both girls were unnerved, uncomfortable accepting help. The distrust in their eyes was evident. Astrid literally stood between Davianna and everyone else. She was a powder keg—about to explode.

My Way - Davianna and Astrid

Astrid prowled her room, anxious and furious. She flicked her knife open and closed as she paced the plush carpet, peeking out the slit in the curtains. "Too high up," she muttered. They never stayed higher than the third floor, ever. "At least a half a dozen people know where we are."

She had not kept them safe all these months by ignoring a feeling of foreboding. "We are going to get caught." The thought looped in her brain, swirling and repeating every thirty seconds. "You are going to get caught. Davianna is going to get caught. They are going to get that device. Caught—this is a trap—run!"

The knife opened and closed with every beat of her pumping heart.

Davianna was in the room next door. This was ridiculous. They had to get out of here. She crept to the door and eased it open. Four men sat in the living room, talking.

"Agnor." She stopped, listening closer. "At Marco ben Massimo's estate."

"Daddy!" She closed the door quietly and retreated into her room, repeating the name, "Marco ben Massimo, Marco ben Massimo? Where have I heard that name?"

Her eyes lit up. She remembered. She heard it on the news, saw an interview with him at his mansion in Singleton Gardens. He was the founder of Facetec, a tech company that was all the rage. Of course, that made sense. Her daddy was a tech investor. He would be friends with tech people!

She pulled her gear out of her bag and reviewed it, discarding the disguises of the day. They needed their trusty tunics and leggings, and they were getting the hell out of here.

Astrid slipped out the door and into Davianna's room.

Davianna was already dressed in her Gune Black. Astrid could tell she was feeling it too, the tension, the anticipation, the sense to run. It kept them alive, despite the odds. Davianna's bag was packed.

"We've got to go," Astrid hissed. "I've got that feeling."

Davianna nodded, but she looked drawn and weary.

"I found Daddy," Astrid whispered. "I heard them talking, they know where he is."

Davianna's heart broke. In that instant, she knew what she must do. There was one safe place for Astrid, and it was not with her. "Where?"

They whispered their plans, just as they did for months, in one accord, together.

December 25, 999 ME

Perfect Storm

Guan outsmarted Marco ben Massimo and escaped with his life, barely. The bastard stole his 'Shoplifter' side project, froze his bank account, and sent his goons after him. Guan's experience in Greece taught him not to hang around and try to collect a reward from a madman. That wisdom saved his life again, but now he was in dire straits.

His room was being watched, and he had enough money in his pocket to buy a falafel and not much else. One person owed him money, and he was the same yahoo who might just lead him to that big reward, computer program or not. Guan just had to dodge Massimo's goons to collect.

Zanah stalked toward the big man slumping in the lounge chair by the frigid swimming pool. A half empty glass of whiskey sat on the table beside him, and a cigar stub spiraled gray smoke into the still night air. Bubba was a prisoner here, same as she. They were bait, and she was no longer deceiving herself.

Marco ben Massimo was certainly no fool. He knew exactly who Bubba was, and of course, he knew she was Davianna's mother. If the girls were discovered, and Marco did not get that reward, they were dead. She was ready to leave, and Bubba, the only man not on Marco's payroll, was going to help her.

The concussion grenade made Josiah feel like his head

was being cleaved in two. He coughed and vomited into the sink. Residual flashes of light blinded him, and he fell to his knees. The acrid smell of gas and bile fouled the back of his throat, burning like fire and acid.

Reuben moaned from the living room. The other agents coughed, and one retched. Panic hit his nervous system—the girls!

He staggered to their rooms. They were gone, captured! He yelled, "Men, rally! We must go!" But something about the room caught his attention, made him pause. Their gear bags… They were not kidnapped. Those little idiots gassed them and ran.

A horrible premonition told him where.

Stephen ben McSwilley watched the monitors in his basement computer lab with detached interest. Astrid ben Agnor and Davianna ben David were fleeing the Mossad safe house. He studied the third monitor, Guan ben Sheldon skulked about Marco ben Massimo's mansion, while Agnor ben Randall and Zanah ben Joseph were chatting by the pool. Stephen activated the speaker on screen four to listen to the pool conversation.

"We have to leave. They are going to kill us."

Stephen rolled his eyes and muttered, "That stupid woman is just figuring that out?"

Screen five showed the Palace. Marco ben Massimo, the charlatan and mafia boss, was being escorted inside. Facetec's software was going crazy, tracking Astrid ben Agnor and Davianna ben David across the city all day. Massimo would give a report that would set the final pieces in motion, which meant Stephen had about thirty minutes.

Five minutes later, monitor number one showed a staggering Prince Josiah ben Eamonn climb into a green sedan outside his hotel. Screen six lit up with multiple Facetec hits.

Across the city, all three high value targets were being tracked.

Fifteen minutes later, multiple messages fed through to the police dispatch system. He watched with delirious amusement as they all began converging in a single spot.

Stephen ben McSwilley had devoted two hundred and seventy-two days of unrelenting work, gathering the information, data, and technology that unfolded before his eyes, in real time. Live.

He studied the dossier, reading it again, making final adjustments. Dates, times, crimes, videos, murders, tortures, sacrifices, it was all there, ready to press send, straight to Mossad, straight to the true King. A second communique was ready, to the head of The Resistance, Prince Peter. Stephen laughed, bitter and humorless. King Korah's fatal flaw was his failure to value those around him. He planned to send it in care of the Prince's accomplished associate, his former friend. It contained all the codes and the back doors to the network Stephen built.

The text from Korah came through with predictable, unhinged rage. Stephen was summoned to the Palace to give an account of himself, and his final failure to deliver the device, and the fugitives. It was the last text he was ever going to read from that homicidal maniac.

Stephen watched in fascinated horror as all the parties converged, Agnor, Zanah, Astrid, Davianna, Guan, Josiah and then a hundred police officers.

McSwilley viewed a few of the torture tapes. Falling into Korah's clutches would not go well for any of them. But he did not care. He was finished. He pressed send on both messages, checked to ensure they went through, then turned off the monitors.

He dimmed the lights and turned on his favorite album. With the deliberate methodical care that governed his professional life, he destroyed every piece of equipment. With tears streaming down his cheeks, he knelt with the Bible in one hand, a picture in the other. He kissed the picture and sent up a prayer for forgiveness. Then Stephen ben McSwilley blew his head off.

Part 9 - The Palace

December 25, 999 ME

Jail

Davianna guessed as far as jails went, the cell she found herself in was not as bad as the ones her imagination conjured. It was sparkling clean, all white, with a built-in plastic bench. The accommodations included a folded thin blanket and a small pillow. After the freezing cold flight, the room was not frigid, though she realized she was numb to the actual temperature.

She pressed her fingers into her cheeks and jawline; they were numb. "That's odd," she thought with absent disassociation. Her heart raced and her insides were shaking, yet her outward appearance was calm, rock solid, still. She examined her hand. "Steady, interesting."

There was an ominous white toilet and sink in the corner. No privacy. The cell's camera appeared to be aimed right at the toilet. "Not optimal, glad I don't have to pee." Her voice sounded hollow in the empty cell.

She considered the orange jail uniform, tunic top

and pajama pants. The rough material creased where it had been folded. The pants were too long. Their hems dragged the floor as she paced. A white reflective stripe ran the length of the outfit; it felt stiff and produced an odd crackling sound when she traced her finger over it.

Weariness hit her, and she sat down hard, staring at her feet. She wiggled her toes in the slippers, also orange, thin and cheap with scant padding and a paper-thin rubber sole. Exhausted now, she pulled the blanket to her chin. The light made an odd buzzing noise, and Davianna wondered how many holes were in the ceiling tiles.

Davianna could not think of what happened three hours ago. She could not process it, could not contemplate what happened next. So, she stared at the ceiling tiles and created cloud shapes in her mind.

Astrid sat motionless, afraid if she moved the headache would seize her. So, she sat with her spine and neck aligned, her eyes closed. With each pound of her heart, she felt the left side of her brain. People were not supposed to feel their brains, yet Astrid knew what hers felt like.

She wanted to think of her daddy's big hug, but he smelled like whiskey and cigars, and that might make her vomit. She wished she could recapture the joy she felt when she saw Guan's gorgeous smile. She concentrated, trying to relive the moment when she forgot she was running, when she was just a girl reunited with the two men she loved.

Astrid blocked the confusing moment afterward when Guan bypassed her and kissed Davianna. The utter betrayal of that Judas kiss drew a small whimper. She quelled her fury at that damn doctor, reasoning his pursuit brought the police. She would not think about being caught. She would not think of the device. Astrid knew with complete certainty if she entertained any of these dark thoughts the icepick would find its mark and smash through her temple. There was nothing in the world she feared more, or so she tried to convince herself.

Josiah's cell opened, Officer Elias ben Phillip, studied him with a quizzical eye. A sixteen-year veteran of the Metropolitan Police Department, Elias came from a long line of cops with a knack for sniffing out trouble. Something niggled him about tonight's arrests, specifically the man sitting in this holding cell. Elias trusted niggling.

"Captain Einar ben Yane, we received word that you are being transferred to the jurisdiction and authority of the Alanthian National Armed Service." The man's face remained neutral, without a word, the prisoner seemed to dismiss him. His soldier's demeanor never wavered, though his color was greenish, ill.

Elias delivered the same message to the remaining two cells on his wing. The other perps arrested tonight were not his problem. They were being processed through the system. Back at his desk, he watched the screens, studying the three, staring at the face of the captain. Elias' memory was legendary, and the man in the cell seemed familiar. He just could not place him. "No matter," he thought, leaning back in his chair. "It will come to me. It always does."

Code Black - Peter

Jarrod ben Adriel, Peter's valet and faithful companion, did something he never did in all the years of his long service, he shook the Prince awake in the middle of the night. "My Esteemed, wake up. We are in Code Black."

Peter awoke with a start. The air in his Penthouse bedroom was cold, and he could hear the low whistling howl of the wind outside. Jarrod helped him sit, pressed a shot of espresso into his hand, and disappeared into the wardrobe. Peter drained the shot and jumped out of bed. Jarrod dressed him in seconds.

Behind the wardrobe wall of shoes, a hidden elevator provided a quick escape. As he descended, he thought, "Code Black, bloody hell."

Entering the underground garage, the anticipation of riding his new motorcycle *momentarily* overshadowed the dire situation at hand. Code Black prompted specific protocol, and this bike was purchased for exactly this reason. He eyed the machine with masculine delight and mounted it. Placing his hand over the screen, he made his menu selection, and rode out of the garage into the frigid night. The bike was silent, fully electric. Without a headlamp, Peter was almost invisible in his black gear.

A mile from his penthouse, he engaged the headlight and the gas-powered engine. It roared to life like a dragon between his lean muscular thighs. The vibration went through him, primeval, powerful. He opened up the throttle, exhilarated by the speed as the dark landscape flew past him. He took a sharp corner, leaning in, accelerating through the turn. He shot out of it like a rocket and sped away, not feeling the cold.

Peter was the first to arrive at the rendezvous site. He hit the garage door button on the motorcycle. The chain drive door opened with a jerk and a clatter. Gray wood smoke danced out of a squat chimney, smelling earthy and pleasant in the crisp air.

The interior garage door opened and standing with her arms braced against the cold was one of his favorite people in the world, his former nanny, Genevieve ben Willard, Auntie G. She rubbed her pudgy hands over her forearms against the chill, her smile bright, her eyes worried.

Peter removed his helmet and gloves, bounded up the steps, and swept her off the ground in an extravagant bear hug. She expelled her breath with a great whoosh tinged with exasperated laughter. "Hello, darling, you look amazing." Peter kissed her cheek and set her down.

Her cheeks were pink and her hair mostly white. Genevieve's dismissive wave telegraphed the absurdity of being fifty-five, awakened at 3:00 am, and wearing clothes she went to the market in. The last thing she looked was amazing. All the same, he could tell she liked it.

"Come in, it's cold. I have coffee."

He squeezed her hand and followed her through the narrow corridor, careful to wipe his boots on the knit rug.

She handed him a heavy crock of coffee, sweeter and milkier than he drank it, but he did not mind.

"Are you hungry? I baked buccellato." His face lit up with a boyish smile so beautiful she wanted to pinch his cheeks.

"Buccellato?" He widened his emerald eyes, and she could see their golden bursts of sunshine. "You are spoiling me already."

"Pfft! I am Italian, it is what we do."

Peter chuckled with dark humor. "Let them eat cake."

They exchanged a serious look, Code Black hung in the air, unspoken.

"He loves my buccellato, too," she said quietly, serving Peter a generous piece of the fig and nut pastry.

The garage door sounded again, and Peter licked the sweet icing from his finger, going to greet the new arrival. He ushered tiny Himari into the warm kitchen. Genevieve greeted her with a cup of Ujicha tea and a traditional Japanese bow.

Himari smiled, but her expression registered dubious speculation at her surroundings. The homey kitchen was decorated with painted geese, wooden hearts, and dried flowers.

Moments later, Alaina arrived, flushed and bleary. She took the proffered coffee mug as if it were a sacred offering. Himari gobbled the remaining bite of buccellato, and at Peter's nod Genevieve directed them to the basement.

Narrow steps descended into a hodgepodge of discarded rubbish, decades of cast-off junk. Two old computers sat on a card table in the corner.

Himari put her hand on her hip. "Peter, Code Black?" Her acid tongue got the better of her. "We are in Grandma's basement."

Peter laughed. 'Were you expecting an abandoned warehouse on the waterfront with a secret room and tons of computers? Maybe a brooding group of pale hackers with tattoos and body piercings?"

Himari bristled. "Well, yes."

"You have been watching too many dystopian films from the Last Age, Himari," Peter teased. "You were looking for a lair, perhaps? Somewhere to wreak havoc on Korah as we wage revolution?" She shot him the evil eye. Alaina yawned. Genevieve rummaged around, moving boxes. "Auntie, shall we show Himari her new abode?"

Genevieve emerged from the boxes triumphant. "Yes." She pressed the button on an old-fashioned baby's toy and a wall opened.

Himari beamed, and Alaina seemed to wake up for the first time since arriving. Beyond the door stood a luxurious fallout shelter from the Last Age. It was enormous.

Peter bowed, and in his best imitation of a major domo, made a grand sweeping gesture. "Sunflower, Miss Pink, welcome to the bunker."

Himari and Alaina exchanged mystified glances. Peter and Genevieve grinned. The space was three years in the making.

Genevieve conducted the tour. "There are five bedrooms, three bathrooms, this large communal living area, and a kitchen through there."

Peter looked around, speculating he might have to hide out here. "We have stocked enough food, water, and provisions for ten people to live in relative comfort for years. It is the reason we bought Auntie this house."

Himari had eyes for one thing, the large bank of computers, servers, and equipment housed in a cold room which had originally been the sixth bedroom. The computer lab dominated one end of the main living area and boasted six adjustable height worktables, dual monitors and three styles of chairs. All new, all top of the line, theirs to wage war and wreak havoc.

After settling in the living room, they turned to Genevieve. The grandmotherly facade fell away, and she said, "At 12:32 am, Metropolitan Police apprehended Davianna ben David, Astrid ben Agnor," her voice caught as she added, "and Prince Josiah ben Eamonn aka Doctor Einar ben Yane."

The room fell silent. Code Black was protocol for Prince Josiah. Peter feared the girls would also be taken. He looked at his watch, 3:47 am.

"At 12:46 am, we received an email into one of our encrypted accounts from an anonymous source. Peter, it is addressed to you, in care of Himari." She paused and looked from face to face, "I am no hacker, but it appears we have the keys to the kingdom."

They got to work.

At 5:42 am, Alaina pushed away from the middle desk she claimed as her own and said, "I have added the extra layers, Peter. No hacker in the world could trace us back here."

Himari snorted, conveying that there was one hacker who could, and she sat in the room.

Alaina rolled her eyes and ignored her friend. "Given what we already had in place for Code Black, the redundancy makes us impenetrable."

Peter nodded. "Do your thing, Himari. Tell me what we have."

He stretched out on the couch while the computer wizards tapped away. There would be only one place Korah would take the captives, the Palace.

By 7:15 am, Himari paled and her hands shook violently.

Alaina was crying tears of joy, making inarticulate sounds of wonder. "Peter, we have everything. Back doors, passwords, logins, access to every site the government operates. Utilities, defense, justice… everything! Oh, my heavens, this could have only come from one person."

Himari groaned and kept typing.

Genevieve monitored several screens and said, "Oh, here they come."

Peter leaned over her shoulder, staring at the camera feeds

of the police station where Josiah, Davianna, and Astrid were being held. Fifteen armored vehicles moved into position. He ran to an empty terminal. "Himari, you grab the five to the west, Alaina, you get the five to the east. I have the ones in the center. I am relatively certain where they are taking them, but we have to make sure."

Dread made his movements rigid. An hour later, the prisoners were delivered to the one place he knew they would go. The last place Peter wanted to put himself was in the vicinity of his father. In the best of circumstances, Korah was a viper, in the worst, a dragon.

Prince d'Or left, off to face the dragon.

Brandy with the King - Davianna

The winter sun cast long shadows down the marble hallway. Flanked by four guards, Davianna looked around, trying to see any avenue of escape. Music played over invisible speakers, old and haunting. She had no idea where the Hotel California was, but she had a sick feeling, she might just be there.

They stopped in front of a big carved door, and one of her stone-faced guards announced, "My Esteemed, Davianna ben David."

King Korah sat in an overstuffed armchair, reading a book, and smoking a fragrant pipe. He looked up as Davianna, dressed in her black tunic and leggings, took several timid steps forward, propelled by a guard.

He laid the book aside and rose to greet her with his hands extended in welcome. He flashed a charming smile and took her trembling hands in his larger, manicured ones. "Welcome, my dear Davianna. Welcome to the People's House." Korah's hazel eyes sparkled, his words seemed sincere, disarming.

Davianna bowed her head and curtsied with her hands still in his. "My Esteemed." She managed to say, just above a whisper.

"Come in, please, and sit down." He guided her inside, saying to a servant, "Shulah, brandy, please."

He led her to a matching chenille chair beside his and asked, "I trust you found your room comfortable, and you were well taken care of today?"

Davianna nodded, scanning the room, looking anywhere but at him. She prowled the luxurious room all day, jumping at every noise. The doors were locked and guarded, the windows sealed, and even if she could have broken one, the fall would have killed her. The guards brought her breakfast and lunch. No one had been cruel, no one questioned her. She did not know where everyone else was, but she knew, without a doubt, she was in more danger than she had ever been in in her life.

The servant placed two crystal snifters on the table between them and departed. The guard said, "My Esteemed, we will be outside."

"Thank you, Reginald," Korah said, then lifting his glass, he motioned for Davianna to do the same.

She hesitated, scared out of her mind, but she had to ride this out. With a trembling hand. she reached for her glass.

Korah stilled her hand with his own. His touch was gentle, warm, and reassuring. "It will be all right, child. You have nothing to fear. You are my guest."

"Th-th-thank you," she stammered and bowed her head looking into the amber liquid. She took a deep breath, gathering her courage. She knew she could not hide; she had to face him. So, she looked up, straight into his intense hazel eyes.

He held her gaze and asked, "Have you ever enjoyed brandy, Davianna?"

"No sir. I mean, no, my Esteemed." She felt a blush spread over her cheeks.

Korah smiled with paternal indulgence, the hint of a dimple visible on his left cheek. "Well, then we will have a lesson, shall we?"

"As you wish, my Esteemed."

Korah raised a golden eyebrow, sprinkled with white and thickening with age. He made her feel like a specimen under a microscope.

"The glass you are holding is designed for brandy. Hold it like this." He cupped the bulb, with the stem resting between his middle and ring fingers. "The heat of your hand will warm the beverage." He watched the liquor in her glass, it quivered. "However, this, we do not rush. It takes patience." He relaxed back into his chair and crossed his Italian loafer over the knee of his tan silk trousers.

Davianna cut a quick sidelong glance at him. He was incredibly handsome, distinguished, with an air of virility and power that beguiled and intimidated by turns. He smelled like pipe tobacco and bergamot, masculine and pleasant. The room was warm, the walls paneled in rich wood, and the shelves stuffed with books. Opposite their beige chenille chairs was an aquarium which cast a soft blue glow. The hum of a pump soothed her ears with its steady bubbling water. Rainbow colored fish flashed among the coral, dazzling the eye with an ever-changing display of exotic creatures. As she watched, a piece of coral animated and speared a small crab. She gasped.

His eyebrow lifted in a half smile. "A cuttlefish. Ingenious, aren't they."

Her eyes widened, feeling like the small crab.

Korah took a lazy pull on his pipe, sweet earth smoke perfumed the air. They continued watching the fish, sitting in silence.

When he spoke, she jumped. "Examine the color in your glass. Good brandy should be deep gold and amber with a pale line along the edge. Do you see it?"

She held up her glass to the shimmering blue light and nodded.

"Good," he said in a hypnotic tone. "Now swirl the liquid around the glass to release the bouquet." He chuckled softly, the sound disarming and light, "Now, this appears the most undignified, but I assure you, it is an essential part. Put your nose in the glass and inhale. Tell me what you smell."

Davianna gave a sidelong glance and ventured a guess, "Vanilla?"

He affirmed with an encouraging smile. "Take a small sip and let it roll over your palate, coating the interior of your mouth before you swallow. Inhale deeply to enjoy the finish. Like this." Korah demonstrated, then raised his glass indicating she should try.

Terrified, the mimic kicked in, and she managed to do as he bade.

His smile did not quite reach his eyes, but he said, "Good, now you know how to properly enjoy a brandy."

They sat in silence, sipping their spirits.

Korah studied her. When she spoke, her voice sounded low and husky, not a girl's but a woman's, although her lack of a southern accent surprised him. She was not stammering, crying, or trying to fill the silence; that intrigued him. He knew quite a lot about Davianna ben David, but the girl herself, was not what he expected. "You have a gymnast look about you. Did you compete?"

Surprise registered on her pretty oval face that was nothing like the sketches. "Yes, my Esteemed, for many years."

"Were you good?" Korah asked matter of fact.

Davianna shrugged. "I had talent," then she laughed, "but I lost my nerve. I took a bad fall."

Korah nodded. "I played polo in my younger years. Did you know that?"

"No, my Esteemed, I did not." A hint of a smile touched the corners of her mouth. "Were you good?"

That amused him. The girl had spunk. "I had the talent," he parroted, "but I too… took a bad fall."

Davianna cradled the glass in both hands and leaned forward, intent on the fish tank, still and quiet.

He was content to watch her, to take the measure of her, his prey. At length he continued. "I no longer ride. The demands put upon me do not allow for it. Yet, sometimes I miss it. Do you feel the same? Do you wish for simpler times, happier times, Davianna ben David?"

Beneath the wariness and fatigue, a hungry innocence lurked, she bobbed her head. He pressed his advantage, tempting her. "A time perhaps to return to Taylorsville, back to your home with the big front porch?"

Davianna wet her lips.

He smiled. "It was nice then."

Davianna blinked and nodded imperceptibly.

"But it does not have to be there, you can go wherever you want." Korah gestured with an open hand. "Something like this might be more to your own preference? I can give you whatever you want, you and your mother. You can even take your friend Astrid with you."

"Are they here?" Davianna's calm veneer slipped.

"Astrid is our guest. Your mother is at her residence," Korah reassured her.

"May I see Astrid, my Esteemed?"

"Of course." Korah smiled and stood, offering his hands for her to rise. The innocent hunger lurking behind her eyes fed the monster inside him. He was going to enjoy devouring her. She placed her hands in his.

The beast struck.

He twisted her wrists backward and screamed in her face. "Give me the device, you little bitch!"

Davianna cried out, pain shooting up her arms. She tried to wrench free, but he held her in a vice grip.

"Tell me where it is!" His pupils elongated, snakelike. They were nose to nose. She smelled the tobacco and brandy; he spit when he yelled.

Then as abruptly as he attacked, he released her. His face softened. With a gentle manicured finger, he brushed her hair out of her eye, patted her wrist, and sat down.

"I am sorry about that. My temper sometimes gets away from me." He rubbed his temple and closed his eyes, looking weary. "You see, the pressures of this kingdom are so great, it overwhelms me." Korah gave her an apologetic smile. "I am usually a nice man. I have been nice to you, have I not?"

Davianna blinked and rubbed her wrists. "Well, um, yes?"

Korah smiled in pure diabolical manipulation. "I want to continue to be nice. Do you want that, Davianna?"

She swallowed audibly. "Yes."

The look in his eyes held such cold menace that her blood turned to ice. He whispered behind bared teeth, "Then give it to me."

Davianna's mind raced, and she resisted the urge to touch the left pocket of her tunic. Her mind ran over the possibilities. All day she had wondered, "How did the police not discover it when they searched me? They took my clothes, my weapons, my bag. How did they miss the device in the hidden pocket?"

Staring into the viperous eyes of King Korah ben Adam, she realized the truth. When the device was in her pocket, it was protected by Gune power. She drew strength from that small hope. Then with perfect earnestness, she delivered the line she and Astrid agreed they would say if they were ever caught. "I do not have it, my Esteemed. It was taken from me in London, by a Gune."

Caged Lion - Josiah

Josiah was thirsty. He was also enraged. He strained against the manacles and knew with inhuman certainty these fetters also bound his father. He would never forget the sight of those bruised wrists. These were the instruments, and to-night their royal blood mingled.

The utter blackness of his cell was disorienting, the stench of sulfur disgusting and pervasive. His doctor's brain understood that sulfur was the one odor the human nose could not adapt to, forever inescapable and vile. The smell of Hell, in his father's home. This is where the rebellion was born. This noxious hole in the ground was the nexus for the undoing of the entire world, Korah the catalyst.

The wicked bastard came down to taunt him. Josiah refused to speak, falling back on his military training. He wondered how he ever thought Korah's smile kind? How did his uncle ever appear anything other than who he was, Cain, a defiant, self-serving rebel, who clothed himself in genteel solicitude and duty, but was nothing more than a cursed, eternally damned, fratricidal lunatic.

Josiah vowed, unlike his father, he would escape. Korah had not killed him outright, and Mossad knew where he was. However, a direct assault on the Palace was a declaration of war, and Josiah, who waited on the Iron King for rescue once before, was not inclined to place much hope in that quarter. But somehow, he would find a way out of here.

He was the only one down here. He did not know where Korah held the girls. Bile rose in the back of his throat, thinking of Davianna in Korah's clutches, even Astrid with her flashing blue eyes that hated him. What would become of them if he could not break free?

His mind followed his body down the moldy steps into the dungeon. He steeled himself against the terror, lest he go mad, alone in this pit of Hell.

Examination - Astrid

Astrid was thankful for the blindfold because it blocked most of the horrible light they were shining on her. For the first time in her entire life, she concentrated on the ice pick, accustomed to its familiar pain. It was preferable to what was happening to her.

She could not move, strapped naked to an examination table with her feet in stirrups. Hands touched her everywhere, examining, lifting her breasts, talking in low voices, then probing her. She wanted to die of humiliation and fear. She willed the ice pick to kill her. Then came the oil, they were rubbing her with oil, stroking and caressing and oh,

God... chanting.

She wanted to scream but terror strangled her vocal cords, and she could not make a sound.

Then it stopped, and she heard them all leave.

They left her exposed, under the lights. Her breathing became labored, the pain in her head so great she could hear nothing except the thundering of her heart. She realized she was not alone when a shadow fell over the blindfold.

A hand caressed her cheek. She felt a smooth finger slide under the fabric and pull it free. The light blinded her, and she gasped in agony, trying to turn her head away. The fingers turned cruel, grabbing her jaw, and turning her face.

"Open your eyes, my sweet, if you want to live another moment."

She believed him. So, Astrid ben Agnor met the hazel eyes of a devil. He should have been ugly, hideous, with horns and a red face, but he was not. Korah ben Adam looked like a beautiful angel with golden hair streaked with silver and snow.

His face paled, and he pulled his hand away as if she burned him. Then his gaze swept her with incredulous wonder, and he threw back his head and laughed. "Oh Alexa, you have returned." Korah murmured to the ceiling. "How beautiful you still are, and what a wonderful way to finally bring our Peter to heel." He lowered his gaze and trailed a delicate finger over her face in reverence. "You are a gift."

When the hooded man returned, he gave her an injection, and everything stopped hurting. She stopped caring that she was naked and bound. Everything faded to black.

December 26 - 31, 999 ME

Wicked Game - Davianna

Davianna was rarely allowed out of Korah's sight, rarely free of his ubiquitous presence. At first, he treated her with paternal courtesy, and on occasion fed her. He taught her things and spoke of his reign, his dreams for Alanthia. They discussed Alanthia's journey from technological darkness to light. He was passionate. He was charming.

Then, out of nowhere, he struck like a viper.

Other times, he painted a picture of what her life could be like if she would just give him what he wanted. A beautiful home with servants, a position in Alanthian society, money, all of it, right at her fingertips. He would give her anything she wanted.

Then he hurt her.

He rarely let her sleep. Sometimes she just dozed off. She tripped when they were in his stables, and the ground felt so nice she just laid there and fell asleep. He took her riding, and the easy gait of the horse lulled her to sleep in his arms. Eating dinner, she face-planted in her pasta. She became so disoriented that he finally let her nap.

But when she was alone, her body's relentless adrenal response refused to stop. Her heart kept hammering, her inside shook. Her thoughts grew erratic. Overwhelmed with fear and exhaustion she could not make her brain reason. She could not plan.

Korah became her whole world.

She actually liked him when he was kind and engaging. Her rational mind knew her growing affection for him was illogical, a product of her captivity. After months of running, hiding, and days without sleep, the King was breaking her.

Korah was quite charming when he chose to be. He brought her presents, made her laugh. They shared stories. They tried each other's favorite food.

Then he snapped.

She was seconds from dying, but then the mean king went away.

He broke her heart. He seemed sad when he did it; she could tell. Astrid left without saying goodbye. "I am sorry, my dear. She said she did not want to see you, that you betrayed her, and you were no longer her friend."

Davianna broke down. Korah held her as she cried. He let her watch from the window as Astrid left on the arm of one of the guards, Reginald. Astrid got in the big black car and drove away without a backward glance.

Tears coursed down Davianna's face. She could not believe it. After everything they had been through, Astrid left without saying goodbye. It was Guan... his kiss. She had lost her best friend over a would-be rapist's kiss. Davianna felt like she was falling off a cliff.

Korah caught her as her knees gave way. Lifting her chin, he whispered, "I will not hurt her. She will be safe, on one condition."

Days with him convinced her that Korah had the power to do anything he wanted. "What condition?"

He cupped her cheek, and she could not tell if he was the good king or the mean one, but he held her eyes and said tenderly, "Stay here, my dear. Do not try to leave." Then he leaned in and whispered in her ear, "If you do, I will kill her."

A panting sob caught in her throat.

He wrapped his arms around her and hugged. He was so strong, and he smelled nice. Where was she going to go, anyway? She had no home. Now that Astrid was gone, she had nobody. She rested her cheek against his heart and could feel it pounding. "With you? You want me to stay with you?"

He leaned back, looking slightly chagrined, and shrugged. "It is your choice."

That was when things got very confusing.

The Dark Prince haunted her nightmares. She imagined him in a dungeon, chained, and beaten. Davianna awoke sobbing. But Korah was there, and he assured her it was just a bad dream.

"You are overtired. No one else is in the Palace. You should sleep. Honestly, Davianna you should take better care of yourself."

"I'm sorry. You're right."

"I know I am, my dear. I'll take care of you and watch

while you sleep." He pulled the covers over her. "If you have another nightmare, I'll wake you."

Her eyes drooped, and she looked down at his hand, holding hers. "You promise?"

"I always keep my promises, Davianna." As she dozed, she thought she heard him add, "And I always get what I want."

She slept for a little while then, and he watched over her.

He woke her up when she had another nightmare. "Come, you need food. Look at how thin you have gotten."

She looked down at her hand; she had shrunk. "I should eat better, shouldn't I?"

He chuckled. "I enjoy having you for dinner."

After dinner, he asked, "Do you like music?"

She answered honestly, it took too much effort to lie. "Yes."

"Good, come with me." He rose and offered his hand.

She walked with him to an unfamiliar part of the Palace. Anytime he took her to a new place she was afraid. She never knew what waited for her, and some of the rooms were not nice. She breathed a sigh of relief when he opened the door. It was only his music room.

They took turns selecting the songs.

He teased her because her taste was quite different from his. "You perhaps have your own music, Davianna?"

They swayed together. She felt the weight of the device in her pocket. She almost gave it to him, but something stopped her, the last piece of herself, or perhaps something beyond herself. Instead, she rested her arms over his shoulders and smiled dreamily. "I like this song."

Korah smiled back. "It is a wicked game, my dear."

They kept dancing.

On the sixth day, she realized she loved him.

He was a good King, so beautiful and kind. He sacrificed everything for Alanthia, indeed he brought the kingdom out of the Dark Ages and into the light. The evidence was everywhere: cars, planes, television, the internet. Of course, he should have the device she carried, it held secrets that would ensure the security and peace of this great land, the land of her birth, the land she loved.

Over breakfast, on December 31st, she rose from her chair and fell at his feet. "My Esteemed, as your loyal and humble servant, I am honored beyond measure that you would deign to invite me to the gala tonight."

There were tears in her eyes. "That the king would insist I accompany him as his special guest is an honor well above my station. Tonight, I shall show my gratitude, with my token, to my kingdom and to my king." She rose from the floor and walked from the room, like the queen he promised to make her.

Too Late? - Peter

It was a gamble, waiting until the last minute. Peter knew it, but he had to wait. The timing, everything hinged on the timing. They had one shot, one chance. Himari, Alaina, and everyone worked around the clock, adjusting the plan.

Peter lived in agony, using every ounce of control he could summon to play his role, Prince d'Or. The only saving grace during the interminable week was that for the first time in almost fifteen years, the Palace was free of the monster's malignant presence. But his absence illuminated the other evil stalking the hallways, his father.

Unleashed and unfettered, the single-minded determination of Korah was horrifying to witness. He ruthlessly and systematically psychologically raped Davianna ben David. That innocent, brave girl, who escaped and eluded the pursuit of the world for months, fell prey to Korah in six days, and Peter could do nothing to stop it.

Josiah fared better in the dungeon. His rage burned hot, keeping him alive. Jarrod ministered to him in secret, doctored his wounds. and told him of the plans—tonight.

Astrid, the cat eyed firebrand, was held in a sealed off wing, the one Peter had not entered for thirteen years. Korah staged a departure for her. It fooled the servants. It fooled Davianna. Astrid was drugged. He used binoculars to watch her as they ushered her into the car. He knew that dazed look. He knew what they were doing to her. He just hoped she would survive it.

December 31, 999 ME

My Burden is Light - Davianna

Davianna dismissed the lady's maid. "I will dress myself, thank you."

"Are you certain?" The maid bobbed a curtsy, eager to please. "You do look pretty."

"Thank you, that will be all." When the door closed, Davianna tilted her head and looked in the mirror, staring at a stranger. Her hair, longer than it had been in months, curled in pretty waves around her face. It was thick and shining with an auburn cast in the warm light. She smoothed her brow. The maid had known her business, the eyeshadows, pink blush, and lip gloss highlighted her features. She looked beautiful.

An elegant white gown lay on the bed behind her, diaphanous and lovely, with gold thread woven through the glimmering silk. She stroked it in wonder, the king's gift. She was his treasure, his special one. He loved her.

Then she noticed the tiny hooks running up the back of the dress and panicked. "Why did I dismiss the maid?" She dug her fingers into her hair, squeezing her head. "Put it on."

But she could not. With trembling hands, she pulled on her Gune Black, but the effort made her dizzy. Disoriented, she collapsed to the floor, shaking.

She felt him enter. "No, no," she said into the rug.

She would be punished horribly now. She was not ready.

She was supposed to be ready. Why could she not dress? She did not weep, it would ruin her makeup, and then he would hurt her. He hurt her so much.

When he spoke, her mind did not register it, would not believe, could not hope.

"Davianna?" The voice was cracked and raw.

She did not turn. "No, you left me. You are not real."

Josiah fell at her side, afraid to touch her, lest she shatter into a thousand pieces. "Nay, little one, I would not leave you nor forsake you. Thou art not alone."

"You left me," she sobbed. "You all left me. Daddy, Momma, Astrid, all of you abandoned me… everyone. Only he loves me now."

Rage and pain contorted Josiah's features. He clenched a fist over his face to block out the huddled mass before him. He struggled for control, trying to hide his anguish. He held his bloodied wrist in front of her face. "Look at my hand, I have struggled to get free. My feet have been bound, lest I would have flown to you. My voice is raw from calling out. Davianna, I did not leave you."

Davianna blinked and looked at his bloodied and bruised wrist. Her gaze traveled up his arms, and she met his red-rimmed eyes. Tears fell over his black lashes. She covered her face, not trusting her vision. "No, I am alone."

Josiah spoke the words he heard his father recite a hundred times, "The true King calls to thee, 'Come to me, all who labor and are heavy laden, and I will give you rest. Take my yoke upon you and learn from me. For I am gentle and lowly in heart, and you will find rest for your souls. My yoke is easy, and my burden is light.'"

The glass wall around her shattered. Her Father's words penetrated the darkness. Like a drowning person going down for the last time, Davianna stretched out a hand, and Josiah caught her.

Alexa's Chamber - Peter

The dark passageway Peter traversed led to his personal version of hell. He swore he would never return, and he had not, until tonight. It had been years since he had been in this passage, and as he ducked under a beam, he realized he was much taller now. Memories assailed him, a hundred times he had walked this narrow hall to his mother's room. But the last time... he saw something so terrible that he never let his mind dwell on it.

He was a witness. The monster held him mute and paralyzed, while his father beat his mother to death in this chamber.

The one room in the Palace that was his haven, the only safe place, was forever destroyed. The dungeon held no power over him compared to this room. Yet, that is where they held her and where he must go.

When the wainscoting opened, she sat at her dressing table, like she always did. The dark circles under her eyes, that she always thought he did not notice, were still there. The room remained as it had been. The aching familiarity overwhelmed him, and he was transported back in time. He was five and could run across the room and hug her, his mother.

When she turned, the illusion shattered. Instead of love, the black-clad figure glared hatred and a desperation he knew all too well.

"I know what they have done to you," Peter said in a low voice. "They will come in a few minutes and give you another shot. It will stop hurting, but you will die." He took two steps forward and held out his hand. "Or you can fight them, you can come with me, and get the hell out of here. Then, we make them pay."

He watched it, the power of addiction already upon her, creating war between mind and body. Her eyes darted. Her breathing became rapid. She was sweating and shaking, convulsively clenching her fists at her sides, at war.

"You can do this," Peter urged.

Then he saw what he hoped for, the girl who drew the attention of the Greek Captain and eluded the pursuit of the whole world for months, Astrid ben Agnor fought back.

Escape

Josiah held Davianna by the shoulders. "You must be silent. It is dark and narrow through these passageways. There are people within inches of where we will travel. The house is full tonight."

She shook with such violence he feared she would collapse. He considered throwing her over his shoulder and carrying her out, but he was despicably weak. "Are you ready?"

Her mouth opened and closed, but she made no sounds.

"Remember Orleans?"

She looked at him, confused, blinking her eyes. She shook her head, violent tremors wracking her body. He wanted to hold her until it passed, but they did not have time. Davianna beat at her left side and stuttered, "This... this... feels more like C-Calais... get me out of here."

She dug her painted nails into his arm and held on for dear life.

"When was your last shot?" Peter whispered low and urgent.

Astrid bit her lip and looked away.

"Tell me! We do not have much time, and I do not need you cramping and shitting, or having a fucking seizure while we are running through these passageways."

Astrid wiped her running nose and pulled at her sleeve. "I don't know, maybe eight or nine hours."

Peter pulled a pill from his pocket. "Here, hold this under your tongue. It will help."

Rage and tears blazed out of her blue eyes as she reached for the pill. She hated herself and him. The moment she held it under her tongue, she saw he was right, relief. "Davianna?"

Her voice came out hoarse and strangled.

"We have her. Be quiet." Peter took her hand. "Let's go."

Peter's heart thundered as he raced through the passageways. For her, he held a flashlight, but he could run these places blind. They kept him alive in this house. More than once, he fled his father's rage, escaping to safety through the darkness. Prince Peter ben Korah knew the secret to hiding in shadows.

He saw the outlines of Josiah and Davianna ahead at the rendezvous point. The girls fell into each other's arms, weeping. Josiah moved in front of them, his arms on his hips, feet spread wide, looking belligerent. The ferocious glare he shot Peter was almost comical.

Peter quirked a golden eyebrow. "Cousin."

This was his world, his house, his plan. He had nearly died a hundred times getting to this moment. Indeed, the last time they saw each other was in these passageways.

Remembrance raced through the dark tunnels and hit them both. Survival, terror, grief, but something else… a bond. One of blood, a vow. They would not allow the evil that ruled here to destroy them. Josiah would come back, and one day, they would fight.

Peter swallowed a sudden lump in his throat. "If you want to live, follow me."

Josiah's nose flared. "Dammit, Peter, it's good to see you."

The two cousins embraced.

When they broke apart, Peter knuckled a tear from his eye. "Fifteen years and I am still pulling you out of trouble."

Josiah wiped his own eyes. Despite his vow to escape, there were times in the dungeon when he knew he was going to die. Gratitude welled in his heart, and he asked, "You got a plan, Prince d'Or?"

Peter smiled with immense satisfaction. "One I have been working on since the last time I saw you, Cousin. Let's roll."

At the end of the tunnel, assorted gear and escape vehicles were staged for every contingency. Peter threw gear bags to each of them, Astrid and Davianna gasped in amazement as their Gune bags flew into their hands. Power surged through Davianna when she strapped on her gauntlets and her knives, Astrid and Josiah did the same.

Peter opened the doors to a sleek black sports car. "Get in."

Astrid and Davianna stumbled and fell over each other climbing in. Josiah took the front, with Peter behind the wheel. Peter placed a hand on the screen, selected three options from the menu.

Himari's voice came through the speakers. "Falcon, you have an all clear in thirty-two seconds."

The cavern was dark except for the red numbers on the dash. Four pounding hearts, four heaving chests, four souls, and four lives hung in the balance as they watched the count down. With fourteen seconds left, Himari shattered the silence. "Falcon, GO!"

Davianna jumped so hard her hand hit Astrid's face. Josiah rolled down the window, his huge assault rifle poised and ready to annihilate anyone who came near. Peter floored the accelerator and shot out of the cavern like Marduk was on his tail. They careened onto the road, tires squealing. Davianna sobbed a prayer as Astrid clung to her.

"Falcon, head east 3.2 miles. They have sounded the alarm and are locking down the perimeter."

Peter screamed into the speaker, "Sunflower, you jam that damn signal now. Send them the false report. Decoy in place, confirm!"

Thirty interminable seconds passed before Alaina's voice came over the speaker, "Falcon, decoy deployed, signals jammed. They are diverting."

Peter let out a long breath. "Pink, confirm Route 3 is viable."

A third voice came over the speaker, to Davianna it sounded like someone's grandmother, "Falcon, confirm Route 3 viable. Honey, you're off the grid."

Peter pulled the wheel hard, his face in full concentration. "G, confirm off the grid?"

An incredulous laugh came from the underground bunker, and in an awestruck whisper she said, "You've got an angel, Falcon. We are going silent. Run, boys, I love you."

The purr of the engine and the rumble of the asphalt filled the silent car. "Was that... was that Auntie G.?" Josiah asked in a strangled voice.

Peter smiled with great affection. "Who else?"

Josiah ran his hands through his hair. "Well, I'll be damned."

Peter shot him a sideways glance; all traces of humor gone. "Not if I can help it."

Not One Angel

There was not one angel guarding the escaping car but one thousand. Millions swarmed the planet. Every elohim not bound by the Black Key guarded the Earth that night. Sky watchers went berserk as comets raced across the sky and flashing stars lit the heavens in a stunning display of celestial fireworks.

At the stroke of midnight, the Archangel Michael, made the long descent into the bottomless pit with a great iron key, his mission foreordained three thousand years before. The stench of sulfur billowed out of the pit, noxious and foul.

Heavy chains rattled and a mighty beast roared. "Release me!"

Michael's wings sounded like crashing thunder. He loomed over the bound Lucifer and taunted, "Thou art brought down to Sheol, to the far reaches of the pit. Those who see thee will stare at thee and ponder: 'Is this the man who made the earth tremble, who shook kingdoms?'"

Lucifer hissed, "I am no man, and I've no inclination to banter with you." He thrust forth his hands and was taken aback at the difference in their size. He resolutely refused to flinch or comment. The irons fell away with a clattering thud.

He pumped his wings and escaped the cursed hole. As he shot forth, a trail of black smoke in his wake, he shouted with triumph.

The triumph was short-lived. He flew into a gauntlet of a thousand enemies who met him without reverence, without fear. He evaded and feinted, outmaneuvered and sought escape in genuine terror. He was alone, his mighty companions sealed and hidden. The expediency of hiding became glaringly apparent when the phalanx of Michael, Gabriel, Uriel, and Raphael descended upon him. He was not foolish enough to fight the entire Host of Heaven alone.

With a powerful thrust of his wings, he shot into orbit, into the silence of the air. He hovered above the crowned jewel of the universe, Earth. He flew over, finding it changed, different. The land masses had shifted, closer together in a manner reminiscent of pre-flood Earth.

To his shock, he saw that it was truly dark, except for two large sections of North America. He laughed at the irony of it, leave it to those people to have light when the rest of the world sat in darkness. The great cities shone like beacons, but one, glowed like a diamond against the jet, San Francisco. Oh, he liked that place. He flew lower, feeding off the energy from it.

As he began his descent, a colossal pulse hit the Earth; electronics blinked, sputtered, cycled, then crashed. The Earth went dark.

Lucifer was released—on parole.

Part 10 - The Cabin

January 1, 1000 ME

Walking Wounded

There was comfort in the running, familiar. Change directions, change vehicles, run!

Astrid was sick, sweating and shaking, her nose and eyes running a steady stream. She cramped and dry heaved but would not let Davianna or Josiah touch her, though they both tried. When Davianna pressed, Astrid screamed, "Leave me alone!"

Davianna retreated to the corner of the backseat, huddled into herself, and did not say another word.

Josiah shot a questioning look to Peter, whose grim expression confirmed what the symptoms told him two hours before, drug withdrawal.

Six hours after they escaped, they pulled into a large warehouse. In one of the bays, sat an ambulance. The two men exited the car. Peter said to Josiah, "We have to take care of Astrid, Doc. It is about to get bad."

Josiah looked around, noting a small office and a restroom. "Let me get Davianna settled first. She's in shock."

Josiah expected an argument, instead Peter said, "There is a medical bag in the truck and more meds in the ambulance. Bloody hell, what a night."

Peter moved around the side to try to coax Astrid from the back seat. Josiah eased Davianna out of the car. "Come on. You can go to the restroom and then get some sleep. I am going to give Astrid some fluids and medicine to help her feel better."

Davianna complied, moving as if she were in a trance. For days she had done as she was told, her survival depended on it. Exiting the bathroom, she stumbled over her own feet, and Josiah caught her around the shoulders. Making incoherent protests, she tried to go back for Astrid.

Josiah steered her toward the office. "I know you want to help. I know you want to sit with her, but you need to rest. Tomorrow it will be much better. I promise."

He eased her onto the small bed and felt her shaking. He took her pulse, it was racing. Reaching in the medical bag, he retrieved a light and checked her pupils. They were huge. "Davianna, you are having a massive stress reaction. Your body is on overload, but I assure you, we are safe now."

"My heart won't stop pounding." Silent for two hours, her voice cracked. "I keep seeing Korah's face, keep hearing his voice." Her expression glazed over, becoming bewildered. "I am supposed to be at a gala, aren't I?"

Josiah adopted a clinical tone, lifting her legs onto the bed. "No, that is all over. You have not slept, and that can be confusing, but everything is going to be okay." He pulled the blanket over her. She was shaking violently.

Astrid screamed.

Davianna sat bolt upright. "What's happening? She's dying, isn't she?" She craned her head and saw Peter struggling with Astrid. "What is he doing to her?" Abject terror overtook her, and she started to fight. "He's here! Look, Korah is here. He has her!"

Josiah gripped her arms. He had not wanted to forcibly

sedate her, but he did. She gawked at him, looking hurt and betrayed. He eased her down. "It's okay, Davianna. You will sleep now."

Heaving himself off the bed, he rushed to help Peter.

"Come on, Red. Get out of the car."

"If you touch me, I will kill you."

"You could not kill a bug right now." He lifted her to a sitting position. "Do your bones hurt?"

Astrid wiped her nose with the back of her hand. "Among other things."

"Come on. I have the medicine you need in the ambulance."

She dropped her hands to her lap, turning in extreme aggravation. "Who the fuck are you?"

Peter shot her a quizzical glance. He could not remember the last time, if ever, he had been asked that question. "Hi, my name is Peter, and I am a recovering heroin addict."

Astrid gave him a one-eyed glare. "Is that what they were giving me?"

"That and more," Peter answered gravely and helped her out of the car. He caught her as she staggered and steered her toward the bathroom. Davianna and Josiah were in the small office, and Peter confided, "They did it to me once. I lived through it. You will, too."

Astrid's head fell back, and she stared up at him. The overhead lights blinded her, when she tried to focus on his face, all she could see was that left dimple and his golden hair. She wrenched away and came up swinging. "You did this to me! You were there!"

Peter blocked the blow, preventing her from stabbing him. He had forgotten her weapons, stupid mistake. He held her wrist as the knife convulsed above their heads with her pitting her killing rage against his superior strength. "No, no, sweetheart, not me."

"It was you. It was you! I saw you!" Astrid accused him

through gritted teeth, her eyes wild. "You kept calling me Alexa. You kept touching me and telling me I was going to be a gift for your son. I am nobody's fucking gift! Do you hear me? I am not a gift—"

Astrid collapsed in Peter's arms as her knife clattered to the cement floor.

Josiah stepped back and capped the syringe.

"Oh, bloody hell, Red," Peter croaked as he eased her to the floor, cradling her as they went down.

When Peter looked up, Josiah saw the little boy he had forgotten, a bewildered, terrified expression frozen on his face.

He kept calling me Alexa. Astrid's accusation seemed to echo in the empty warehouse.

Josiah fell to his knees. Peter's hand trembled as he brushed a curl from Astrid's eye. Josiah gasped. "Oh, saints in heaven, Peter. She is Aunt Alexa's twin."

Peter stroked Astrid's cheek. "I know." Deep, racking sobs shook his body. He pulled the sleeping girl to his chest and held her close.

Shame! Wretched and bitter, shame washed over Josiah.

For fifteen years, if he spared a thought for his cousin it was contempt, jealousy, or anger. Believing Peter had thrown his lot in with Korah, he became the enemy, an obstacle to be overcome, a rival to defeat. Even if Korah died, Josiah would have to fight for his throne. Alanthians loved Peter. They thought Josiah was a madman, a murderer, a delusional, disturbed Prince. Given the chance, they would choose Peter over Josiah. Given the chance, they had chosen Korah. It was the reason he had not made his move, why he bided his time and waited for the Iron King. But in the waiting, his anger grew until it consumed him. Every news report, every publicity picture, every fawning article about Prince d'Or fueled his rage.

Until Jarrod snuck into his cell, he believed Peter had become as twisted as Korah. The hushed whispers of the valet shattered his misperceptions. His cousin was not his enemy, it shocked him. Watching Peter weep over the girl, looking at the vehicles, the ambulance, reviewing their escape, the truth hit him. He had willfully chosen to overlook and refused to consider the possibility that Peter was still his ally.

He believed their parting words were long forgotten, sacrificed on the altar of the Alanthian throne, given up for ambition and power. Like a ghost rising from the grave, they came back to haunt him. 'This will not stand, Josiah. My mother and I will hold the kingdom until you return. Be careful. We will be here when you get back.'

But Alexa was gone, years in the grave. He never imagined Peter was still fighting.

A flash of Korah's deranged face came to mind. Despite his resolve, Josiah had looked into his uncle's eyes and saw the maniacal madman. Evil festered in him, becoming a malignant cancer. It was palpable, evidentiary. Korah wore his wickedness like a mantle.

And Josiah had left Peter to live under the authority of that twisted bastard. He was Korah's son, his prey, an easy victim. Prince d'Or had survived, but the broken man weeping at his feet, hugging a facsimile of his dead mother must have paid a price. Josiah began to realize how high it had been.

He felt like a worm, the lowest of the low. Every tear was a blow to his honor, every wretched groan an indictment. His cousin put him to shame.

Josiah wrapped his arms around the prostrate figures and held on.

January 3, 1000 ME

Three Days Later

Davianna slept forty-eight hours straight. She woke up, used the restroom, drank a glass of water, and slept another twenty-four. Her dreams were violent and frightening. Several times she woke to find Josiah holding her, and she fell back to sleep.

Astrid was in for a much harder time, but Peter never left her side. She railed at him, he let her. She cursed him, calling him every vile name she could conjure. He critiqued her style and offered suggestions and improvements. She cried. He wiped away her tears and assured her it would be over soon. She begged him for a fix. He told her funny stories.

On the morning of the third day, he opened his eyes and found her staring at him, lucid. "What are you looking at?" he grunted, his voice raspy with sleep.

"You are so freaking beautiful it's a crime." Astrid flipped over and showed him her lovely little backside.

"It is not a crime," Peter disagreed, stretching his long lean body on the ambulance cot.

"You don't even deny it," Astrid said to the wall.

Peter yawned. "I have many things to answer for, Red, being pretty is not one of them."

She snorted. "Is there coffee?"

"There is if you make it. How about you take care of that this morning? You wait on me, while I laze about in this luxurious bed."

"Show me where it is."

He closed his eyes and said, "Well, that would defeat the purpose, would it not?" He heard her get out of bed, felt her lean over him.

"Thank you," she whispered in his ear and kissed his cheek. "I'll make the coffee."

Davianna snuggled into the warm body pressed behind her, big, strong, and male. She knew the minute he came awake because he tensed and lifted his arm away.

Josiah struggled to sit up, pressed between the wall and her backside. He groaned and tried to shift. His morning cock had no morals. God help him, she had wiggled against him, and he wanted her to do it again. He was slightly embarrassed, sore, and beat-up, but thoroughly aroused.

She felt like herself, or at least a version of herself, one shattered into a thousand pieces then hastily puzzled back together with cheap glue, but herself. Then the memories flooded back, and she covered her face. "I went crazy."

"You did not go crazy," Josiah said through a jaw popping yawn, taking shelter in a professional tone. "You suffered a severe psychological trauma. There is a difference."

"I thought I was going to become the queen," Davianna groaned.

"Hey, look at me," Josiah coaxed.

Davianna covered her head with a pillow. "No."

Instead of forcing her to do anything, he burrowed under the pillow. When he spoke, his breath tickled her ear. "Listen to me, this is not your fault. You were a victim of psychological torture, like a prisoner of war. You did nothing wrong. You survived, you escaped, and you are okay."

"Josiah," Davianna asked in a tiny whisper, "is that your real name?"

He draped an arm over her belly and told her the truth. "Yes."

"Did I see…" She began to tremble again. "Did he make me watch you being tortured?"

"I'm sorry," he soothed. "Davianna, I am okay. It's over."

"He… he hit you."

She looked up with eyes so frightened he wanted to drive back to the New City and kill Korah. "Yes, but I am okay."

"He was going to kill you." She nodded quickly as the truth registered. "He was going to kill me." Out of habit, her hand skimmed over her left pocket, feeling the familiar shape. Fear sent a bolt of lightning through her body. She threw off the blanket and rolled on top of him. Grabbing his face with both hands, she said, "You kill me before you let him take me again. Promise me!"

He grunted as she jostled his cracked ribs, but managed to say, "He is never going to touch you again. I promise that. I swear on my life, Davianna. He will never lay a finger on you again."

"He won't stop. He won't. I still have it!"

"You still have it? How?" He could see the panic building in her eyes.

"They can't see it unless I give it to them. Do you feel it?"

She moved his hand to her left side, he felt curves and nothing more. Josiah blinked in surprise. "No, I thought surely you handed it over."

Davianna's laugh held an edge of hysteria. "I was going to, at least a dozen times, something stopped me."

"Thou art not alone."

She fell onto his chest, still weak, still exhausted, still scared. "Don't leave me, Josiah. Take me to the Iron King. Only he can save me."

He ignored the stabbing pain in his ribs and carefully wrapped his arms around her. "That is what I have been trying to do."

January 4, 1000 ME

Who's Driving?

The news that Davianna still carried the device increased the urgency to put as much distance between themselves and Korah as possible. Peter explained they were headed to a safe house to lie low for a couple of days, then they would change vehicles and continue. At the mention of vehicles, their first big argument erupted over the simple question, 'Who's driving?'

Astrid concluded that Peter was as stubborn as he was gorgeous as their heated words reverberated off the high ceiling of the warehouse. She insisted Peter teach them to drive, arguing that the safety of the group depended on it.

Peter and Josiah agreed the idea had merit, in theory, but neither wanted to put their lives on the line with a brand-new driver behind the wheel. Both men agreed they needed more distance between themselves and the New City before even attempting it.

Davianna countered that it should be sooner rather than later, especially if the danger was high, the likelihood of them being required to drive became more pressing.

Peter put an end to the discussion with brutal, blunt honesty. "Look, Red, you are still shaking from withdrawals, and your reflexes are not going to be worth a shit for at least a month." He gave her an apologetic shrug and turned to Davianna. "Sparrow, you are jumping at shadows. I dropped my lighter an hour ago, and you nearly leapt out of your boots." He looked Josiah up and down. "You learned to drive a car, what, three weeks ago?"

Everyone got quiet.

"I, conversely, have been racing cars since the first ones rolled off the assembly line. I am arguably one of the best drivers in the world, and I am certainly the best driver in this motley crew." He cleared his throat and drew himself up in absolute regal authority, "Besides, it is my bloody car. So, get in. The lot of you are making my head hurt."

Davianna and Astrid looked at each other, amused with feigned indignation mirrored in their lively eyes. "My bloody car," Davianna mimicked.

Astrid stuck her nose in the air. "And we lot are making his head hurt."

They slipped into the back seat of the large SUV, laughing.

Josiah snorted at Peter's thunderstruck expression. He surmised no one had ever mocked him to his face and recognized offended royal dignity when he saw it. "Welcome to the outside world, Prince." He slid into the passenger seat with a snicker, holding a large assault rifle across his lap.

Peter threw up his hands in exasperation, then drove them to a remote mountain cabin, their second stop on a long trek across the globe.

Camp Eiran Recap

Later that afternoon, Josiah approached Astrid as she exited her room. "May I speak with you privately?"

Astrid became wary but motioned him inside.

The muscles in his jaw were working, and his grave expression did not bode well. He stood erect just inside the door, in what she recognized as his full military mode. "Please, sit down." He gestured to the chair in the corner. "I have something to tell you."

Dread flooded Astrid's gut, but outwardly she appeared calm. "Okay."

He cleared his throat and assumed a clinical tone. "On April 9th, I arrived at Camp Eiran. As you know, this was twelve days after the attack. My mission was, and is, to recover Davianna and escort her safely to the Golden City. When I arrived at the camp, there were no survivors. To ascertain if Davianna was among the dead, I conducted an intensive investigation."

Astrid's insides began to shake. She knew what he was going to say, and she did not want to hear it. If she did not know, there was a chance, ever so slim, that one day she would be walking down the street and find her mother. If he kept talking, that dream, that hope, would die and Emaline truly with it.

"I'm sorry, Astrid, your mother and stepfather were among the dead. I thought you would want to know."

She closed her eyes, hiding the pain, and gripping the arms of the chair so har her knuckles turned white. Fresh grief washed over her, crushing her. Through strangled vocal cords she croaked, "Thank you. Can you please leave now?"

"Of course. Please let me know if I can do anything." He pulled the door shut softly behind him.

Astrid covered the sobs with her hands, keeping them silent, keeping them quiet, refusing to lose control. But as bad as the wracking grief was, the sudden and intense hunger for the oblivion was even worse.

Royal Wedding Shocker

"Good evening. I am Ebenezer ben James of News 1, bringing you breaking news.

"We take you now to the New City Palace, where we expect to have confirmation that the wedding between Princess Keyseelough and Prince Peter has been canceled. The union, long speculated to be ill-suited for the pair, is scheduled to take place on January 10th."

A picture of the couple glaring at one another flashed on the screen.

The Alanthian Secretary of State, flanked by the Egyptian foreign minister, moved to the podium. "The kingdoms of Alanthia and Egypt have always been close allies and friends. To strengthen our ties, the betrothal of Prince Peter ben Korah and Princess Keyseelough ben Mubarak was negotiated three years ago. But over the course of their betrothal, it became apparent that the two were not well suited."

Cameras flashed; reporters shouted questions.

The Secretary continued, "In a manner, sadly in character with Prince d'Or, he dishonored our kingdom, his father, and his fiancée by running away on New Year's Eve."

The crowd gasped and grumbled their disapproval.

"Our Esteemed King is deeply distressed by the actions of his son and presumed heir. As we all know, King Korah has selflessly dedicated his life to the betterment and enrichment of Alanthia. However, he has done so at great personal cost. From the tragic deaths of his brother's line, to the murder of his beloved wife, Princess Alexa ben Seamus, at the hands of anti-technology terrorists, and now to the abandonment of his son, King Korah has found himself very much alone." He paused for dramatic effect, his lugubrious tone reminding the kingdom of their grief over the lost Princess and the burdens the king bore on their behalf. "King Korah ben Adam has mourned his family's deaths, specifically his wife's these many years."

A picture of the long dead Princess Alexa filled the screen.

Davianna drew in a sharp gasp.

The Secretary paused and cleared his throat. "Princess Keyseelough's has made many trips to Alanthia over the course of the betrothal. Prince Peter's disregard for her, his frequent absences, and neglect became a source of pain for her. To soothe her feelings and to keep the honor of Alanthia, the King and the Princess developed a deep and abiding friendship. They share common interests and goals, as well as a strong sense of duty and honor toward their respective kingdoms."

Peter snorted in derision, then his mouth fell open. He saw what was coming.

The screen flashed a photograph of Korah and Keyseelough at a formal dinner, dressed in royal attire, looking regal and stately.

The Secretary gave an ironic turn to his head. "It is hereby announced the royal union between Alanthia and Egypt will commence as scheduled with King Korah taking the hand of Princess Keyseelough."

Shouts erupted from the crowd, the Secretary held up his hand for silence and continued, "The royal couple appreciates your congratulations and best wishes."

Then without answering a single question the two ministers left the podium.

Peter stared at the screen unblinking, then uncoiled with the grace of a leopard and stalked out of the room. Astrid held a pot under running water, the contents overflowing.

Josiah came into the living room, drying his black hair with a towel and looked at their ashen faces. "What's happened?"

"That bastard Korah is going to marry Peter's fiancée," Astrid said through gritted teeth.

But the sight of Korah had triggered a post-traumatic attack in Davianna. She stood frozen, a spatula in her hand, stir fry sizzling behind her, forgotten.

Josiah sprang into action. He turned off the stove and the

water, took the spatula from Davianna's hand, and guided her gently and purposefully to the couch.

"Turn off that blasted television," he barked at Astrid, who raced around him. "Bring me my medical bag, now!"

Astrid tore out of the room, her running feet echoing up the wooden steps.

Josiah counted the pulse in her wrist, strong and fast, one forty, too high. "Breathe, deep breaths. Come on, you can do it." He placed his hand over her belly and pushed. "Like the night in the park, remember?"

She did not respond.

"Do you remember how we laughed about Nacho Libre?"

Davianna stared at the blank television screen. "He was going to make me Queen. I think that was bad. I think that poor girl is in trouble."

Peter's scornful laugh startled Davianna, and she jumped.

Josiah shot him a ruthless glare.

Peter waved him away and got on his knees in front of her. "Hey, Sparrow, look at me."

Davianna blinked and tried to focus, then drew in her breath with a cry. "You look like him."

"Bloody hell, what an insult. Look closer. Come on, you can do it." Peter waited patiently.

Astrid approached on silent feet and set the bag beside Josiah's thigh.

Peter took Davianna's hands and brought them to his face as if she were blind, which with her eyes closed, she was. "Feel my hair, it is soft and thick, not like his. His is coarse and thinning, remember?"

She kept her eyes closed and nodded.

"And here, here is my hairline, you feel how it is low on my forehead, his goes way back, does it not? You know he is starting to go bald, that bastard, even though he tries to hide it with his comb over."

Davianna's mouth twitched.

"Now open your eyes. You know I am not him." Peter spoke to her as if she were being silly.

Davianna responded to the tone, opening her eyes.

"Now, do my eyebrows look like those overgrown cater-pillars he sports? I surely hope not. They have a life of their own when he speaks, bobbing up and down like creatures have taken up residence on his forehead. Am I right?" Peter waggled his eyebrows in comical imitation.

Davianna snorted.

"And my eyes? Come now, they are nothing like his." He batted them prettily, the long golden lashes almost brushing his cheeks.

Dark chocolate met emerald sunshine. She stared into his eyes and saw kindness, humor, and understanding. Her chin started to quiver.

He teased her out of it. "How about my nose? There are no gray whiskers protruding from it, are there?" He sniffed at her like a hedgehog.

She giggled and shook her head.

"My teeth," he pulled his lips back for inspection as if he were a prize horse at market. "They are perfect and pearly white, not all yellow and crooked on the bottom, like a jack-o'-lantern."

She flashed her own pearly whites at his silly expression.

"So, you see, he really is a funny looking fellow, not at all scary when you think of him like that, Sparrow. Just a bald-ing, great jack-o'-lantern with caterpillar eyebrows, and nose hairs coming out of his huge proboscis."

There was a light in her eyes.

"You hold on to that image, it helps. Trust me." He smiled, the left dimple showing, but it lacked the cruel twist his father had.

Davianna leaned forward to hug him. "Thank you, Pe-ter." She pulled away, staring into his beautiful face. "You don't look like him at all." Then she tried to wink, pitiful yet playful.

He drew himself up in royal dignity, his shield. "Well, of course, I do not." He lifted her up and maneuvered her back toward the kitchen. "Now, go finish my supper, wench. I am hungry, and it smells delicious."

Astrid and Josiah sagged in relief as they walked away.

"That was close." Astrid covered her eyes.

Josiah furrowed his brow. "No more TV." He stalked from the room, taking his medical bag with him.

Smoking on the Deck

It was snowing. Snow had not fallen on Millennial Earth, ever. Peter watched it in wonder as a deep silence enveloped the mountain cabin. He could hear the flakes hitting the deck. The porch light illuminated them into great white diamonds. It was late, but sleep eluded him, so he was smoking, a habit he tried to give up. Alas, there was so much he had to give up, he did not begrudge himself a cigarette.

He heard the sliding door open but did not turn. He wished whoever it was would just turn around and go away. Five full days of people, ugh. He was bone tired and sick of talking, sick of them, sick of it all. He simply wanted a smoke and some peace.

Astrid took the cigarette from his fingers and drew deeply. "You shouldn't smoke."

He shot her an impatient look. "Shut up." Resisting the urge to add, 'You are not my mother.'

"Snow," she stated flatly and handed him back the cigarette. She touched the railing, the snow melting under her ungloved finger.

Despite his fervent desire for solitude, he answered, "Not a good sign."

"Nope," she agreed, "Guess we're not leaving tomorrow."

Peter gave her a sidelong look and said, "Not unless I call a helicopter in here."

"You have a helicopter?"

He shrugged. "A couple."

She threw snow at him. "You are rotten."

Then he turned it on her, full force, almost blinding with

its radiance and splendor, Prince d'Or. "Of course, I am, Red. Are you just now figuring that out?"

Astrid sucked in her breath, regarding him intently. Her instincts, honed during their months of running, dulled by the drugs, began to return. She narrowed a blue cat eye and said, "I don't think I have even begun to figure you out." Without a backward glance, she disappeared through the door.

Prince d'Or lit another cigarette, watched the snow, and knew what must be done, but he also knew he would be putting his own soul on the line to do it.

It Can't be Like that, Can it?

"You know I have to have sex with you, right?" Peter said, stepping into the semi-darkness of Astrid's room.

Astrid snorted, "Like that is ever going to happen."

He chuckled, deep and confident. "You are not going to like it, and neither am I, but we have to do it."

"We have to do it?" she mocked, getting out of bed, facing him. "Why?"

He advanced on her like a great cat. "Because Korah only sacrifices virgins, you stupid bitch."

Strange heat and fear mingled with rage, jolting her upright. "Shut up!"

He scoffed and said hatefully, "Why do you think they examined you?"

"How do you know about that?" she hissed.

He laughed, bitter and humorless. "I was raised in that torture chamber."

She turned away, her breath coming in deep gasps.

"Do not worry," he growled. "I will make sure you hate it. It is going to hurt." He moved behind her, stalking her in the darkness.

"Because it cannot be any other way, can it? It cannot be stroking hands and soft caresses?" He jerked her roughly to his chest and sneered in her ear, "Or scented oils?"

She made a strangled gasp.

He bit her neck. "It cannot be nice and gentle, teasing? No murmured words or tender kisses, can it?"

Astrid balled her fists at her side, breathing in short pants.

He pinched her breast.

She clawed his thigh, going rigid under his touch.

"Because if it was gentle, it would be like then. If it was nice, it would feel like they were touching you, and you would die."

She dug in her fingernails, he let her.

"You would die from the shame of it. Die as you squirm under me, trying not to respond. Dying of humiliation as you did, hating yourself every second, not able to help it, because your body betrayed you." He cupped her between her legs, thrusting against her from behind, and whispered, "Because I will not stop. They would not stop. They never stop, do they, Red?"

She pushed him away, turned, and slapped his face.

He smiled, feeling her fingerprints grow livid on his cheek.

"I'll kill you," she promised.

He jerked the shirt over his head, fire green eyes dared her to try. "You do not have the courage. You left it back in those stirrups."

Astrid shrieked and flew at him. She ground her mouth into his. He pulled her hair, plunging his tongue down her throat. She raked her fingers down his back as he arched into her with shock and pain. He shoved his hand down the front of her panties entering her roughly, rubbing hard. He pulled her to him, his body heaving in great gasps.

She sank her teeth into his chest and bit him. She tasted blood as she arched into his questing hand.

He gasped, the bite mark on fire. He was aflame.

Astrid ran her palm down the flat of his stomach and grabbed his pulsating manhood, squeezing without mercy. His loose pants dropped to the floor.

He pinched her swollen clitoris. She convulsed under him. "I am going to split you in half!"

She scratched him. "I will rip the hide off your back."

"Do it," he growled and tore her panties from her body, pushing her against the wall, spreading her legs, pressing into her. "I am taking you now."

"No!" Astrid hissed in his ear, dragging him down to the floor. "I'm taking you." She grabbed him with inexpert hands and impaled herself. It hurt, burned and ripped. She bit her lip, stifling the grunt of pain.

He spread her cheeks and shoved, ruthlessly driving into her. He felt the barrier break, felt her blood, touched her womb. Peter pushed deep inside, where no man had ever been, and took possession.

She burned with every stroke, tasting blood, sweat, and tears.

"Damn!" he swore and moved his hand to where their bodies joined, rubbing with expert skill. Her rhythm became erratic. He felt her falling and stroked without mercy until she began to convulse. When she cried out, he lost himself with a deep, wracking shudder.

She collapsed on top of him. "Oh, I hate you."

He ran a hand down her back and kissed her cheek. "I hate you, too."

She looked at him with a slanted blue eye. "Are you going to do that to Davianna, too?"

His laugh dislodged him from her body. "No. I will let Josiah take care of Sparrow."

Astrid snorted. "The good doctor is never going to have sex with Davianna. She is his patient, his mission. She's doomed."

Peter rolled on top of her, his charming grin flashing in the faint light. "Which is why he is supposed to be the Ruling Prince. I am far too wicked." Then he began to move against her again, to prove his point.

January 6, 1000 ME

Pancakes for Breakfast

Davianna sang under her breath, spooning pancake batter onto the griddle. She smiled as it spread perfectly across the bubbling butter. Bacon sizzled in the oven; the rich aroma snaked under the bedroom doors like smoke from a genie's bottle.

She flipped the pancakes. "Superb!" she said to herself, amused that it sounded like a 'Josiah' word.

Returning her attention to the fruit salad, she decided it needed a little sugar and lemon juice to perk up the frozen fruit. Munching a piece of pineapple, she said, "Satisfactory."

Still humming, she set the table, placing the coffee in a neat carafe nestled beside dried cream and sugar. She sipped her cup, not bad for a drip machine, a French press would have been better.

Josiah was the first riser. He came downstairs with his hair mussed from sleep, wearing loose gray pants and a blue t-shirt. The dark circles under his eyes were less pronounced than the day before. Beard stubble gave him a pirate look

He took in the scene, Davianna in her customary black tunic and leggings with a speck of flour in her hair by her right ear. She looked less haunted, more substantial. "Coffee?" he asked in a voice gruff with sleep.

She smiled and nodded to the table. "Just there. Have a seat. Breakfast will be ready in a few." Davianna turned back to the griddle, flipping pancakes, and humming some little tune.

He watched her over the steam in his mug, concern creasing his brow. "Did you sleep?"

She shrugged a shoulder, looking down at the pancakes. "A little." Then resumed her humming.

When she turned, her eyes seemed overly bright. He swore under his breath, trying to keep his voice steady. "How much is a little?"

She waved his concern away. "A couple hours. I slept for three straight days. I wasn't tired." She put a bowl of fruit on the table and returned to the kitchen. "Did you see the snow?"

Josiah's brows shot up, so intent on Davianna, he failed to notice. "Wow, that is magnificent."

Davianna giggled. He was always so serious, to catch a glimpse of him off guard amused her. "I know! Today, you must help me make a snowman, but after breakfast." She grinned, delighted at the prospect.

"Well, perhaps you should eat then go upstairs and have another rest," Josiah said, employing his strict doctor's tone.

"Pft." Davianna wagged a spatula at him. "No way, Doc. This is the first snow I have ever seen, and I am not missing it to go take a nap like a three-year-old."

The commanding officer, the doctor, and the Prince could well order her to do anything he wanted, and she better get used to it. She suffered a serious trauma and may well be slipping into a manic episode. He was not going to have it. Just as he was about to inform her of that fact, she put a plate of bacon in front of him and flashed a pretty smile.

"Pancakes, coming up!"

She swished away; her incredible ass covered by a handprint of flour. He nearly choked on his coffee. Damn, undone by bacon and a tight little ass.

A huge stack of pancakes followed the bacon, and she sat down beside him. "Are you hungry?" Her expression looked innocent and eager.

Josiah nodded. "Are you?"

With an emphatic nod, she said, "Starving!"

He watched her eat and absently took a bite of the pancake. Josiah moaned in bliss. Buttery crisp, soft, and sweet exploded on his tongue. He closed his eyes, savoring the moment. He loved pancakes and bacon. He loved breakfast. She was an amazing cook. She was enchanting.

"Do you like it?" she asked with a hopeful gleam in her brown eyes.

"It's delicious," he said between mouthfuls.

As his stomach filled, he considered that perhaps she was not manic, maybe she was simply happy. Maybe Davianna ben David was just sweet. He had only seen her in dire circumstances. The Prince was wary, the doctor alert, the man knew he was in serious trouble. Davianna dabbed the syrup from the corner of her pretty pink mouth, and he wanted to groan.

"I feel bad that we did not wait, but I was hungry." She bit her lip, looking up at the open hallway where the other bedroom doors remained closed. "Astrid likes to sleep late, and Peter, I don't think he slept at all while Astrid was sick, didn't you say?"

Josiah nodded. He slept nearly as long as Davianna and Astrid, though he was ashamed to admit it. Chained in a dungeon and tortured for a week took a lot out of a guy. So indeed, Peter had taken care of all of them in one way, shape, or form. "He did."

Davianna cleared the empty plates, leaving the food on the table for the late risers. "There are jackets and warm clothes in the hall closet through there," she called from the kitchen.

Josiah gave a bone popping stretch. "How long have you been up?"

"I don't know," she shot back. "Don't be a sleep monitor."

She ran the water for the dishes, and he joined her by the sink, drying and putting away where she directed. He noted with some amusement that she already had the entire kitchen memorized.

"Come on." She took him by the elbow and pulled him to the hall closet.

With mischief dancing in her eyes, she deposited a fur hat on his head, a ridiculous thing, with long ear flaps that dangled to his shoulders. He crossed his arms and scowled at her.

She shrieked with laughter. "You look like a big growling bear." He continued to scowl, which made her laugh harder.

She pulled the matching fur coat from the hanger and moved to put it on him.

He held out a hand to stop her. "No."

"Please?" she coaxed, holding an absurd creation of long white fur, better suited for a huge woman than a man like Josiah.

"No," he warned.

She bit her lip, judging whether she might needle him into putting it on for her, simply so she could laugh at how ridiculous he looked in it. Deciding it was a lost cause, she removed a more sedate gray one and held it out to him.

"Too small."

"How do you know?" she challenged.

He shot her an exasperated look.

"Fine." She hung it back up and handed him a black one.

He put it on for her.

"Perfect!" she declared, bouncing on her toes. Then she dug out a bag of gloves. "Here find some gloves." She waved a pair at him. "I already have mine."

Reaching into the closet, she pulled out a tunic length royal-blue coat with white fur trim. She shrugged it on and turned with an expectant expression. "How do I look?"

Warning bells went off in his brain. He was on perilous ground. The girl before him was as fragile as spun sugar. Six days ago, he picked her up off the floor in the Palace, absolutely destroyed. She needed something from him right now. She needed him to be kind, to treat her like a lady, not a patient. He would have to draw the line later. It would be necessary, but if he did it now, it might crush her, and he knew it. So, he spoke from his heart and told her the truth, "You look perfect."

Davianna preened and spun around, with her arms stiff, palms flat to the ground. "Put your boots on, Jo. Let's play in the snow." She dashed off, laughing over her shoulder. "Ha, I made a rhyme!"

He could hear her repeating it as she ran to get her boots.

Birthday Boy

The slamming door woke Astrid, that and the fact that Peter was moving on top of her, again.

"I thought they would never leave," he whispered in her ear.

She tried to squirm away, to push him off.

He captured her wrists and held them above her head. "No," he brushed his lips against hers, "it is my birthday."

She tightened around him, and he made a strangled groan. Astrid narrowed her eyes, and he met her look with a wicked grin.

"Sore?" He punctuated his question by pushing fully inside her.

She pretended to be bored. "You wish."

He gave a throaty moan and felt her body quivering underneath him. "I've never slept with a virgin before, novel experience." Holding her wrists above her head, he moved his other hand between them, teasing her. She sucked in her breath.

"There is so much to explore."

Astrid was sore, but she would never admit that to him, ever.

Peter watched her face as he touched her. She turned her head away, refusing to let him see her eyes. Refusing to give him anything, refusing to move.

But he saw the pulse beating in her neck, felt her grow slick beneath his finger. Her breasts began to rise and fall as her breath quickened.

Astrid knew she could break free any time, he held her lightly. He was dominating her, but in her submission, she was the one in control. It was highly erotic. Powerful.

Peter moved to his side, keeping her arms captured above her head. It changed the angle, giving him deeper access to her. He began stroking his long, elegant finger down the cleft of her bottom, coaxing her, opening her, taking her. Sliding his finger deeper, more dangerous, teasing.

"Let me," he whispered across her lips. He pushed his finger harder, entering her, demanding she give him what he wanted until she let him have everything.

The instant she submitted, the orgasm started, deep in the pit of her stomach. She stiffened and arched, fighting it and him, but it was too much, too intense, utterly erotic. It washed over her in violent waves and swept her away. She took him with her. He shuddered, pounding into her body as if he could not get close enough, deep enough.

They lay, joined together, boneless and spent.

Then he licked his lips and stared at her with an eager expression. "Come on, there is bacon."

Astrid pushed at him, suddenly mortified at all the things they had done. "Go away."

He rolled from the bed with fluid and easy grace, standing before her like a golden god, long and lithe, muscled. In the light, she saw the marks she made on him, bites and scratches, her blood mingled with his. She pulled the blankets up.

He jerked them away.

She resisted the urge to grab them back, instead met his gaze with a challenge.

He knelt beside the bed and pulled her breast roughly into his mouth. His hand teased and pinched the puckered nipple of the other.

She reached around the back of his head and yanked his hair, until he broke the kiss, but his hand continued its exquisite torture. She leaned forward and bit his ear. "Bring me coffee. Now." She released his hair and swatted his hand away.

Peter rose in an excellent imitation of a manservant, albeit a naked one and said, "Certainly, my Esteemed." Then he settled the sheet around himself and exited the room like a Roman Emperor.

Snow and Wolves

"Come on, let's go look." Davianna grabbed Josiah's arm, urging him up the mountain.

The snow crunched under their boots, up to their ankles as they climbed. Josiah cringed. His ankles were still raw from the fetters, and the boots chafed in exactly the wrong spot. The last thing he should be doing was trudging up a mountain. Beneath his clothes, he had at least three cracked ribs, likely four. He was covered in contusions and an assortment of hematomas, two which bore the unmistakable shape and size of Korah's twisted weapon. The sight of the bruises, swollen and livid purple, made him burn with impotent rage. No, he should not be out here. However, the ethereal fey quality that surrounded Davianna seemed to have blown away with the snow. She was going outside, whether he came or not.

He paused, leaning against a tree to catch his breath. A pile of snow fell from an overhead branch, splattering on his head. Davianna exploded with laughter as he blinked white crystals from his eyelashes. He narrowed his eyes and shook the tree she was standing under. Huge globs of snow fell all around her.

She covered her head in gleeful outrage.

Josiah laughed and scooped up a big handful of snow.

"Don't you throw that at me," she said, backing away.

"You wanted to play in the snow." He advanced on her with mock menace.

"Ahhh!" she screamed and scampered up the hill, treating him to an amazing view of her tight, round, perfect ass. He shook his head, reminded again of how fast she was.

He topped the vista and a snowball hit him right in the solar plexus.

"Why you!" He formed a snowball and pelted her with it. It smashed against her shoulder. She whooped and reached down to make her own.

Mayhem ensued.

Finally, pelted into submission, Davianna surrendered, defeated by his superior accuracy and snowball making skills. Her cheeks were bright pink, her hood had fallen back, and wet hair framed her face in wispy tendrils. Adorable. He pulled her in for a playful hug, still laughing.

She flicked a bit of snow from his nose.

He leaned in for a kiss, it was the most natural thing he had ever done, but he stopped himself, aborted the kiss, and rested his lips on her forehead. He was dying… she was killing him. Raising her hood against the cold, he stepped back and looked over her head, trying to cool his ardor.

For the second time in a minute, his breath caught, overwhelmed by what lay before him. Beyond the mountain, as far as he could see, sat an enchanted land of white crystal and snow castles. "Look, Davianna."

She followed his gaze and brought a gloved hand to her mouth. "Josiah," she breathed his name like a prayer, "it is wondrous."

They stood in awed silence, side by side, their millennial eyes partaking of a vision that no one in over a thousand years had seen, snow-covered mountains.

"Alanthia." A lump in his throat made his voice catch. "Look at it."

She leaned her head against his shoulder and gazed up, her big brown eyes full of innocent wonder. "This is your kingdom."

He could not look at her. He could not look at the mountains. So, he closed his eyes and brought his head to hers. With his arm around her waist, standing with her in the silence, he absorbed the moment and realized he would be content to stay here for the rest of his life.

The moment was shattered by a low, menacing growl.

Josiah pushed Davianna behind him, crouching, bracing for attack. This time it was no dachshund. Unsheathing his dagger, he felt rather than heard Davianna do the same. "Stay behind me."

He scanned the woods, looking for the beast. The gray shadows made it impossible to discern what stalked them. Thick undergrowth could have hidden one or a hundred wolves. He could see the roof of the cabin, downhill, three hundred yards away. If they ran fast, they might make it. He hoped. Shit.

He pulled her to his left, keeping his right side open. "Get ready to run."

Josiah shouted, bellowing a war cry at the top of his lungs. It echoed through the trees and down into the valley. Whether it traveled into the house or was buried in the snow, he did not know. "Go!" he roared.

Davianna stayed at his side, keeping up. They flew head-long into the woods, knives drawn, ready to fight.

He checked their retreat. A huge beast broke cover and loped after them. "Run!"

Davianna looked back, hit an icy patch, and slipped.

Josiah swooped in, catching her before she fell. He did not break stride, but the impact jarred his cracked ribs, making his lungs burn like hellfire.

They careened down the mountain, dodging saplings, jumping impressions. His boots filled with snow. Every step shot excruciating pain up his legs, and the fetter wounds opened anew, leaving a crimson trail in the snow.

The wolf smelled blood.

They topped the last ridge, and he spotted Peter on the back porch, barefoot, shirtless, and in boxer shorts. He aimed a rifle, covering their retreat. If Josiah had breath, he would have whooped.

A shot split the cold mountain air, echoing for miles.

Davianna flew on the feet of Hermes into the house. As she cleared the threshold, Astrid shouted, "What the hell is going on? Have they found us?"

Davianna bent over, trying to catch her breath, and shook her head no.

Peter scampered in, shivering, and leaving Josiah with

the weapon on the deck. "Wolves," he answered succinctly. "Bloody hell, it is cold out there."

"How many?" Astrid demanded.

Peter shrugged. "Only one that I saw. Josiah will take care of the rest; if there are any." He walked over to the table and ate a piece of bacon.

Davianna straightened up, still gasping. After the cold outside, the cabin felt like a sauna. She started to take off her coat, but her hand froze on the zipper. The mutual state of undress of her two erstwhile companions registered. They looked like they had been fighting. Peter had scratches all over him and what looked suspiciously like a bite mark on his chest. Astrid stood in the living room in nothing but a sheet.

Davianna's eyes bulged. "Tridi, you have a hickey!"

Astrid blushed in spectacular fashion, the way only a true redhead can manage. She shot Peter a vicious look and ran up the steps, slamming the bathroom door behind her.

Absolutely incredulous, she turned to Peter, who was reaching for another piece of bacon. He raised it in salute and devoured it in a single bite. Then he drained a cup of coffee and strolled up to her, completely unconcerned with his near nakedness. He kissed her cheek and said, "Thanks for the breakfast."

Davianna's mouth dropped as he sprinted up the steps and joined Astrid, in the bathroom!

"What in the world?" she said to the empty living room. Shaking her head, she stripped off her coat and gloves. She looked at the remnants of breakfast and took a cold pancake, eating it while she watched Josiah through the window.

The snowy backyard was silent. Josiah stood guard, poised with the weapon, ready to annihilate anything that came over the hill. As she finished her pancake, he shouldered the weapon and came inside.

Leaning the rifle against the door frame, he shucked off his coat and gloves. Davianna took them from him and poured him another cup of black coffee. He mussed his hair, still damp from the snow, his cheeks red with cold.

"Here," she said, pressing the cup into his hands.

"Actually," he cleared his throat and winced, "I need an ice pack, please, and my medical bag."

Davianna's eyes widened. "You're hurt."

He shook his head. "Just a twinge. Souvenirs."

"Oh." She looked around, not sure what to do.

"Freezer first, my bag is upstairs." He forced himself not to limp to the couch. While she made the ice pack, he bent over to unlace his boots, then thought better of it. The socks were wet with melted snow and blood, but the wounds on his feet and ankles were superficial. His ribs were the most pressing concern. He had taken a hell of a beating down in that dungeon.

"Where do you need it?" Davianna asked, presenting him with a tea towel full of ice.

"Just give it to me and go get my bag. It's on the chair in my room." He did not want her to see his ribs. It was bad enough that she had to take off his boots.

He heard her run up the steps and gingerly lifted his shirt, palpating the ribs to make sure none of the cracked ones had broken. That would put him in a world of hurt, and he did not fancy performing surgery on himself. Ribs six, seven, and eight on his right side sustained the worst damage, but they felt fine. It was the pesky three and four ribs on his left side that took the impact when he grabbed Davianna.

"Damn, this is cold," he hissed and settled the pack over the injury, holding it in place with his arm. He heard Davianna coming down the steps and composed his expression.

"Okay, now what?" She gestured to the bag. He could tell this upset her. She was flushed, her voice breathless.

"Thank you for the ice pack. It's just a little tweak on my ribs. Could you do me a favor and pull off my boots and socks?" He winked. "I am giving my diaphragm space."

"Oh, I remember that. You said that in the park when I

got the wind knocked out of me." An odd expression crossed her face, and she absently rubbed her stomach. "That hurt."

"Indeed." He closed his eyes, hiding his intense discomfort. The frayed nerve endings in his ribs had turned into live wires, sending showers of sizzling zaps across his chest.

"Your poor feet," she murmured as she pulled off his sock, daintily holding it between the tip of her finger and her thumb and dropping it with a splat on the cold hearth. She looked up at him and said, "You have hairy big toes."

The laugh hurt. He had expected her to say something about the injuries, how he sustained them. He expected her to go back to the dungeon with him. Instead, she made him laugh. "I have never noticed," he answered honestly.

"Who doesn't notice their own toes?" She held up her stockinged foot. "I know what my toes look like."

"They're pink."

She craned her neck in surprise. "Oh? You know what my toes look like, but not your own?"

"I just noticed them when you were sleeping." To cut off further conversation of what else he noticed about her while she slept, he gave instructions on how to clean and dress his ankles. She did a fair job of it, though had she been an intern or a nurse, he would have chewed her out.

She sat beside him on the couch, tucked her left foot under her, and sighed.

He could feel her shaking. "You're trembling."

"I just got chased by a wolf, Josiah. I think that is normal."

He shot her a patronizing glare. "Nothing about this last week has been normal, Davianna." Then he could have kicked himself. The shadow missing from her face all morning returned. He felt her draw into herself. "Sorry," he apologized in a low whisper.

She gave a little shrug. "Not your fault."

He slung his arm around her shoulders and pulled her gently to his side, feeling the deep trembling in her body. It was a residual effect of the trauma, but this time, he had been the one to bring it on. He felt like an ogre.

"You are still cold," she said, pulling a soft throw over them.

"It's the ice pack." Yet it was more than that. His injuries were making it difficult for his body to regulate his temperature. The stress of their flight down the mountain had not helped, nor had the snowball fight.

She drew both her legs up and curled into his side.

He settled her more comfortably, not caring that it hurt. He could smell her hair, a mixture of snow, shampoo, and her. They sat that way, in comfortable silence for a time. Then Josiah said, "I think it was a lone wolf."

Davianna sighed and looked up at him, the haunted look of Korah's dungeon retreated to the shadows. "It was a good shot."

Josiah nodded. "Men in my family have always been expert marksmen."

Davianna toyed idly with a button on his gray flannel shirt. "And you, are you a good shot?"

He rubbed his hand up and down her back, pleased to note that the trembling had subsided. "I am not bad."

Her expressive eyes signaled that she suspected he was being humble. "Astrid and I need to learn. Neither of us knows how to shoot."

He lifted her wrist, fingering one of the arm guards hidden under her tunic, each held a four-inch switchblade. These were in addition to the lethal six-inch hunting knife she wore at her side. He wrinkled his forehead and said, "You are pretty well armed, Minx."

She shrugged, silently conveying that it had not been enough when they were captured.

Unfortunately, she was right. He needed to teach them to shoot. "Where is my cousin, anyway?" Josiah looked around the cabin.

Davianna buried her face in his chest, squinting her eyes. "In the shower, I think."

Josiah settled back on the couch. The roaring adrenaline ceased, making his limbs languid. Ice and a mild analgesic took the edge off the pain. He continued the steady stroking of her back, and she relaxed into him.

He realized he was always holding her, as if he could not stop touching her. Under normal circumstances, he would never touch a female in his care, but she felt so nice sitting there, he did not have the desire or the energy to extricate himself. Besides, he was comforting her, just like he did after they escaped.

In the warehouse, he prepared a pallet on the floor. Soldiers can bunk anywhere. However, her dreams were so pitiful that he laid down with her. She ceased her restless moaning, and they slept.

A niggling thought mocked him. It was not just in the warehouse. That night on Waterloo Bridge, he was drawn to touch her, and that kiss in the park? Even under the dangerous circumstances, he remembered the way she felt underneath him, the way she moved, the way his body reacted. And now… in this isolated cabin, all alone, she snuggled beside him and made a soft feminine sound as she settled in. Wiggling her great ass, brushing his arm with those perky little boobs, and looking up at him with dark chocolate eyes, blood rushed to his groin. "Damn!" he swore and got up.

Davianna startled and darted a look upstairs, wearing a guilty expression. "What?"

Josiah narrowed his eyes.

She turned red.

"What's going on?"

Davianna got up from the couch, busying herself with the breakfast dishes. "Nothing. Do you want any more breakfast?"

Josiah pulled the ice pack out from under his shirt, motioning upstairs to distract her away from his injuries. "Did they eat?"

Davianna shrugged. "I think so." Looking at the table, she nodded. "Yes, they did."

"Well then, where is Astrid?" A sneaking suspicion, perhaps influenced by the debauched turn of his own thoughts, occurred to him. His cousin had been standing on the deck in his underwear.

Get Your Own Bathroom

"Get out of here!" Astrid hissed as Peter sauntered into the bathroom right as she flushed the toilet. She stood, pulling the sheet over her chest.

"I have to wee." He brushed by her.

Her mouth opened in outrage. "Go to the other bathroom, you pig. I am in here."

"So am I." He sighed with pleasure.

She stared at him, dumbfounded as a strong stream of urine blasted the commode. "You have no shame."

"You do not know the half of it." His voice sounded low and seductive. "You liked that didn't you?"

She blushed for the second time in three and a half minutes. "No. You are gross. Go away."

He strutted toward her, naked and glorious. "I am sticky."

He brought her hand to him. She felt moisture and blood, remnants of their long night and morning of passion.

He nipped at her earlobe. "Get in the shower with me, Red. Let's get clean."

If she got in the shower, the last thing she was going to get was clean, and she did not care. She pulled the hair near his groin, her pressure insistent, the power thrilling. His sudden intake of breath told her she made her point. He grew rigid under her hand.

Her sheet fell away, and he drew her into the tiled shower. She admired his backside as he turned on the water, rivulets running over his skin and down his back. He turned to her with a grin, took her in his arms, and kissed her. Pressing a bar of soap in her hand, he breathed, "This could be dangerous."

She dug her nails into his buttocks, closing her eyes. She understood what he meant. It could be too much like the oil, too much like those damn hands, too much like them.

"Keep your eyes open," he demanded in a harsh whisper. "Do not go there. Stay here with me."

Astrid blinked back the water and stared up at him.

He smoothed her hair back, and said, "I am not going to hurt you." He brushed a kiss down her neck and pulled her claws out of his buttocks. "And you are not going to hurt me."

Real fear crossed her face, and he responded by backing her into the shower wall, pressing his body against hers, covering her. "Do not look at me that way." He could not stand it. When the terror did not flee, he banished it. "No!" He kissed her mouth hard, reminding her of who he was. "They do not belong in here, in us, or with us. Do you hear me?"

The strength he knew she possessed, had seen it on that video tape a hundred times, came into her eyes. Steel, they were both going to need.

"Kiss me gently, Astrid. I need you."

She was sobbing as she put her mouth to his, not so much a kiss but a mingling of breath, her breathing life and pain into him, him doing the same. Somehow the sharing of it made it better, less raw. Their pain and terror evaporated into the mist.

He fell to his knees, soaping her body. She was exquisite, perfectly made. His hands glided over her skin in gentle caresses, and there was reverence to his touch. She had a faint dusting of freckles, here and there, where the sun kissed her. Her fair skin flushed in the hot water. She was not a stick-thin model, not one of those pouty-lipped, plastic beauties. Astrid was real, a natural redhead. He groaned, nuzzling her, kneeling at her feet in tender worship. He rested his cheek against her belly, alabaster silk, so soft, not concave and bony. It felt as if this place had been created for him, and she was the most beautiful woman he had ever seen.

Looking up, he saw her eyes were open, watching him. He stood and handed her the soap. "Your turn, Red."

He backed under the waterfall, raised his arms above his head, and clasped the shower nozzle. His Adam's Apple bobbed as he swallowed. Unfathomable depths of fear swam behind his emerald eyes as he stood before her, vulnerable and naked. He shook with the force of the moment, offering her a gift beyond measure, a sacrifice beyond price, in an act of bravery that he did not even know he possessed.

Astrid read it all.

This beautiful, damaged, and broken man let her hurt him, and then surrendered himself to her care. She began with the bite on his chest, crusted with dried blood, bruised. She kissed him as he had her. She washed his fine-boned face, his neck with the love marks. She ran the soap over his rip-cord arms, the golden-brown hair in his armpit, and smiled when he flinched at the tickle. Exploring the lean planes of his torso, she reveled in the artistry of his creation. Her hands went up his back, feeling his muscles shift and tighten in response to her touch. He hissed when the soap touched the scratch marks, and she wanted to cry.

Their gazes locked, unblinking and intense.

She moved the soap between his legs. His eyes flashed as she touched him with tenderness, running the length of velvet steel. There was a pleading in his eyes, a reluctant trust. This was costing him. He did not move, standing perfectly still with water raining down his shoulders and back. Slowly, she moved further down to the most vulnerable part of him. With infinite gentleness she cupped him in her palm, washing lightly. He let out a ragged shudder, tilted his head back, and kept his hands suspended.

Resting her head against his chest, she felt his breathing, heard his heartbeat, strong and rapid. She moved down his lean, strong thighs, running her finger over the dents of muscles that ran from hip to knee. She noticed an old scar from a skinned knee and kissed it. His calves were covered by a wealth of curly blond and brown hair. His feet were as perfect as the rest of him. She sat on her haunches and looked up at him in wonder. He was exquisite.

He lifted her to him and brushed his lips against hers. "Astrid, I want you. But after last night, after this morning… I do not want to hurt you. Is it okay if I just kiss you?"

She smoothed his eyebrow and said in a throaty whisper, "You can kiss me anywhere you want."

He closed his eyes for a moment, then looked up, as if he were giving silent thanks. He turned off the water and stepped with her into the fogged bathroom. He wrapped her in a towel, affixed one about his waist, and guided her to his bedroom.

The mid-morning light peeked through the drawn draperies, casting his rustic cabin bedroom in red and umber shadows. He took the towel from his waist and dried her hair. After attending to every drop of water on her skin, he laid her down and fell in beside her. Their bodies were cold from the chill of the air and the shower.

She kissed him shyly.

He fought down the urge to mount her, to possess her, but this was something different, something wondrous. He caressed her side, finding she was ticklish at the point right above her hip. He nestled his hand in her rich red curls, feeling precious dampness and heat. He whispered into her mouth, "Open your legs for me, love. I need to touch you."

Astrid moistened her lips and opened to his questing hand. His delicate fingers caressed her, finding the shape of her, soothing, playing, teasing, before sliding into the slippery wetness that waited for him. Gently, softly, and with infinite patience, he touched her.

She began to move and make little noises in the back of her throat.

"Look at me," he coaxed, "feel how I am touching you."

A broad grin broke across her face as she pushed against him. "I feel it."

"Good," he chuckled.

Starting with her breast, he kissed his way down her body. She groaned as his tongue touched her engorged skin, and she felt a familiar tightening come over her, the quivering in her legs. Spasms of warm pleasure came wave after wave, cresting one after the other.

He did not stop. He was like a starving man at a banquet.

He played and licked and coaxed, sucked and probed, and the waves kept coming. She cried out and raised her hips. It was too much, but he held her firmly and kept going, forcing her to continue. She clawed at the sheets, kicked her heels, and tried to pull away. He drove her onward, merciless. Surely, she would die of this; it could not go on, but it did. Deeper and deeper, until she ceased being Astrid, ceased being a person, ceased being anything except this experience with this relentless beautiful man, taking her further and further, until in absolute desperation, she cried out his name.

He moved beside her, continuing his gentle stroking. She was shattering all over his hand. "Do you trust me?" His voice sounded ragged and hoarse.

"Yes," she whimpered.

Her soft wet folds were making him crazy, and a possessive madness gripped him. "This is mine. No one else's, ever. Say it!" he demanded, desperate to hear here say the words.

"Yours!" she cried. "Oh God, Peter... only you, only you. Yours."

"Mine." He was raw, exposed, and completely undone. "Mine."

Pushing deep inside her, they became mindless with sensation until the world exploded. They soared together into heights of oblivion and boundless ecstasy. When the pieces of themselves came back together, they were forever mingled, forever mixed, forever bound—together.

What Do You Know?

At 12:30 pm, Josiah could take no more. He stormed up the steps, and with a thundering crash, banged on Peter's bedroom door. "I would speak with thee. Now!"

Peter lifted his sleep creased face. His hair had dried while he slept, and it plastered to the side of his head. He collapsed back into the pillow with a groan. Opening a green eye, he said, "Ugh, he threw a 'thee' at me. This ought to be fun."

The corner of Astrid's mouth lifted into a smile. "Good luck."

Peter rolled his eyes. "You got me in trouble." He kissed her nose and got out of bed.

She snorted at him. "I did not get you in trouble. You did that all on your own."

His grin was pure rogue. "My kind of trouble, Red."

Astrid huffed, hiding her smile behind the blanket. "You are impossible."

Peter pulled on his jeans, stretching and yawning after he buttoned up the fly. "I am very possible, as you well know." He donned a long sleeve athletic shirt and strode from the room barefoot and rumpled.

Josiah waited for him at the end of the hall, breathing fire. Peter anticipated this confrontation all morning and honestly did not give a rat's ass.

Josiah jerked his bedroom door open and ground out, "What are you doing?"

Peter adopted a bored expression, honed from a thousand such encounters with his father, who was infinitely more frightening than his cousin. "I was napping until I was rudely awakened."

"Napping!" Josiah growled. "You have defiled an innocent!"

Peter gave an indolent shrug and said, "She is not innocent anymore."

Josiah straightened, growing rigid with fury. "You have

dishonored her, dishonored your name, but worse, you have brought dishonor upon our house!"

Peter sneered, "The honor of our house died on a sacrificial altar stained with the blood of your father, Josiah."

Josiah recoiled as if he had been struck.

Peter advanced on him, becoming ruthless. "The same bloody altar where they planned to murder you if I did not save your ass—again. They were going to kill you. You were the main attraction. What do you think the gala was for?"

Josiah stepped backward, horrified. However, he had seen Korah's eyes, read the bloodthirsty madness, and knew it was true. "That is abominable." He rubbed his hands over his face, trying to block the image. "But to sleep with that girl, Peter? What were you thinking? That is the last thing she needs right now."

"What do you know about what she needs? Do you think you are some type of expert on how to survive Korah's House of Horrors?"

"I know one does not sleep with innocent girls to help them!" Josiah barked.

"Really?" Peter shook his head. "You do not know the first thing about what she needs, about what any of us needs. Yesterday, you were ready to sedate that poor girl downstairs because she saw a picture of Korah, a picture!" he yelled. "Do you plan to sedate her every time that happens? What about when his name is mentioned? Are you planning to carry around your trusty needle and keep her comatose?"

Peter rubbed his hands over his face, disdain dripping from his lips. "Because that is the extent of your knowledge, Doctor. Drugs!"

"Hey—"

"Who helped her?" Peter took two steps forward.

Josiah looked away.

"Who?" Peter demanded. "Me! I made him funny, not scary. I gave her something to hold on to, something she is going to need."

Peter bowed his head, old anguish and dead certainty cut through the air. "I know him. Once he sets his mind on something, he does not give up. He will never stop chasing that girl. She might have to face him one day, and when she does, she will need more than your injections to get her through that."

When Peter raised his eyes, they burned copper fire. "So do not judge what you do not understand."

Just Lunch

Sitting in the empty living room, Davianna looked up at the second floor, listening to the argument or at least trying to. She could only make out muffled voices and shouts. Astrid peeked around the corner, looking disheveled with her hair flattened to the back of her head and still dressed in a sheet. She looked both ways and sprinted to her bedroom, presumably to put some clothes on, or so Davianna hoped. Peter stormed out of Josiah's room, disappearing down the hall. The house grew quiet.

She wanted to sprint upstairs and have her own words with Astrid. However, Astrid could have a temper, and Davianna was not up for a fight just now. So, she retreated to the kitchen.

The cabin was well provisioned, albeit with frozen and shelf stable foods, which posed no challenge for a pilgrim girl. She defrosted fish for lunch, and there was a chicken for dinner. It was cold outside, so she decided to make soup.

Peter leaned his head around the corner. "What are you cooking?"

Davianna jumped. "Do not sneak up on me!"

"I did not sneak up on you. You are as skittish as a colt."

"I know. It's terrible. I've always been that way."

"Could be entertaining for the rest of us," Peter teased.

"You wouldn't be the first one who thought so." Davianna patted the fish dry with a towel. "Back in Taylorsville, there was a boy, Joseph," she paused in remembrance, "lost his front teeth and wore this strange bridge. Anyway, he thought it was great fun to scare me. Kept jumping out at me, at recess, around corners, sometimes just sitting there he'd yell, BOO! It was awful. I ended up with a twitch in my eye."

"What did you do?" Peter asked, perusing the contents of the refrigerator.

Davianna flipped the fish into the flour. "Nothing. I told my dad, and he told the teacher. They told Joseph, if he kept doing it, he would get detention. He kept doing it, so he got detention. Then it stopped."

Peter studied her, wearing an enigmatic expression she could not interpret. "So, you did not fight back?"

Davianna washed the flour from her fingers and moved on to the veggies. "No, I suppose I should have, but I am not very good at that."

"That surprises me. You do not seem the type." Peter picked at the pickles she was slicing, eating a handful.

She sighed. "I know. I have my moments." Flashes of her encounters with Korah swam to the surface, but she pushed them away and said, "Most of the time, well, I suppose I let people walk all over me."

Davianna smacked his hand as he reached for another pickle. "I am hungry," Peter protested and moved back to the refrigerator. "What are you cooking?"

"Fish sandwiches for lunch, and I think chicken soup for supper would be nice."

Peter poured a glass of orange juice. "I am glad somebody can cook, because I cannot boil water."

That always surprised Davianna, who loved being in the kitchen since she was a toddler. "Who can't boil water? Why not?"

He narrowed his brows and answered in a measured tone, "Because someone always brought me my food?"

Davianna dropped the knife with a clatter and laughed. "Oh crap, sorry. I keep forgetting who you are."

"Charming, actually." Peter moved around to sit at the

bar, keeping her company while she cooked. "Considering that I am on the run, excellent idea. Keep forgetting."

Davianna stopped dredging the fish and looked at him. "You have one of the most recognized faces in the world. If we are running together, we are going to have to disguise you. You can't be strolling into a store in the middle of nowhere all blond and fabulous."

Astrid joined Peter at the bar at that moment and gave Davianna a speculative look.

Peter turned to her and said, "Your friend here thinks I am fabulous. What do you think?"

"You know what I think." She leaned in and kissed his cheek. "You are hideous."

"Hideous?" Davianna laughed. "Lunch will be ready in a bit." She felt Josiah come into the kitchen.

"You need help?" he offered.

"Yes, that would be nice. There were some potatoes in the pantry. Get me out five or six. If I am going to fry this fish, I may as well make chips." Davianna turned to Peter and Astrid. "We are limited on the fresh food, but we'll make do."

"Any more wolves?" Astrid shuddered.

Josiah turned from his search of the pantry. "No, just the one." He spied the spuds. "Davianna, catch." In rapid fire succession, he started chucking potatoes at her.

She caught them with a little yelp.

"Did you bury it?" Astrid shifted her gaze out the window, trying to see if the carcass was still there.

"No." Josiah's voice oozed condescension. "It is frozen out there. To bury it, I would need Peter guarding my back. However, Peter has been unavailable all day."

Silence descended on the kitchen, save for the running water as Davianna washed the potatoes.

"It is my birthday. I do not bury wolves on my birthday," Peter retorted.

Davianna looked up, smiling. "It's your birthday? How old are you?"

"Twenty-two, right?" Josiah said, standing at Davianna's arm.

Peter held open his arms and smiled. "I made it."

"Oh fun, then you get to pick supper tonight." Davianna paused, mentally reviewing the contents of the pantry. "I don't think I have what I need for a cake, but I bet I can pull together cobbler or even a pie."

Peter gave Astrid a salacious grin, stroking her leg behind the bar. "Peach pie is my favorite."

Davianna was the only one in the room who did not understand the double entendre. "I think I have the stuff for peach pie."

When everyone, even Josiah, burst out laughing, Davianna asked, "What? Why are y'all laughing? What's so funny about a peach pie?"

There was a hint of southern accent when she said pie that made Josiah want to sit on a porch swing and sip sweet tea.

After lunch, the group voted Davianna the official cook. She sat at the bar, watching Josiah and Astrid do the dishes. Since it was Peter's birthday, he received, what all decided, was a onetime reprieve from clean up duty.

Josiah nodded toward Peter. "You have to watch him. He got out of everything when we were kids."

Peter pointed at himself. "Who, me?"

Josiah remembered well. "We could not keep him in class. He gave our tutor Mr. ben Merriweather fits. We would usually find him with the horses or with his mother."

Peter stiffened.

Josiah caught his eye. "Sorry."

Peter glanced at Astrid, who was putting away the big fry pot. "No worries. She has been on my mind."

Josiah made a face and mumbled, "Oedipus."

Peter shrugged and said for Josiah's ear's only, "I am a sick bastard."

Davianna was vaguely aware of the interplay, but she was preoccupied, calculating how long the pie crust took and wondering whether there was enough sugar.

Exile

As night fell, Astrid and Peter disappeared upstairs, leaving him and Davianna alone in front of the fire. Josiah fiddled with it, making the flames dance, adding another log. The wind howled, but the cabin was warm, blanketed in snow. Isolated and cut off from everyone, for the moment they were safe. Despite the tranquil environment, Davianna's face revealed the troubled turn of her thoughts. In repose, the horror of her captivity caught her. Josiah had something that could help, but it was going to cost him.

"I was fifteen when I escaped the Palace the first time," he said it into the flames.

That gained her attention.

"Peter, his mother, my Aunt Alexa, and Auntie G., the lady you heard over the speaker the night we escaped, helped me." He scratched his head, lost in the memory.

"We faked a suicide, so Korah would not come after me. The plan was for me to go to the Golden City, present myself at court, and seek the help of the Iron King. I made it all the way to Macedonia. Then, I was captured." Josiah met her eyes.

Davianna hugged herself and looked at him in surprise. "I did not know that."

"Nobody knows, I have never told anyone." He pressed his lips in a grim line and swallowed. "I spent the first six months locked in a room, held for a future ransom. But I wouldn't tell my captor who I was, so we were at a bit of a stalemate."

"Who held you?"

Josiah cleared his throat. "A crazy revolutionary named Yane ben Sandanski."

He moved to the window, staring into the dark. His face reflected in the black glass, his mind far away. "He lived alone and would sit outside my door and talk. He was an anti-royal revolutionary, hated Antiochus, hated anything to do with the monarchy. So, he'd talk."

Josiah turned to face her. "It is hard to explain. I was disillusioned, young, scared. I kept waiting for the Iron King, day after day, but he never came." He looked away and said, "I hated Korah. Inside those four walls, it consumed me." Speaking of it, brought it back. He closed his eyes, fighting an urge to punch his fist through a wall.

Davianna sat perched on the edge of the sofa, watching him quietly.

"After a while, at least in my mind, I began to agree with Sandanski. I started talking back." His laugh sounded bitter, full of self-recrimination and regret. "After six months, he let me out of the room. I worked the farm with him. At night, he locked me back in. One day, he stopped locking the door, and I stayed."

Josiah settled in beside her. "I was there for two years. I stayed on that farm, with a man who held me hostage, for two years."

Davianna stared at her lap. "How did you escape?"

Josiah gave a bitter snort. "My dog died." At her quizzical frown, he elaborated, "I cannot explain it. He was old, a gift from my father. It just seemed to wake me up, so I left."

"Did you ever go back, ever confront him?"

"Last spring, I went to the farm, but he was gone. I don't know where he is, or what I would have done if he had been there."

They sat still and quiet, the fire crackling, lost in their own thoughts.

When she spoke, her voice was low with unspent tears. "Thank you, Josiah. You know I needed to hear that. I've been beating myself up about what I did."

He put his arm around her, drawing her close. "You didn't do anything, Minx. You just survived."

Her hand went to the side of her head, and she gripped her hair. "When you escaped, why didn't you come back to Alanthia?"

His chest rose and fell with a deep sigh. "I found out they

fought a Civil War while I was held captive. Korah won. I think I was still a bit messed up in my head after enduring years of anti-royal propaganda, and I thought, to hell with it." He laughed with old bitterness. "I also knew, if I came back, I'd have to explain where I'd been."

Her eyelids were heavy, her expression grim. "It's embarrassing, isn't it, being held prisoner? Especially when they make you believe you have a choice, and you stay."

He raised a black brow at her and said, "You may be one of the only people in the world who actually understands that."

January 7, 1000 ME

What's the Plan?

At breakfast the next morning, Josiah called a meeting. "We need to talk about our strategy and our plan, both immediate and long-term. We are all coming into this with different levels of intelligence and information. For our plan to be effective, we need to share information. Agreed?"

They spent the afternoon discussing what they knew. Astrid shared about their time on the run, how they evaded capture and learned to change disguises and accents. They all agreed the girls' greatest strategy was their unpredictability.

Josiah came at it from a hunter's angle, but he also shared with them the results of his negotiations. Peter grinned when he learned the Iron King would give his support once he safely delivered Davianna to the Golden City.

Peter's role was more enigmatic. "About three years ago, I began putting together an organization. It is a bit hackneyed, but we called it The Resistance. They are the ones who helped us escape and will assist as we make our way to the Golden City. We acquired a number of safe houses and vehicles along the way. There are also assets if we run into trouble.

"We caught a break the night you lot were arrested, someone sent us the codes and back doors into the government's systems, so we can monitor what they are doing. Some of the best minds in the kingdom are working on our behalf, and they will be able to give us advance warning if Korah makes a move."

Davianna went last, relaying her visit with the Iron King, the Gune, and then the incredible discovery that only she and Astrid could feel the device when it was in her tunic.

Peter held out his hand. "I need to see it."

Davianna shook her head. "No, we can't touch it. I haven't looked at it since the Gune's Cottage. Jelena put it in my pocket, and I never took it out. It's a wicked thing."

Peter shuddered. "You have no idea what is locked up with that device."

Josiah asked, "You only looked at it twice?"

Astrid scowled at him. "Yeah, the massacre and that whole earthquake thing sort of put a stop to it."

Peter ignored Astrid's sarcasm. "What concerns me is the biometric scan you two did when you opened the device."

"Why is that a concern?" Josiah asked.

"It means the device, if it gets in the hands of someone else, must have one of you to open it." Peter sat back on the sofa and took Astrid's hand. "Up to this point, I thought we might be able to extricate you, get you somewhere safe, but you will not be safe outside the Golden City, any more than Davianna will."

"We figured that out," Astrid said with a matter of fact nod. "Even if my print wasn't on that thing, the fact that I have been here since the beginning locks me in. The die is cast. I don't have an escape."

"Damn," Peter said staring out the window. "I need to see it."

"Why?" Josiah demanded in a low growl.

Peter gave him a long-suffering look. "Because I need to have replicas made. If we get caught, we need a decoy."

Astrid wet her lips, considering. "You can get that done?"

"Of course."

Davianna backed up. "I'm not touching it. It has a mind of its own. The first time we opened it, it started talking. The second time, it just went crazy. Astrid could not get it to turn off, and it was playing this horrible devil music. It only stopped when I put it back in my pocket. No, you can't see it."

Astrid moved in front of Davianna and met Peter's stare. "She cannot open it."

"I do not want her freeing any more monsters, but I cannot make a decoy if I do not know what it is." Peter widened his eyes and looked at Davianna.

"It's an iPhone, but not like I've read about before. The box had a label on it," Astrid said.

"What did it say?" Josiah asked.

Davianna answered, "Prototype 1.C, NSA - Project Rusor."

Josiah sucked in a hissing breath. "Rusor is Latin for rising. It is also the name of a Roman god and it means the god to whom everything returns."

Davianna grabbed the back of her neck and looked away.

Astrid exhaled and wagged a finger at Davianna. "That lines up exactly with what Jelena told us."

"Hang on." Peter rose from the couch, returning a moment later with a tablet, opened to a blank email. He handed it to Astrid. "I want you to type everything you remember about the device, markings, label, size, everything. With the backdoor codes we have into the government's system, plus the team we have in place, we might be able to pull together what we need to make a couple passable decoys."

Josiah rubbed his chin, considering. "That would make sense. Nobody has seen it except these two, so as long as it looks ancient, it could fool somebody."

Davianna's heart pounded. "I don't have to take it out?"

Peter met her eyes. "I need you to remember everything you can about it, every detail, including the things it said and the song it played. My people will take care of the rest."

"And sending this message? That won't get us caught?" Astrid tapped the tablet with her fingernail.

Peter shook his head.

Astrid turned to Josiah. "You take that grenade launcher and every freaking weapon we've got on that back deck and shoot down anything that comes out of the sky." She stood, going toe to toe with Peter. "You better know what you are doing."

He leaned forward and whispered something low, personal, and utterly between them. She kissed his cheek, opened the email, and started typing.

January 8, 1000 ME

Weapons at Dawn

Astrid thought Josiah was joking about weapons at dawn, he was not. At 6:00 am, she looked blearily at him over her cup of coffee as he lectured about weapon safety. "Just let me hold the damn thing."

Josiah gave her an admonishing stare. "No, not until we have reviewed the appropriate safety and operational precautions for handling a firearm."

There was no dissuading him. Astrid recognized the stubborn set of his jaw, and his patient lecturing tone. As much as he might irritate her, he was a good teacher, and such an utterly decent man it was hard not to like him, even if he was a bit patronizing and bossy.

Two hours later, three broken nails, and a shoulder that was already turning purple, Astrid appreciated why Josiah insisted knives were a better weapon for the girls than the heavy guns. Her hands ached, and even with the protective earmuffs, a headache was threatening. She wanted breakfast, and she wanted to crawl back in the bed with Peter, who was still asleep. He was exhausted, even if he would not admit it. When Josiah dismissed the class, she ran upstairs and jumped in bed with him.

He rolled over, sleep rumpled and ready to snuggle. "You smell like gunpowder. I like it," he said, nuzzling her neck.

"I'm a good shot," Astrid giggled and moved away from his tickling breath.

Peter smiled. "Texans. Why does that not surprise me?"

Astrid gave him a coy look, pleased with herself. Control of a gun gave her back a measure of safety taken from her at the Palace.

He understood that. "And Sparrow, how was she?"

"Well, she's okay." Astrid hunched her shoulders and threw up her palms. "She is very smart and figured out how to break those guns down in record time. She can load and unload a weapon in seconds, mastered all of it, much faster than I did."

"But she could not hit a thing, could she?" Peter pictured it.

Astrid laughed. "No, she couldn't. Poor Josiah, he is so patient, but her hands shake like crazy, she has no aim, and the gun hurts when you fire it, especially the revolver. They are also loud, and you know how jumpy she is. She tried, but she hated it. She fired about ten shots, then escaped into the kitchen and is making sausage biscuits and gravy."

Peter's stomach growled. "Well, at least she knows how to handle a weapon, and somebody has to be the cook. She can load if we ever need her."

Astrid grew still. "You think we will?"

All humor and teasing evaporated. "Bloody likely, Red."

The Golden Prince and the Danish Bear

Disguises came next, Astrid's forte. She became adept at them while they were running and devoted considerable time watching videos on latex and prosthetics while they were holed up in the hotel. To her absolute frustration, she did not have the tools to practice while they were hiding. Peter foresaw the need, and with great ceremony and flourish, presented Astrid with a case full of stage makeup and assorted paraphernalia. She hugged his neck like he had given her the crown jewels. Josiah surmised, under the circumstances, the case was the more valuable of the two.

As they were discussing various ways to disguise each of them, Davianna exerted her will. "No, I am not doing it. I'm not cutting my hair and playing a boy again." She crossed her arms, a mulish expression on her face. "Besides," she glanced down, looking left and right, "I can't hide these anymore."

Heat exploded in Josiah's groin, unwanted, unwelcome, unstoppable. He looked away with a ragged exhale. She was correct. There was no denying she was anything other than a curvy, busty, round ass, little female with big, beautiful brown eyes, a pretty oval face, and those pink heart-shaped lips. "I agree, thou canst no longer pass for a lad."

Peter exploded with laughter, which he tried to smother, turning away, and acting like the melting snow was fascinating.

"What's so funny?" Davianna put her hands on her hips.

Peter could not look at her, or he would lose it. "Nothing, Sparrow." He held up his hand to stop her. "You do not have to be a boy."

"Good," Davianna declared and stomped off into the kitchen.

"You," Astrid said, pointing at Josiah, "sit down. I have some ideas for you. That Carsten ben Hansen persona was an excellent disguise."

Peter sputtered, "What?"

Josiah rolled his eyes. "It was not my idea."

Astrid shook her head. "It was brilliant. Just the nose and ears, changed you completely, and of course, that blond wig."

Peter guffawed. "That was you?"

The laughter was contagious.

Josiah scowled and threatened in a thick Danish accent, "Little Golden Prince, do not make Danish Bear kick your ass."

Agile as an acrobat, Peter jumped to the back of the sofa,

raising his arms in challenge. "The Golden Prince rules the cabin in the mountains. Give it your best shot Danish Bear!"

An absolute melee of good natured, furniture crashing, wrestling erupted. Peter, younger and agile, had quickness and wiry strength. Josiah outweighed him by forty pounds of solid muscle, but he was fast and wicked strong. Astrid and Davianna scattered, looking with fascinated pleasure and a touch of consternation as the testosterone contest ensued.

At some point, it shifted, changed from play to something more important. Despite their physical differences, they were evenly matched. Amid sweat, strain, and pain, it became a contest of will and strength, one of strategy and endurance. It asked, 'Will you be there? Are you strong enough? Can I depend on you?'

It passed between them and settled. When they broke apart, a tension as old as their relationship dissolved, and in its place, respect.

January 9, 1000 ME

Alanthian Royal Cry

At half past one, Peter rolled over in his warm bed, unable to sleep, his mind running over the cryptic warning he received three days ago.

"Falcon, it is not safe for me to discuss the situation over the line, but trust that we have this in hand. In the interim, stay put, and only communicate with us in an emergency. We are going dark."

When pressed, his contact refused to elaborate on the nature of the threat, but Peter could tell from his tone that the breach was serious. Peter had not heard from anyone since. However, as much as they all wanted to move, Korah's hostages needed the respite.

Astrid lay on his left. She was a stomach sleeper and always kept one foot outside the covers with her other knee drawn up. Astrid did not like to be touched when she slept and grumbled at him when he tried. He slept with women regularly, kept them in his bed when he was done with them as a sort of insurance policy. The monster did not attack in front of witnesses. They never discerned their actual purpose and tried to hold him all night long. Their clinging always irritated him, and thus, the irony of his current sleeping arrangement was not lost upon him.

He was thirsty, and his dry mouth reminded him for the dozenth time that week how much he missed Jarrod. Normally, there would be a tray on his nightstand. Not quite awake, he wondered idly if he could convince Davianna to make one up before he came to bed, but immediately rejected the idea. Astrid would get prickly about it, and he did not want her prickly. He wanted her warm, soft, and sexy.

He groaned and rolled out of his cozy bed, shaking his head because getting his own glass of water and leaving an enticing woman were novel activities, to be sure. He shrugged on a pair of jeans and a sweater and padded barefoot out the door.

Downstairs, Josiah laid on the couch, reading a book by the firelight. He rested the novel on his chest and looked up as Peter descended.

"You are up late."

Josiah stretched. "I woke up and could not go back to sleep."

Peter walked past him into the kitchen. "I suppose that is a good sign. No lasting effects from your vacation in Korah's dungeon."

Josiah rose from the couch and stretched his arms over his head, his shoulders popping. The gray t-shirt lifted, showing Peter the dark bruises on his torso. His wrists bore the chafe marks of the manacles, and his bare feet were still swollen and discolored. He limped when the girls were not around. "I hurt like hell. That wrestling match did not help."

"You are strong as an ox," Peter laughed.

"Me? You are fast as lightning and agile as an acrobat. Where did you learn to fight like that?" Josiah joined Peter in the kitchen, perusing the contents of the refrigerator.

"I train six days a week." Peter raised his glass of water in a mocking toast. "They won't take me again."

"I have no doubt about that." Josiah pulled out a bowl of leftover pasta salad, not bothering with a plate.

Peter took a fork from the drawer and helped himself.

The two Princes of Alanthia stood in the dim kitchen, eating Davianna ben David's macaroni salad in companionable silence. They made quick work of it, fighting over the last bite with their forks and laughing as they did it.

Peter gestured toward the living room, "Let's go sit down. We have some things to discuss. Now is as good a time as any, the girls are asleep."

Josiah put another log on the fire, stoking the flames which cast dancing shadows across the oak planked floor and ceiling. Peter hit the light in the kitchen and the two settled on the sofas, relaxed, but with an air of expectation. To date, they had not discussed their long-term plans for the kingdom. The immediacy of survival, escape, and recovery had taken precedence over any speculation about the future.

Peter cleared his throat, his demeanor serious, without the customary teasing gleam in his eyes. "I am sorry to admit, but I remember very little about your father. He did not have much time for me, not that I blame him, running the kingdom occupies a man's time. However, I do remember one afternoon. He brought the two of us into his study for a history lesson. Do you recall?"

Josiah's brown eyes bore into his cousin's green ones, and he nodded. "I do."

"That was the day he made us swear our loyalty to one another. We promised to protect and defend each other and stand against anyone who might seek to destroy us." Peter sighed, his expression far away. "It was also the day he taught us the royal cry, the one you shouted from the mountain when the wolf came after you and Davianna."

"And you answered that call," Josiah said quietly.

"Without a moment's hesitation, though I was naked at the time." The corner of Peter's mouth lifted.

Josiah closed his eyes and laughed. "You managed to pull on your shorts and bring a weapon. That was a good shot, by the way. I do not believe I thanked you for that."

"No, you were too busy being angry at me for debauching an innocent, but I will make that right."

"You will?" Josiah raised his eyebrows in speculation.

Peter shrugged a shoulder. "She is different."

"There are many obstacles to a relationship between the two of you. If I recall, that was part of the conversation we had with my father that day." Josiah gave Peter a pointed look.

"I remember the whole lecture about our duty to our line, the brides they would choose for us, and the responsibilities we would both bear." Peter shook his head, the corner of his mouth lifting. "That never sat right with me, for obvious reasons."

Josiah stared into the flames. "Aye."

"I never forgot that conversation, and I have done everything in my power to prepare the kingdom for you. The organization I built will be the mechanism by which we will destabilize Korah's government. By the time we reach the Golden City, we will expose him for who and what he is. It is my hope that the people will rise and demand the true and rightful heir take the throne, avoiding another Civil War."

Josiah leaned forward, resting his chin on his knuckles, considering. "That would be my preference."

"Mine as well," Peter agreed. "I would beg your indulgence, Prince."

Josiah dropped his hands to his lap and sat erect. Peter's formal address prompted his reply. "Please proceed, Prince. I shall grant thy request if I am able."

Peter gave a nod of acknowledgment. "I will do my utmost

to secure your throne and see that you returned to power. I
will assist, aid, and protect you. I will transition leadership
of my organization and step aside. They will follow you." He
took a deep breath and continued, "In exchange, you will release me from further obligation to the kingdom of Alanthia.
You set me free."

Josiah was shocked by the request, but he quickly recognized the strategic advantages to Peter's proposal. Prince d'Or
was Alanthia's darling. Eliminating him as a contender for
the throne solidified Josiah's position. It also quashed factions
that might emerge in opposition to his rule. It would be preferable to have Peter by his side, but his father had paid the
ultimate price for keeping his popular brother close at hand.
"Where will you go?" Josiah asked.

Peter flashed a smile. "Wherever I want. I envision a
yacht on the Mediterranean and a winsome redhead by my
side. I shall play the exile and enjoy every damn moment of
it. You will be bogged down, running the kingdom, while I
enjoy living in a house where no one wants to kill me. A fair
exchange, do you not agree?"

"I suppose a handsome allowance is in order?" Josiah
grinned.

Peter hid a secret smile. "I am not opposed, but it is un-
necessary. I am comfortable in my own right."

"Is that so?" Josiah asked, amused.

Peter swept a hand around the cabin. "You do not think
my allowance financed all this, do you?" He laughed. "The
old bastard barely gives me enough money to pay for my
wardrobe, let alone finance a revolution."

Josiah shook his head, admiration glowing in his whiskey-colored eyes. "You have always been full of surprises,
Prince. Korah's biggest downfall will be underestimating
you."

Peter rubbed the bridge of his nose. "I had a friend say
that to me on New Year's Eve." He looked up, deep sadness
registering on his face. "They shall be the only people I will

miss in exile. I want your word that you will see to their protection and the protection of the rest of my people. They have put their lives on the line for our cause."

"I give you my solemn word, as your sovereign. I will do everything within my power to ensure their safety."

Peter nodded, emotion straining his voice. "My honor and my allegiance remain with you. I swore it to you that day in your father's study when I was six years old. I have never wavered in my commitment. I have never broken that vow."

Josiah took a deep breath, a firestorm of nerves shot up his spine. Peter spoke the truth. In all ways, he lived up to his oath and had been the most loyal of the two. Josiah realized that in the warehouse, but it hit him full force tonight.

"I would have you at my right hand, for there is no one I trust more. However, I will honor your request if that is what you choose. Know this, I reaffirm my vow of loyalty to you. Our royal blood binds us to each other and to this land." Josiah offered his hand, a gesture of an equal, a friend. "When you finish floating around the Mediterranean, come home."

Contingencies

The next morning over breakfast, they determined it would not be safe to always travel together. There would be times where they split up, otherwise it would be too easy to find them. Vehicles and safe houses were scattered across the route, but only Peter knew them all. As a precaution, no one else did. On the days they traveled apart, they would each know the next two rendezvous points, never more. If the safe house was compromised or either of them were being followed, they would proceed to the second stop. If the second stop proved dangerous, they were to wait for the third day and access a single use email account where there would be an ad for a product with the address encoded in the flyer. In case of absolute emergencies, they memorized a phone number, a phrase, and prayed they would never have to use it.

Funding was not a concern. Peter was well provisioned.

And the Gune gold that appeared in the girls' boots fascinated Josiah. "I wondered how in the world you two were getting funds. I expected to find a trail of thefts, but I never did. I could not figure it out."

"Well," Davianna said with a saucy tilt of her head, "I'm just full of surprises."

That you are, little minx, Josiah thought. but would never say, mad at himself for thinking it.

Peter suppressed a smile and raised a knowing eyebrow at him.

Josiah ignored him, irritated by the perceptive looks his cousin kept giving him. Josiah wanted to punch him, he wanted to kiss her, and he wanted to get on the road. It was maddening, especially the sounds coming from Peter's bedroom. The guy was insatiable. All those two did was go at it like rabbits, day and night. It was more than another guy should have to bear.

He was dying, and he knew better than anyone, he was only a man, as much as he might tell himself otherwise. Davianna was just so adorable, pretty, funny, sexy as hell, cooking for him all the time. She was so sweet. He loved her laugh and the way her eyes sparkled right before she said something outrageous. She was oblivious to half the stuff going on around her, the undertones, dirty jokes. She also did not seem to notice that any time Peter paid her the slightest attention Astrid bristled.

Josiah needed to do the honorable thing and leave her alone. He did not want to force her out of this respite, back into that tough girl he met on the bridge or at the park. The soldier in him knew they were facing battle. This may well be the last time she ever got to be this girl. He would not let anything, or anybody take it away from her, including himself.

The mountain cabin wrapped them all in a temporary cocoon. They all needed it, for their own reasons, but Davianna was the most fragile, the vulnerable one, and in the wickedest twist of the tale, the one they hunted most.

Not Now, Not Ever

The brass knob felt cold under Davianna's moist palm. Her heart pounded in her fingertips as she pushed open the door. Moonlight cast a silver glow on the wood framed queen-sized bed. Josiah's body seemed to occupy every inch.

It was the soldier who woke up. "Is everything okay?"

"Yes."

"Did you have a nightmare?" The protector rubbed sleep out of his eyes.

"No."

"Well, are you sick?" The doctor asked with impatience.

Davianna let out a frustrated breath. "No, I am not sick, Josiah."

"Then what are you doing in here?" Alarm bells sounded in the man's brain as the fog of sleep blew away.

The pale winter light silhouetted her. She was wearing a long tee shirt, standing in bare feet. Davianna bit her bottom lip and said, "I know I shouldn't, we shouldn't but... I just don't want to be alone tonight."

Oh God, do not do this to me! The very lonely exile thought.

But the Prince answered. "I'm sorry, Davianna, but that is not going to happen, not now, not ever."

She covered her face with her hands. "I'm sorry," she whispered in mortification and fled his room.

The door did not quite close. He heard her heart wrenching intake of breath and a stifled sob as her footsteps pounded down the hall.

He wanted to go after her. With everything in him, he wanted to throw open that door, take her in his arms, and kiss her tears away. He wanted to cherish her, love her, protect her. But if he moved from this bed, he would be doing none of those things. He would be destroying her, dishonoring her, defiling her and in the process himself. It would destroy everything he ever worked for.

He draped his arm over his eyes and used every ounce of willpower he had to stay put. Because above all, above everything else, Josiah ben Eamonn was an honorable man, and that was rarely easy.

Utterly humiliated, Davianna wanted to die of shame.

'Not going to happen, not now, not ever.' The words tumbled over and over in her mind, followed by the litany that plagued her these nine days, 'You went crazy! You thought you were in love with Korah. You thought he was going to make you a queen.'

She buried her flaming face in the pillow and wished the earth would swallow her whole.

"Do you really think Josiah would want you? He saw you on the floor, out of your mind. He saw you freak out in that office. He saw you go comatose in front of the TV."

Not now, not ever.

Sobs of the deepest kind, the ones that made no noise, contorted her body. She could not go to Astrid; Astrid was with Peter. She would never tell anyone this.

Not now, not ever.

January 10, 1000 ME

Make Your Own Breakfast

After much discussion and consultation with The Resistance, they determined they would not leave the mountain cabin until January 11th, the day after the Royal Wedding. Peter would be too much on the public's mind to risk even the best disguise, and the mountain pass still had patchy spots of ice according to the scouting mission Josiah conducted the day before.

Thus, the place that seemed like a haven yesterday, now felt like a prison cell. Sleep eluded Davianna, and when the dawn light peeked through the windows, she dressed and rose.

Armed with her knives, she put on the blue coat, and slipped out, intending to watch the sunrise from the crest. Something had carried off the wolf carcass, and she did not care if she met whatever had. She would kill it or let it kill her, then all this would be over.

Poor, stupid, naïve, Davianna. Crazy... she knew that was what they thought about her. She caught how they were always laughing behind her back. She was a joke, a crazy joke. Crazy...

The snow had melted, leaving a stark landscape, majestic, but bleak. A north wind carried the smell of wet earth and moldering leaves. Looking up at the ice-blue sky, her eyes filled with tears. "Why? Why have you brought me here? Why me?" she prayed for the hundredth time.

She stood at the top of the peak, a solitary figure among the mighty mountains. The answer that came to her mind on the frozen wind, "Thou art not alone," was not enough, not today.

Abandoning any hope of peace, she stormed from the vista and back to the cabin where she was sure more fun awaited.

Josiah came out the backdoor as she walked down the hill. He wore an expression full of solicitude and concern. She wanted to punch him. "What are you doing out here by yourself? Are you crazy?"

Wrong. Thing. To. Say.

Until that moment, Davianna ben David had never lost her temper at anyone—ever. When it happened, the explosion was on par with a nuclear bomb, southern style.

She hit him full force with a stiff arm, pushing him out of her way. "No, I am not crazy. I went for a walk, which I am perfectly capable of doing, and if I decide I want to go for a walk, I will go on a fucking walk! Do you hear me?"

Josiah drew back. "Hey, now," he started, but she was having none of it.

"I am not your patient, and I am not your sister. I don't give a shit about your mission, or your army, or your damn kingdom. Stay the hell away from me!" She stormed into the house.

Astrid made a face. "Somebody is grumpy."

Davianna whirled on her. "And you! Damn you! You think I don't see those looks you've been shooting me all week, every time your precious Peter says a word to me?"

Davianna charged straight at her. "You think I don't see? You think I don't know where that shit is coming from?" She pushed Astrid down to the couch and leaned over her. "Like I am blind, naïve, and stupid? You think I don't know that you believed that lying sack of shit Guan... over ME? You stupid, fucking bitch!"

She stalked off, screaming, "He is the one who attacked me! I didn't cheat with your mean-ass boyfriend. I hated him! I was only nice to him because you liked him."

Davianna's face turned crimson as she looked from Astrid to Peter. "And there you go again, Astrid, throwing down with a world-renowned playboy."

She sneered, ugly and jealous, "You're just a piece of tail to him. When this is all over, you think you got some kind of future? You think Prince d'Or will keep you around when every leggy blonde on the planet is trying to get in his pants? Do you think for one damn minute, if we were not locked in this cabin, he would even give you a second look?"

Davianna laughed and added scornfully, "Well, maybe he would, considering you look exactly like his dead mother. And if that ain't some sick twisted shit, I don't know what is."

She pounded up the steps, and before she slammed her bedroom door, shouted, "So you all can make your own fucking breakfast!"

Is She Right?

Astrid watched a stranger storm up the steps. She felt her face begin the telltale blush, and before either man could say a word, she fled to her own room. The range of emotions crashing in on her ran the gamut.

How dare Davianna speak to her that way?

But she was right, she had been giving her mean looks, believing the worst of her. Why hadn't she told her about Guan? All those months, she never breathed a word.

And what she said about her and Peter? She fell on the bed with a groan. Did she look like his dead mother? She buried her hands in her face and realized it was true. That was why Korah kept calling her Alexa. The thought made her sick.

But did she care? Did she really care? Because she wanted him, and that desire was so strong it wiped everything else away. It was dark, this passion. A need, to claw and to kiss, to love and to wound, and to utterly possess Prince Peter ben Korah.

Worse than all the other emotions, a new one crawled in. Addiction pulled at her, beckoning her back, promising oblivion and euphoria, the ability to forget for a while.

Astrid stood up, her chest heaving, and closed her eyes against the swirl. Her breathing slowed. She clenched and unclenched her fists, set her jaw, gathered herself. "I will think about this later."

She went back downstairs, dry-eyed.

Peter cocked his head in silent inquiry.

As she moved past him, she growled, "I'm fine, just don't talk to me."

Peter smiled at her retreating form, looked at Josiah with a self-satisfied smile, and quipped, "The woman of my dreams."

Josiah leaned back in his chair, staring up at Davianna's locked door. "That one will be the death of me. I know it."

Peter was fairly certain that was not a jest.

Come on, Fireball

Mortified, Davianna determined she would die of starvation before she left her room. She was a peacemaker, not a fighter, and even if she had spoken the truth, she did not know how to make it right, having zero experience with this type of thing.

The knock on her door sounded around five. She let out a sigh and called for them to enter. It was Peter. Of the three of them, he was the last one she expected.

He stepped in and closed the door. "Are you going to hide up here all day?" His level gaze was full of teasing humor.

She hid her face with her hands. "Yes."

"Sort of ruins the whole badass thing you had working down there."

Leave it to Peter to make her laugh. "I'm so sorry. I owe you an apology. I was mean."

He blew her off. "Davianna ben David, I grew up in Korah's household. You could take lessons for a thousand years and still not be mean." He flopped down on the bed beside her.

"Well, I guess when you put it like that, but still."

"For the record, I know at least a half a dozen leggy blondes who do not want to get in my pants."

His charming smile disarmed her, and she collapsed on the pillow beside him, laughing. "All six of them?"

"Maybe, five."

She giggled, and they lay there in companionable silence.

Then Davianna moaned, "Astrid hates me."

"Red needed to hear the truth," Peter said matter of fact. "At least about that asshole Guan. What a douche."

"Oh my gosh, I adore you." Davianna smiled. Then she added hastily, "But not in that way!"

He rolled his eyes. "I know, Fireball."

Davianna snorted. "I like that better than Sparrow."

"Well," he drew himself up on one elbow and in mock seriousness declared, "I, Prince Peter ben Korah of Alanthia, do hereby dub thee, Davianna ben Fireball, to be known as such throughout the land. henceforth and ever after."

"Good." She nodded. The matter settled.

"Good." Peter smiled.

"Fireball, ugh, who am I kidding? I made an ass of myself in front of Josiah. I could just die." With renewed humiliation she hid under the pillow.

"Fireballs do not hide under pillows." Peter lifted the edge and smiled, the dimple in his left cheek showing.

"It was awful," Davianna groaned and pulled the pillow back down, hiding her flaming face.

"Bloody hell, what did you do? What I saw on the porch was not that bad."

"I can't talk about it. It is humiliating," she said in a muffled voice.

Peter let out a long sigh, and after a moment whispered, "I can guess."

Davianna lifted a corner of the pillow. "Am I that obvious?"

"No, you are not that obvious, but I have eyes. Come on out of there. Let me tell you a few things about my cousin."

Davianna crossed her arms over her chest, staring at the ceiling, refusing to look at him. "Go ahead."

"Prince Josiah ben Eamonn is the most decent and honorable man I have ever known. Where the rest of us mere mortals talk about duty, honor, and fealty, Josiah lives it. He was born to it. It is who he is. Which is why I have spent my entire life doing everything in my power to forsake my legal position and restore him to the throne. He is the better man, certainly better than Korah, better than me, as evidenced that I had no qualms about 'compromising an innocent'. Which is another discussion we will have, by the way. But Josiah, even though he is about to explode with pent up lust for you, will never give into that."

Davianna snorted. "He doesn't lust after me."

"You do not see half of what goes on around you, although after this morning, I realize you see more than you let on, but you do not see it. He does not show it. However, I know him, and I am also a man. I know what a man in rut looks like."

She giggled. "You always look like you are in rut."

He unleashed his legendary grin. "Because I am." Then he narrowed his brows and pointed a long finger at her, his tone becoming serious. "Which brings me to my last point, and that is what you said about Astrid and me."

Davianna crinkled up her face. "Sorry."

"Under ordinary circumstances, you would have probably been correct. I will grant you that," he said, slow and deliberate. "But you are wrong, and I will leave it at that. Okay?"

Brown eyes bored into emerald ones, searching for deception. This was the most important point, more important than anything they discussed, and he was telling her the truth. "Okay."

"All right then." He got off the bed and offered her his hand. "Come on, Fireball. Shall we dine?"

"Did you cook?" she teased.

"Hell no, none of us wants to die."

Black Wedding

It was like a scene straight out of the classic Sleeping Beauty. The rich, the powerful, the royals, and the gentry from across the globe, gathered to celebrate the royal wedding of King Korah ben Adam of Alanthia to Princess Keyseelough ben Mubarak of Egypt, when an unexpected and uninvited guest showed up.

The lavish celebration was in full swing. The bride and groom sat at the head table, surrounded by gifts and flowers. Guests, dressed in their finery, enjoyed the world's most delicious food from overflowing banquet tables. Souls were merry from dancing and the copious amounts of alcohol that poured from bottle and tap. Every kingdom, save one, came to make speeches and give honor to the esteemed couple, when the hall was plunged into darkness.

The enormous double doors blew open in a thunderous

crash. The wedding guests panicked, jostling each other to escape, but calmed when an enchanted breeze blew through the ballroom. It smelled heavenly, of sea, wood, or earth, afterward, no one could agree. Collectively, they inhaled, and exhaled euphoria.

Music began, quiet at first, then building until it engulfed the hall. It was a song of such tender beauty that men wept to the depths of their souls for the joy of hearing it.

Blue orbs of cold lightning rolled through the open doors, performing a buoyant dance among the crowd. They were devilishly delightful, breathtaking. Spiraling upward and moving in brilliant colors. They merged, creating shapes that drew gasps from the crowd. The lights converged into the flags of the world, then united under a single banner.

The sky show transformed into a white tornado of magnificent strength and awesome power, culminating in a brilliant flash.

When their mortal vision cleared, they fell to their faces. Elegantly attired in ebony and jet, radiant in beauty and power, stood the long-exiled king. The ruler of the Earth for six thousand years, who reigned over the great and powerful age of technology and personal freedom, Lucifer, in the flesh.

For Keyseelough, it was not her husband who laid her down that night, not a tender lover, a handsome Prince, or even an aging King seeking an alliance. No. On her wedding night, they did not usher her to the royal bedchamber. She was not perfumed and dressed in a shimmering peignoir. She did not luxuriate on a canopy bed draped with silks and satins, tempting her new husband.

Lucifer demanded, *jus primae noctis,* the lord's right of first night.

In the dungeon, Keyseelough was stripped naked before a select audience and spread before Lucifer on a slab of stone. She had vied for the role of Ba'alat Ob, had burned with indignation when they passed her over, taking second place, but she thought by doing this, she would supplant them all and become the most powerful woman in the world.

However, when the dark angel fell upon her, Uriel's prophecy came true, and death, that she so ardently wished for, did not come. In her body and soul, she suspected that Hell would be a reprieve from what he was doing to her.

Korah stood alone on the dais, clothed in his wedding finery, watching with detached horror. A new master was in his dungeon, more terrifying than the last. Lucifer clearly had no use for him, nor did he have plans to form an alliance. The Devil demonstrated that vividly by splitting his new bride in half, right before his eyes.

Part 11 - Road Trip

January 11, 1000 ME

Anarchists

The disguise of the day, anarchist. Davianna spiked her hair and sprayed it with temporary black and purple color. Her makeup was severe, onyx eyeshadow and crimson lipstick over pale foundation. The jewelry she wore was appropriately rebellious, big silver hoops, and a black studded collar. She studied the temporary tattoo on the back of her hand, a jagged 'A' enclosed in a circle. She belted her tunic with a silver chain and pulled purple socks halfway up her thighs. She looked wicked.

It did something strange to her. She felt drawn to the girl in the mirror. That girl did not take any shit. That girl would not hide in her room. She would tell the whole world to take a flying leap. That girl said, "If you mess with me, I will hurt you." She pulled her knife. The deadly click of the switchblade cut through the air. Manipulating it, she rolled it between her fingers: dexterous, competent, deadly.

An impulse seized her as she grazed her left pocket. She wanted to pull it free. Feeling the shape, she imagined the sleek black surface, knew the power. She could play a song, just for spite. Her hand closed over the device.

The eyes that stared out of her mirror were not bewildered; they were brazen. And it was not the first time she had seen that look. In Korah's Palace, she stared into the hazel depths of the mad king and saw eyes that seized what they wanted, that promised destruction to anyone who stood in his way. Korah's eyes were powerful. And he had poured that power into her, channeling every ounce of his charisma to draw her into his world. She now understood how he seduced the kingdom and led them all into rebellion. She felt his energy, was drawn to it, foreign and enticing. Korah wielded a power that took what it desired, by force or seduction.

But then she remembered the way his hazel eyes narrowed, flashing insane anger and evil. She saw the hatred eating him alive, like a cancer. Then she felt his hands on her neck, remembered the press of cold steel at her throat, and knew the catastrophic force of his wrath. Davianna had stared into the eyes of a beast.

She pulled her hand away from the device as if it burned her.

Josiah's call from downstairs jolted her out of Korah's clutches. She spun away from the mirror, away from those eyes. Davianna grabbed her gear bag and did not look back.

Two doors down in the master suite, Astrid was applying a second coat of mascara while Peter leaned against the wall, watching her. The transformation was astounding. He would not have recognized her, which was, of course, the point. But to his male mind, the fact that she looked so different excited him beyond measure. The thin diamond studded collar around her neck was the *pièce de résistance*. He shifted, the black leather pants growing much tighter.

When she turned to face him, the heat that passed between them melted the paint off the walls. His breathing became labored. "Josiah will kill us."

"Josiah is a prude." Astrid's eyes devoured him. The green hair set off his eyes, and the leather fit him like a glove. He was the hottest thing she had ever seen.

He flew to her; she turned her head away. "Don't kiss me. You'll mess up my makeup. Hurry!"

When Josiah saw Davianna walking down the steps, he thought, "What kind of brand new hell is this?" The sweet, innocent, bewildered Davianna was gone, in her place a hard-eyed vamp strutted down the steps like the star of every adolescent boy's wet dreams. A good girl gone bad. Lust exploded in his loins.

The look she gave him told him she was still furious. Clinically, the doctor knew this was a trauma induced stage, the man railed against it.

Emboldened by the power coursing through her veins, she looked him up and down. Screw him, she could look if she wanted to. He had not shaved, which made him look like a reprobate. Temporary tattoos covered his bulky arms, and he still had dark circles under his eyes. The only addition to his black leather was a heavy spiked belt. A silver skull earring dangled from his left earlobe, which Astrid insisted he wear because it lent him a piratical air. He looked dangerous. He was gorgeous. She hated him. "You look properly dystopian."

"And you look nothing like yourself," Josiah answered in a cold clip.

She raised a lip at him and struck a provocative pose with her hand on her hip. "That's the point, Dark Prince."

He glared. She glared back.

"Keep a civil tone, if you please."

Her nose flared. "I'm in character. Deal with it."

Josiah stepped forward. "No, I will not. I will not have you behaving like a petulant snot from here to the Golden City."

"And I'll not have you behaving like an overbearing, condescending, jackass who thinks he can control everything I say or do," Davianna retorted.

"Hey, hey!" Peter called from the staircase. "Are you kids ready to roll?"

Josiah shot Davianna a look that conveyed their conversation was not over and said to Peter, "All packed and ready. I shut the house down and have gone through the list. Here, be sure to wipe down the railing for fingerprints like we discussed."

Davianna grunted, exasperated at the delay. "I forgot my dressing table. Hang on." She took the cloth and ran upstairs.

Astrid looked at Josiah. "Did you get her riled up again?"

Josiah growled in frustration, pivoted, and went to wait by the vehicle.

The cold air felt good. He was stewing at her, at himself. He crossed the line and knew it. Now he was paying the price for not keeping his distance, garnering the consequences of relaxing his own personal discipline.

Pacing the garage, he tried to silence the nagging part of his brain that taunted him. "Fool. Why are you keeping your distance? Look at her! Think of what she offered you. Only an idiot would have rejected that. Would a single gentile Ruling Prince, including Korah, have sent Davianna ben David back to her room? And how different would the last thirty-six hours have been, if you had said, yes?"

Playlist

A dented, dirty van wound its way down the steep mountain roads, appropriate for a disreputable bunch of anarchists. The engine was loud, the ride bumpy, and the seats uncomfortable. They rode in charged silence. Astrid sat in the passenger seat with Peter behind the wheel. Josiah took up the back bench, keeping company with an impressive arsenal. Davianna sat in the middle, alone.

Forty-five minutes after leaving the cabin, the mountain lay behind them, and a flat dry road lay ahead. Peter put the van in park, turning in the bucket seat and meeting their eyes. "All right, here is road rule number one." He reached in the small pocket of his leather vest. "The driver picks the music."

The three passengers straightened, their eyes wide at the tiny pink square in his hand. "What is that?" Astrid asked.

Mischief lit his green eyes. "Music."

Davianna's mouth hung slightly agape. "That's ancient."

Josiah growled, "Where'd you get it?"

Peter wagged it between his thumb and forefinger. "Filched it from Korah's desk when I was eight or nine. He has a ton of these things."

"You did not!" Astrid was shocked and supremely delighted.

Peter plugged it in. "I sure did, and I know every word, to every song."

Davianna looked around. "Won't they track us?"

Peter shook his head. "Nope. It is not a connected device, simply a storage mechanism." He held up his hand ending further protests. "And before you ask, it will not release anything. If it did, I would have released two hundred and fifty-three monsters a long time ago. Besides, pirate radio has been broadcasting old music for a couple years now. Sunflower pulls this stuff off the old internet all the time. It is your device, Davianna, that is the key, not the songs themselves."

He turned on the speakers and gave a half-lidded look to Astrid. "I used to listen to this song and dream about what we are doing. I suppose it is a good way to start our adventure."

The speakers crackled with static and then like magic, the cab filled with the opening riff of a guitar, haunting sounds behind the tinny scale, building, and a man, weary to his core sang about being wanted dead or alive. Bon Jovi rocked the Millennium.

Peter sang along, in a voice perfectly pitched and nuanced. Astrid and Davianna shared their first true smile in days. Josiah said nothing, just closed his eyes and listened. As

the song wound down, the mood shifted, the tension evaporating. They were in this together, all of them.

The next song queued up, and at the opening guitar
chords, Peter turned his legendary charm on Astrid. "Red,
this might just be our song."

Bass and drums chimed, holding a steady beat that had
all of them bobbing their heads. Astrid screamed with delight. "I did shake you all night long!"

Davianna laughed, and Peter kept time on the steering
wheel. Josiah disapproved of the lyrics, clearly dark music
from the Last Age, but they were having fun. Davianna sang
along, and Astrid kissed Peter, laughing. Josiah was sick of
himself, so he enjoyed it.

When the song ended, Peter said over his shoulder, "I
have one, just for you, Davianna." He skipped through several tracks, having memorized the order of the songs a week
after stealing it. A Latin beat filled the van, an abrupt change
from the rockers a moment ago. Davianna started bouncing
to the music, the singer began, quick, hard to decipher, fading in and out, the Latin rhythm swelling.

Davianna threw back her head and laughed, "They made
a song about fireballs? Ha-ha! I love it!" Then snapping her
fingers, she began to shimmy and dance on the bench seat.

Astrid joined in from the front. Peter, knowing every
word, every pause, pointed, gestured, and had a blast behind the wheel. Josiah watched Davianna, happy again, and
thought the fireball was in his pants. Outwardly, he nodded
his head to the beat and smiled.

"Okay, Cousin." Peter glanced over his shoulder. "This
always made me think of you. So, I guess, this is your song."

He skipped ahead several counts. It had been years since
he had listened to them, did not know what possessed him
to put it in his pocket the night they escaped, but found he
appreciated the music anew through their ears. This one he
did not sing, he let Tom Petty do it.

As it began to play, Josiah templed his fingers and pressed

them to his lips with a brief nod of appreciation for the compliment. The lyrics spoke to Josiah, a simple song that captured Einar, the lone warrior, Josiah, the exiled Prince.

Davianna leaned against the window, her legs stretched on the bench in front of her, covertly watching him. The words rang true. He would not back down, not this man. No matter if he did not love her, he would see her safe. Decent, kind, and trustworthy he was her protector, her friend. The smile she bestowed upon him held it all.

He read it, closed his eyes with a sweep of long black lashes, and gave her a small formal bow.

Truce.

The Prince's Love Child

Las Vegas had always been a wicked city, but there was an undertone to it now that made Astrid grateful for their disguises. They fit right in. As they drove in, an atmosphere of depravity, violence, and desperation invaded the van. Astrid shifted in her seat, eyeing an emaciated prostitute in bright yellow leaning into a car. "I've got a bad feeling about this place."

Davianna glanced over her shoulder and said, "Which means we get in and get out."

Peter pursed his lips, ignoring the drug deal going down on the corner, and said, "We cannot do that. They are finishing the decoys, and we are making the exchange here. There is no reason to change the time or the place." He squeezed Astrid's knee in reassurance. She jumped under the tickle and slapped his hand away. So, he did it again.

"I still have reservations about the second part of your plan, Peter." Josiah studied the road, negotiating the strip traffic. "It is risky."

"I have mitigated the risk, and it is a critical component," Peter countered.

Davianna looked from Peter to Josiah. "Apparently I missed something."

It was a wide opening to slam her for her tantrum yesterday. Any of them could have gone in for the kill, instead, by mutual accord and silent understanding, they dropped it. Astrid graciously filled the gap. "Peter is going to plant pictures of him and Josiah in Vegas on the conspiracy sites and perhaps release them to the media."

Josiah watched Davianna's face as her mind worked. Her left eyebrow dipped, then her right one raised as the answer came to her. She bit her bottom lip considering, then began to nod. "Well, timing of course, we have to be gone," then she smiled in pure mischief, "but that is brilliant!"

"They will go nuts." Astrid agreed and made air quotes, saying, "Princes plot Korah's overthrow. That story has kept them busy for years."

"Well, my team has been circulating the rumor that Korah had me killed to steal my fiancée." Peter shuddered. "The story has gained traction, especially because I have dropped off the face of the Earth."

"Lost Prince sites," Josiah made a deep growl, "they are everywhere."

Peter stretched and yawned. "Half of them were founded and run by The Resistance."

Josiah snapped his head around. "I am going to kick your ass when we get out of this van." Nobody was sure how serious he was, including Josiah. "Those people are crazy. Tell me you had nothing to do with the 'I have the Prince's Love Child' site?"

Davianna and Astrid both guffawed, knowing Josiah as they did now, it was absurd.

Josiah failed to see the humor. "It's not funny. According to those lunatics, I have about two hundred bastards running around the kingdom, ready to take my place in court."

Davianna's hand covered her mouth, her eyes alive with merriment.

He tried to scowl at her, but damn if the humor wasn't contagious. "It's not funny! Some of those kids are awful looking."

Davianna lost it. After a moment, she held out a hand to stop him. "Is it?" Laughter overtook her. Astrid was not helping, howling in the back seat. "That they are saying you fathered all these children," she struggled for control, giggling, "or that they are ugly, that bothers you so much?" Her chest shook as she regarded him.

He felt the blood rush to his face. She was laughing at him, laughing about something that gnawed at him for weeks, since Reuben brought it to his attention. His scowl did not quite reach the quivering corners of his mouth. "It is unseemly and undignified, not to mention false. Most of those women are Alanthians, and I have not been here for fifteen years."

"Are you sure that site isn't dedicated to Peter?" Davianna teased.

"Oh, Peter's section is a whole lot bigger than mine." Josiah smirked at his own zinger.

"That is not the only thing of mine that is bigger than yours, Cousin."

The entire van erupted.

Astrid was crying and hitting at Davianna, begging for a tissue from the glove box, her black mascara leaking everywhere. Davianna could not breathe. The two Princes, their lives to date largely devoid of frivolity, laughed more in the last week than in their entire lives. Two more souls grabbed ahold of the driftwood and held on.

Help Us Find Our Girls – New City – Bubba and Zanah

In a New City news studio, Zanah dabbed at her dry eyes. "I just miss my little girl. All these months," her voice trailed off, and she looked away. Bubba patted her hand solicitously, "I thought she was dead."

The *cafe au lait* skinned reporter, Sondra ben Pierson, leaned forward. "Tell us about the morning you arrived at the camp."

"Oh, Sondra," Zanah's voice cracked, "it was devastating.

Bodies were everywhere, tents burned to the ground, children dead." She collapsed onto Bubba's shoulder, posing for the camera.

"Did you see a body you thought was your daughter Davianna?" the reporter asked, barely hiding her salacious curiosity.

Zanah nodded in mute horror and placed a hand over her heart. "She was burned, but yes, I thought it was my daughter. That image haunted me."

"Afterward, you fled?" The reporter's cocoa eyes were sympathetic.

"Oh, yes. We did not know who did it, or if we were in danger, so we ran."

The reporter patted Zanah's hand. "I realize this is hard for you, but can you tell our viewers about the difficulties and the dangers of your journey? The stories we hear from the pilgrim road are frightening these days."

Zanah launched into a fabricated tale of narrow escapes, sleepless nights, bandits, brigands, and wild beasts. She wore royal-blue, one of her best colors and could see herself on the monitors as she talked. She looked great on TV.

"Finally, I arrived in the New City, which is how I met Agnor." Batting her eyelashes, she stared up at him with adoration.

Sondra resisted the urge to roll her eyes. The woman was over the top. She would take over the interview if Sondra did not reel her back in. The camera turned on the flushed big face of Agnor ben Randall. This guy had the potential to be interview gold. Sondra felt a surge of excitement and resisted the urge to lick her lips. "Now, this is an amazing part of the story, how you two came together, please tell us."

"Sondra, it was just one of those moments of fate. I am an investor, you see, and I was in the city. A good friend of mine invited me to a social gathering, where I met Zanah. She and I hit it off."

He patted Zanah's knee. She blushed.

Before Zanah could start talking again, Sondra prompted. "Tell us about the night you first discovered your amazing connection?"

"Well, we just finished dinner, and the news was playing, and they showed that picture of our girls on the screen. We both said," he paused, looking at Zanah. They had rehearsed this moment and said in unison, "That's my daughter!"

Sondra threw up her hands in amazement. "Wow, what a moment! Amazing! Then what happened?"

"Well," Zanah dabbed her dry eyes again, "then I started to cry, and I think Bubba started to cry a little too." She squeezed his shoulder. "Though he would never admit it."

Bubba gave an awe shucks look. "Sondra, it was one of the greatest moments of my life. I was mighty tore up about my little girl." He turned away. His mouth tightened with genuine emotion. "Until then, we both believed our daughters were dead."

Sondra knew she had it, if she could just keep Bubba talking, "Bubba, I know this is hard, but can you tell us what happened the night of December 25th." His brows narrowed, and Sondra saw clearly, of the two of them, he was actually concerned for his daughter.

"Well, it was like a scene straight out of a play. Zanah and I were out for a stroll, and then, bam!" He clapped his beefy hands. "Out of nowhere, our girls came running. It was a miracle, one of the greatest moments of my life. She was there." He swallowed. "Truly, there. We just stood there hugging and crying. I don't even remember what we said. It happened too fast. One minute we were together, and the next," he shook his head and knuckled a tear away, "the police surrounded us with weapons. They handcuffed us, arrested us, for nothing. I couldn't do anything. I just watched helplessly as they took my girl." He looked down at Zanah and amended, "Our girls. They took 'em away. Wouldn't let me see her, wouldn't tell me why she was being held, and now? They refuse to give us any information. We don't know where they are."

Zanah lied straight into the lens, "We've been to the police station, but they won't tell us anything. We don't know what's happened to them."

"There have been no charges, no court hearings, nothing!" Bubba's face flushed. "I know my daughter, and I will tell you one thing, she's no thief, and neither is her friend. We have a right to know where they are being held, and our girls have a right to defend themselves."

Sondra's made for TV face became serious. "So, you believe that your daughters were falsely accused and are now being held without merit by the government on false charges? Why?"

Zanah sniffed. "We do not know, Sondra, and that makes it even more distressing. These are our girls today, tomorrow it could be your girls."

Sondra had a big story. If the viewers could not see on screen what was so obvious in person, she might just pull this off. She gambled and asked, "What would you like to say to your daughter tonight, Zanah?"

"Davianna, I'm so glad you are alive, my sweet angel. I will not stop fighting for you. I miss you."

Sondra wanted to grin, instead she adopted a suitably grave tone and said, "I am so sorry, Zanah, a mother's pain. I am sure you must be devastated." Turning, she added, "What about you, Bubba? Do you have something you would like to tell Astrid?"

Bubba cleared his throat, "Astrid, don't you be scared. I'm here. Daddy is fighting to bring you home."

The camera cut to Sondra. "We here at News 1 will continue to follow this story. So far, Metro Police and the Alanthian Government have refused to comment on the arrest of Davianna ben David and Astrid ben Agnor. If you have any information about these two girls, please call our hotline on the screen below."

"Cut!" the director yelled.

Sondra leaned forward. "That was great. You both did really well."

Zanah's smile did not reach her eyes. She was ready to leave.

Bubba shook Sondra's hand. "You were fantastic, sweetheart. Had me crying, you did. Where'd you learn to do that?"

When the couple exited the studio, they breathed a sigh of relief. In hiding since their arrest, they came up with this scheme to earn some fast cash, each was now a quarter million shekels richer. Marco ben Massimo, flush with the reward money, no longer cared what happened to them. Yet by doing the interview, they made a new enemy, King Korah.

Flip the Switch

The ramshackle hotel on the outskirts of Vegas was their destination for the night. The foursome sat in a diner across the street, eating a quick meal. A television droned in the background, ignored, until Astrid sucked in her breath and froze.

Davianna dropped her fork, and salad dressing splattered all over her wrist. "All these months, I thought she was dead." Her mother's voice cut through every perceptual filter in her brain, Davianna's mind laser focused, her eyes bulging with shock.

Josiah scratched his head, hiding his face to look at Davianna. He grabbed her hand under the table, squeezing.

Peter took Astrid's chin between his fingers, murmuring, "Be cool, you got this." Then he kissed her. The public display of affection made anyone looking, turn away.

Davianna clutched Josiah's hand hard, pretending to be lost in his eyes, while she watched her mother on TV.

"Eat," Josiah said under his breath.

The food so delicious a moment before, lost its appeal.

Her panicked expression spurred him into action. "I'll go pay."

The interview finished, Astrid's pale face was even more pronounced with the dark makeup and bad overhead lighting.

Josiah returned with a couple to-go boxes. He was starving.

They walked across the street as Josiah breathed a litany, "Keep it together. We have to check in. Act normal. Keep it together."

Peter saw them both change, like the flip of a switch, back in character. Runners! In that instant, he began to appreciate the skills that kept them alive.

Astrid made an imperceptible flinch and transformed. Davianna's walk changed, she grabbed Josiah's arm, and in the nasal Alanthian accent of the middle of the kingdom cooed, "Axle ben Diesel, it has been a long ride from St. Cloud, as I am sure Jewel and Christopher will agree. You boys unload the van. Jewel and I will check in." She raised up on tiptoes and kissed his cheek.

Damn! Josiah loved when she did that. The mimic turned him on. She was so good at it. Astrid caught him watching her, raised a well tweezed eyebrow, and made an open palm rolling flourish toward the departing fine actress, and her very fine ass. He sighed, looking heavenward, then busied himself unloading their gear. The night was about to get a whole lot worse for the frustrated Prince.

He dropped their gear inside the room and shot Davianna an incredulous look.

She pushed past him a bit too forceful. "I couldn't help it. The guy at the front desk was a pervert." Throwing her small bag on the king size bed, she turned. "And it's not like we've never slept in the same bed. You slept beside me for three days."

"You were nearly comatose," he choked.

Aggravated, she turned on him. "Well, I am not anymore." She was sick of him treating her like a patient. With jerky movements she dug around in her bag for her toiletry kit, snatched it up, and stomped to the bathroom. "Don't worry, I got the message loud and clear. Not now, not ever. You're safe." She slammed the bathroom door.

"Oh, but you're not, little minx," he muttered, "not by a long shot." Running his fingers through his hair, he knew he was not made of stone. He was flesh and blood, a grown man. She was killing him, and when the shower turned on, he decided it was a superb time to go for a run.

The Real Reason

Davianna emerged from the shower to find the room empty. Twenty minutes later, she got worried. Reluctant to knock on Astrid and Peter's door, she had no choice. Peter's hair was damp, no longer green, but they were both dressed, for once. Davianna slipped inside, Josiah was obviously not there. "Sorry, Josiah was not in the room. I thought he might be here."

Peter peeked out the curtain. "The van is here. He might have gone out to get something else to eat." He shrugged. "I would not worry. He can take care of himself." Peter had a sneaking suspicion Josiah was cooling off somewhere. He looked like he was about to spontaneously combust.

Davianna flopped down on the bed beside Astrid. "That interview, Tridi!"

"What the heck? That came out of nowhere. Our parents though, eww!" Astrid crinkled her nose.

Davianna laughed at her silly expression and rolled to her side. "Hey, if they get married, that makes us sisters."

Astrid's blue eyes sparkled at the thought. "It would."

A deep look passed between them. Emaline had called them soul sisters. She had been right, and sisters did not leave festering wounds.

"I'm sorry," they said together.

"I shouldn't have said those things about you and Peter," Davianna whispered, since Peter sat across the room, tapping on his tablet.

Astrid picked up Davianna's hand and squeezed. "And I should've asked you about Guan. However, you should've told me. All those months, you said nothing, why?" Astrid was not angry, just puzzled.

Davianna shrugged. "It just never seemed like the right time. Then your mom died, and we were running. After a while, it just did not seem important, with everything else we had going on."

Astrid bit her thumbnail, remembering the camp and the months of intense grief. "You told me at Jelena's cottage that the man who attacked you also saw the device. You said yesterday it was Guan."

"Yes." Davianna pursed her lips. "I've thought for months it had to be him who tipped off the Greeks."

Astrid's eyes flashed a deadly glare. "And they killed my mother and sent us running. That bastard!"

"I know," Davianna said gravely.

"What exactly did he do to you?"

Davianna pulled at a fabric pill on the hotel comforter. "He... he followed me back to my tent one night after meeting."

"When?"

Davianna looked away, rolling the brown fabric pill between her thumb and forefinger. "The last night he was in camp. He tried to force me inside my tent. When he picked me up, he must have felt the box." She shrugged and tapped her left pocket. "You know, I did not have my tunic back then. Anyway, he saw it. But then George was there, and he jerked Guan up by his collar." The corner of her mouth twitched. "It was not funny at the time, but I can still see his feet pedaling in the air like he was riding an invisible bicycle."

"You're not right," Astrid said, then moistened her lips and cut a sidelong glance at Davianna. "Poor George."

Davianna turned, this was the first time Astrid ever mentioned anyone in the camp. "Yes, poor George. Your momma was not the only person the Greeks killed, was she?"

Astrid pinched the bridge of her nose in a pensive expression that was so reminiscent of Peter that Davianna would have pointed it out if the topic were not so grievous. "No, she was not."

A gurgling lump lodged in Davianna's throat and she covered her mouth. "They killed Nico, sweet little Nico. Tridi, he was two. I promised him… I promised him I would say goodbye before I left the next day. I promised."

As they had a hundred times on the run, the girls fell together and held on. The strong one holding the weaker one, which always varied, and often changed during the embrace. Neither had the strength in the early days after their escape to probe the circumstances that sent them to Korah's Palace. The cocoon of the cabin kept the questions at bay. As they wiped away the tears and broke apart, a silent understanding passed between them. The time had come. They were strong enough.

"All right. I want to know," Astrid began, "why was Guan there the night they arrested us?"

Davianna threw up her hands, befuddled. "I have no idea. How the heck were we all there? We went to find your daddy, and then, bam! I don't know, it was bizarre."

Peter cleared his throat again. "I do not mean to eavesdrop, but you are in my room, five feet from me." He flipped his tablet over on the small table and leaned forward in his chair. "I can fill a few holes on how everybody ended up at Massimo's that night."

That got their attention.

"My team has been all over this. It starts with Massimo and his facial recognition software company, Facetec. We have discovered that he is a mobster, a nasty character, into all kinds of illegal activities." He waved his hand, encompassing a whole world of evil.

"Is he the man my mother met? The one who brought her to the New City?" Davianna gasped.

Peter nodded. "Yes, but she got away," he gestured to the miniature TV, "as you saw on the interview."

With the memory of Guan's attack fresh in her mind, a new horror dawned. "I was supposed to go with them. They were coming to get me that morning."

Peter cringed. "That would not have turned out well, Fireball." He did not tell her what they learned about her mother's life in Massimo's mansion.

Davianna bit her bottom lip. "Where is she staying now? Do you know, Peter?"

Peter shook his head. "After the arrest, both of your parents dropped out of sight. You two come by your hiding skills honestly. Who knows how that reporter got them to come forward? I suspect they got a nice payoff for their story. Which is good, they will need it. I think they are both smart enough to realize, Korah will be furious when he sees it. He is not stupid enough to do anything to them right now, but he is a diabolical bastard with a long memory. They are in danger." He saw the effect his words had on Astrid and added, "We will find them first, and when we do, my team will get them to a safe house."

Astrid scrambled off the bed and pressed a quick kiss on Peter's cheek. She and Davianna exchanged glances. Neither Bubba nor Zanah were candidates for parent of the year, but it was a relief to know Peter's organization was on their side. "Thank you."

Peter leaned his head against the wall, looking at Astrid through hooded eyes, and said, "Anything for you, Red."

Astrid grinned at him and resumed her place by Davianna on the bed.

Peter continued, resting his hands on his knees. "As far as what brought you all together that night, we believe Guan worked at Facetec as a desk filler. That is someone hired to fool investors. It looks like there is a large workforce. Hell, Korah sent me to open the place. Nobody knew what Massimo was up to, but it was a scheme. Whether to launder money or just to bilk investors, we are not sure. But he hired a bunch of geniuses, besides desk fillers. He killed some great minds. Bloody waste of talent. Anyway, he fooled a lot of people, including your father, Astrid." Astrid's eyes grew large. "He invested in Facetec."

Davianna jumped in, putting the pieces together. "So, Astrid's dad goes into business with Massimo and meets my mother. Since Guan is working at Facetec, he meets him, too?"

Peter lounged in the cheap chair. "Exactly. A few days after they posted the reward, we found search criteria on Facetec's system that varied from the sketches everyone else was using. Your parents' images also went into Facetec's data searches."

Astrid studied a fingernail, and said, "So Guan figures out that Bubba is my daddy." In an aside to Peter she added, "Everyone calls him Bubba. They meet or Guan follows him, then sees Davianna's mom, who he recognized from the camp."

"It's possible Massimo brought my mother to Facetec. Either way, Guan would have recognized her." Davianna added for Peter's benefit, "You saw her. Men remember my mother."

Astrid rolled her eyes. Zanah had been one hot momma in the camp. If Davianna was not so sweet, Emaline would have never permitted their friendship. She never shared that with Davianna, never told her the things she heard about her mother while they were in camp. It was the one decent thing Frank had ever done, he stood up for Davianna, and Emaline relented.

"Well, Massimo knew I'm my mother's daughter, and it isn't a far stretch to figure out that Agnor is Astrid's dad. His name is not common. When they put the bounty out on us, Massimo must have figured it out."

Peter quirked a golden eyebrow, impressed. "Very good, Fireball. We had an asset inside Massimo's mansion. He confirmed Massimo was holding both your parent's hostage, using them as bait. He needed the cash and figured between Facetec and your parents, he had a good shot at collecting."

Davianna paled. She remembered what it felt like to be held hostage. Grabbing Astrid's hand, she said to Peter, "Go on."

Peter looked grim as he continued, "So the day of the capture, Facetec gets several hits on you two. The notifications go to Massimo. Facetec sees the images garnering the hits are not the sketches and tracks the source to Guan's workstation. It is not difficult. We figured it out. Massimo needs the cash, and mobsters are not noted for their charitable contributions, so he sends his boys after Guan. He must have seen something that tipped him off, realized he was about to end up like Massimo's other dead employees, and scooted, but nobody knew your location at that point, and the reward was still out there." Peter's face darkened as he said, "So, the douchebag figures his best chance of collecting the reward is to stick close to your parents."

The cloud of confusion blew away with the revelation, and Davianna exclaimed, "That's how we ended up at the same place at the same time!"

Astrid was still not clear. "Then why did he kiss you?"

Davianna hung her head, dragged back to that night, and Guan. "I think it was his plan all along, to hurt us. He was very nasty when you weren't around."

"Again, why didn't you say anything?" Astrid hit the flat of her hand on Davianna's thigh, exasperated.

Davianna jumped, then furrowed her brows, and reminded her. "Camp Eiran was miserable, you know that. And at first, he was just looking at me weird. Then he started saying things, but he phrased them in a way that if I repeated them, it would make me sound paranoid. Either that or he could deny they meant anything, and say he was just making a joke."

She shifted, uncomfortable. "I tried to convince myself that I was just imagining it. You know I am not good at reading people. What was I going to say?" Davianna threw up her hands in frustration. "Guan said he caught you a big rabbit. How in the heck is that bad? It's not. But when he said it, he rubbed himself and had that look in his eyes."

She gave Astrid a pointed stare. "If I told you now, you

would believe me, but back then, before we went through what we've gone through, would Astrid from Camp Eiran have taken me seriously? Or would you have just shrugged it off and told me I was being silly?" Davianna looked away and murmured, "I think the real reason was," she paused and let out a shuddering breath, "because I was afraid."

"Afraid of what?" Astrid squeezed Davianna's finger.

"You know what they thought of me in the camp. I heard them talking. I heard what they said." She looked up with her eyes swimming. "I thought you might start to think, maybe, I was like my mother." The air grew very still. "I'm not stupid, Astrid."

"I know you're not, Davi."

"The night he attacked me, that's what he said, 'I know you're like your mother.'" She swallowed hard. "He told me he was going to say I came onto him, that I was asking for it, but I wasn't. I swear to you." She wiped her mouth, feeling his bruising kiss, remembering his hands on her body, remembering the terror. "He tried to rape me."

"Davi—"

"I fought him, I swear, as hard as I could." Her voice climbed. "He was so strong and-and my freaking mother deserted me. There was nobody around. He had his hand over my mouth, but even if I yelled, they might not have come. They thought I was a whore. You know they did." She buried her face in her hands. "It was awful. His eyes, I saw that same look in Korah's eyes."

"How did I not see what he was?" Astrid's chest caved in. "I strut around, proud as a rooster, crowing that I see through everyone, and I missed that?"

"He hid it from you. I was around you two enough to see that. It was part of the reason I kept telling myself it was all in my mind. He did not act that way around you."

Astrid stared at the ugly painting on the wall, a faraway look in her eyes. "No, you're wrong. He did. I just ignored it and saw what I wanted to see. I knew Frank didn't like him and that made me—" She gasped, her jaw dropping.

"What?"

"Frank threw him out of the camp because he attacked you, not because he was trying to break us up."

Davianna hung her head, ashamed. "George must have told him what happened." She remembered the night at the campfire, all the men looking at her with veiled expressions after Astrid stormed off. She did not comprehend the meaning of it then, and secretly, she had liked Frank. "I think you're right."

"Damn." Astrid swore under her breath, uncomfortable with her dead stepfather cast in the role of protector instead of villain.

Davianna pressed her fingers into her eye. "I guess, in the end, he got his revenge on us, and everyone in camp."

Peter cleared his throat and grabbed a bottle of water, draining it in one gulp. Typing on his tablet, he pretended to ignore them. If either girl would have been paying attention, they would have seen the dangerous look in his eyes.

Out for a Run

After recuperating in the cabin for days and riding in that rattling van for eight hours, Josiah's body needed exercise. Half the reason he was such a grouch was lack of physical activity, the other half was back in that hotel room. However, he was not quite recovered from his vacation in Korah's dungeon, and his cracked ribs did not care what he thought he needed.

Despite the aches, he pushed his body to its limits. Reasoning if he wore himself out, he might fall asleep, in bed, next to that fine little ass, and not touch her.

He kept running.

Vegas was not a safe place, but he would rather face a gang of thugs than a hot little minx. She was in the shower when he left, naked, with soap… oh he envied that soap.

A few more miles ought to do it.

Two hours later, he put the key in the lock and eased into the dark hotel room.

She was not asleep. "Where have you been?"

"I went for a run," he grumbled, digging in the dark for a change of clothes, drenched, as much from pain as exercise.

She turned her back on him with a huff. "You could have told me."

"You were in the shower." He tried desperately not to imagine it. Otherwise, he would have to run another mile.

"Pff," she snorted, "whatever."

He felt like a cad. She was worried. He knew the tone. "Sorry."

"All right," she said with a long sigh. "Good night, Josiah."

"Good night, Davianna." He did not look at her, and he tried to keep his mind blank while he showered, for all the good it did him at 2:30 am.

The nightmare came on hard. Real and imagined horrors swallowed her up. She could not move, Korah held her trapped in a python grip, a knife pressed to her throat. A scream caught in her chest, but she could not make a sound, or he would kill her.

"You want to play, little girl?" Korah hissed in her ear, as he forced her to go with him. She saw Josiah, beaten and bleeding, chained to a dungeon wall. In the cell beside him, Astrid was naked, tied to a bed. "I am going to kill your friends if you don't give me what I want."

"No, no, no!" she screamed as Korah pulled her down a narrow hall.

"Come with me, my dear. I am going to make you my queen."

She could not stop him. She could not run. He was going to consume her. "Please, let me go."

"Davianna, wake up! Wake up!" Josiah shook her.

She came awake with a cry, but the dream came with her, sheer terror. She was panting and sobbing, pushing at him, trying to escape.

"I've got you. You are safe. It was just a dream."

"It wasn't a dream!" she cried, and in her mind, she was back there.

"No! It was. You are here now." He took her face in his hands. "You are with me." He gathered her quaking body. "I do not hurt you. I protect you. You are safe."

"That's what he said." Davianna's hands were trapped against his chest. "He hurt me, Josiah." She sobbed his name in short gasps, repeating it over and over.

"Shh," he soothed, kissing the top of her head, moving down to her forehead, "I've got you." He kissed her eyes. Her sobs turned to sniffles. He kissed her lips softly, quieting her. The kiss was gentle, chaste. He moved to her ear, her jaw, her neck. She made a small moan and arched into him.

Josiah was undone. When he kissed her again, it was not chaste.

Davianna met his lips in an explosion of passion. Her arms encircled his neck, returning his kiss, touching him. She ran her hands up his back. His hand slipped under her t-shirt, cupping her breast, the size and shape of a perfect martini glass, the nipple taut under his caress.

Terror turned to liquid fire, and she burned for him. Her tears dried up, the nightmare melting away. Here, now, this man, this bed, she gave herself over to it.

He broke the kiss. "We can't do this."

"Then just kiss me." She was mindless, rubbing against him. "We won't, we don't have to."

"Oh, but I want to." He pushed his erection against her, showing her how much. He lifted her chin, staring into her eyes and breathing like a winded stallion.

Her eyes widened in trepidation at the reality of him, large, demanding, intimidating. Josiah was a virile, full grown man in his prime, on the verge of losing control. She understood, unlike the night in the cabin, if she kissed him, if she touched him, she could have what she wanted, but at what cost?

They did not move, but their hearts pounded as desire coursed through their veins. In a Vegas hotel room, honor and chastity battled the flesh for control.

At length, Davianna said, "Okay, sorry I woke you. Perhaps you should remove your hand from my breast now."

She felt the chuckle start deep in his chest as his hand slipped from beneath her t-shirt. "Minx, you are killing me."

Davianna closed her eyes. "I don't mean to, Dark Prince. I really don't."

They fell back to sleep, still in each other's arms.

January 13, 1000 ME

Bad Luck Guan

Bad luck… always with the bad luck. Guan sat at the bar watching a rerun of that nauseating interview with Bubba and Zanah. He was so close, but instead of being six million shekels richer, he was broke, unemployed, and well on his way to being drunk. Guan was smart enough to still have his skin, but worse off than he was in December. Damn, he thought his luck had turned.

The golden bubbles of his beer tickled his nose as he brooded. He at least had one decent memory of that night, the horrified look on Astrid's face, right before they were arrested. Sweet revenge. He still wanted to get his hands on them. He could not explain it, even though the reward was gone, he felt a burning need to find and possess that device.

"Can I buy you a drink?"

Guan took stock of the woman taking the barstool beside him, money, nice shoes and purse, heavy makeup. She looked like the trophy wife of an old rich man. "Sure. What is your name, pretty lady?"

"Does it matter?" She leaned forward, running a hand up his thigh.

Guan gave her his most charming smile. "I guess it doesn't." His luck was turning.

The next morning, Metro police found his body floating in the river, garroted.

January 15, 1000 ME

Limelight

Agnor and Zanah's interview went viral, sweeping across the kingdom. In the minds of every parent, Astrid and Davianna became their own children. Mothers empathized with Zanah and rallied behind her. Fathers lingered in the doorways of their children's rooms, saying good night, thankful their children were safe. The thought that it could happen, made them angry, and the question burned in their minds, had their long beloved king kidnapped two young girls?

Even more disturbing was the wedding. The union was not well received. It was unseemly, the age difference between Korah and Keyseelough. The circumstances were troubling, and her immediate departure after the ceremony added to the overall distaste they felt over the whole sordid business.

In the public eye since he was two years old, Peter's legions of fans clamored for news of his whereabouts. Dark speculation began to swirl. Had Korah killed Peter to marry his fiancée? Where was their favorite Prince?

Persistent whispers of foul doings at the Palace gained momentum. Old rumors about the death of Prince Eamonn and his family reemerged. Long a favorite of the conspiracy crowd, Prince Josiah's name became linked with Prince Peter's. What if they were together, plotting an overthrow of the corrupt King Korah?

The lost girls reminded the Iron King's loyalists of the slaughter at Camp Eiran. Once the overwhelming majority, their numbers were dwindling. They were persecuted, harassed, and even killed for their faith. Pilgrims were treated like scum, targeted as easy prey, and their plight gained no sympathy as they were regularly portrayed as intolerant, hateful, bigots. Davianna and Astrid became symbols of their movement. The righteous got down on their knees and prayed.

Anarchists crafted wild tales about the antics of Astrid and Davianna, casting them as heroes in their struggle against tyranny of all kings and governments. They launched rock throwing campaigns, with Davianna and Astrid's names scrawled on the stones.

Republicans seized upon the story. The girls became the poster girls for everything wrong with a hereditary monarchy. They rallied for a return of the federal legislature that would balance and curtail a power, that by the nature of its unaccountability, was doomed to become corrupt. Falsely imprisoning innocent citizens was just a symptom of a kingdom on the verge of collapse. They built websites and launched social media campaigns.

The anti-technology jihadists saw the girls as whores and infidels, but their fame made them into high profile targets. Their followers began hunting in earnest.

The Ruling Princes and their governments were under no false illusions, holding no romantic notions about anyone. They had received instructions from Lucifer at the Alanthian wedding, "Find that device now, or suffer the consequences." They watched in horror as Lucifer grabbed Korah by the throat and escorted him and his new bride out of their own reception. There was a new power to contend with, who wanted control of them, their kingdoms, and the Earth. And Lucifer was no choir boy.

January 20, 1000 ME

It's Not All on You - Duncan Texas - Peter

Life on the run was routine for three of the fugitives, but for Peter it was an upheaval of epic proportions. His life to date, at least in public, was largely singular. He was surrounded by servants and guards, his every whim or need catered to, but the loss of prestige and comfort did not trouble him as much as the responsibilities pressing in on him.

The girls' notoriety brought a myriad of new complications, but he took solace that the mechanism to make the adjustments in their escape was in place. The Resistance, his creation, his rebellion, and his secret would see them through. It was his crowning achievement.

Conceived in terror, in the depths of the dungeon, through the haze of drug addiction, he emerged from that hell hole ready to fight. And he got away with it. For three years, Peter dedicated his life to ensuring that Korah or his monster did not discover the truth. As the heir to the throne, no one suspected he was leading a rebellion because on the surface he had everything to gain.

He funded The Resistance through a labyrinth of trusts, shell companies, charities, and foundations, some legitimate, some not. They produced products, developed new technologies, and dealt in secrets. Those secrets he sold, sabotaged, or used. No one knew Prince d'Or had a brain, let alone a vast fortune and a secret empire.

Now, everything and everyone depended on his ability to wield it, and he feared he was not up to the task.

"No, you are not carrying it." Peter put the decoy in his pocket.

Astrid squared off with him. "They expect me to have it."

Peter rubbed both temples, weary of this argument. "No."

"Fine, then you teach me to drive today."

"One month, you have ten more days."

She crossed her arms, planted her feet, and shot him a look of brewing fury. "I'm fine."

He wanted to shake her. "Bloody hell, Red, you forget I know a bit about what you are going through. I am not risking it. Stop asking me."

"We risk it daily." She scowled at him. "You just don't trust me."

He grabbed her by the shoulders, dangerously close to losing his temper. "It is not about trust. You, of all people, cannot say that to me."

"We are not in bed, Peter!" Astrid gave him a penetrating stare.

"You do not know what we are up against, what we fight, what has been loosed." He ran his fingers through his freshly dyed dark hair, turning away. "I do."

"Tell me."

He whirled on her. "Never!"

She noted the stubborn set of his jaw and realized she had scratched a wound. They did not speak of pain; they did not share. Instead, through passion, they forged a soul deep connection, which warned her to back off. He was closed up, impenetrable. Her instinct was to fight, to force him to tell her what was behind the look in his eyes. But she read it. He would not tell her a thing, not in the state he was in. All morning, he had been on edge, vibrating with an energy that filled the room like electric static. Would she fight, or would she trust him? She bit her thumbnail and whispered, "All right."

Peter's eyes widened. She could tell her capitulation knocked him askew, but he recovered fast, retreating behind that inscrutable mask. "Good. Grab your gear. Let's get out of here."

"Hey," Astrid called him back from the dark place swirling behind the emerald depths in his eyes. Instinctively, she knew he did not need her affection, but he needed this. "It's not all on you, Peter." Without another word, she grabbed her bag and left the room.

Outside, she stared up at the yellow sky and wondered what caused such a look. They were all wounded.

Josiah was physically injured, though he never complained. He thought no one noticed, but she did. It was obvious by the tentative way he moved in the morning, or the little flickers of pain that crossed his face if he lifted anything heavy.

Davianna was inexorably changed. Her outburst in the cabin was just a symptom. She refused to speak about what happened during those six days with Korah, but she had not forgotten. Astrid could tell when she went back there because she would grow still, pale, and silent. Most telling was the compulsive way she rubbed her stomach as if she was remembering something terrible.

As for herself, she refused to dwell on the dark shadows hovering at the edge of her mind. Physically, she was recovering, though there was a gnawing need. It stalked her like a beast out of a sterile nightmare. That part remained, like a hunger she could not satisfy. It made her mouth turn dry, her breath come quick, her palms sweaty. When it hit her and she could not fight it alone, she took Peter by the hand, and fed it something else. She drowned the addiction in a sea of lust. She doused the inferno with the cool water of Peter ben Korah… her new addiction.

However, while the three of them bore their wounds openly, Peter hid behind that mask. It took many forms, sarcasm, humor, bored cynicism. He sometimes lapsed into a caricature, the indolent, lazy Prince. She sort of liked that one. He was amusing when he morphed into Prince d'Or. Her favorite, though, was when he became stuffy, oozing royal dignity. She loved when he did that because she teased him out of it. She adored the look on his face when she refused to acknowledge his spoiled privilege, it caught him off guard. She would cut out her tongue before she ever called him, my Esteemed. Sometimes though, when he was making love to her, she would feel the desperation in him, she would touch the deep brokenness inside him, and it made her want to weep. They had been visitors in Korah's House of Horrors; Peter had lived there a lifetime.

He loaded their gear and slammed the trunk. For this leg of their journey, they were driving a nondescript family style sedan. He opened the driver side door and waited. His jaw was set, his hair and whiskers darkened, his eyes shielded behind sunglasses. "Come on, Red."

Astrid bit her nail, looking at him. He could try to hide,

but she saw through him. "I guess I'll let you drive."

The corner of his mouth lifted, and his left dimple made a beguiling appearance. "Thanks."

That smile... that damn smile could convince her to go anywhere with him, do anything. She got in the car but did not touch him. He did not want to be touched. As they pulled off, part of her wanted to say, "Take me back to the cabin, lay me down. I will hide you. I do not want whatever is behind your eyes to find us." But she sat quietly, staring at the flat road looming ahead. Miles to safety, thousands of miles to go, every one of them dangerous.

"It starts today." Peter did not look at her as he said it.

"I know. It's weird not having Davi here. You think they will be safe?"

Peter made a hollow sound in his chest. "My cousin has proven himself more than capable. Nothing will happen to her."

"You're right."

He did glance at her then, a small crack in his veneer. "I hope I am, about everything. Because if I am not, if I have miscalculated... my team, on my orders, is about to launch a proverbial nuclear strike. If I am wrong, then it will take us out."

"No. It will take Korah out. It will work."

"Bloody hell, it better." He smiled and shook his head. "If not, then you and I are going to go down in flames, but I swear to you, Red," he grinned, "we are going to have a little fun before we go."

Astrid laughed. "Mardi Gras, here we come."

Don't Ask it of Me - Texas - Prince Josiah

Thirty miles outside Dallas, behind an abandoned store, an old pickup truck waited. They were leaving the beat-up van, donning new disguises, and taking a different route to their next rendezvous with Peter and Astrid. Josiah dressed as an aged farmer. Davianna played the role of his daughter.

"No." Davianna put her hands on her hips and stomped her foot. "I will not ride in the back of that truck, hidden under a blanket for three days. I will not be cowed by you, your big loud voice, or your patronizing tone. I have had enough of it and enough of you." She bulled up at him and had the temerity to poke him in the chest. "You are not my father. I do not care what disguise you are wearing. I do not have to listen to what you say."

Josiah thought with some irony that the raging cock stand plaguing him for weeks was not fatherly. She stood toe to toe with him, her shoulders back, her lips pursed in fury, but not rage, just feisty minx. He looked down on her and tried to glower, but her pert breasts heaved, and there was a fleck of mascara under her right eye. She faced him down like a spitting kitten.

The corner of his mouth quivered.

She pushed his chest in exasperation. "You are not laughing at me. You," Davianna sputtered, searching for a word, "you self-important, royal butthead!" She started mussing her hair, as she was prone to do in fits of frustration, it got bigger.

He snorted in amusement.

She gaped at him in outrage, curling her little hands into claws about to tear him apart.

His snort turned into a chuckle, which grew into a laugh as she hurled a rock at him and missed. He covered his head as she threw another, which also missed.

She charged.

He brought her down with him as he collapsed on the grass, hilarious. She squirmed and struggled, still trying to claw him, but laughing in frustrated amusement.

He suspended above her, merriment dancing in his eyes. Then he leaned down, and whispered, "It's not nice to throw rocks at people, Minx." He nipped her ear. "I was teasing you about the bed of the truck."

"Teasing?" She got a look in her eye, then arched her back and moaned, rocking her hips against his.

He bolted off her, growling. "You have to stop that."

She sat up, batting her eyelashes, playing the temptress. "Stop what?"

He narrowed his eyes at her in warning. "I am a man."

She rose and stopped a hair's breadth from him. "And I am a woman, and you know it."

"Do I know it?" His breath became ragged. "You tempt me beyond reason. You prance around half-naked in our hotel rooms, snuggle up to me with that hot little body while you sleep. Then those sounds you make when I can no longer keep my hands off you? It is unendurable." A pleading note entered his voice. "Davianna, stop. You do not understand what you ask of me."

"Then tell me." Her voice shook with frustration.

"Don't you understand? Everything I have ever done, my entire life, since the day I was born has been for honor, to be worthy of my position, my kingdom, my father, my King."

He grabbed her and pulled her tight, pressing his arousal against her, the thrum of need coursing through his body. He looked down at her, desolated. "I have sacrificed everything; my personal wishes have never mattered. What I desire, what I want?" Josiah released her and stalked away. "I am the Prince, albeit exiled. The Iron King, for reasons I have never fathomed, allows Korah's sins to go unpunished, my father's murder unavenged."

Determination, half a lifetime in the making, rang in the air. "But I will not stand before the Iron King like Korah, filthy in sin, with the shame of your dishonor crowning my head. He would throw that in my face, and I will not allow it! I have a case against him, for I have lived as a righteous man, and will not give up my honor, no matter how much I want you."

She covered her mouth, blinking at him.

His laugh tasted bitter. "Do you know why?"

She shook her head and the look she gave him nearly shattered his control.

His frustration boiled over. "Because it would come to nothing! Nothing! Do you hear me?" His voice strangled. "I cannot have you. You are not mine."

"But—"

"Stop." He held up a hand and turned away. Staring out at the flat Texas landscape, he said, "When I defeat Korah, and I will defeat him, there will be alliances that must be formed. There will be a bride, that I must take."

He turned, silently begging for understanding, for mercy. "I will not make you my whore and drag you into sin, for my own pleasure. I will not! I could not bear it, and you should not ask it of me."

In that moment, she finally understood. She had been playing with fire, watching Peter and Astrid, wanting what they had. But he was right. It was wrong. There could be no future for them. She was the daughter of a whore, and he was the Prince. Her chin quivered and the tears that fell down her cheek were the first of a thousand. "Not now, not ever," she whispered.

He closed his eyes against the pain, against the anguish. His shoulders slumped in defeat, his heart, sacrificed on the altar of honor.

Pair of Jacks - New City, Alanthia - Sondra

News 1's, Sondra ben Pierson opened the tenth anonymous email of the day with skepticism. Since the viral interview, she was flooded with purported pictures of the mysterious Davianna ben David and Astrid ben Agnor.

Her source at the Metro Police Department, Officer Elias ben Phillip, speaking off the record, confirmed his department had indeed arrested the young women and several others the evening of December 25th, but they transferred the prisoners to the Alanthian National Armed Services the following morning. From there, the trail went cold. The Military was stonewalling.

Her career, boosted by the story, was on the rise. She needed another break if she was going to unseat Ebenezer ben James and get that anchor chair.

She jumped up from her desk when the picture opened. "Oh, my stars!"

Her French manicured fingers shook as she dialed the station's IT department, the photo already forwarded, on its way for validation. If the photo was authentic, this was a career maker.

Genevieve ben Willard, the sender of the email, looked at the photograph on the screen, her two Princes. Peter's face, familiar and beloved, never failed to warm her heart, but it was Josiah's she studied. The faint lines around his eyes were from a life lived outside, not smiles. The black hair and golden-brown eyes were from his Italian mother, Princess Marguerite ben Alfonso. His facial structure and bearing were his father to a tee. He was tall like Eamonn, but burly, more muscled than his father had been. The black leather clung to him like armor, royal warrior encoded deep in his DNA.

He had been a sober child, thoughtful, and steady, which always made the rumors around him seem so ridiculous. She could not fathom how anyone believed them, but they had. She resisted the urge to reach out and touch the screen, to touch the man in the photograph. He possessed a competent fierceness that could not be denied.

She sat back, looked at Himari and Alaina, her companions in the bunker. "I think we just set the world on fire."

A Single Photograph - New City, Alanthia - Sondra

At 2:00 pm, Dwayne, Sondra's contact in IT, called with bad news. He could not authenticate the photograph. The validation of Prince Peter was simple, Prince Josiah was not. "No baseline photograph exists, even the royals did not have cameras in Eamonn's day."

"Shit, what about paintings?" Sondra pressed.

"I thought about that. There are four of him, but only one as a teenager. The rest were painted when he was a baby or a little kid. He disappeared when he was fifteen, and the last portrait was for his Bar Mitzvah at thirteen. Even if we had one of him now, paintings are not scientific. I couldn't use it."

"Dwayne, you are killing me."

"Find me a picture, Sondra."

She pounded her fist on her desk, racking her brain. A picture? Then an idea hit her. She scrambled to her computer, typing madly. When was that? Last fall? Something about Greece, right? Where was it? London? Was it London?

"There you are!" A fuzzy photo taken outside a Windsor police station came up on her screen. Her hand shook as she redialed the phone. "I got it! Dammit, if you can't validate off this, I'm running with it. I don't care." But she clamped her mouth shut.

Ebenezer ben James moved into his office doorway, listening. The old dinosaur built his career on Prince Josiah's suicide, a story he still bragged about breaking. He had the damn thing framed in his office, alongside pictures of him and King Korah at a dozen events. Any whiff this photo was fake, and he would scuttle the story. Her editors would bury it.

"Dwayne," she turned her head away, whispering in the phone, "I just sent you another. Ignore what I said before. I need rock solid proof."

Twenty minutes later, she could barely stand it. Ebenezer sniffed something brewing, and when he started toward her, she jumped up and bolted to the ladies' room.

Instead of going back to her desk, she snuck downstairs. Dwayne's cube sat in the back corner. They were friends, though he would like to be more. He was cute, but she had bigger ambitions than a molasses-voiced black boy in a cube.

"Do you have it?" She ducked inside and pressed against the wall.

He pulled off his glasses and tossed them carelessly onto his desk. With his fingers laced behind his neck, he leaned back and said, "Yep."

"Are you sure?"

He motioned her around his desk. A facial map showed ten correlating data points. Several paintings of Prince Eamonn and Princess Margaret were up for reference. "With mapping, you can then use the paintings. Look at this, he is the spitting image of his father."

Sondra clenched her fists and squeezed her eyes shut, trembling with excitement. "Dwayne, I am going to blow the lid off this thing. After that interview with the parents?" She pressed a kiss to his cheek. "That anchor chair is as good as mine."

He looked up at her with his soulful brown eyes and moistened his lips. "I'm already working on tracking that email, but whoever sent that has got some serious skills. Every time I run a trace; it sends me to a different destination. So, it either came from Veracruz, Montreal, or Miami. But I enhanced the background of the picture they sent you. Look here." He pointed to a section in the upper right corner. "That's the Rockvale Hotel in Vegas."

Sondra leaned forward, reading the marquee. "Oedipus - Live."

"I called 'em. The band's engagement is running the month of January."

She threw her arms around his neck and jumped up and down. "You're a genius. I owe you dinner."

"You owe me drinks."

It was the scoop of a lifetime, and despite Ebenezer ben James' howling, they ran with it. At 4:20 pm, News 1 started teasing the story. By 5:15 pm, the wires picked it up. The public began to chatter. At 6:05 pm News 1 went live and confirmed a scoop of epic proportions would air after the commercial break. The accountants were ecstatic. Sondra ben Pierson was ready.

At 6:18 pm, New City time, Sondra ben Pierson looked straight into the camera and smiled. "Our top story tonight, focuses on the royal family."

On screen, Prince Peter's familiar face unveiled. "This picture, taken within the last three weeks, confirms that Prince Peter ben Korah is alive and well."

Sondra paused, imagining his legions of fans celebrating.

"And as relieved as we all are to have confirmation that Prince d'Or is okay, we now understand that he is not the lone Prince of Alanthia. His companion," the blacked-out portion of the picture slid away, "is none other than Prince Josiah ben Eamonn."

She imagined the shouts across the kingdom.

Then she launched into a discourse on the methodology used to validate the photograph. On screen, she watched the live audience count grow, and grow, and grow. Using digitized video, the computer mapped the Windsor photo with the one from Vegas.

Sondra confidently declared to Alanthia and the world, "The science does not lie, but see for yourselves."

A portrait of Prince Eamonn and Princess Margaret with their newborn came onto the screen with the cropped photo of Josiah beside it. Even the skeptics could not deny, the resemblance was striking.

"Alanthia, if this photograph was of Prince Josiah alone, it would still be rock solid proof that he is alive, but consider," she paused while the original photograph came back on screen, "he is with Prince Peter, so there is very little doubt about who he is."

She waited. She waited for them to study the picture. She waited for them to come to the same conclusion. She waited for the earth to shatter.

The Prince was not the man they expected, but his ghost seemed hauntingly familiar, and she could feel them, glued to their screens.

"Alanthians, one and all, mourned the tragic death of

Prince Eamonn, but for Prince Josiah? His name and memory have been tainted in our minds. We have diminished him, but perhaps we were as wrong about his mental state as we were about his suicide."

Sondra turned, staring at the man who perpetuated the story for fifteen years. They had set him up. He was pale and sweating in the chair he occupied so comfortably the day before. "I do not know, Ebenezer, this man," she tapped the photo, "does not look deranged to me."

News 1 brought the closeup on the screen, a vibrant, confident warrior.

"Many questions remain, where has he been, and what has he been doing for the last fifteen years?" The camera cut away from the photograph and zeroed in on Sondra ben Pierson's arresting features. "But more importantly, for all of us, what are these two royals planning? With King Korah's recent troubles at home, we can only speculate. However, one thing is crystal clear, these two royal Princes are a power unto themselves, a force to be reckoned with."

The Millennial World exploded.

The Resistance and News 1 threw the second most powerful kingdom on the planet into chaos with a single photograph.

When the newscast started, Josiah and Davianna were sitting at a feed store counter in Terrell Texas, sipping iced tea and waiting for their dinner. Dressed as farmers, no one spared them a second glance. A shout came from behind the bar, and the TV volume blasted. Service in the restaurant stopped. The cooks came out of the kitchen, dishwashers ran to the front of the bar. Word spread like wildfire; something was happening. Waitresses, with trays held aloft, froze. Diners got out of their chairs and walked toward the television set. When Prince Josiah's face came on the screen, their collective gasps were audible.

Toward the back, someone cheered. "Hell yeah! That sum bitch is alive. Look at him!"

Davianna covered a smile but could not meet Josiah's eyes. She feared she would give them away; afraid she would give herself away. He might see it, then she would be exposed again. She wanted to hug him, to share the moment, but she could not. There was a royal wall between them now.

At the same moment, a hundred miles away, Steve and Joseph, two fashionable gentlemen of a delicate persuasion, stepped into a Dallas hotel bar. Steve, a. k. a. Peter ben Korah, the more flamboyant of the pair, smacked his lips and said, "That is one gorgeous man."

Joseph, his smaller companion, glared.

Back in the New City, off-duty police officer, Elias ben Phillip nodded in satisfaction, his suspicions confirmed.

Princess Keyseelough of Egypt and Alanthia had a psychotic break and flew into a murderous rage. The Palace doctors, who were giving her around the clock care, sedated her, and discussed their long-term strategy to keep her that way.

Yane ben Sandanski, the old revolutionary from Macedonia, raised his glass in a Moscow bar, toasting the young man he had not seen in more than a decade, appreciating the strategy, even if it was a royal war.

Jarrod ben Adriel and the other Palace servants exchanged looks at the racket coming from the King's study. Korah went on a rampage. Seven kitchen maids, two gardeners, the head steward, and three footmen left that night. They never came back.

January 23, 1000 ME

Ordinary Man - New Orleans - Josiah

The ancient city of New Orleans was pulled out of the swamp around the turn of the last century. A group of Alanthians, who balked at the puritanical rule of the Iron King, conceived the scheme in a brothel. The Bayou Folly, as it became known, floundered for decades, cursed by disease, disaster, and corruption. Hundreds of investors lost their fortunes, even more laborers died in the Louisiana miasma.

When the city emerged, it brought up more than memories of Bourbon Street, something old and wicked lurked beneath that Mississippi delta mud.

However, those drawn to its winding streets, soulful jazz and spicy gumbo were not overly concerned with the dark side of the Big Easy. It became a destination for the disenfranchised and rebellious, the raucous and the wild. They came to party, drink, and sin, just as they always had.

New Orleans was a perfect place to hide, regroup, and perhaps have a bit of fun. Josiah was against sneaking out among the masked Mardi Gras celebrants, deeming it a risk. Unfortunately for Josiah, he was outnumbered, outvoted, and until he took the throne, not in charge. They gave him an ultimatum, either come along or stew by yourself.

Street music floated through the open windows. Raucous crowds laughed and sang. Josiah brooded in the dimly lit sitting room, waiting for his companions. Surrounded by luxury, he gave not a second thought to the well-appointed flat, nor the madness taking place on the streets below. He was preoccupied with the girl down the hall.

The tension between him and Davianna had grown, manifesting into long hours of silence as they traveled the back roads in that loud pickup truck. And in the silence, he thought, "If I was just an ordinary man?"

It haunted him through Texas, Mississippi, and down into Louisiana. It played with repetitive monotony.

"If I was an ordinary man, what would I do?"

She sat beside him on the bench seat of the truck with her feet on the dash, adorable.

He would marry her, take her to bed, and never let her leave it. He would go to sleep looking into her big brown eyes and kiss her awake in the morning. He would eat her cooking and sit with her in the quiet. He would bring her flowers, play her music, and sing her songs. He would tickle and tease her until she tackled him, then they would roll around on the floor, laughing. He would make up corny jokes that only they thought were funny. If she cried, he would hold her. They would vacation, some place that had snow, and she would throw her arms around his neck and kiss him with playful abandon.

He would practice medicine. She could teach school, she loved little kids.

He would give her babies.

He would love her with his life.

They would grow old together, walking their miniature dachshunds. In their twilight, they would welcome grandchildren for Sunday dinners and play bingo on Tuesday nights.

But he was not an ordinary man. These were not ordinary times, and the fantasy world he created on that long silent drive would never exist.

He felt like someone died.

When she emerged from her bedroom, dressed and ready to go, he knew there was going to be trouble—the epic kind. The sort that started bar fights and drove men to smash beer bottles over each other's heads. Trouble strolled into the sitting room, sporting a second-skin, curve-hugging, peacock-blue mini-dress.

Josiah gulped.

Astrid had cut Davianna's hair into an elfin fringe that framed her oval face and set off her big brown eyes. She painted her lips a shimmering pink, ripe for his kisses, and so much more. He could just make out a faint outline of a knife strapped to her upper thigh. Dangling carelessly from her left hand, she held a peacock feather mask. Five feet two inches of dangerous, cute, hotness balanced on spiked heels. Fireball, indeed.

"You are going to cause a riot in that get up."

She rolled her eyes, dismissing the comment. "I am a brunette. People notice blondes, redheads, and girls with black hair. Brunettes are invisible. Besides, Josiah, it's a party. This is a party dress. I blend." She looked him up and down, all black leather and scowl. "You look like you are going to a funeral."

Given his thoughts a few moments ago, she was not far off the mark. "Deal with it," he dead panned.

She laughed, remembering she had said the exact thing to him at the cabin.

A loud crash came from the master bedroom, Josiah sprang to his feet, pulling his jeweled dagger. Telltale sounds of lovemaking inched their way under the door. Besieged from all sides, he stormed out.

Taking refuge on the balcony overlooking Royal Street, New Orleans celebrated with raucous abandon. The breeze carried the briny smell of the bayou, booze, and a faint hint of urine and vomit. The latter were not as vile as they would have been to 'an ordinary man'. He was a doctor, but honestly, was he even that anymore?

Medicine, the one thing that made him feel alive in exile, was gone. He felt desolate, empty. And tonight, he experienced the loss as deeply as he had that day in the Golden City. Standing alone on the balcony, surrounded by laughter and gaiety, he was a man with neither kingdom nor profession, but most painful of all, the woman he loved.

He was more miserable than he had ever been in his life.

The door slid open. He sensed her presence at his side, smelling of white soap and hair spray. She took his arm, her first touch since Dallas.

"Dark Prince," she said in a husky whisper, "this life is hard, but every once in a while, we get a break, a moment of respite." She squeezed his arm with both hands. "I want to give you one of those moments."

He could not speak; he could barely breathe.

Davianna met his gaze with a sad smile, her voice wistful. "Take me to dinner. Take me dancing. Drink a hurricane with me. Let's have fun tonight. Tomorrow, it will all be here."

"If I was an ordinary man…"

She closed her eyes, her long black lashes casting shadows on her cheeks. "Then be an ordinary man with me tonight, Josiah."

"Minx," he whispered. It was the plaintive cry of a desperate man, losing the battle, crossing a line.

She stared up at him, earnest, vulnerable, her precious heart swimming behind her eyes.

He lost the battle. "Let's go."

Her face lit up like a sunrise, and she bounced on her toes, making the tiniest squeal of excitement. "Come on, get your mask, nobody is going to spoil our fun."

Josiah smiled as she scampered through the sliding door. He took up his mask and rapped on Peter and Astrid's bedroom door. "Hey rabbits, I'm taking my girl out to dinner. See you later."

Davianna turned, a flirty hand on her hip. "Your girl?"

He felt a slow smile build and said, "If I'm an ordinary man tonight, then you, Davianna ben David, are my girl."

For as long as he lived, he would never forget the smile she gave him or the little yelp she made a moment later when he finally, finally, smacked that hot little ass. The gratifying pop felt so nice, he did it again.

First Date - Davianna and Josiah

They walked a while, finding a little bistro away from the crowds. There were six tables and only one other couple dining. They sat in the back corner at a table with a single candle and a bud vase. The small place and the darkness gave them the freedom to remove their masks, eating dinner in relative safety. Their meal began with hot French rolls, served with salted butter. They both moaned in ecstasy. Dinner was a spectacular feast, fish *meuniere* topped with seared shrimp and crawfish, served by a feisty waitress, who made Davianna laugh.

Davianna closed her eyes and moaned. "This is amazing."

Josiah smiled, thinking she was the most beautiful girl in the world.

She picked their personas for the night, George and Zoe from Alabama, on a New Orleans adventure. The inspiration came from some ancient TV show she watched while they were hiding in the New City.

She was amazing; the accent, the southern charm, and the stories she told of their life in a zany small town, where he practiced law, and she was a family doctor. He loved it. Because tonight, he got to play the role of an ordinary man.

After dinner, properly masked and disguised, they strolled arm in arm down the crowded sidewalk. She bought an enormous, rum-heavy hurricane from a street vendor which they shared as they took in the sights of New Orleans.

A warm pleasant glow bloomed in his gut.

She pulled him into a bar where audience members were singing with the band. Drinks flowed, and the lively spirit of fun was contagious. Davianna smiled, breezy with a little rum, full of mischief. "So, as the story goes, George sings Zoe a song."

Josiah stroked her delicate jawline and asked, "You want me to sing you a song?"

"Yes. I have heard you sing in the car. I know you can."

Princes were born to have an audience; ordinary men were free to make extravagant gestures. He kissed her, full on the mouth, soft and sweet. "For you?"

She nodded, blinking up at him.

When the bodacious lady in the black feather boa finished her rendition of "The Way That I am," Josiah volunteered. Ensuring the mask was secure, he mounted the stage, knowing this was the most spontaneous, reckless action of his life. He saw her expression behind the elaborate peacock mask. He shocked her. Good.

He turned to the band and made his request. Then seized the microphone with both hands and set his legs firmly on the ground. The New Orleans violin began the opening notes, joined by a soulful trumpet, trombone, then drums, and in a song that Peter played for them countless times, Josiah ben Eamonn sang "O Mary Don't You Weep" for Davianna ben David.

The crowd danced and sang along. He was an extraordinary talent, the song apropos. On the last verse, he pulled her on the stage. The crowd raised the roof. Emboldened, and with the flair of a natural born showman, he dipped her for a kiss. Refusing an encore, he struck a formal bow, and beat a hasty retreat.

As they scampered from the bar, she laughed and hugged him around the waist. "Our New Orleans adventure was brilliant."

He laughed, free and easy. As he did so often, he relaxed in her presence, letting his guard down.

"Where did you learn to sing like that?"

"I have no idea." He shrugged, slightly embarrassed. "Don't tell Peter I did that. I'll never live it down."

Davianna looked up at him with a teasing glint in her eyes, but then looked away, biting her bottom lip. "I won't tell him. I won't tell anybody."

Josiah hugged her to his side, as their flat on Royal Street came into view. "Do you think they made it out of the room?"

Davianna laughed, leaning her head on his shoulder. "I doubt it."

A pair of women pushed passed them, clearly inebriated, a redhead and a brunette. Festive costumes began to look a bit wilted. Pedestrians staggered a bit more, and a darker mood crept over the street.

"Come on, Zoe, time to go home."

As the flat drew nearer, the charade came to a close.

"Thank you for a wonderful night," she said, touching his arm.

He gathered her close and kissed her.

It was a kiss for the sake of kissing, for the simple joy of it, not as a prelude to something else. It did not promise or seduce. The kiss Josiah and Davianna shared was complete in its own right. It was a celebration.

When he pulled back, he leaned his forehead against hers. His voice was warm, his eyes tender. "Davianna, you made this the best night of my life."

The pain did not come until he was upstairs, in his own bed, alone.

January 24, 1000 ME

Beignets - Josiah and Davianna

The next morning, Astrid and Peter were still not out of their room. It was ridiculous. He and Davianna dressed to pick up breakfast at a cafe down the street.

She wore big black sunglasses and her Gune clothing with the hood pulled up against the chill. Under normal circumstances, he was intimidating, but the dark glasses, skull earring, and leather added an element of menace. Most people gave them a wide berth. He scowled at a college kid, leering at Davianna in overzealous alcohol fueled lust. The youth held up a hand and staggered off, muttering.

Desire lingered about New Orleans, seductive and inviting. Josiah was firmly under its spell. Though Astrid and Peter could not use the Big Easy as an excuse. They were on a record setting pace for the most sex by two people in the history of the world. He hoped they were using some sort of birth control. The doctor in him started watching for signs. A pregnant woman would be a disaster.

As he and Davianna walked, he broached the subject. "I do not mean to be indelicate, but have you spoken to Astrid about birth control?"

She bit the bottom corner of her lip and cleared her throat. "I have not, but I am not worried about it."

His forehead wrinkled. "How so?"

"I am not going to tell you that; it's embarrassing." Davianna turned pink.

"I am a doctor, Minx."

She rolled her eyes and whispered, "It was part of the gear that Jelena left us. Once a month, we take a pill. No period." She looked away, her face turning crimson. "It was a blessing on the road."

"The Wonder Girls never cease to amaze me." Josiah linked his arm with hers. "Did I mention I've met her?"

"The Gune, Jelena?"

"Black hair, violet eyes, tall, bossy, Serbian?" Josiah did not add, unbelievably gorgeous.

"Yes! When did you meet her?"

"In the spring," Josiah said, looking up at the cloudy sky. "I'll tell you about it one of these days, but not today, Zoe." He smiled, his eyes lidded, his voice husky. "I think I'd like to be ordinary George for just one more day."

She leaned into his side, blushing. "Then you shall be."

He put his arm around her waist as they walked. Then, because he was just an ordinary man, he moved his hand lower and gave her a firm squeeze. She rewarded him with a fetching yelp.

They purchased their beignets and chicory coffee from the bustling outdoor market and strolled back to the flat. Outlandishly costumed people still filled the streets, some clearly intoxicated. The party during Mardi Gras made no distinction between day and night.

"Did you notice something odd last night?" he asked.

Her eyes widened, then she sighed with relief. "Oh my gosh, I was not going to say anything. I thought I was imagining it."

Josiah chuckled. "That about half the women were in costumes and makeup to look like the sketches of you two? No, you were not imagining it."

Davianna covered her forehead and squeezed her temples, her chest vibrating. "There were Peter and Josiah characters everywhere, too."

"Did you see that guy with the big crown?" Josiah smirked.

"The half-naked, fat guy with the purple cape?" Davianna snickered. "He was dee-lux."

"They were everywhere." He handed her his cup of coffee and opened the door to their flat.

Upstairs, they stood at the counter, munching warm donuts. He wiped powdered sugar from her nose. "When you think about it, if half the city is dressing up like us, New Orleans is perhaps the safest place in Alanthia for us to be."

Davianna sipped her chicory coffee. "There are worse places to hang out for a few days." She took a bite of her donut and gestured to him with it, sugar falling to the counter like snow. "These are tasty."

Josiah leaned in, kissing away another powdered sugar fleck. "So are you."

The door to the master bedroom opened, interrupting them. Peter emerged, looking shaken with Astrid's wooden tea chest in his hand. "Davianna, will you please put on some water for tea? Astrid has a headache."

"Of course!" Davianna sprang into action.

"I have something better than tea." Josiah went to get his medical bag.

Peter looked relieved. "Thank you." He turned to Davianna, snatching up a beignet and stealing her coffee. "It started last night, out of nowhere."

Davianna set the water to boil. "A lot of times she won't

tell you, not until she can't move or see, and she's throwing up. Even then, she'll just tell you to go away and leave her alone." She turned toward him. He needed to know this. He needed to understand. "She won't tell you things, sometimes nothing that is going on inside her head. Be careful with her, Peter. Astrid is not nearly as tough as she pretends to be."

"I have never seen anyone hurt like that." He sounded scared.

"Hey," Davianna touched his shoulder, "look at me. I know the protocol for this. Her mom taught me. Put that coffee down, she won't be able to take the smell."

In quiet and patient tones, she gave Peter the gift passed to her by Emaline, the knowledge and method for taking care of Astrid. As she spoke, she realized it was no small thing.

Bug Out

The alarm, dreaded since they began, shattered the silence of the flat. Astrid writhed in agony, and for a second, they all froze.

Josiah took charge. "Peter, get Astrid dressed. Davianna, grab your gear, wipe as you go like we practiced." Then he shot from the room, the sound of the arsenal being readied, rang in the air.

Peter's tablet, from whence the alarm sounded, came to life. "You've got four minutes Falcon. Get out!"

Only the knowledge of what awaited them if they were captured kept Astrid from fighting him. Instead, she channeled the iron will he admired, and stared back at him through red eyes, dilated with pain. "Get my tea chest." With a herculean effort, she donned her Gune Black, grabbed her bag, and let him guide her down the stairs.

Peter breathed a silent prayer of thanks that their getaway vehicle was fast and exceedingly common. From alarm to departure, they were out in two minutes, thirty seconds. Loaded into the car, he yelled into the tablet, "Who have they got?"

"Doc and the Sparrow," Himari sounded shaken, "get them down, hide them."

Josiah let out a string of foul words that would have put his drill Sergeant to shame.

"Give me eyes, Sunflower," Peter yelled as he pulled out of the parking garage.

"Right on St. Peter's. You need to go, Falcon. They are shutting down the Quarter."

"I have traffic, Sunflower. Get the lights!"

Alaina came over the speaker. "On it."

Auntie G's soothing voice entered the cabin. "Stand by for second locale."

"Right on Dauphin, they blocked St. Peter's!" Himari sounded frantic. "Right on St. Louis, then right on Basin. You've got one shot at this."

His heart hammered, everything inside of him wanted to floor the accelerator.

"Don't." Astrid clutched his knee. "The secret to running is to do it without being obvious." She squeezed her eyes closed. "Steady. You mash that accelerator they got us for sure. You can do this." Her native Texas accent emerged from the depths of her pain.

Davianna and Josiah were under a blanket in the back-seat. Peter could hear her praying.

A police car roared up on them, sirens blaring, lights flashing. Peter's hands gripped the steering wheel, white knuckled. "Bloody hell, here they come."

Astrid twisted in her seat, gasping. "Peter!"

It was time to panic.

Then Peter stared in open mouthed wonder as the police car screeched tires, turning right on Burgundy, and disappeared around the corner. "Bloody hell, what happened?"

"I don't know!" Astrid moaned and pointed out the windshield. "There's another one."

The police cruiser sped by, headed in the opposite direction.

Auntie G's voice came over the speaker, joyful. "You're off the grid again, Falcon."

Peter floored it, and the four fugitives shot out of the Quarter.

Alaina was out of breath when she came over the line. "I have no eyes on you, but we have an asset in place, sending you the coordinates. Go there!"

A text message blipped, and Astrid clicked on the icon.

Himari said, "Falcon, we will send revised instructions ASAP."

Peter felt a low burn in the pit of his stomach, dangerous. "Trigger?"

Josiah had a sick premonition, before she said it, he knew.

Genevieve delivered the blow. "Mary just about wept this morning."

Both occupants in the backseat groaned.

Astrid resettled her sunglasses and growled without moving her lips, "What did y'all do?"

"Thirteen million views and counting." Auntie G's voice had that odd mix it always held when Peter was in trouble, but she was amused by his antics. "Quite a finale, Doc. You are still dark, Falcon. Praise God. Signing off."

Peter felt as if his vocal cords were strangling him. When they broke free, he shouted in a guttural voice, "Bloody hell, an asset? Do either of you have any idea how dangerous that is?"

And I You

The asset turned out to be a striking French Cajun man from Delacroix, Louisiana. He directed their vehicle into a metal shed and pulled the door shut, blocking the daylight.

Astrid breathed a shuddering sigh of relief.

The stranger leaned into the open driver's window and said, "Sir, grab your gear. We'll get you out of here. I've got a boat waiting."

Peter nodded his thanks and turned to Astrid. "Are you all right?"

"Can we just sit here a minute?"

"Be still. I will get us settled," he whispered and gave her knee an encouraging squeeze. He could not even look at Davianna and Josiah. He simmered like bottled fury.

They exited the car into the filtered orange light of the shed. Peter nodded. "Thank you, sir. I'm Peter ben Korah."

The man gave a formal bow, his manner friendly, but the tick in his cheek reflected his amusement at the absurdity of Peter introducing himself. *"Mon Estimé,* I am Beau Landry, an old friend of Alaina's."

He made a formal bow to Josiah. *"Mon Estimé,* welcome. Glad to be of service to you both."

When he turned, his cobalt blue eyes registered surprised recognition. "Miss Davianna ben David, I presume?" His accent, devoid of distinct consonants, held the rich cadence of the bayou. She offered her hand in greeting, which he raised to his lips in a courtly kiss. "Beau Landry, *mon chèr."*

Beside her, Josiah made a deep grunt. Davianna flushed, and Beau Landry shot her a riverboat pirate's grin.

Peter helped Astrid from the car. She pressed an open palm over her left eye and made a quiet whimper. Davianna took Astrid's gear. Josiah managed the weapons. Beau hefted Peter's case out of the trunk and shouldered one of the heavy assault rifles.

Beau moved with the languid grace of a man who spent a lot of time on the water. Peering out the door, he saw no one around and motioned them down a long dock. A flat-bottomed boat waited. *"Allons,"* he said and motioned them to come.

The smell of the delta swamp hit them, thick and fecund. "If I get on that boat, I might die," Astrid moaned, then vomited over the dock into the dark water.

Peter looked at Josiah with a frenzied, pleading expression.

Josiah nodded grimly. "Get her aboard. I'll take care of her."

"Mo chagren, chèr is ill?" Beau Landry asked.

"Headache," Davianna said, stroking Astrid's arm and handing her a bottle of water.

"The boat will be hard, but we won't let her over the side. There's alligators."

"And snakes?" Davianna shuddered. "I hate snakes."

Beau chuckled. "There are plenty of snakes in the bayou, *chèr*. You stay in the boat, too."

They settled Astrid into a fisherman's chair and loaded their gear. The boat rocked and swayed, which caused her to scramble to the bow and dry heave over the edge. Wiping her mouth, she sat, limp as a rag doll, while Peter secured her life vest. "It will be all right. You are okay. We are safe now."

"I can't do this." A small sob caught in her throat.

"Yes, you can." Peter pressed his lips to the pink shell of her ear. "You can, Red. I have seen you."

"Here, this will help." Josiah took Peter's position and administered a mild, but fast acting, sedative.

Beau Landry readied the boat, waiting for his passengers to vest up.

As the medicine took effect Astrid sagged with relief. "Is that what you gave Davianna when we were in London?"

Josiah made a hollow laugh. "No."

"Okay, good because I was going to be mad at myself if I threw that away." Her head lolled to the side and in a slurred voice she drawled, "I'm still gonna die, but I sorta don't care."

The corner of Josiah's mouth lifted. "That means it's working, Astrid."

"I wanna kill you and kiss you at the same time." Her voice trailed off as she melted into the bucket seat.

Peter lifted her hand to his cheek and murmured, "That is what you always tell me. I am jealous."

She reached out and pulled his head to hers. "Don't be jealous. You know I love you."

He froze. Emotion swept over his face, and in a cracked voice he murmured, "And I you."

Astrid smiled dreamily, resting her eyes behind the dark glasses. "I know."

Bayou Safehouse

The slow ride through the bayou became a fascinating journey into an enchanted world of green shadows and gray moss. Sunlight filtered through the massive tree canopy as they wove their way through a series of canals and channels. Beau Landry proved to be an excellent guide, pointing out features of the landscape, species of trees and animals, including several ridge backed alligators hiding among the logs and muddy banks. They exited the murky channels into a pristine lake of deep azure blue.

"Now, Miss Davianna, La Petit Pishon is safe. We don't follow King Korah around here. He won't find you."

"Thank you, Mr. Landry." Davianna looked around, the place was beautiful, wild, and prosperous.

"Call me Beau, *chèr*." He winked. "You make me feel old, calling me mister."

Davianna flushed. Beau Landry was not old, no indeed, he was the very definition of priss-teen. She looked up to find Josiah glowering at them both. She blushed and pointed to a house. "That's pretty."

"Thank you." Beau turned the rudder toward the house. "That's where I live."

She had expected a swamp house, perhaps a metal roofed ramshackle, but the well-appointed home of cypress plank siding and plate-glass windows was not a hovel. She narrowed her eyes, staring at him. Who was this man?

Beau guided the boat into its slip, beside a new ski boat, pontoon, and an old sailboat he was restoring. He turned off the loud engine and steered up to the dock.

Astrid let out a sleepy sigh of relief.

Beau gestured to the grounds. "This property is isolated and gated. There are cameras, so we can watch if anyone is coming. The only other way to get here is by boat, and we will lock it down."

Josiah scanned their surroundings. "By we, you mean?"

Beau gave an ironic shrug of his shoulders. "My family, the folks around here, we won't let anybody in that's not supposed to be. We've stayed loyal to the Iron King, it's why we've still got rain, and we liked your father." He turned to Peter with a shrug that expressed they did not like his.

Josiah met his eyes, assuming a regal, dignified air. "I am honored and humbled by your service, Mr. Landry. You have my appreciation, and we are in your debt."

Peter moved to stand beside Josiah, with the sunlight hitting his hair. Light and dark, they were beautiful and together.

"Your loyalty and support are noted, Beau Landry, and all who offer their aid and succor to our cause, today, and in the future. If we can ever be of assistance, you must not hesitate to call upon us."

Davianna sat very still, watching them in awe. It was easy to forget who they were, but a few simple words reminded her forcefully. For the sake of Astrid's heart, Davianna was glad she missed it.

As if summoned from the dead, a sepulchral moan drifted across the calm waters. "Somebody get me off this boat."

Cajun Moon

The night brought a low bright moon. Davianna chopped vegetables in the kitchen, and Astrid kept her company, sitting on the sofa, drawn but lucid. Peter and Josiah were outside on the deck with their host. Beau Landry had allowed Davianna the run of his kitchen, which was the most organized space she ever worked in.

The atmosphere in the house was formal, strained. Peter was furious but holding it together in front of their host. Davianna and Josiah were both chagrined. Their easy banter and fanciful plans to spend a few days as George and Zoe were blown to smithereens.

Hovering twenty thousand feet above New Orleans, Lucifer watched. "Appropriate it was New Orleans," he said into the ether, "it brings it out in people."

The Prince of the Power of the Air, Lucifer had not done reconnaissance since Eden, having minions for that in times past. Alas, the only lieutenant at his disposal was a quivering weakling, bleeding to death from wounds that even Lucifer could not staunch. It was troubling, this mortality of Marduk's. When he first discovered it, he flew into a murderous rage. However, since Marduk was, for the moment, the sum total of his elohim, he decided not to kill him.

Pathetic as he might be, he still had his talents. Marduk's wild men, among his favorites in the Last Age, were adept at spreading violence and terror. Lucifer was pleased to learn they had not changed.

Marduk, for all his perfidy, had at least started the mechanisms they would use to see into the darkest corners of the world. Lucifer had not expected to find the planet almost devoid of technology. It was pervasive at the close of the Last Age and enabled him to see with unprecedented clarity and accuracy to events happening across the globe. The lack of it made his current task more difficult. It would be tedious, time consuming, relying on traditional intelligence gathering. Even that was hindered by the imprisonment of the demons and his remaining elohim.

One step at a time.

The foundations were there. Man's heart had not changed, that was evident. Marduk knew his business, though Lucifer dismissed any true genius in his second in command. It was rather simple to manipulate men. Promise them freedom, wealth, and power, throw in some nice sounding words, sugar coated blasphemy, and they would do anything he wanted, always. His resumption of power would go as planned. Albeit, slower than he intended or wanted.

To that end, he scanned the marshland below, attuned to any violence. He knew men, once they felt safe, those two Princes would battle it out, and when they did, he would be ready. The devilish grin that split his face contained no trace of beauty, held no joy. Lucifer's smile was pure evil.

On the expansive back porch overlooking the lake, Peter stood up, and addressed their host with strained politeness, "Mr. Landry, I must beg your pardon. I require a private word with my cousin. If you will excuse us."

Peter turned a murderous glare on Josiah and stalked off. He did not speak to either of the girls as he walked through the living room, exiting the house, and slamming the door with a bang.

Josiah rose slowly from his chair.

Beau looked up at him with a sympathetic expression. "Best to have it out in the open, I suppose."

"Indeed." Josiah nodded and left their host, prepared to take his lumps. He deserved them. As he walked through the kitchen, he looked at both girls. "Stay inside." It was an order.

Astrid had Peter's tablet in her lap. She looked up at Davianna and said, "Forty-seven million views and counting."

Davianna cringed and continued stirring the etouffee she was cooking.

Peter prowled the lawn like a caged animal.

Josiah stepped into the light and waited.

When Peter spoke, it was through gritted teeth, his face ferocious. "What were you thinking, making a viral video of you and Davianna two hundred yards from where we were sleeping?"

Josiah met him head on. "It was impulsive and reckless. There is no excuse. I am sorry."

Peter's voice was savage. "You are sorry?"

Josiah lifted his chin, stoic. "Yes."

Josiah's cold veneer enraged Peter. "Do you have any idea

how many people have put their lives on the line for you?"

"I think I have a pretty good idea."

"No, you do not! You do not know them. You do not know their faces. You do not know their stories, their children. You do not know what they risk, every single bloody day. And they do it willingly, to help you, a man they do not know, because I asked! They know the cost if they get caught; if WE get caught." Peter pointed an accusing finger at Josiah. "You risked everything. You risked their lives and ours! How many of my people are going to die because of what you did last night? How many people have already died, trying to help you?"

Peter gripped the sides of his head. "You know they killed Mr. ben Merriweather?"

"No, I did not." Josiah looked away, deeply saddened by this information.

Peter bared his teeth like a rabid beast and snarled, "And my mother!"

Josiah balked at that. "I had nothing to do with your mother's death."

"No? Were you there? Did you hear the argument? She helped you. She gave you her escape, hers and mine. She did not make it out. You did!" Peter clenched his fist at his sides. "I saw it. I saw it all. It made me watch, while he beat her to death."

Josiah gasped. Aunt Alexa... Father... Mother... the horror of it all crashed over him like a tidal wave, pulling him under. They were all dead. Murdered. His family wiped out. This was not his fault. How dare Peter stand there and accuse him of perpetuating the atrocities that Korah had inflicted upon them all?

Enraged, Josiah shouted, "Did you know your mother? Do you have memories of her? Because I don't! He killed her when I was a baby! He killed them both, my father and my mother! He stole my kingdom, sent me into exile. He took everything!"

Something snapped in Josiah's mind, and poisonous re-sentment gushed out. "I lived the life of a captive, a fugitive, an outlaw, while I watched you, with your cars, and your women, and your money, going to parties, getting drunk... living the life that should have been mine! It was mine!" he thundered. "So, for one damn minute, I let my guard down. For one lousy fucking minute, I was reckless, and you, the most reckless of all, condemn me?"

"A life that should have been yours?" Peter turned his blazing green eyes on Josiah, maniacal madness lurking just below the surface. "You do not have an inkling about the life I led under that monster. You would not have lasted two weeks in that house, not two weeks! Do you know why? Because my father is not the only monster in the Palace, Cousin."

Peter's face turned into a mask of black rage. "That's right he has one. It stalks the halls, stinking of sulfur and death." He shoved Josiah and said, "You want to know who its fa-vorite target was? Me!" Peter screamed, coming completely unhinged. "It would brain rape me regularly. Throw me up in the air and spin me around my bedroom until I puked or pissed myself. Then it would slam me up against the walls. And for fun, it would show itself to me. It is a fucking mon-ster! A fork-tongued, black devil with hair like snakes, and claws he can dig into your brain!" He was sobbing in furious anger. "I was eight when it started, the night we buried my mother!"

Then the wrath he had held in check his entire life broke free, sending him into a blind rage. "So, do not ever speak to me about my life, about the life I lived that should have been yours. You got off easy, you son of a bitch!"

When the blow came, Josiah was relieved.

Violence erupted.

"Josiah!" Davianna screamed from the doorway.

The panic in her voice penetrated the frenzy of flying fists. He shoved Peter and stumbled backward, spitting blood.

Peter staggered sideways, holding his ribs.

Astrid left the shelter of the house. Pushing past Davianna, she ran toward Peter.

"It's on!" Davianna clutched her left pocket, it was vibrating, calling forth the ancient evil that created it.

"Davianna!" Josiah's voice faded away as a black veil fell, extinguishing all light, all hope, and all love.

For Davianna, night turned into day, and she was alone.

Whatever You Want

Poised to bolt, Davianna looked around. Her hand flew to her mouth, and she gasped. The vibrant intensity of her surroundings overwhelmed her. It was the world as it had been, before drought, before rebellion.

Paradise.

Flowers bloomed in blinding profusion, perfuming the warm air. She touched the fuzzy bud of a tulip magnolia, one like her daddy planted on her fifth birthday. She turned, her boots making a soft crunching sound on the white pea gravel drive.

A tiny whimper escaped her lips. Her chest rose and fell in an erratic rhythm. She forgot to breathe. A small carriage house and stable sat at the end of the drive. She knew where she was and knew what she would see when she turned because this place was indelibly etched in her memory; Taylorsville, her old house with the swing.

"Davianna?" a familiar voice called from the backyard.

Davianna squeezed her eyes tight, not daring to hope or believe. Her fists balled at her sides, her knees shook, and she breathed, "Daddy?"

"Davianna."

And there he stood, smiling with his arms held wide. His wavy brown hair blew in the breeze, his eyes shining with love. He wore his favorite shirt, the one she gave him when she was eleven. She ran with a cry, her arms thrown wide. "Daddy!"

"Oh, Davianna." He swept her up in an exuberant hug and kissed her cheek. "How is my girl?"

"Daddy, what are you doing here? Where are we?" Davianna looked around. The backyard seemed a vague representation of her memories, but not quite right. She looked closer and realized the houses behind them were out of focus, blurry. As she stared, they came into sharp relief.

"We're home, the place where you and I were the happiest. It's where the Lord let me come to see you. Just for a bit." He brushed her bangs away from her forehead, his face alight with love. "I know this has been hard for you, but you can rest now, your work is over. You don't have to fight and struggle anymore."

"Am I dead?" Davianna looked down at her body and gave a tentative push on her belly. She seemed real, still flesh and blood.

"No, but the Lord is coming to speak with you, to walk with you." He smiled down on her, his brown eyes, familiar and warm. "I want you to listen to him and do what he tells you."

He kissed her cheek and vanished.

"Wait!" she cried into the silence.

The scene shifted, becoming the woods outside Camp Eiran. Golden light surrounded her, warm and comforting. When she turned, she knew who would be there. She bowed her head and fell to her knees. "My Lord."

"Davianna." He held out his hands to her.

She remained frozen, unable to move, unable to speak.

"Arise, my child. Let us walk."

Without moving a muscle, she was lifted to her feet and came to his side. Her heart thundered, and her palms began to sweat. Now that she knew who he was, she was terrified.

"You have done well. I have come to tell you that you no longer have to carry this burden."

She blinked up at him, surprised. "I don't?"

He smiled down at her, indulgent and full of understanding. "No. You were never meant to hold it forever, Davianna, just for a time."

He touched her shoulder and cold dread shot down her spine. She had opened the box. He had not given her permission to do that, just keep it safe. "I am so sorry, my Lord. I did not understand what it was. I was curious. Please forgive me."

He shrugged, dismissing it as a trivial thing. "It is no matter. You did not know. Did you?"

Davianna blinked up at him, relieved. "No, my Lord. I did not. I would never have done such a grievous thing if I had known."

He nodded, a fathomless look in his eyes. "You are a good girl." He pointed to her pocket. "I never meant for that to cause you so much trouble. I am sorry, Davianna."

Davianna's lips parted, a cry stuck in her throat. "It has been very hard."

"Indeed, you have suffered for the burden I placed on your young shoulders."

To receive sympathy, when she tried to be strong for so long, caused a dam of tears to break. She turned away, sniffing back a sob.

"But it was not for nothing."

She swallowed thickly and ventured a glance at him. "It wasn't?"

"No." He directed her gaze, pointing down a long path. Josiah appeared, resplendent in royal robes, a crown gleaming on his head. "I put you together so you could help him regain his throne and become his queen."

Her clothes changed from her Gune Black to a glorious white gown. She looked down in wonder. Raising her arms in surprise, the flowing sleeves almost reached the ground. The fabric moved like water, clear as spun glass, twinkling like snow.

"This is for you, Davianna ben David, Queen of Alanthia." He brought forth a magnificent crown and offered it to her.

Davianna's eyes widened, dazzled by the gold filigree and red velvet crown. Rubies, emeralds, and diamonds blazed in the magnificent light. "Truly?"

He smiled with the wisdom of the ages. "Oh, indeed. You will make a splendid Queen."

He swept his arm and a huge crowd appeared, waving Alanthian flags and cheering her name. A trumpet sounded, and Josiah moved to her side. He waved at the crowd, smiling. He put an arm around her waist and pulled her close. "They love you, as do I." He leaned in and whispered, "This is everything we ever wanted, isn't it, Davi?"

Davianna rested her hand against his jaw, staring into his whiskey-colored eyes. It was everything. He was everything. She loved him with her whole heart. "It is."

Josiah nodded, closing his eyes, and resting his forehead against hers. "You were never meant to carry that burden. It's time to give it back to him. Then we can have it all, everything, you and me."

Davianna turned.

The Lord held out his hand. "Give all to me, who are burdened and heavy laden, and I will take it from you. For my burden is light, and my yoke is easy."

She moistened her lips, her forehead creased in confusion. "That's not the Scripture. It's come to me, not give to me."

She shook her head, stepping back. "Josiah doesn't call me Davi." Her words came out in a rush. "And my daddy called me Dee-dee." Her heart began to thunder, and she swallowed. "I have walked with the Lord before, and you're not him. You're not any of the men I love."

His lip lifted in a snarl, and there was no light, no love, in his evil black eyes. "Give it to me."

The illusion shattered.

She stood frozen on Beau Landry's back stoop. Peter and Astrid were still as statues. Josiah was in mid stride, a drop of blood from his nose hung suspended in midair. A glittering black dome covered them, reminiscent of the Gune's golden one, yet there was no peace inside this space.

"Oh, so you want to do it the hard way?" Lucifer narrowed his eyes and smiled.

Davianna whimpered.

With a wave of his hand, time resumed. The drop of blood fell to the ground. However, a second wave of his hand arrested Josiah's forward momentum. The occupants of the backyard were lucid, conscious, awake.

"Good evening," Lucifer said smoothly and turned with a formal bow toward Josiah. "Prince Josiah ben Eamonn, it is lovely to meet you, at last."

He turned to Peter, repeating the bow. "And Prince Peter ben Korah, your father sends his regards, as does Marduk."

He looked between them. "Trouble between you two boys?" He laughed in wicked delight. "That amuses me, considering what you have been stirring up." He made a tsking sound, shaking his head like an admonishing schoolteacher. "It does not bode well for your prospects, this infighting. However, you royals do kill each other on a regular basis."

He looked between the girls and pointed with his thumb at Peter. "The smart money is on Korah's son, history bears this out. The apple," he looked over at Davianna with a wicked grin, "rarely falls far from the tree."

"Although," he tapped his cheek, appearing to consider, "I have a simple solution to your calamity. I can restore your kingdom, Prince Josiah. Would you like that? Would you like to be on your throne tonight? I can give it to you." Josiah started to protest, but Lucifer cut him off. "Think about it."

He turned and said, "And you Prince Peter, I know what you want, to be free." He looked between Astrid and Peter. "Free to have your woman, free from a royal life of responsibilities. Free."

He turned his evil eyes on Astrid, and she recoiled. "Miss Astrid, intrepid young lady, I always admire a red-headed rebel. The best friend, the companion, but you are so much more, aren't you?" His voice became sensual, seductive as he drew close. "You can choose your own destiny, be in control of your life, released from those headaches. One even plagues you now, you will be free from them forever." He touched her left temple.

The mystified expression on Astrid's face showed that the headache was gone.

When he turned to Davianna he possessed a special look, an ancient one, "Miss Davianna, our very own proverbial Eve. The irony is not lost upon me, I believe this time, you give me the apple." His glittering black eyes held her in their grip.

Josiah's voice penetrated the trance. "No, Davianna, don't give it to him."

Lucifer tilted his head and narrowed his brows, looking at Josiah. "Hmm, more irony, amusing." Then, with a cajoling smile, he said, "Prince Josiah, admirable as the sentiment may be, you and I both know you are powerless to keep me from taking what rightfully belongs to me. However, I am a gentleman, and I am prepared to offer you a bargain."

The air was pregnant with temptation.

"Korah is finished. The people already clamor for you. Tell her to give me the device. She will listen to you. She loves you. Stand aside, and tonight you will again rule Alanthia with the woman you love at your side. Josiah ben Eamonn, you will be King."

"No, Josiah. Don't do it," Davianna cried.

When Lucifer turned, his face lost all its coaxing charm. It held a malevolent hatred reserved exclusively for Davianna, who stood alone. "I have tried to be nice, but you want to do this the hard way. Give me the device, Davianna ben David, or I will kill your friends."

He snapped his fingers. Vipers appeared everywhere, writhing, hissing, and slithering around her legs.

Astrid screamed, surrounded by rattlesnakes. A king

cobra rose in front of Josiah ready to strike. An anaconda, twenty feet long, moved toward Peter. They stank of lethal poison and fetid pits, the stench of pure evil. The rattlers sang a song of death. The cobra opened its mouth and hissed. The anaconda began a slow-motion circle of death. The ancient enemy of man came to take their final revenge.

"No," Davianna whimpered. "No."

Lucifer transformed into a dragon and roared.

She stumbled backward and fell. The snakes moved to strike, and she screamed, "Yeshua, help!"

The name enraged the Dragon. He lunged at her, his wicked teeth flashing, black slime dripping from his jaws. "Give it to me, or I will rip your throat out."

Josiah bellowed, "Davianna!"

The Dragon struck.

The instant before Lucifer devoured her, the Archangel Michael intervened. He scooped Davianna ben David out of the dirt and carried her away.

Astrid watched in abject terror as two rattlesnakes uncoiled, flying at her in an open mouthed, deadly strike. Rafael snatched her up, out of harm's way, rebuking the vipers who disintegrated in a fiery explosion.

Peter launched himself in front of Josiah, dodging the anaconda, prepared to take the king cobra's strike. But Uriel snatched him out of harm's way and disappeared.

Josiah stumbled, pushed off balance by Peter's sudden move. He turned on Lucifer. Their eyes held. "No!" Josiah screamed, a split second before Gabriel took him around the waist and shot into orbit.

Lucifer howled, unfurled his wings to give chase, but he was thwarted by a dozen mighty angels, who swarmed Beau Landry's backyard, swords drawn, ready for battle. They attacked the Devil with righteous fervor and vengeance that went beyond the age of man. The angels were there when he tempted, tricked, and deceived their friends, their comrades, their companions. They remembered, and they unleashed their fury.

Wounded, Lucifer was forced to retreat.

The Most High declared from the night sky, "How you have fallen, morning star, son of the dawn! You have been cast down to the earth, you who once laid low the nations!"

The Devil fled into the swamp.

Part 12 - Penthouse

January 25, 1000 ME

On the Wings of Angels

One moment, she was about to be devoured by the Great Dragon, and the next she perched on the edge of a bed with the Archangel Michael standing over her. Michael laid his great hand upon her head, and supernatural peace enveloped her. "Thou hast done well, Davianna ben David, daughter of Eve. As thy journey continues, do not be afraid to take thy place. Be courageous. The Most High is with thee."

Astrid never conceived a face more beautiful than Peter's, but gazing at Rafael, she beheld one. "Astrid ben Agnor, thy sacrifices and stalwart heart are esteemed. As thy journey continues, find thy bravery and surrender."

Josiah knelt at the feet of Gabriel, the Messenger of God. "Prince Josiah ben Eamonn, the Lord is well pleased with thee. Do not be afraid to take thy love to wife, for Davianna ben David has been chosen for thee."

Peter knew the second he regained his wits where they were, his New York penthouse, his bedroom. Uriel's golden wings filled the room. "Prince Peter, son of Alexa, remember the mercy and grace thou received from the King in this very room. It is the Lord's will that none should perish, but all should come to Him. Doubt no longer, finish thy journey well."

As quickly as they came, the messengers were gone. By human standards, the encounters took less than ninety seconds, for the four stupefied mortals it was the most impactful moment of their lives. With the divine still upon them, they walked to their respective doors and opened them in unison. Ecstatic relief overwhelmed them, and they came together. Peace surrounded them in the quiet hallway, as they held each other.

Davianna broke the silence with a tiny snicker, Josiah tilted her chin up. "What are you giggling at, Minx?"

Amused disbelief lit her eyes. "I can't say it. Y'all will kill me."

Astrid bumped her shoulder. "Say it." She knew it would be something inappropriate and outrageous.

Davianna's lips pursed, and she tried to hold the laughter bubbling up like a spring. "Okay." She cleared her throat and said, "I'm sorry I missed the play, the Devil was trying to eat me."

Astrid threw back her head, laughing.

Peter and Josiah looked on with bemusement as they became uproarious, falling to the floor in hysterics. At length they wore themselves out, exhausted.

"Well, at least my head doesn't hurt anymore." Astrid sat up, weaving like a drunk. "Does anybody know where we are?"

Peter helped her up. "At my Penthouse, in New York."

Astrid snorted, her eyes sparkling. "Good then you know where the bathroom is, I've had to pee," another bout of laughter seized her and she stammered, "s-s-since Louisiana!"

The two girls stumbled down the hall, peals of laughter in their wake.

Josiah watched them, one of Astrid's sayings on his lips. "They are not right."

Peter burst out laughing. Josiah's southern accent was spot on. "They are not boring." He slapped his cousin on the back. "Come on Star Search, can I offer you a drink."

A slow smile spread across Josiah's face. "Yes. It is said that a king may not drink lest he rule unjustly and pass unrighteous laws, but we are not making any laws tonight."

"No, we are not." Peter rubbed his jaw. "My jaw hurts, by the way. You have a nasty right hook."

"My ribs don't feel so great either." Josiah countered, then added, "I am sorry."

"Cousin, we were just rescued by angels. I think I will let it slide."

Josiah nodded, suppressing a grin. "Appreciate that."

Peter sidled up behind the bar. "What are you drinking?"

Josiah looked at the selection. "I have no idea. The first drop of alcohol I ever tasted was last night when I split a hurricane with my girl in there."

"Rum it is." Peter tilted his head, puzzled. "Honestly, you never had a drink?"

"Nope. Grandmother Mary told me I would die a horrible death if I ever drank alcohol. It scared the shit out of me."

"I believe Grandmother Mary scared the shit out of everybody." Peter grinned. "We should have had her with us tonight."

Josiah cracked up, remembering their formidable grandmother.

Peter passed the shot across the bar.

Josiah raised the rum in toast. "To new adventures and changes." He drained the glass and flashed his own version of Peter's lecherous grin.

Peter poured a soda and took a sip. "What did that angel say to you?"

Josiah held out his empty glass. "I'll tell you later. Hit me again."

Davianna plopped down beside him.

Josiah draped an arm around her shoulder and pulled her tight. "Do you still carry it?"

She touched her left pocket and made a face. "Yes." Then shaking off the thought asked, "Peter, what do you have back there?"

Peter sent her a wry look. There was enough alcohol to start a nightclub.

"How about a hurricane?" Her eyes sparkled in memory.

He cocked his head and adopted a stuffy royal demeanor. "I am not a bartender. I am a Prince. Someone else makes the drinks. Shall I call in the staff?"

"That would be lovely," Davianna mimicked his haughty tone. "In the meantime, rum is fine."

Peter turned to Astrid. "Red, what can I get you?"

"My head has stopped hurting, something non-alcoholic and cold."

He winked at her; their sobriety maintained. He poured her the rest of his can of soda and they toasted, sharing a private victory, together.

They moved to the comfortable living room. Josiah steered Davianna onto one of the luxurious cream-colored sofas, holding her close. Peter and Astrid followed, both yawning. Beyond the twenty-foot-tall windows, the city of New York bustled, but at this height, the sounds were muted.

Josiah winked at Davianna. "As memorable nights go, I'd say that's two in a row."

Davianna tilted her head back, relaxed and misty. "I'd say you are right."

Their eyes locked.

"I love you," he whispered.

She swallowed audibly, blinking back tears. "I love you, too."

He pulled her to his side and let out a deep sigh of contentment.

Peter and Astrid both beamed with pleasure. "Finally," Astrid said in a long-suffering tone.

Josiah kissed the top of Davianna's head. They sat in companionable silence.

At length, Davianna yawned. "I am too tired to even talk. Let's take this up tomorrow."

They murmured agreements, but no one moved. Moments later they were all fast asleep, angels watching over them.

House Calls

Astrid woke in Peter's bed. She smiled in sleepy pleasure as his tongue flicked over her left nipple. "Good morning," she said, yawning. He bit down hard, and she gasped. Her eyes flew wide in shock and pain.

It was not Peter.

Hovering above her body was a great black reptile, baring fangs that dripped blood.

She screamed.

Peter sat straight up. Smelling sulfur, he shouted, "Get out!" He threw her behind him, shielding her body. Several flashes of light came in from the roof, and he heard the monster bellow in rage. Then a trail of black smoke shot out the window. "You evil bastard!"

Astrid became frantic.

He pulled her tight, holding her, refusing to let go, even as she fought him.

Josiah burst in with his weapon drawn.

Peter pulled a sheet over Astrid and said, "It is gone. I have her. Go to Davianna. If you smell sulfur, yell."

Josiah looked confused but left without further questions.

Astrid was wiping her skin, sobbing, pushing him away, then clinging to him.

Rage erupted inside him, with nowhere to go. Burning with fury, Peter said to the empty air, "How dare you touch her!"

Clutching her breast and crying, she said, "It bit me! Peter, it bit me."

"Let me see." He had to pry her hands away. Blood gushed

out of a series of deep punctures. Instinctively, he stemmed it with his fingers. It ran copious and warm. Panicked, he said the only thing that came to his mind, "I pray healing over you, in the name of Yeshua."

Astrid felt her breast go from blazing hell fire, to normal. She stopped struggling and looked down.

The bite mark healed before their eyes.

She began to sob in earnest, clinging to him. He held her tight. Their breath coming in deep gasps, adrenaline flowing like a fire hose.

"Come on." He pulled her out of bed toward the shower, knowing from experience she would want to be clean. "It knows this place. I am sorry, love. I do not know why the angels brought us here. I never wanted to come back here. I intended to sell it." Peter's voice shook as he washed the blood from her skin. "We will go somewhere it cannot find us, okay? Where we will be safe, both of us. I promise."

"That was one of those monsters, wasn't it? One of those beings the Devil is trying to release." At his nod, she grimaced. "It was horrible. How can there be such a thing in this world?" Her face contorted. "Peter, did Davianna and I free that thing?"

"No." Peter shook his head, his eyes solemn. "Korah did, when he killed his brother."

Her voice broke. "That is the monster that lived in your house, who has attacked you since you were little?" She sobbed on his chest, her heart breaking. "That is who made you watch while your father beat your mother to death?"

He paled. "Yes."

Held at bay since she heard him screaming at Josiah last night, the full comprehension of the horror he endured washed over her. Her heart broke for him. As she held him, a dark understanding dawned. "No! You were just a little boy. Peter, oh I'm so sorry." She curled into him, hoping this was a nightmare.

"Shh. You are okay."

"But are you?" She reached up and cupped his face. "That thing hurt you." She saw the truth in his eyes and began to weep. She wanted to pull it out of him, take it upon herself. The spray of the shower equaled the tears she cried.

He tried to pull away, unable to bear her sympathy, ashamed. Memories flashed. He saw himself slammed against the wall, heard his skull as it smashed into the plaster. He felt himself floating above his bed, contorted in a backbend that was one of the monster's favorite tortures. His toes touched his head, knowing any moment his spine would crack. Then he spun, caught up in a tornado that would never end. He staggered. The cold ceramic tiles under his feet reminded him of lying on this bathroom floor, violated and broken. Raped. He covered his eyes, and a horrible groan erupted from deep within his soul.

They sunk together to the shower floor.

"I'm so sorry. Oh, Peter."

He put the flat of his hand between their faces and turned away.

"No, don't pull away from me!" Her vehement cry echoed off the tile walls. "You don't hide from me."

The horrible spinning stopped as her words penetrated his panic.

"Remember? They don't belong in here with us or in us? You said that to me that day back in the cabin, and you were right." Blue, savage fire flashed in her eyes. "I won't ever let that thing hurt you again! I will kill it if it ever comes near either of us again. Do you hear me?"

"Red," he choked, "you are going to kill that thing for me?"

"Yes. That's a wagonload of horse shit, him picking on you. I'll rip his heart out."

"He is not that easy to fight."

"I don't care. We will find a way. I won't let him." Astrid cupped his face. "I won't."

Peter blinked up at her in wonder. She would fight for him. Someone would come. Someone would finally come.

For a moment, she saw him, that little boy, Princess Alexa's pride and joy. She experienced a fierce wave of protectiveness. "I will stand in the gap for you, and together we will break free."

She made love to him, gently, tenderly. She gave him her heart, with the warm shower washing away all that had come before, before her, before this moment.

Afterward, she got to her feet and held out her hands to him. The man who rose from the shower floor was a little less broken than the man who fell down.

Future as an Entertainer

Peter blessed Davianna ben David for her superior barista skills, sighing with pleasure as he sipped the French pressed elixir of life. Their gear reappeared while they slept, apparently delivered by Angel's Express.

Peter fiddled with his tablet, "Sixty-eight million views, Star Search," he teased. "You know, if the whole Ruling Prince thing does not work out for you, it looks like you have a future as an entertainer."

Josiah looked up from his pancakes. "I am never going to live that down, am I?"

Peter took a pancake off the top of the stack, munching it without syrup or a plate. "Nope."

Josiah met his cousin's eyes with half-closed lids. "Okay, just checking."

Astrid kissed Peter's cheek. "Leave him be. I think it's sweet."

Davianna brought the last batch of pancakes and took her place at the table. "Are you okay?" she asked Astrid. "My heart nearly stopped this morning when you screamed."

Astrid and Peter exchanged a look.

"I'm fine. Just your average, every day fallen angel come to cop a feel."

Davianna's forehead furrowed, then she nodded and said, "Oh, if that's all, please pass the syrup?"

Josiah glanced around the table. "I'm in an insane asylum."

One corner of Peter's mouth lifted. "Certifiable." He munched on a piece of bacon. "Can we eat first?"

Josiah threw up a hand. "Of course, Satan and the holy angels last night, fallen angels this morning, definitely difficult on the digestion."

Astrid raised her coffee in salute. "Welcome to the madhouse, Doc."

The Drawbacks of Being Royal

They settled in the living room, the great city of New York visible through the windows. Peter paced as he spoke. "I have to debrief my team this morning. They were frantic last evening when we disappeared." He stopped, and his shoulders drooped a bit. "There is something I need to clarify. I kept it from you all, but I should not have. I rarely speak of it." He made a hollow snort and shook his head. "That is until last evening, when I thoroughly lost my mind, and screamed it to the heavens."

Josiah grew very still. Peter's confession, while overshadowed by the appearance of Lucifer, was not forgotten. "You lived through hell. I did not understand."

Peter shrugged, feigning a casualness he did not feel. "It is not a normal conversation topic."

"I would think not," Josiah agreed. He understood why Peter kept quiet. Stoicism was bred in their bones. Royals do not complain. They get on with life and keep their private pain, private.

They shared a look, unspoken understanding passing between them. It was something the girls could not comprehend: the responsibilities of being royal, the rules that governed their lives, and the innate isolation of their world. The press fed on royal gossip. Weakness or peculiarity was blood in the water to media sharks, and truth did not matter in a feeding frenzy.

Looking into Josiah's eyes, for the second time that morning, Peter felt a little less alone. "I expect you do."

"Aye, go on." Josiah nodded with the hint of an encouraging smile.

"That device you carry," Peter pointed at Davianna's left pocket, "is legendary. My father and his cronies have been looking for it for quite some time. The story goes that there were twelve such devices, yours being the most powerful. Around '83, Korah got his hands on one. I know this because I stole it from his desk."

Davianna covered a gasp.

"My mother forced me to put it back, fearing he would kill us if he discovered its theft. She was probably right." He swallowed, looking pained, but he had to tell Josiah. "I believe he used it, in conjunction with your father's murder, to release one of those things."

The room fell silent.

"The Gune confirmed that to me, back in the spring." Josiah moistened his lips. "She said an evil entity broke free and aligned with Korah."

Peter stared out the window. "Korah calls it the Dark Master. He is a nasty, stinking bastard."

Davianna looked horrified. "You can smell them?"

"Yes. He smells like rotten eggs."

"Bloody hell." Josiah shook his head. "Korah's dungeon reeks of it."

"Not surprising, I think that is where he lives."

Davianna brought her knees up and curled into a ball.

"Okay." Peter resumed his pacing. "According to our bayou visitor last night, the monster's name is Marduk. I heard him called that once before." He swallowed hard and confessed, "But I was in a bad way, and I forgot."

Davianna gasped. "Wait, Marduk? I know who that is. He was a Canaanite god, or Babylonian, an abominable creature. He goes by a bunch of names, Moloch and the Prince of Persia are specifically mentioned in scripture. That's him."

Peter scowled. "To my great misfortune, I know him well." He cleared his throat again and cut a glance to his bedroom door. "Back in November," he paused, choosing his words carefully, "I had a particularly rough night. After it was over, I had a visitation."

"By whom?" Josiah asked.

"Yeshua." He shrugged and turned away.

The room fell silent.

Peter met Astrid's eyes and said, "He said that they could not touch me again. That it was over." He closed his eyes, grabbing the back of his neck. "Later, I thought I imagined it. However, the monster was gone from the Palace when I returned, and last night the angel said to me, 'Remember the mercy and grace thou received from the King in this very room. It is the Lord's will that none should perish, but all should come to Him. Doubt no longer, finish thy journey well.'"

"Those are powerful words, Peter," Davianna said.

"Finish thy journey well." Josiah nodded and gave Peter a smile.

"If he was in the Palace, it would have made our escape even harder." Davianna took a sip of her cold coffee and said, "I think the Iron King is still imposing rules on them and sending his angels to fight them. They are powerful, but they are not omniscient, nor are they omnipresent. I think they are restrained in what they can and cannot do. Otherwise, Satan would have followed us here."

Peter gave Davianna a wide-eyed look, impressed by her. "I believe you are correct, Fireball. They chased the monster out of our bedroom this morning."

"Well, I would much rather wake up looking at your face than his." Astrid chuckled and kissed Peter's cheek. "You are priss-teen."

Davianna giggled.

Peter's left dimple showed when he flashed her a smile.

"If we are all done fawning over Peter's pretty face, perhaps we can continue?"

"Shut up, Cousin. You are just jealous."

Josiah ran his tongue over his teeth and confessed, "Perhaps I was. That was misplaced, wasn't it?"

Peter rolled his eyes and quipped, "I do not believe so. Look at me. I am priss-teen."

And just like that, the angry words of the night before were diffused.

"Indeed," Josiah said, smiling. "There was always more to you than met the eye, Prince d'Or.

Peter chuckled and rested his forehead against Astrid's. "Yeah, I am complicated."

She whispered, for his ears only, "I think I am starting to figure you out."

"Be careful, Red. You might not like everything you find."

Gabriel's Message

Josiah drew Davianna to her feet. "I need to talk to you." He turned to Peter and Astrid. "If you will excuse us."

He led Davianna to a sitting room that connected their bedrooms. Dominated by floor to ceiling windows, the room commanded a stunning view of the Hudson River. Intent on his mission, Josiah took no note of the scenery, did not bother to look outside. He directed her to one of the large low-backed chairs and dropped to one knee.

His whiskey-colored eyes shimmered with gold in the bright sunlight. She caught her breath, hope battling fear. He broke her heart, time and again, but he said he loved her last night, and Prince Josiah did not speak idle words.

"I think I fell in love with you before I even saw you. I fell in love with your spirit, your spunk, and with the stories I heard from the people you met. They painted a picture of the feisty girl, giving me a merry chase across half the planet."

She smiled. "I did, didn't I?"

"Yes, you did." Josiah's head fell back in entreaty.

He lifted her hand and pressed a soft kiss to the back of her knuckles. "Then in London, when I saw you on Waterloo Bridge, you were much more than the phantom I was chasing. You were so lovely, with the wind blowing your hair, smelling like flowers. I will never forget how turned on I was when I realized you were armed to the teeth, or what it felt like when you hugged me and thanked me for Calais." He swallowed a tightening in his throat, thinking of the fear in her eyes.

"You saved my life that night in Calais."

He nodded. "All I wanted to do was take you to safety, but I couldn't because Korah was trying to kill me. And you disappeared like smoke, gone again. I went crazy with worry. That night in the park, when you finally let me find you, I'd been half out of my mind." He dropped her hand and scrubbed his palms over his face at the memory. "You ran from me again." His eyes flashed, dangerous. "Then at the hotel, you gassed me."

Davianna's face went crimson. "Sorry about that."

Josiah held her gaze. "Don't run from me again." His voice grew hoarse. "We almost died because of that. I thought Korah was going to kill you in front of me." He looked away, remembering the impotent rage and terror of the dungeon. "In the end, I realized that wicked bastard intended to murder me and make you watch. He had you, Davianna, and there was nothing I could do." His face contorted, and he laid his forehead on her knees. "You stopped him."

"I don't remember," she whispered, a haunted look in her eyes.

"I'm glad. Don't try to recall it."

She nodded.

"After we escaped, I got to see who you were, my Davianna." His voice shook. "Sweet, playful, funny, smart girl who refused to let all the terrible things that happened steal your joy or your laughter. I died a thousand deaths in that cabin and in the weeks after." He smiled at her ruefully. "You thought I did not want you."

"Well, that is what you said."

"No. That's not what I said. That would have been a lie, and I won't lie to you. It was my honor and my kingdom that barred me from you, like an impenetrable wall around a lonely castle. I built those walls, and they stood for so long I knew nothing else." As he spoke, he felt them crumbling and rejoiced in their destruction.

"That is lonely." Davianna rested her hand on his bent knee.

"More than you know. I filled the space with my work, with medicine, and it was enough to get me through the day. At night, I planned, but I was angry. I could not understand why the Iron King sat by and let it all happen. When I arrived in the Golden City, I expected him to give me an army to defeat Korah. He did not. Instead, he sent me after you. I was furious. I wanted my plan, but he had another, you and me."

Davianna's breath caught.

"The other night in New Orleans, I wanted nothing other than just to be your man because that is who I was made to be, yours."

She put her hand over her mouth, her eyes glistening.

"I do not know what the future holds, but I know I do not want a future without you by my side." His eyes shone with tenderness, his voice deep and husky. "Davianna ben David, I love you with all my heart. Will you do me the very great honor of becoming my wife?"

Josiah watched the emotions play over her pretty little face; her nod started before she answered. "It would be the greatest honor and privilege of my life. Yes."

Prince d'Or in Residence

Agreeing to get married and accomplishing it were two separate things, when one party was a long presumed dead Prince, and the other an international fugitive, of common birth, and no connections. Further complicating the matter was the fact that the current ruler of Alanthia had no intention of stepping aside or stopping his diabolical plans to murder the groom and seize the bride. Throw in Lucifer and a key that would release hell on Earth and the newly engaged couple faced serious obstacles to their happily ever after.

None of these facts dampened the happy occasion. When Astrid raised the questions, Josiah answered simply, "Sufficient unto the day is the trouble therein. We will figure it out. Today, we celebrate."

"And we stop hiding." Peter pointed at Josiah.

Josiah nodded. "It's your plan, Peter. I see the wisdom in it."

Donning the cloak of royal authority, Peter picked up his phone. "I am not running from the local police again. That was absurd, and I will be damned if I let those wicked bastards keep me prisoner any longer."

"What are you going to do?" Davianna touched her pocket, looking scared.

Peter flashed her his famous smile. "Prince d'Or is officially back in residence."

Davianna and Astrid exchanged dubious glances.

"Today, we launch the second phase of the plan." Peter pressed the call button and mobilized The Resistance.

His trusted and elite security force flew in and took up positions, guarding the Penthouse. Jarrod arranged for the Princes' personal comfort from afar, and deliveries began pouring in. The press got wind of it and camped outside the building, vying for a photograph. They openly speculated about Josiah's presence.

The story led every broadcast in the kingdom. Absent from their reporting was any mention of Davianna and Astrid. The press was in the dark by design. Prince d'Or was back, and King Korah, besieged on all sides, could not do a single thing about it. The angels on the roof ensured that neither could Lucifer.

January 27, 1000 ME

Propaganda

The gray video background offered no clue to their location, but where they were did not matter. The most sought-after fugitives on the planet went public, and Alanthians were captivated the second they saw the girls. Their performances were worthy of an ancient Oscar. Peter, with a flair for the dramatic, directed the films.

For the first one, Astrid wore a navy-blue blouse with a sailor's collar, Davianna a turquoise knit top. Dangling from delicate gold chains around their necks, each wore half a friendship heart, popular with every schoolgirl in Alanthia. As the camera rolled, they clutched each other's hands and stared wide-eyed into the lens, reality TV at its best.

Davianna opened with a shaky voice. "Hi, Mom."

Astrid's lips tightened into an encouraging smile, then she turned to the camera. "Hi, Daddy."

Davianna blinked and said, "We saw your interview, but we cannot come home. It's not safe. No one is safe as long as Korah rules Alanthia."

"Daddy, you were right. We didn't do anything wrong." Astrid's eyes flashed defiance. "Korah had us arrested. It was terrible." She looked down at their clasped hands, true emotion clouding her face. "We got away, but we are hiding. Please keep fighting for us! We love you."

The video faded out with Davianna in the background, crying.

Josiah startled Davianna with his applause.

Peter flashed a devilish grin. "Every parent in the world is going to go crazy over that."

Josiah leaned down and kissed Davianna's cheek. "That little girl act is freaking me out. I feel like a lecherous old man."

The look she gave him was anything but childish. "Do you like it?"

"No, not really." His pained expression made her laugh.

Peter looked Astrid up and down, the dimple in his left cheek lent him an exceptionally roguish air. "I do not know what you are talking about, Doc."

Josiah rolled his eyes. "You are twisted."

Astrid blew Peter a kiss. "Just the way I like him."

"All right," Peter smacked Astrid's bum as she scampered off. "Go change for the next one."

They created four thirty-second videos with one objective, to destabilize Korah's support and bring him down. Precise, nuanced, and sincere, the scripts delivered specifically targeted messages. The line they walked was razor thin. Taken as a whole, the videos could not contradict, pander, or jeopardize their futures.

For the Iron King's loyalists, they dressed as pilgrims and recounted the Camp Eiran massacre. They changed their clothes and hardened their appearance for the Anarchists, describing life on the run from the world's corrupt governments. Republicans saw two thoughtful young women, imprisoned without due process.

Purposely oblique, their message reverberated throughout the kingdom. Though deceptively simple, they were released as part of the strategic campaign started with the Vegas photo. Davianna and Astrid already notorious, skyrocketed to worldwide fame, becoming cult symbols on the global stage. Behind them, stood two Princes, their lives and kingdom hanging in the balance.

Their supporters went online and went to war.

January 28, 1000 ME

Photographs

Astrid became the campaign's official photographer. Her Vegas picture of Peter and Josiah was perhaps the most important of the age. Her shots in the New York Penthouse were breathtaking. Artistic and instinctive, she captured the essence of the moment and her subjects; Josiah holding papers for Peter's consideration, Peter skeptical. There was one of Peter standing in shadow, light illuminating the left side of Josiah's face, another of the two opposites sharing a laugh, gold and black, masculine beauty. She documented the subtle interplay between them as they discussed strategies, risks, and plans—their future.

It was Peter's shy beauty, the kind he possessed when he was not trying to be charming, that was so endearing. The public was always drawn to him because of it, but Astrid's pictures revealed a side of Prince d'Or they had never seen, quick intelligence, intensity, purpose.

Josiah's rugged masculinity, inherent decency, and honor evoked a powerful sense of calm, steadiness. In his eyes, they saw a future of safety and prosperity. Reminded of Prince Eamonn, they reminisced about Alanthia before rebellion, when the world was lush, peaceful, and safe. They were weary of drought and violence and began longing for the days of paradise. Through pictures, Astrid revealed the Alanthian Princes the kingdom had forgotten or discounted but would soon clamor for.

For posterity, Astrid captured Davianna and Josiah in the first blush of betrothal. Josiah's half smile over a cup of coffee, while Davianna cooked breakfast. Davianna teasing a ferocious scowl off Josiah's stern face. The dreamy faraway glow in Davianna's eyes when she admired her heirloom engagement ring, which had arrived in one of the parcel deliveries. She snapped a photo of Peter with his head thrown back, laughing at one of Davianna's outrageous quips. The last, of the three of them, with their heads pressed together discussing strategy, their plans… their future.

With each shot she felt herself slipping further and further away. Outside their royal cocoon, no longer part of them, Astrid began to fall far beyond their reach.

Nothing

Astrid stood alone on the Penthouse balcony. The setting sun glowed orange and red over the city. It looked warm from the window but was bitter cold in reality, which seemed apropos. The frigid wind buffeted her, ruffled her hair, and turned her cheeks pink. She took no real notice of the temperature or the view.

Craving solitude, she wanted time to think, alone.

On the run, there was no time for contemplation, no thought to the future beyond tomorrow. For months, she lived by instinct, in survival mode, but standing still, no longer fleeing, everything she pushed aside swallowed her whole.

Grief struck like a venomous snake, and she ached for her mother. Certain smells triggered the horror of her captivity and torture. The drugs clawed at her, beckoning her back to oblivion. She could not even begin to process encounters with supernatural beings or Peter's painful confessions. For days she felt a growing unease that she could not put a name to.

On the windswept balcony, she pinned it down and made it surrender. It was this place, this Penthouse, the guards, the staff… his closet, Prince d'Or's real world.

A fat pigeon landed on the railing and watched her with expressionless beady eyes. She ignored it, lost in thought.

Peter spent a lifetime convinced he wanted nothing to do with the kingdom, but the days of planning and strategizing with Josiah revealed the truth. What he craved was freedom from his father. His beautiful scarred mind made Korah and Alanthia one and the same, they were not. Collaborating on the videos, his passion, love, sense of duty, and honor became crystal clear. Alanthia was Peter's kingdom, as much as it was Josiah's. It coursed through his royal blood, an undeniable reality.

As darkness fell, she felt as trapped as she had been in Korah's Palace, except Peter was the addiction now. Her fairytale Prince, beautiful and broken, was more intoxicating than any opiate. A cold wind blew through her spirit, clearing the haze, banishing the misty dream. Her life with him was nothing but a fantasy, a delusion, and she was coming down hard. Even now, as she stood apart, she craved him.

Peter needed her now, but for how much longer? She could see the changes in him. He was growing stronger as she grew weaker. She saw him blossom, back in his element. It was only a matter of time before he realized his mistake. Davianna warned her of this back at the cabin. The angel told her to be brave when it came time to surrender, now she understood what he meant.

A soft blanket came around her shoulders, lean strong arms pulled her against his chest. With hooded eyes and a lazy smile, Peter kissed her cheek. "What are you doing out here alone in the cold, Red?"

Astrid could not look at him. "Nothing," she whispered into the darkness.

January 29, 1000 ME

Lawyers

Teams of them arrived, lawyers. First up, the criminal defense lawyers, who came over coffee. The girls were overjoyed to learn that Korah's reward for their capture was a ploy, not precisely illegal, but far outside the boundaries of established law and precedent. Astrid and Davianna were never indicted, never formally charged with a crime, and there was no evidence against them. The lawyers' left, armed with sheaves of documents, heading to court to have the warrants withdrawn.

Accountants and lawyers from Peter's legitimate trusts, businesses, and charities descended on the penthouse in droves. His long absence created a backlog of documents to sign, decisions to make, and expenditures to authorize.

Josiah met in private with Prince Eamonn's personal attorney, the honorable Sir Preston ben Worley of the venera-
ble firm of Worley, Blake, and Standish. Ninety, if he was a
day, his bright gray eyes shone with excitement as he shook
Josiah's hand with arthritic vigor. Josiah did not recall ever
meeting him, but Sir Preston assured him they had met on
many occasions.

The legalities of the resurrected Prince were monumen-
tal. Personal property, estates, and trusts were all absorbed by
Korah when the court declared Josiah dead fifteen years ago.
The old lawyer did not appear daunted, instead he seemed
rejuvenated. Through conversation, Josiah discerned that Sir
Preston despised Korah and seemed gleeful at the prospect of
taking him on in court.

"Sir Preston, at this time, I do not wish to seek a restoration to the throne through the court system. If such an
edict is to come, the Iron King must issue it, otherwise, the
kingdom may well erupt into another Civil War, which is not
my desire."

"But my Esteemed, the timing is perfect. Prince Korah
is at his weakest point since his usurpation. To wait, affords
him the opportunity to sway public opinion and shore up his
defenses," Sir Preston advised.

"Your counsel is wise, but I shall not be swayed on this
matter. It is enough, at present, to establish that I am alive."

Sir Preston did not appear pleased but demurred. "As you
wish, my Esteemed."

"There is another matter, of the highest confidentiality,"
Josiah intoned, his eyes boring into the old solicitor. "I can
trust your utmost discretion?"

"Of course. How may I be of service?" Sir Preston leaned
forward.

"I am getting married. The timing of it is uncertain at
this point. My companions and I are traveling to the Golden
City next week." Josiah cleared his throat. "To be frank, the
journey is fraught with danger. As such, I wish to establish

a trust for my betrothed, in the event I am killed before we wed."

The shrewd old lawyer twisted the end of his prodigious moustache. "My Esteemed, first allow me to offer my sincere congratulations on your pending nuptials. We will, of course, make the necessary arrangements as you request. However, I must urge you to reconsider. Leaving Alanthia now is not politically expedient." Sir Preston's gray eyes flashed with intensity. "The kingdom has suffered great injustice under Korah. It would be devastating to lose you again."

"I appreciate your concern, however, above being a Prince of Alanthia, I am a servant of the Iron King and must do as he commanded. I will return to the Golden City."

Sir Preston's voice quivered with age and resignation. "You are Eamonn's son to the core."

Josiah bowed his head. It was a compliment of the highest order. "Thank you, Sir."

A glimmer flashed across Sir Preston's ancient face. "And the marital and betrothal contracts?"

Josiah smiled, lawyers and their fees never changed. "Will be drawn up in the Golden City, thank you."

Sir Preston raised a woolly brow. "Of course, my Esteemed, as you wish."

They discussed the details of the trust and the estate. Sir Preston predicted that the documents would be available for Josiah's signature by the close of the week.

As their meeting drew to its conclusion, Sir Preston asked, "My Esteemed, may I perhaps have a private word with Prince Peter?"

"Certainly." Josiah rose. "Please, stay here. I will tell him you would like to speak with him."

Several minutes later, Peter sat across the desk from the solicitor, his indolent Prince d'Or armor firmly in place.

Sir Preston studied him. "You have her look about you, your mother. Did you know that?"

Peter drew back, surprised. Even to his own eyes, he bore a strong resemblance to Korah.

"It is not your countenance, but your mannerisms and expressions that bring her so vividly to mind." Sir Preston paused, his old eyes penetrating. "Also, the way you use your good looks to hide a keen brain."

Peter remained impassive, revealing nothing.

The solicitor laughed. "She was my goddaughter. Did you know?"

Peter blinked in surprise, the veneer of indifference dropping. No one spoke of Princess Alexa, and his foggy memories were buried deep in his mind, becoming mere shadows as the years passed. "No, I did not know she was your goddaughter. I knew your firm managed her estates. I get the reports."

The corners of Sir Preston's eyes crinkled as he smiled. "She set those trusts up for you. Came to visit me several months before she died." He rubbed the grisly stubble on his chin and turned his head away, but not before Peter caught something in the watery gray depths of his eyes. "I should have advised her differently that day."

Peter's face turned to stone. He had a vague recollection of an outing with his mother. As he looked across the desk, he remembered the solicitor. The moustache was unforgettable. "Yes, perhaps you should have."

"Alas, I have carried that burden since she died," Sir Preston confessed. "I did not comprehend the danger she was in."

Peter flared his nose at the old man. Another lost chance, another person who failed them, sat across the desk. "If we are done," Peter said coldly and began to rise.

"If you will indulge me just a moment, I have something I need to give you."

Peter reluctantly sat back down.

"Alexa was a spirited child. She saw what she wanted, and she went after it. She turned into a wonderful caring person." He swallowed, audible in the silence. "She was a good mother, and she loved you very much. She wrote of it often." He dug around in his battered, overstuffed leather briefcase and produced a letter, yellowed with age. His large veiny hand trembled as he passed it across the metal and glass desk.

Peter stared at the handwriting before accepting it. "What is this?"

"It's a letter for you, my Esteemed. She gave it to me that day she set up the trusts, with instructions."

Peter studied the letter for a long moment. "What sort of instructions, may I ask?"

Sir Preston pursed his lips. "She asked me to give it to you if you ever escaped your father's house." His voice turned cold and lethal. "I have held it, these many years, waiting."

"I see we are of one accord." The corner of his lip curled into a smile.

"Aha," Sir Preston declared and pointed an arthritic finger at him. "That little half smile, right there, is your mother to the life."

A Mother's Letter

After the lawyers departed, Peter collapsed into the low-backed chair in his bedroom, exhausted. He handed Astrid the letter. "Read it to me, I find I am weary, and my head is throbbing after all the legal wranglings of the day."

Astrid took the letter. The paper was fine vellum, soft with age. The glue loosened at the slightest touch, pulled away without tearing the envelope. Blue ink, from an old-fashioned pen, flowed across the page, written in a fine script. The words made her eyes blur, but she took great care to keep any tears from falling on the priceless paper.

August 14, 986 ME
Dearest Peter,

My darling little monkey, please forgive the baby name but as I look upon your sleeping face that is who I see. You are so handsome, with your cheeks flushed pink and innocent, your golden hair falling over your green eyes. It is morning, and you are asleep. I adore watching you sleep. I can still see the baby you were, and I fear I will not live to see the man you will become.

The greatest joy of my life has been being your mother. I have loved you with all my heart, every day of your life. No matter what happens, you will always be my baby, my beloved only son.

You may wonder why I never took the final steps to leave. I could write you a volume of letters, but even then, I doubt I could make you understand. Suffice it to say, it was a solemn vow I made to your father the day we wed. And as royalty, you understand the significance of such a promise. I have done my best for him, though, I fear it has not been enough.

If you are reading this letter, I am gone, and I am so sorry, Peter.

I do not know the life you will have lived, but I have a dreadful fear it will not have been an easy one, your father being who he has become.

But since you are reading this letter now, you have escaped him, like we planned. If possible, if he survived, find Josiah. Eamonn was a good man, and Josiah is made from the same mold, as are you, Son. Together or alone, you can defeat Korah and stop this wicked rebellion he is fomenting.

Your father is blind, consumed by the things that have happened. His rage never had anything to do with you. He just broke, and try as I might, I could not fix him.

Use your strengths and take your place, take your kingdom, your birthright. Be strong, be brave, and never forget how proud I am of you.

Your loving mother,
Princess Alexa ben Seamus

Peter sighed as she finished. "I could hear her voice as you read that. I have not heard her voice in so long."

The letter trembled in Astrid's hands. This message from the grave confirmed what she knew, what she feared. Tears stung her eyes, and she wished desperately for a letter from her own mother. Fresh grief swamped her, swirling in the emotional tornado that propelled her into his arms. Nothing could have stopped her from touching him. "She sounds like an amazing mother, Peter." She felt him nod and said in a strained voice, "She is right you know."

He pulled back, looking at her. "No, I do not want it."

There was denial on his lips, but reluctant realization dawning in his eyes. Astrid smoothed his eyebrow and whispered, "I know you don't, but I don't think you have a choice."

"That is where you are wrong." Peter pulled away and stalked over to the window. "You read what she wrote. My whole life I have dreamed of this, to escape, to be free." His face and voice became resolute. "You and I, when we get to the Golden City, we are never coming back."

He turned, gesturing to the city with a wave of his arm. "This kingdom is Josiah's; it always has been. I never wanted it. I decided that as a little boy. And after spending three years creating a mechanism to put him back on the throne, I am done!"

She wanted to believe him. He was offering her a fix, a lifeline, a gossamer thread that she could seize, a hope. She was so weak. Desire to possess him, to bind him, to keep him by her side made her say, "Okay."

His eyes turned a rain forest green, stormy with emotion. "You do not believe me."

Astrid put her index finger to her mouth as if she were considering him. Then she took shelter from the storm, seductively tracing her finger over her full bottom lip. "Convince me."

He responded with a low growl. "Take off your clothes."

"And how is that supposed to convince me?" she asked, still toying with her lip.

He looked at her like a golden stallion. "Because I am in charge. I do what I want."

She ran the flats of her palms up her thighs, pushing her skirt higher. "And what do you want?"

Peter spent the better part of the night showing her.

What if We Don't Make It?

Josiah bade the guards in the hall good evening and locked the front door. Davianna was laying sideways on a loveseat reading a book. Josiah hovered over her with an ironic smile. "I forgot how demanding servants and lawyers are."

Davianna rested the book on her chest. "Well, I suppose we must get used to it."

He gave a deep sigh and took the book from her chest, wedging his way onto the loveseat with her. "Scoot over."

She chuckled and tried to make room for him, which was difficult. His large frame took up most of the love seat, but she did not mind.

He kissed her forehead and snuggled next to her, lazy and relaxed. "I made arrangements for you today, in case something happens before we get to the Golden City."

She stiffened. "Do not say that."

"It is a distinct possibility, Davianna. You know that." His voice was steady as he continued, "No one knows what tomorrow might bring, and I will not leave you unprotected or without resources."

She turned to face him, her body pressed firm and solid against him. He wrapped his arms around her to keep her from tumbling to the floor. "Then I don't think we should wait."

"I've been thinking about that, particularly after Sir Preston left." He brushed a kiss over her lips and said, "We could become handfast."

"Handfast?" She smiled and kissed him back, murmuring, "People have not done that for hundreds of years."

"It's still the law, still legal. The Iron King sanctioned it." Josiah's eyes were veiled, the dream of a life with her firmly upon him.

Davianna toyed with his hair. "When people were few, and they couldn't get to a church."

Josiah shrugged. "Well, there are more people, to be sure, but you cannot deny, right now, we cannot get to a church."

The obstacles were indeed daunting, even after they reached the Golden City. But as she considered it, her heart sped up. She continued stroking his hair and asked, "So, how is it done?"

"The couple holds hands, makes a blood vow, and they marry each other." He nuzzled her ear. "Then they make love and promise to have a formal ceremony in a church before the year is out."

She admired the ring on her left hand, the weight of it still unfamiliar. "When do you want to do it?"

He nipped at her earlobe and growled, "Now."

She laughed and rolled from the couch, scampering away.

"Hey," he called after her, his arms suddenly empty, "where are you going?"

"To shower and get ready. I'm not marrying you in this." She motioned to the conservative attire she wore for the lawyers.

"Wear that blue dress!"

One corner of her mouth lifted as she disappeared down the hall. "I have something better. Jarrod, the Wonder Servant, sent it over. I will see you in an hour, Dark Prince."

Perfect

Josiah's hand was steady as he lit the candles in the sitting room that adjoined their suites. A lone boat trudged down the river, shining a spotlight to illuminate its ponderous progress down the Hudson. The windows reflected the golden glow of the candlelight and the striking figure of a well-made man in formal attire. Josiah wore a suit of the deepest ebony, white shirt, and a red sash festooned with the military and royal medallions of his station. He had no idea how Jarrod managed it, but he had, and Josiah was grateful.

The door to the sitting room opened, and Davianna stood with nervous hands clasped in front of her. She wore an elegant black party dress piped in white. It fit her to perfection, highlighting all her gorgeous curves, showcasing strong shapely legs.

"I don't own anything white. Life on the run, you know. White is not practical." She took in his elegant suit, and her courage faltered. "Jarrod sent this yesterday. Is it okay?"

"It's perfect," he said, moving to take her hands in his. "I promise, you will have the most gorgeous wedding gown ever created for our formal ceremony, but honestly, Davianna I have never beheld a more breathtaking vision than you tonight."

She let out a sigh of relief. "Good answer."

He closed his eyes with a laugh and drew her to him. "For that and a million other reasons, you have made me the happiest man alive."

"And you, my Dark Prince, have made me the happiest woman alive."

"Are you ready?" he asked. At her nod, he picked up a silver scalpel from a cloth on a side table.

She smiled at his forethought, knowing he would have sterilized the blades. He guided their hands, his surgeon's cut, precise and exact. They put their wounds together, pressed firm. Their blood mingled as they gazed into each other's eyes.

He smelled of soap, his strong jaw scraped clean of the black stubble that tickled her neck earlier. Josiah squeezed her uninjured hand and spoke the words that would bind them together.

"Let it be known, from this day forward, that I, Josiah son of Eamonn and Marguerite, from the royal house of Alanthia, take thee, Davianna ben David, to be my wife. I bequeath all that I have upon thee. In so doing, I bestow all legal rights due unto thee as my Princess, my wife, my chosen bride. I give my solemn troth and vow to love, honor, and to protect thee, all the days of my life. I will esteem no other but thee, giving fully and freely to thee, as long as I shall live."

When she began, her voice was soft, quietly reverent as she pledged herself to him. "I, Davianna, daughter of David and Zanah, from the humble house of Alanthia, take you, Doctor Josiah ben Eamonn, Prince of Alanthia, to be my husband." She smiled up at him, then looked at their clasped hands. "I vow to honor and cherish you, to make you laugh and bring joy to your heart. I pledge my undying faithfulness and loyalty to you as my husband and my Prince. As your wife, I will support you, protect, and stand beside you no matter the cost. I promise to love you fiercely, with my whole heart, all the days of my life."

Josiah nodded; his face sober as he prayed. "Heavenly Father, we ask you tonight to bless the words of our mouths and the meditations of our hearts, may they be acceptable in your sight. We pray for you to sanctify our union, bless us, and show your favor on us, all the days of our lives. May we serve you in honor and in truth. In the Savior's Name."

"Amen," they said together.

Josiah kissed her, soft and tender, all the love he held in his heart shimmering in his eyes. He smiled down at her. "May I have this dance?"

She lifted her chin and tilted her head in surprised wonder. "Of course."

Peter's little pink iPod was plugged into a speaker. He pressed play and took his bride into his arms. The song was tender, poignant, and utterly romantic, "Perfect".

Davianna wept.

He held her close, swaying to the music, his heart overflowing.

When the song finished, he dried her tears, and held her face between his strong hands.

"Wife," he said in awe, kissing her.

She locked her hands around his waist as she kissed him.

"Come," he murmured, dancing with her toward his room, their lips never parting.

Josiah kicked the door closed behind them, desire coursing through his veins, so hot his hands burned where he touched her. He fought the urge to devour her like a wild animal. Pent up masculine passion unleashed, he pulled her against him hard, kissing and touching her. Davianna's moan drove him to the brink. With the last vestige of control he possessed, he broke contact. "We should probably slow down a minute."

Her arms rested on his shoulders, her fingers playing with the dark hair at the nape of his neck. "Okay, I guess one of us knows what they are doing." Virginal fear and desire made her voice shaky.

His face flushed, and with slight chagrin, he pressed a kiss just below her ear, whispering, "I have never lain with a woman, Davianna."

Her breath caught. She cupped his cheek, Josiah, valiant and honorable. She assumed a virile military man would have experience; she should have known better. Holding him close, she whispered, "Thank you."

A sense of destiny fell upon the room, as if the world aligned. They basked in the glow of love.

She ran her fingers over the medals on his sash, before lifting it over his head. He took it from her and placed it over the back of a chair.

"Sit down." He nodded to the edge of the bed. With jerky movements, he shed his coat, tie, and shoes.

She perched on the edge of the bed, devouring him with voracious eyes. He moved like a black lion, all 6'3" of Dark Prince, coming to make love to her.

Kneeling before her, he removed her black leather pump. He massaged the instep and kissed her toes. Davianna giggled, her foot jumping in his hand. "Ticklish?"

"Terribly," she admitted.

"Good to know." He kissed the inside of her knee. She leaned her head back, enjoying the exotic feel of his lips on her skin. She heard him murmur, "Also good to know."

He rose bringing her with him. In a singular motion, he lifted the dress over her head. She stood before him in black lace. Her body was strong and curvy, with the athletic grace of a gymnast turned woman. "Divine," he breathed.

She bit her bottom lip and looked down, very shy, but she was not a coward. Moving her hands to his chest, she worked the buttons of his white shirt.

His fists clenched and unclenched at his sides as she made slow progress. Her fingers elicited sparks of electricity through his body. When she ran the flats of her hands over his bare chest, he let out a strangled groan. His shirt joined her dress on the floor.

His restraint broke. He lifted her off her feet, into a bruising kiss, walking her backward. He laid her down, none too gently, leaving his britches behind, his knit black boxers showing her his full desire. Josiah pulled the lacey cup to one side, freeing a perfect breast, its tiny pink nipple straining toward his devouring mouth.

Davianna arched, holding his head with both hands, giving over to the succor that pulled deep in her womb, and set her aflame.

His hand slipped over the flat of her belly, into the black curls below the lace, hot and moist, awaiting his touch. He tore his mouth away. "Minx, I can't wait any longer!" He slid off the end of the bed taking her lace panties with him, freeing himself of his boxers.

She arched her back unsnapping the bra and throwing it aside. Josiah crawled up the bed, naked and feral. She opened her legs to receive him, her breath coming in short gasps. He positioned himself at her entrance and pushed, finding her slick and tight.

"Look at me." His voice strangled, barely audible. She opened her eyes as he made her his wife. "I love you," he growled as he took her.

She gasped as the barrier broke. His unfamiliar invasion hurt. He felt impossibly large for her small body. Throwing his head back, the cords of his neck straining, he began to move. In his passion, he dislodged. She whimpered in pain. He gave a frustrated fumble, an incoherent apology, and impaled her again, driving deep. His body began to shudder with a sudden, violent climax. He groaned, his face twisted into ecstatic agony, and he collapsed atop her.

Davianna stroked the curve of his back as his breathing steadied. She felt his chest shaking with laughter.

"Forgive me, Wife. That was a bit ignominious."

"Ignominious?" Davianna snickered at the word.

He rolled off her, his elbow thrown over his eyes as the embarrassed chuckle took hold. "Not exactly how I imagined it."

The bed shook with their shared laughter.

"Me neither," she admitted.

His eyes met hers. His inky-black hair was disheveled, and he looked younger with the stern expression wiped from his face. "We shall practice. Forsooth, I promise I will do better next time."

She gave him a pained expression of helpless mirth. "I am a bit sticky."

He kissed the tip of her nose. "We can fix that." Josiah slipped out of bed and went to the bathroom to prepare a warm washcloth. He closed his eyes with humble appreciation when he saw her blood on his body, her sacrifice, a gift to him. He returned to their marital bed, determined to make amends.

Davianna pulled the blankets over herself while she waited, becoming modest and shy. He slipped in beside her, the warm cloth in his hand. Josiah kissed her gently and pulled back the covers. He ran the tip of the warm cloth over her stomach. She clamped her thighs together.

"Shh," he soothed.

Drops of crimson mingled with his seed, staining the sheet where she lay. He set the cloth aside and lifted her to the other side of the bed. Then with infinite care, kissed her stomach, and ran the cooling cloth over the blood at her thighs. He opened her before him, feasting his eyes, carefully cleaning her. The cloth soothed the discomfort.

Davianna drew in a sharp breath as he buried his face where the cloth had been. Trying to pull away in shocked embarrassment, she asked in a high-pitched voice, "What are you doing?"

"Mmm." He gave a low groan, nuzzling, breathing the scent of her, moaning with bliss, here at last. Thousands of barracks tales flooded his mind, his turn now. She blossomed under his hand, like a delicate flower. He teased, stroked, and caressed until she forgot her virginal modesty, and began to toss her head back and forth on the pillow. He was patient, watching her body react to his touch, tasting her, learning. When the deep shudders began, he felt like an artist who just created a masterpiece.

Entering her this time, his way smooth and sure. She panted in pleasure, not pain. He stroked her deep, timing his thrusts with the spasms rocking her body. She cried out in release, and he joined her in ecstasy.

As their breathing returned to normal, she murmured, "Now, that is how I imagined it."

He pressed a kiss to her fingers and said with moisture in his eyes. "Better, perfect."

January 30, 1000 ME

Coffee

Peter looked around the empty kitchen with a mixture of frustration and bemusement. He was spoiled, and he knew it. Neither fact was going to make him coffee. He stared at the empty French Press, no clue how it worked. With his arms crossed, he stared it down as if it were an enemy that would suddenly produce the elixir of life.

Half-heartedly, he called from the kitchen, "Davianna, how do you make the coffee?"

Craning his neck, he looked around the door frame, hoping to see her sleepy figure stumble from her room. Instead, the Penthouse was eerily quiet. The clock on the wall read 9:27 am. He scrubbed his hands over his face, confused. Breakfast was always ready by now. She and Josiah were normally up and finished eating. He grunted in frustration and padded down the hall, a slight worry buzzing in the back of his mind at the change in routine.

Smothered laughter coming from Josiah's bedroom, arrested his hand midway through a knock at her door. Peter's mouth fell open in dismay, followed by an unaccountable surge of anger. His cousin, Prince Upright and Honorable, was getting it on.

Bursting into his bedroom, Astrid opened a sleepy eye at him, and he said, "They are having sex in there."

She came fully awake. "No way!"

Peter threw his arms wide, palms upturned to the ceiling. "I swear they are, and there is no coffee."

Astrid's face split in a huge grin, laughing at his expression. "Oh, Prince, there's no coffee?"

Golden brows came to a point over the bridge of his fine straight nose. "No," he sulked. "You make the coffee."

"I think I will have tea this morning." Astrid stretched with lazy amusement.

He made a moody groan deep in the back of his throat and jumped on her. "Listen, wench, I served you well last night. You make the coffee."

Astrid smiled up at his angelic face, the golden stubble giving him a rascal's air. "I'll make the coffee," she pulled him down for a kiss, "later."

The Morning After

When Davianna and Josiah left their marital chamber an hour later, they heard Astrid singing in the shower and found Peter waiting at the end of the hallway. He looked like an angry father who just caught his daughter in bed with a boy. "And who is the debaucher of innocents now, Cousin?"

"Wife." Josiah moved past him.

Peter made a dismissive snort. "Wife? Yeah, right."

Davianna, absolutely oozed sated lover, and said with a smug smile, "Husband."

Peter stepped in front of them. "I am serious, Josiah, after all the grief you have been giving me."

Josiah and Davianna exchanged looks. Davianna leaned forward and gave Peter a peck on the cheek. "Someone is cranky because he hasn't had his coffee."

Peter scowled at her, the corner of his mouth twitching. "Well, that is part of it."

Davianna burst out laughing. "Poor baby, I'll make your coffee, Prince d'Or."

Now that coffee was on the way, he was a little less perturbed. Turning to Josiah, he asked, "Wife?"

Josiah shrugged. "Handfasted."

Peter cocked his head to the side, considering. "Interesting." As the answer came to him, his eyes widened, and the corners of his mouth drew down. He nodded. "Actually, quite brilliant."

Josiah rubbed his beard stubble, watching his pretty young wife in the kitchen. "I thought so."

Peter grinned. "Congratulations, Cousin." He pulled Josiah in for a back-slapping hug. "Did you bleed?"

"Shut up."

Guileless

Five innocent words, uttered over brunch, sparked a maelstrom between Astrid and Peter. Davianna flush with happiness, giddy with love, looked from Peter to Astrid and declared, "You could do it, too." As soon as she said it, the table froze. She wanted to suck the words back, but it was too late.

Astrid paled. Peter's eyes widened in stunned shock. Josiah scrunched his face into a closed eyed grimace.

Davianna glanced between her breakfast companions, breathing an apology in a low frantic tone. "Oh, I am so sorry."

Astrid did not say a word. With calm deliberation, she put her fork beside her plate, stood up with a jolt, and retreated from the room.

Peter closed his eyes, frowning and holding the back of his neck.

Mortified, Davianna slid down her chair, repeating, "I'm so sorry."

Josiah patted her leg under the table. "You did not mean anything by it."

Peter did not meet either of their eyes, but with a resigned sigh he rose and trudged after Astrid, mumbling, "This ought to be fun."

"Oh, I cannot believe I said that."

Josiah dismissed her concern. "It was bound to happen. This has been brewing for days."

Davianna turned to him in surprise. "It has?"

Josiah shrugged. "Yes, you've obviously missed all the undercurrents between them since we got engaged."

She gave him a rueful look. "I must get better at that."

He tweaked her chin. "It's part of your charm, Minx."

Davianna curled her lip at him. "What? That I am clueless about what goes on around me?"

Josiah pursed his lips, shaking his head. "Not clueless, guileless."

"Well, that sounds a little better."

"Infinitely," he agreed. "Besides, Peter needs to do the right thing." The sound of raised voices from the bedroom punctuated his statement. "But I do not envy him."

Something We Have to Do

Astrid stood at the French doors, looking outside. She heard him enter. She closed her eyes and tried to keep her voice calm. "Leave me alone. I do not want to talk to you right now."

"Red," he coaxed from just inside the doorway.

"I'm serious. Leave me alone."

Peter watched her stiff back. It would be easy to turn around and walk out the door, ignore it, let it pass, then pretend it never happened, like they did in the cabin after Davianna's tantrum. That was a mistake; he realized that now. The time of reckoning was upon them. "I do not think that is wise."

Astrid looked over her shoulder, her face set in suppressed anger, eyes flashing blue fire. "You have no idea. I am warning you now. Leave. Me. Alone." She glared at him unblinking.

He threw up his hands in surrender. "I did not do anything wrong."

With a deep sigh of exasperation, she turned her back on him. "No, you didn't. Don't worry about it. It's fine." She crossed her arms over her chest and stared with unseeing eyes out the window.

He stalked across the room, angry that she would dismiss him like a child. "This does not seem fine to me. You have had a bug up your butt for three days! What the bloody hell is wrong with you?"

She whirled on him and said through gritted teeth, "Nothing."

He stepped closer, his nose flaring. "Liar."

She drew up like a banty rooster and bumped him chest to chest. "Back off!"

He leaned forward, right in her face, and just below a shout, said, "No!"

"Dammit, Peter!" Her voice cracked with angry tears. "What do you want me to say?"

The muscles in his jaw worked as he demanded, "Tell me."

Her control shattered. "Tell you what? That you are tearing my heart out? That I see it every day—" Her voice broke in an angry sob, and she turned from him, pleading, "Leave me alone."

She felt him close behind her, his words were quiet and measured. "What do you see that is tearing your heart out, love?" He pulled her to his chest.

She melted into him, throwing her head back in anguish, eyes closed against the pain. "That you will never be free."

"No, you are wrong." He kissed the side of her neck. "We will escape. We will be free." He paused, holding her tightly. His voice grew low. "Do you think, for one minute, that I would ever let you go?"

She turned in his arms, shaking with silent tears.

He held her; suddenly so afraid he was losing her. He

fought off the urge to take her to bed, to show her what she meant to him, but he did not. They had to learn to communicate outside of sex. They had to do this, or they would not survive, and he feared what would become of him if she left.

After a time, she mumbled into the folds of his shirt, "You say the words now, because we are living in a dream." She lifted her head, smoothing his hair. "But I know the truth. When reality sets in, Peter, I'm no Princess." She shook her head. "I can't be someone, or something, I am not. And you know it."

His head bent forward, his mouth slack in disbelief. "What?" He appeared genuinely baffled. "Not a Princess? Who cares? I know a few. They are not that great." He shook his head as if to clear it. "The Hell Bitch, for example, she is a piece of work. You know she had sex with a horse in front of me?"

Astrid jerked backward, her eyes bulging. "No!"

Peter's face morphed into a dark shadow. "Oh yeah, one of her lighter days." He made a dismissive flick of his hand, shuddering. "Look, the point is, I would take one of you over a million of them."

He drew her hand to his heart, love swimming in his green eyes. "Astrid, do you not know?" He covered her hand, pushing it hard against his chest. "Do you not know that my heart is yours? That you mean everything to me?"

Gazing up into his precious face, she was lost. Prince Peter ben Korah was the most powerful drug ever created, and she, Astrid ben Agnor, was a hopeless addict. She decided, in that moment, she would hold him for as long as he would let her and deal with the inevitable withdrawal when it came.

January 31, 1000 ME

The Resistance

The call came in from Himari, they needed to set up a video conference. Reluctant at first, Peter acknowledged there was ample reason to proceed. Moving around the room, setting up the equipment, he kept looking at Astrid and clearing his throat.

"Spit it out." She crossed her arms, tapping her toe at him.

Peter looked sulky and uncomfortable. "You know I love you, right?"

Astrid narrowed her eyes. "Yes."

Peter pulled at his collar. "Well, there will be several members of The Resistance on the call, among them," he cleared his throat again, "Alaina, Himari, and of course, Auntie G.," he added the latter with a sigh of relief. "Auntie G. is great, you are going to love her, really, you are. She helped raise Josiah and me, amazing lady, like the grandmother I never had."

Astrid indulged him, amused at his uncharacteristic sputtering. "I can't wait to meet her, and the others?"

Peter rubbed the back of his neck. "Alaina and Himari? Indispensable, brilliant minds, both, we could not have come this far without them."

Astrid folded her hands over her belly and gave him a sidelong glare. "Sunflower and Miss Pink," her voice dripped with sarcasm, each consonant enunciated sharply. "And what is it about them you do not want to tell me?"

The boyish innocence he tried to adopt was comical.

Astrid's mouth hung open. "Am I about to meet two of your former lovers?" she asked, placing a heavy emphasis on the word former.

"No! Neither of them. They work for me, or rather with me, or whatever." He dismissed the technicalities of his arrangement with members of The Resistance, growing haughty in royal dignity. "I never fraternize with my staff, that is abhorrent."

She cocked her head at him. "Prince d'Or draws the line?"

He looked sorely put out. "Why does no one ever believe me when I say that?"

"Because you are a world-renowned playboy?" she answered dryly.

"The operative word being was." He sighed in harassed resignation, staring at the video equipment. "They are just beautiful, that is all, predictably, boringly, beautiful."

"And?"

"And Alaina?" His expression grew pained. "Well, she is Alaina ben Thomas."

Astrid's mouth dropped open. "A leggy blonde."

He backed away with his arms held out in front of him, mischief dancing in his eyes. "One of the five or six, I swear."

"Five or six what?"

"Leggy blondes who do not want to get in my pants."

A throw pillow sailed after him as he scampered away, laughing.

Part 13 - Flight

February 1, 1000 ME

An Understanding

"Can you please explain to me why we have to go to London?" Astrid asked Josiah.

"Well, first of all—" Josiah began.

"It doesn't make any sense, and it creates all sorts of dangers and obstacles."

Josiah's lips compressed. "As I was saying, they have always been one of Alanthia's greatest allies."

Astrid held up a hand. "Then we go there afterwards."

Josiah looked down at his watch with growing impatience. "Second, we have received landing rights through back-diplomatic channels." He loomed over her as he added, "Not an easy task to accomplish."

Astrid drew her chin up, refusing to be intimidated. "Davianna and I got around just fine without," she mimicked his accent, "diplomatic channels. I say we throw on some disguises, get some fake IDs, and get the hell outta here."

He gazed at the ceiling, his left foot tapping. "Which might have worked in November before you became an international household name. Perhaps it has escaped your notice that those videos have garnered upwards of three hundred million views, in a week." Josiah ground out the last word through clenched teeth.

The videos were a source of massive anxiety for him. He blew up over the comments, and Peter was forced to disable them. He stomped around for days grumbling about it. Astrid was a bit more pragmatic and thought some of the comments were hilarious. Josiah disagreed. "Yes, I am well aware of the number of views."

"As far as why we need diplomatic channels, a private plane flying under diplomatic credentials, not just a charter aircraft, but one cleared and sanctioned by one of the ten kingdoms, is the only way we will get you two into the Golden City."

Astrid's nose flared, and she crossed her arms, refusing to answer.

"Otherwise, you two would have hopped on a plane after they announced the reward, right? You both knew between security, inspections, and immigration they would have caught you the minute you tried."

Astrid threw up her arms in surrender and turned her back on him.

"Furthermore, under diplomatic asylum, even if Lucifer has turned Prince Edward, they cannot arrest us when we arrive in London."

"Do you think Satan cares about diplomatic credentials?"

He threw up his hands in frustration. "I doubt he does, but I have to believe the Iron King is restraining him. Otherwise, Marduk's little foray into your bedroom would have been followed by an all-out assault. We have not hidden. He knows where we are!"

"He's not after you! That creepy stuff he said to you down in Louisiana was just bull. He was testing, to see if you would bite. He dismissed you as soon as he saw you were not falling for it. It is Davianna that he is after."

"And what would you have me do? Hide out here like a fugitive for the rest of our natural lives? That is not the way we operate, Astrid."

She spun away from him, hiding the stab of pain that shot through her heart.

He kept his voice calm, but even he heard the lecturing tone. He could not help it. "Listen, this is the only logical plan. In London, we will go to the Iron King's Embassy. Prince Yehonathan will provide us sanctuary *and* escort to the Golden City. You tried to book a flight when you were in London, Davianna told me. The first available ticket was a month out, and it is worse now. We either accept their escort or take our chances across Europe. Do you honestly want to do that again, Astrid? Do you?"

"Mossad," she ground out and wrapped her arms protectively around her stomach. "The last time—"

He crossed the room and turned her by the arm. "The last time we got caught because you panicked and bloody gassed me!"

There it was, up to that moment, unspoken. Her chin dropped to her chest. She knew he was right.

When she said nothing, he squeezed her shoulder. "Astrid, you have done well. All those months, you kept yourself and Davianna safe, but you are not alone anymore. You have to trust us."

Her eyes were full of self-loathing as she confessed, "That does not come easy to me."

Josiah drew back his head, surprised at her admission. "Nor I."

Intensity vibrated around her, and she pointed a finger at him. "You better keep her safe."

"To my last breath," he vowed.

Phone Call

The phone call when it came, did not surprise Peter, but his reaction sickened him. His guts turned to hot liquid at the sound of the voice on the line.

"Peter, my son."

"Father."

"I see the depths of your treachery knows no bounds." Korah's mirthless chuckle rang hollow. "In an odd way, I suppose I am impressed."

Peter's lip curled in contempt, and he went on the offensive. "How is my new stepmother?"

"Ill apparently. However, I think a better question might be, how is your mother?"

Peter sucked in a horrified breath.

"The likeness is extraordinary, don't you agree?"

Peter held his tongue, giving him no weapon. He knew how Korah worked.

"I hear the Dark Master paid her a visit," Korah taunted.

Peter's control cracked. "Leave her alone, both of you, leave her alone!"

"Oh, that is not possible now is it, Son?" Korah's face flashed in Peter's mind, pure evil. "You know I always punish your disobedience." A lifetime of depravity and abuse hid beneath his father's words. "Like I punished your mother." Korah's voice grew low and lethal. "Perhaps I'll let you watch... again."

The line went dead.

Astrid found Peter collapsed on the floor, the phone clutched in his hand. When he looked up, she could tell he was seeing a ghost. The anguish in his face ripped her heart in two. She fell on her knees by his side.

"I cannot watch it again!" His chest heaved. "He knew I was there. I was never certain."

His expression turned from agony to wild panic as he focused on her face. His open palm hit her ear hard as he enveloped her in a crushing hold, climbing her body, taking her to the floor, shielding her. Nose to nose, he covered her head, chanting, "No! No!"

He was hurting her. Her arm was pinned behind her back. She struggled to free it, to comfort him, but his mani-

acal strength held her still, as he repeated his denials into the
darkness of their embrace. Astrid tried to soothe him with
desperate small kisses, trying to calm him. When he relaxed
a small degree, she wrenched her arm free. Wrapping her legs
and arms around him like a python, she squeezed with all her
might, holding on as shudders wracked his body.

He braced himself above her, his gaze desperate. She felt
the quicksilver change in him, recognized his need. He fumbled between them, pulling aside her panties and pleading,
"Please."

She nodded, and he entered her with a force that made
her gasp. She was not ready.

"I am so sorry." A tear fell from his eye into her mouth.
"Oh, Astrid. I would never hurt you. What have I done?" His
face crumpled, and he made to roll off her.

She seized him around the waist and pulled him as deep
as she could take him.

He arched, every muscle in his body seizing. Driven mad
by trauma and fear, he drove into her body. He punctuated
each thrust, grinding out a litany. "He. Will. Not. Touch.
You." His orgasm, when it came, was jerky and violent,
wrenching an agonized cry from the depths of his tortured
soul.

In the Air Tonight

Davianna concluded that royal luxury might prove as seductive as her husband. The spacious jet had a bedroom, a
steward, an entertainment center, and an onboard chef. Josiah
did not notice any of it. Lost in his own thoughts, he stroked
the back of her hand as the sprawl of New York shrunk to
miniature out the jet window. She craned her neck, looking
past him, and glimpsed the grotesque statue illuminated by
the setting sun.

She relaxed in the leather seat, giving Astrid a companionable smile. Astrid smiled back, sad and unfathomable. Something dreadful had occurred. Neither she nor Peter spoke of

it, but even Davianna noticed the worry lines around Peter's mouth, the way he kept pinching the bridge of his nose. His animated face and teasing manner vanished. His speech was stilted, and he moved like he had been ill for an exceedingly long time. She recognized that feeling. Davianna's voice when she spoke brimmed with authority, "Switch seats with me."

Astrid drew back in mild surprise, glanced at Peter's impassive face, and shrugged, relinquishing her seat.

Preoccupied, Josiah looked at Astrid through half-lidded eyes when she settled beside him. "Hello," his tone held an unspoken question.

Astrid frowned and indicated toward Peter.

Josiah patted her leg in reassurance, returned his gaze out the window, but tuned into Davianna's quiet voice, barely audible over the roar of the engines.

Peter did not glance up when she settled beside him. She surmised he did not even notice she was there. She took his yielding hands, giving them a shake and a squeeze. He focused, and she saw in his eyes who caused this. "You have spoken to Korah."

A shadow came over him, and he tried to withdraw.

Sudden fire blazed through her body, and she lifted her lip in derision. "What did he say?"

"The usual." He shrugged in half-hearted dismissal.

She remembered in the cabin when he teased her out of her panic, and she could do no less for him. A strong sense of self-preservation prevented her from mining the depths of her six days with Korah, but like Josiah, when he told her about Yane ben Sandanski, she opened a black door and stepped inside.

It was like tumbling backward, into dungeons and tortures, juxtaposed with elegance and manners, at the bottom of the pit, there was madness. She felt the hopelessness, the way Korah consumed her, the way he took control of her mind. He seemed all-powerful, capable of anything.

"Davi, there is so much darkness. Just one of those monsters has caused untold pain, and I am eviscerated."

"No. We survived." Her voice sounded strangled, and she brought her hand to her throat.

"I suppose that depends on your definition of survival."

"You are alive. We are alive."

Alive… the word echoed like a gong in his head.

"Listen to me now. The Iron King says, 'For I know the plans I have for you. They are plans for good and not for disaster, to give you a future and a hope.'"

Peter dropped his head, staring at their clasped hands.

"Peter, be strong and courageous. Do not be afraid or terrified because of him. The Iron King is with you. He will never leave you, nor forsake you."

He brought their joined hands to his forehead and closed his eyes. She leaned into him and joined him in that dark place. Tremors of adrenaline ran through his body like flashes of lightning, but as she prayed, the storm subsided. When he met her eyes, the sigh of relief he expelled ruffled her hair, smelling of coffee and metallic fear.

He kissed her hand and squeezed. "It has been a long fight, Fireball, but I will see it through to the end. We will all see it through to the end."

She hugged him tight. "Thou art not alone." Tears welled up in her eyes. She dearly loved this man.

Peter's dimple flashed, and he pressed a chaste kiss to her lips.

"Hey," Josiah leaned forward and called, "I've got my eye on you, Cousin."

Peter looked across the aisle, puckered up, and gave Josiah a loud kiss.

Relieved to see the light return to Peter's eyes, Astrid stood up. "This is a road trip. We need music."

"Singing!" Davianna added and winked at Josiah.

"And a drink," Peter said, rubbing the back of his neck.

The steward appeared as if by magic. Astrid produced the pink iPod and plugged it into the stereo system. She turned to her companions. "Requests? Peter, I think it is your choice."

He accepted the soda from the steward, leaned back in his chair, thinking. His lip curled as he extended his hand toward the device. "Give it to me, I will cue the song. It is appropriate since we are in the air tonight."

No one asked who or what the song was about. It was obvious. With that phone call, Korah unleashed Hell, his son the avenging angel.

February 2, 1000 ME

Sometimes, I Am Right - London

Astrid got part of her wish. The foursome that exited the private jet resembled nothing more than a group of wealthy, ancient dignitaries. For the better part of the last week, Astrid threw herself into the artistry of latex masks, to the point of becoming a nuisance. Several times, Josiah and Davianna exchanged looks and ran down the hall, preferring their marital bed over hours in a chair while Astrid fussed with latex, spirit gum, itchy wigs, and facial hair.

Davianna delighted in giving body language and voice inflection lessons, as she assumed the role of director. Peter, a life spent on the public stage, was a natural, Astrid, quite good, Josiah, horrific.

While he had pulled off the Carsten ben Hanson persona, he lacked both the sense of absurdity and drama necessary to transform him into anything more than a silent old man with a hunched shuffle. Even then, Davianna used a cane to remind him to stoop, poking him incessantly, mischief dancing in her eyes. Astrid took inspiration from Josiah's lawyer, Sir Preston, and fashioned enormous gray eyebrows for him. She surmised they would be such a distraction that no one would notice anything else about him. Josiah managed to move them up and down, in such a comical manner, they howled with laughter.

As the plane taxied, in full costume for the first time, they regarded each other. A hush fell over the cabin, unspoken hope that one day they might achieve such great age, together.

A contingent of Mossad guards met them. Josiah's friend, Agent Reuben ben Judah, was among them. Davianna felt Josiah vibrating with intensity, hyper-alert, watching for an attack. The Big Easy was fresh on everyone's minds, nobody dwelt on the bayou.

The commotion started outside Kensington. A street corner hawker of the Daily News was knocked flat, papers flying around him like giant confetti. Pedestrians ran screaming, but unaccustomed to the newly imported automobiles, they ran pell-mell into traffic. Davianna watched in slow-motion horror as a man in a business suit and no shoes flew through the air, struck by a careening red bus.

In the next instant, the force of an explosion plastered her backwards. The repercussion sucked the air from her lungs and raised the tiny hairs on her skin. Debris rained down in heavy chunks on their armored vehicle. Josiah leapt on top of her, shielding her.

Peter let a string of foul expletives fly.

Black cloaked riders erupted like demons out of the chaos, screeching and wielding swords. They cut a path of indiscriminate slaughter through innocent London commuters.

Josiah pushed Davianna to the floor and dove for the cache of weapons. He tossed rifles to Peter and Astrid. The first shot from Peter's weapon was deafening in the confines of the car. Josiah shot a millisecond afterward.

"Load!" Josiah yelled over the commotion and placed the spent weapon in Davianna's hands.

Survival instinct took over. With shaking hands, she grabbed the ammunition box from the weaponry cabinet and loaded. Josiah and Peter positioned and fired at the oncoming attackers with brutal efficiency. Astrid positioned her weapon but had not yet fired.

Their Mossad driver wasted no time, driving up on a sidewalk, and scattering fleeing commuters. They sped away from the carnage.

Astrid twisted around, watching the chaos retreat and shouted, "I knew it! I had a bad feeling about London." She whirled on them all. "One of these days, y'all are going to start listening to me! I might not be one of you high and mighty royals, but I know what I am talking about!"

Josiah, feeling chagrined, answered, "Affirmative."

Peter was still cursing. "Three of those demented lunatics tried to kill me in March."

Astrid's head snapped around. He was a news item then. She covered her mouth and whispered, "I forgot about that."

Rifle in hand, his gray wig askew, Peter ground out, "I did not."

A strangled cough came from the floorboard. "Help me up."

Josiah searched the interior of the vehicle, by reflex checking for more danger before lifting Davianna into the seat beside him. Half her latex face had peeled off. Josiah patted her all over, checking for injuries. "Are you hurt?"

She shook her head, but her eyes were glassy. "That man did not have any shoes, but he was wearing a suit."

Astrid gave a convulsive snort. A second later, she realized Davianna was not being droll.

Josiah put his arm around her. "The force must have knocked him out of them."

Davianna tilted her head in abstracted consideration. "Oh." London sped by, billows of black smoke reaching the sky. On the streets, people panicked. Davianna did not see it, her expression dreamy. "I think he's dead."

Josiah sent up a silent prayer of thanks that she was on the floorboard during the worst of it.

Reuben said over the intercom, "ETA one minute."

The button cracked under Josiah's index finger. "Take us in dark. Our cover is compromised." As he spoke, a huge caterpillar gray eyebrow fell over one eye, dangling and ridiculous.

No one laughed.

The Long Hunt

In a windowless workroom below the Embassy, Astrid muttered and grumbled while she stripped every one of her carefully crafted disguises. She demanded they help clean and store her treasures for posterity. Fury and righteous indignation afforded her a measure of dominance not previously exercised among them. At length, her exacting standards were satisfied, and a guard escorted them upstairs to their private apartments. Astrid and Peter exchanged a glance as Astrid was shown to her own quarters, separate from Peter's.

Josiah paused outside the door, a constrained anticipation about him that Davianna did not fathom. With his hand resting on the small of her back, he said, "I have a friend inside that I am eager for you to meet."

Davianna shot him a puzzled glance, other than Reuben, he never mentioned any friends. Feeling self-conscious, she smoothed her old lady dress, not pleased at the prospect of meeting anyone after what they had just been through. "How do I look?"

Josiah grinned. "He won't care."

When he pushed through the door, all hell broke loose. Benjamin sprinted across the tile floor, his nails beating a rapid staccato. Loud barks of recognition turned into high-pitched cries of rapture as he leapt into Josiah's outstretched arms. Davianna watched in slack jawed astonishment as the little dachshund kissed him, writhing in ecstatic glee in the arms of his master.

Josiah abandoned himself to the kissing, wiggling, joy of the moment.

After a time, Benjamin left Josiah to investigate Davianna. He sniffed her foot then made a low, long howl. He barked and ran back and forth between them, before scampering off. When he reappeared seconds later, he had her old knit hat. Davianna gasped. He dropped the hat at Josiah's feet, then ran barking at Davianna, his whipcord tail wagging with vigor.

Benny had found Davianna, at last.

She lowered herself to her haunches and reached out to pet him. He flopped to his back, presenting his tan smooth belly. "Oh, my goodness, he is the cutest thing I have ever seen. Where did you get him?"

A cloud obscured the light in his eyes, but only for a moment. "At the camp. He's been looking for you as long as I have."

"Well, I am glad I let you both find me." She gave Benny a hearty scratch under the chin which elicited a great sigh of contentment from the prostrate dog.

"I know how he feels, and if I did not have an audience with Prince Yehonathan, I'd love to show you just how much."

Pearls

Peter paced Astrid's chamber, waiting for her to finish getting ready and go down to dinner. He knew she was nervous, although she would choke to death before admitting it. The third coat of mascara was a clear indication of her apprehension over dinner with Prince Yehonathan. While he understood it in theory, he could not truly identify. This was his world, and he was comfortable in it.

Astrid made an offhand comment last week, that upon further consideration, contained some merit. Since he was seven, he knew his father was a usurper and by extension, so was he. Consequently, he refused to consider there was a legitimate role for him to play. She pointed out that it was a reaction to his father, not his actual desire.

His tutors and instructors shared her sensibilities. They ignored his disinterest, horrible study habits, and abject failure in the classroom. Paid to ensure he was educated and trained in royal protocol and duties, he made them earn every shekel. In retrospect, that was rotten.

When he was fourteen, he escaped the Palace to attend

military school. There, they did not give a crap who he was. He figured out that if he wanted to stay, he had better study. He had, though it was a painful process. He enjoyed his time at the Royal Military Academy, excelled in military science and strategy, and found his place among the soldiers. Consequently, he was comfortable around warriors, drawn to the men who guarded him. He respected them.

When they launched The Resistance, he made a concerted effort to show public support of the military. He cultivated a reputation as a friend to the troops, attended their parades, and courted them. Peter knew they would play an intricate role when Josiah took back Alanthia. He hoped it had been enough, he prayed that if it came to war that they would side with him and Josiah.

Prince d'Or was not a product of The Resistance, nor if he was honest, a completely fictional character. Prince d'Or was an amplified version of himself at about twelve. He noticed when he put on the character, Korah and Marduk ignored him. Life was infinitely better when they ignored him, so Prince d'Or stayed put.

On summer break, the year he turned sixteen, he discovered being a Prince had other perks. His status made it exceedingly easy to get women to sleep with him. It was minor compensation for the hellish life he lived, and he took solace where he could find it.

Astrid was still putting on her mascara, so he wandered over to the window, studying the Embassy grounds. They were lit with armed guards posted at close intervals. They were on lockdown, and London was still fighting. He fingered the heavy silk curtain. They were safe. Those living outside these guarded walls were not.

A month ago, he probably would not have given it a passing thought. Not in the way he did now. A month ago, he had no true understanding what it was like to be a normal person. He had brief intervals, precious intervals, where he lived in a world where he was simply Peter, but he had never been stripped of his status, not like he was while they were running. It was a novel experience. His planned exile had not included shedding the title. He accepted the wealth and privilege of being royal. He suspected it was like oxygen, only noticeable when it was absent.

Both Astrid and Davianna teased him when he became Peter the Prince, and he found, while foreign, he enjoyed being Peter the man. He dropped the curtain and wandered back into Astrid's dressing room, where she sat, mercifully screwing the mascara lid back on and making the final touches to her makeup. He crossed his ankles and leaned against the wall, waiting.

Though they teased him about being royal and stuffy, they never did that to Josiah. He did hear Davianna periodically muttering under her breath. Her favorite epithet was bossy jackass. He had to give Fireball credit. She had learned to stand up for herself.

He wondered darkly how much his father had to do with that. He suspected more than she knew. People were made in the fires of the furnace. He doubted Josiah would have married her if she had not risen like a phoenix from the ashes. Not that anybody planned to write Korah a thank-you note, but still, their ordeal served a purpose.

His purpose was currently applying a shimmering gloss to her lips and trying not to portray how nervous this dinner made her. The brutal irony of his current situation did not escape his notice. The woman with the lip gloss wand had no interest in becoming royalty. The woman he loved, wanted the man, not the Prince.

As their journey continued, stark reality dawned clear. Prince Peter ben Korah was royalty, whether he liked it or not. For the first time in his life, something other than escape governed his future, and he was coming to terms with how much it might cost him.

Astrid studied her reflection and met Peter's faraway gaze in the mirror. "I swear Josiah brought us to London so we could pick up his dog." She cleaned up her lip line with a tissue. "I wish this was over."

He was not sure whether she meant the dinner or their journey, and he was loath to ask. "You have worked yourself into a frenzy for naught. Think of it as the four of us, having dinner with a guest. No big deal."

She rolled her eyes. He was being absurd. "Help me pick an outfit. I have no idea what to wear."

Jarrod ensured they received appropriate attire for their visit to London. His flawless taste and Peter's bank account meant her request was no mere ploy for attention. Peter reviewed the contents of her closet and emerged with a charcoal slip dress and flowing jacket,

She shot him a skeptical look but relented.

"Here are the shoes." He presented her with a pair of gray snakeskin pumps. After the bayou, he liked the idea of treading on adders. Damn snakes.

She slipped them on and spun, showing off the outfit.

He tapped his cheek, pretending to consider. "It is missing something." He reached in his suit pocket and pulled out a black velvet box. "I have just the thing."

Astrid gasped, her hand over her heart.

Peter opened the box, revealing an exquisite pearl necklace. "Do you like it?" He heard the hope and vulnerability in his voice and resisted the urge to make a joke. Instead, he watched her face as she ran a finger over the strand of pearls.

They were quite fetching if he did say so himself. Ten-millimeter Japanese pearls in cream, gray, and black were studded with half carat round diamonds. The necklace shimmered against the black velvet, capturing the evening light. She ran the strand through her fingers and looked up at him with such an expression of delight, he vowed he would buy her jewelry every week for the rest of her life.

"They are magnificent."

He moved behind her to fasten it, pleased that his hands were not shaking. "Oh, I almost forgot." He pulled a matching box from his other pocket. "Here are the earrings. I had a pair made up in each color."

"You had them made?" Her voice climbed in surprise. "These aren't, I thought these were royal—"

"They are a gift for you, love." Peter kissed her cheek and slipped an earring through the tiny hole in her lobe.

Astrid inhaled at the intimate touch and held her breath in surprise. Then the corner of her lip twitched. "You are seducing me with jewelry. Wicked man."

He kissed the base of her neck. "Is it working?"

She leaned into him, sighing. "Yes, dammit."

Feeling more confident in her pretty clothes and jewelry, Astrid was still reeling as they walked downstairs. She was a simple girl from Texas, out of her league. In the royal hierarchy, Prince Yehonathan ben Hezekiah was the highest ranking official in the world, save the Iron King, and they were having dinner with him.

On the run, it was easy to forget who Peter and Josiah were. In New York, and now in London, there was no denying reality. She longed for the cabin in the mountains.

An informal dinner in mainstream Alanthia bore no resemblance to an informal dinner with royalty. Jet lag hit Davianna after the entrée course, and she stifled a yawn behind her napkin. The two-hour nap did little to offset the loss of an entire night's sleep and a miniature war.

Prince Yehonathan proved to be a gracious host. By the end of the evening, she and Astrid were both relatively at ease. Relative being the key term. They were both subdued, employing none of their typical dinner table banter. To her immense relief, neither disgraced themselves nor their partners.

The news from the outside world was not so encouraging.

Uprising

London exploded. Jihadists, self-proclaimed pure servants of the Iron King, mounted terror bombings across the city. They claimed that the uprising was in response to the Geneva Summit which lifted the ban on Alanthian exports of technology the previous summer.

Anarchists, who had no real beef about technology, joined in the melee, breaking windows, storming train stations, and setting vehicles on fire. Their goal was the obliteration of all forms of government. Prince Edward's government responded with overwhelming force, clashing with everyone, and sometimes mistaking peaceful citizens as agitators. The narrow, twisting streets of London rained shrapnel, fire, and blood.

Standing atop the Persian Embassy, Lucifer watched in satisfied glee at the chaos below. He turned to Marduk. "Your wild men have proven again to be a most effective weapon. I enjoy watching them kill each other."

Marduk, pale and gray, nodded in thanks. "My King, their worship of you has always made it possible."

Lucifer rubbed his chin, assuming an air of modest consideration. He was still furious with Marduk, but at least he crawled out of his Babylonian hidey-hole. "Our plans proceed slower than anticipated. I suspect this little melee will make our manipulation easier. Nothing stirs up trouble like a little terrorism."

"I caution you on that. My experience in Alanthia proved enlightening."

Lucifer wanted to throttle him, instead waved a dismissive hand. "I am certain I will wield that weapon with more dexterity and skill than you."

Marduk nodded and stepped back, surreptitiously adjusting a bandage on his arm, taking refuge behind Lucifer. A bevy of the enemy hovered over the Iron King's Embassy, guarding the Black Key.

"Davianna ben David will have to move, and when she does, I will take control," Lucifer promised and sent a scorching glare at the enemy.

His frustration at being thwarted grew daily. Since New Orleans, the Black Key was under constant guard. Marduk's brief foray into the New York Penthouse had come at a great cost, as the sniveling gray wreck at his back attested, but Lucifer dismissed Marduk and his wounds, they were just punishment for his treachery.

While Lucifer did not doubt that he alone could foment the rebellion, it would be more efficient with the rest of his elohim. He could feel the key within his reach. Yet the night he attempted to wrest control of it, they attacked, and the bleeding sword wound he concealed under his cloak served as a powerful reminder, he too was vulnerable.

It was intolerable, he would not become mortal!

In fury, he struck out, directing a bolt of lightning at his enemies, which was summarily deflected back at them by Michael's sword. The wicked duo scattered.

Davianna shook Josiah awake, pale and shaking, her slack tunic in her hand. "He is here."

London proved to be the match that ignited a powder keg, terror and anarchy swept the globe. From Tokyo to Rio de Janeiro, riots broke out in the streets. Nowhere on earth was the governmental response more ferocious than Alanthia. Seizing the moment, Korah ordered the assassination of dozens of his political enemies. Some had the foresight to evade the onslaught, chief among them, Josiah's personal attorney, Sir Preston ben Worley, who escaped to his farm in upstate New York.

That night, Korah dozed off, convinced the tide was turning in his favor. Nothing could have been further from the truth.

Inside the Embassy, Josiah sat up, staring at Davianna's tunic. The vibration of the device had been brief, but ominous. The sounds of fighting droned on. Tomorrow he would begin two full days of meetings and negotiations with global leaders, who were flying to London in response to his resurrection, and the growing global crisis. The weight of the world rested on his broad shoulders, and he did not sleep.

February 3, 1000 ME

When the Truth Comes Out

Sondra ben Pierson settled into her new position behind the News 1 anchor desk with an arrogance born of sudden success. Tonight, she planned to cement herself in that anchor chair and become the most powerful news reporter in the world. Queued up, and ready to roll, was the story of the century. Sondra ben Pierson had Stephen ben McSwilley's tapes.

King Korah was going down.

Macaroni Salad

"Knock-knock," Astrid called from the entranceway of Davianna and Josiah's apartment.

"Back here." Davianna answered from the kitchen.

"I'm sorry I missed the play. There is a war going on outside."

Davianna countered. "I'm sorry I missed the play. I was attending a reception with the Ruling Princes and their wives."

"Yuck." Astrid screwed her face into a comical grimace and shuddered.

Davianna laughed. "I'm making some macaroni. Are you hungry?"

Astrid munched a carrot out of the bowl. "You know I

will always eat your macaroni salad, as long as you leave out the celery."

Davianna rolled her eyes. "Celery is good. What's your problem with celery?"

Astrid shivered with theatrical loathing. "Texture! It freaks me out, those weird stringy things get stuck in your teeth."

"You are weird."

Astrid helped herself to a glass of juice and shrugged. "I am not weird, celery is weird."

Davianna crunched a big bite and smiled, green celery coating her front teeth.

Astrid chuckled. "Not very Princess-y."

Davianna groaned. "Ugh, I know. This is going to be difficult. The truth dropped on me like a three-hundred-pound crown as soon as we arrived."

"Better you than me, sister." Astrid pursed her lips.

Davianna eyed Astrid. "Is everything okay with you and Peter?"

"The sex is good. Though we are sneaking around. They've posted a steward," she punctuated steward with air quotes, "in the hall outside our doors, like some medieval chastity guard." Astrid moved to the window and looked over the Embassy grounds. "It's all crashing in, Davi."

"What is crashing in?" Davianna kept her voice steady.

"The whole thing." She made a sweeping gesture of the empty apartment. "They are downstairs meeting with heads of state, and you and I are up here eating macaroni salad, which Peter has probably never even heard of, let alone eaten."

"He likes my food." Davianna waved Astrid away. "And he ate about ten bowls of it when we were in the cabin."

"That's not the point, and you know it." She sat down on the floor, and Benny crawled into her lap.

"What is the point, precisely?"

Astrid buried her face in Benny's fur and said, "I'm no Princess, Davi."

"Well, neither am I."

Astrid tilted her head, looking up through her spiky brown eyelashes. "That's where you are wrong. The moment you married Josiah, you became one, whether you like it or not."

Davianna's shoulders slumped. "I don't know how to do this, but I know for certain, I won't be able to do it without you."

Astrid's smiled, sad and enigmatic, but said nothing. Instead, she buried her face into the ruff of Benny's neck and cooed nonsense words of affection.

February 4, 1000 ME

Power Struggle

By sheer force of will and considerable diplomacy, Josiah insisted they leave London for Tel Aviv immediately. The crux of his argument was the attack in London marked the beginning of the uprising, not an assault on them. As the violence spread, his argument rang true. It also closed off all avenues of escape, save one, Mossad.

Josiah and Peter attended round-the-clock negotiations with diplomats from across the globe, but the outcome of their meetings was yet to be determined. The Ruling Princes remained uncommitted on whether they would support Josiah. The tapes of Korah made them lean heavily in Josiah's favor, but unseating the most powerful gentile king on the planet was something they did not approach lightly.

Peter, ever the cynic, summed it up. "They are raking in tax revenues from all the sales of exported technology. Their sphincters are drawn up tight, scared that you will turn off the flow or revert to Uncle Eamonn's policies."

"That has not been my position, publicly or privately," Josiah protested.

"Talk is cheap, Prince. They do not know you; they know

Korah. And they will not risk anymore unrest in their kingdoms, not after this week. If they support you, and you cut
off the tech, this week's riots will seem like child's play. Peter
shook his head. "Prince Chou in Asia has had major unrest,
especially in Japan. He will not risk anything that puts him
in the hot seat."

"But it is baseless. This is asinine."

"They are scared." He lowered his voice so Davianna and
Astrid would not overhear in the next room. "Princess Tati-
anna told me that Lucifer paid them a visit."

"I suspect he has done that with all of them. They are
shaking in their boots."

Peter clapped him on the shoulder. "Nobody said this
would be easy."

February 5, 1000 ME

Tel Aviv

The day the foursome landed in Tel Aviv; peace still
reigned in the Golden Kingdom. Ten years prior, the Iron
King designated Tel Aviv as the lone technology center of
the kingdom. Critics called it hypocrisy; the Iron King knew
better. Tel Aviv abounded with ingenuity, invention, and
wonders beyond imagining. It kept the young from rebelling
and gave the Golden Kingdom the tools it would need—in
the end. Tel Aviv also served as the international gateway for
fleeing pilgrims and visitors. The deep harbor and the airport
received thousands an hour.

Astrid gasped in wonder as they disembarked. The quality of the light, soft and golden, illuminated everything with
glittering luminescence. This was not light from a distant
star. It enveloped them in the purest beauty known to man.
A gentle breeze kissed her cheek, effusing her with weight-
lessness. A tiny cut on the back of her hand healed the instant
she stepped onto the tarmac. The enchanted soil's power shot

through her with electrical pulses, beginning in her feet and exploding like fireworks through the top of her head, leaving behind euphoric bliss. She fell to her knees.

They arrived. Safe, at last.

Peter's voice penetrated her rapture, she brushed her hair aside, struck dumb by the vision before her. Gorgeous, in the dull gray smog of Alanthia, he shimmered with such blinding magnificence her mind could not comprehend it. "You are more beautiful than the angel."

Prince d'Or unleashed his devastating smile. "And you my love, have no parallel." He gazed at her as if seeing her for the first time.

She realized with shock that he was stroking her head in wonder. The hands she raised to his cheek were familiar, long perfect nails, not a boy's manicure. She touched her head, instead of close-cropped spikes, luxurious wavy tresses fell down her back. She held it in front of her, shimmering with auburn, gold, and rich deep red. Tears fell over her magnificent cheekbones, and she gasped, "My hair, my nails." Until restored, she did not fully comprehend the loss.

"Come, let's get off the tarmac. I think we have an amazing day ahead of us." Peter lifted her to her feet.

When she turned, Davianna stood, looking almost like the girl who raced through that tent flap a lifetime ago. In Tel Aviv, a woman smiled back at her.

They fell in each other's arms, weeping.

The jewel of the Mediterranean, Tel Aviv was a marvel to behold. Prince Yehonathan's personal limousine drove them to the long-vacant royal Alanthian seaside villa, where they would stay until summoned by the Iron King. Benjamin, excited to be free of his crate, ran around the immense coastal Palace with reckless abandon, his nails tapping in merry exploration.

Josiah paused in the entryway, lost in a long-forgotten memory.

Davianna put her arm around his waist, looking out at the sea.

"I was here before, a long time ago. I must have been six or seven, just my father and me." Old grief choked the last words, it caught him unaware. Standing in the villa, he felt his father's loss anew.

It traveled from him to her, and her throat tightened. They stood together in silence, remembering their fathers.

Peter pushed past them, breaking the somber moment. "Come on, Red. Let's get naked."

Astrid giggled, and they disappeared down the hallway.

Josiah lifted his chin at the departing pair. "I think my cousin has the right of it." A youthful exuberance and optimism erased the worry lines on his face. His eyes sparkled with whiskey warmth and heat as he took her hand and guided her to the royal bedchamber.

The Master Suite was marvelous with white stucco walls and blue tile the color of the crystalline sea. The furnishings and decor were done in sea green and muted yellow with splashes of blue. Even with the curtains drawn, the incredible light suffused the room and reminded Davianna of the glittering gold dome.

Josiah ran his fingers through her thick hair, amazed by the heavy silk of dark chocolate, umber, and auburn. He buried his face in it, inhaling her scent. "I loved the pixie cut, Minx, but I have to admit I am partial to this."

She tossed her head back, shaking it with delight. "I missed my hair."

As he ran kisses down her neck, her hair receded to somewhat less importance on the scope of his priorities. He ran his hands up her curves, making small love noises as he gathered her close. A deep, abiding, and holy ardor shook him to his core. In a voice husky with passion, he said, "Davianna, I want to make a baby with you."

The thought, which would have seemed ludicrous and irresponsible yesterday, surged through her body with absolute surety. She abandoned restraint, surrendered to his passion, and met his seeking mouth. "Oh, yes."

The conflagration between them rendered mere sexual desire akin to the spark of a match. The combustion burned away their clothing as they sought each other and a greater calling. Skin on silk, rough on smooth, hot on cold, they loved.

He lay on his back, watching his perfect Princess, her dark mane playing hide and seek with her young breasts, a tantalizing pink nipple peeking out at him through the veil. Josiah marveled in her, the way she filled his empty spaces, the curve of her waist, the softness of her hip under his hand.

Davianna's head fell back as she gave a cry that began the deep shudders within her body, he flew with her to a higher place, riding with her as she soared to the heights of human passion. When he could stand it no more, he rolled her to her back. showing her his love with every deep stroke. As he convulsed, a wonder beyond human comprehension, beyond the boundaries of time and space, a miracle occurred. They ceased being two, became one, and then three.

What Others?

On the other side of the villa, Peter ran his finger over the gold and diamond pendant that rested tantalizingly between Astrid's breasts. Since her admission that he was seducing her with trinkets, he showered her with jewelry. She reminded him of a magpie, collecting shiny objects. He found it winsome and endearing. There was a lightness to their mood. Sated and relieved to have made it to safety, Peter was at peace. "Love?" he said, still running his finger over the delicate gold chain.

"Yes?" Her eyes were closed, her voice drowsy.

In a manufactured light tone, he asked, "Will you marry me?" He felt her stiffen, not a good sign.

With the magic upon her, she answered from her heart,

"I love you, more than anything in this world, but I don't believe we should."

He half expected that, encouraged that she did not flatly refuse. He brushed a soft kiss to her lips and said, "I know why you say that, but I have a solution."

Astrid kissed him back.

He saw a glimmer of longing, a tiny spark in her eye.

"Do tell." She stretched in lazy luxury, burrowing into the thick down comforter.

"We take a page out of Josiah and Davianna's book and become handfast. If after a year, it does not work out, which it will, but if you cannot stand me, we go our separate ways."

"Why can't we just be together?" She dismissed the conversation. "Hardly anyone gets married anymore. Josiah and Frank are the only people I have ever known who took it seriously."

Peter gave her a level look and kept his voice soothing. "Well, they take it seriously here." He cleared his throat. "We cannot live together here unmarried, and royals have to get married." With a casual wave, he added, "All the legal stuff, you know." Peter nipped at her ear. "Besides, love, we cannot go before the Iron King without this settled between us. He does not permit fornication, which. if you have not noticed, we have been engaged in three times a day since we met."

It felt like he dumped a bucket of ice water over her head. "Fornication?" It was a disgusting word. It made her feel dirty, and that made her defensive. "Peter, we live in the real world, you and me. Alanthians abandoned those laws decades ago. I have not lived my life that way and neither have you."

She sat up, covering herself, and faced him. "Besides, whoever said I was going before the Iron King? I never agreed to that. I only went on the stupid pilgrimage because my stepfather forced me to go." Her hands bunched at her sides, gripping and releasing the sheet.

Panic hit her, and she scrambled off the bed, pulling on her clothes with quick jerky motions. Her temper ignited.

"All the talk about our happy ever after? That was just bull-shit. I knew it!"

"Stop!"

"That's why Josiah was so mad at you. All this time, I thought he was just a prude, a stiff, holier than thou, over-bearing royal!" She spat the word like a foul curse. Realization struck like lightning, and she pointed an accusing finger at him. "That's why he wouldn't touch Davianna. He knew the rules about being royal and what they would mean when we got here." She felt the darkness closing in, the end coming too soon. "But that didn't stop you, did it?"

She struck a nerve, he leapt from the bed pulling on box-ers, advancing on her. "That is not how, or why it started, and you know it!"

Astrid glared at him, remembering his words that first night. Rage and fear erupted, and she lashed out at him. "Oh, I remember, 'Korah does not sacrifice virgins.' You screwed me to keep me safe? Well, that brilliant plan seems to have backfired now, hasn't it?"

Peter recoiled as if she slapped him. When he rebounded, fury burned in his eyes. "And I will kill him for it, just like I killed the others."

She stumbled backward in shock. "What others?"

He stalked her, a golden lion in defense of his mate, full of menace and masculine grace, and not a bit sorry for it. "The Greek Captain, for one."

True fear gripped her as she retreated, her face stark white.

Peter advanced, snarling. "And that maggot, Guan ben Sheldon," he spat the name, "those two killed your mother. I know exactly what that feels like."

He gripped her shoulders. "I had the Greek killed before I ever met you. Do you know why? Because you look like her, because I watched a video of you a thousand times, each time burning with rage that he would hunt you, hurt you!"

He ran his hands through his hair. "That night in Vegas, when you and Davianna told me what Guan did, how his actions led to your mother's murder, how he tried to rape her?" His voice dripped with scorn. "I ordered it that night, and he is dead!"

His face was inches from hers, a mask of vengeance. "So, do you think for one moment that I will allow my bastard father to live after he threatened to kill you in front of me, like he did my mother? Think again, Red. He is as dead as the others."

Astrid fled from him.

February 6, 1000 ME

Three AM

It did not get dark in the Golden Kingdom. The light merely mellowed to a deep golden hue. However, it was not the unusual light keeping Peter awake, nor did the bottle of whiskey put him to sleep. There would be no rest for Prince d'Or tonight.

He let Astrid walk out of the room, let her stroll on the beach, let her be alone. He did not let her leave. Yet she was gone, had been for ten hours. He might have set a record for the worst marriage proposal in the history of the world.

Stubbing out the cigarette, he realized with insane irony that the last cigarette he smoked was that fateful night at the cabin when he decided to seduce her. He lit another, brimming with self-disgust. The whiskey no longer burned going down, and he had abandoned the civility of the crystal tumbler two hours ago.

It was a relief when Josiah and Davianna retired. He could not bear to see their perfect faces, with their perfect love, their perfect future, and their perfect marriage laid out before them, all wholesome milk and cookies. He and Astrid were like broken glass, torn flesh, and dried blood; passionate, brutal, and destructive, just like he was.

He fumbled with her stiletto, open, close, open, close.

She did that if she became agitated. The sound soothed him, the violence in harmony with his soul, a connection to her. When he saw her walking up from the beach, he wanted to leap from his chair and run to her, bind her. He rose, and the world tilted and spun. He fell back in the chair, lit another cigarette, and waited, presenting an image of cool, indolent rakishness.

She did not say a word as she faced him, merely took the cigarette from between his fingers and turned toward the sea. She leaned against the railing. Gray smoke disappeared into the night as she exhaled. Her long red hair blew in the breeze, disorienting him, like she was someone else. He wanted it short again.

Astrid flicked the cigarette into the dunes and turned. A few swigs remained in the whiskey bottle. She poured it into the empty glass and up ended it. Then she set the glass down with a thud and held out her hand.

He rose unsteadily and let her lead him to their bedroom. He looked down at his free hand, surprised to see her knife in it. With a sheepish grin, he handed it back to her.

She took it with a nod and set it on the dresser.

His whiskey-soaked brain tried to form words, but they would not come. He just looked at her, wretched pain, and longing on his face. He drew in a breath to try.

She placed a finger over his lips, stopping him. Shaking her head, she looked up at him. There were no words needed tonight.

With profound gratitude, he lowered his forehead on her hair and held her.

They swayed a drunken rhythm of his choosing, breathing together in the deep golden light, the waves of the Mediterranean the soundtrack for the night. They undressed, dancing together in a beautiful ballet of their own making. Their lovemaking was tender, warm like the whiskey that coursed through his veins. With his body, he told her everything he could not say. She gave him everything she had left.

As he fell into a deep slumber, his beloved's cry of anguish was heard only by the angel watching over them.

The Morning After

Peter stumbled into the kitchen, seeking coffee. Davianna's devastated expression confirmed what his soul knew about 5:00 am, Astrid was gone. He froze solid, standing barefoot on the hard tile floor. He covered his face and prayed he was having a nightmare, hoped that when he rubbed the sleep out of his eyes, he would discover it was just a dream. Davianna's muffled tears shattered the illusion, cutting through his soul like shards of glass.

Peter's arms fell limp by his sides, and he met Davianna's teary eyes. A letter dangled from her fingertips. On the coffee table, lay an envelope with the pink iPod on top.

His throat closed. His chest hurt. Physical anguish crushed him, and he made an animal sound of pain.

Josiah led him to a chair. He was incapable of moving. He stared at the letter, trying to breathe. A cup of coffee appeared, and he accepted it without taking his eyes off the letter. The coffee revived him, but that was not necessarily a good thing. He turned to Davianna, and his head lolled. He realized he was still drunk. "She left?"

Her lips quivered, and she looked down at her feet. "I'm sorry, Peter."

"She wrote you a letter?" His voice sounded foreign to his own ears.

"You have one, too." Her words came in halting gasps.

It was a death blow. It hollowed out his chest, and he caved. His hands dug in crazy torment through his hair.

The suffering on Peter's face made Josiah turn away.

Davianna fell on him, sobbing.

He collapsed listless, unable to move, unable to sob, knowing that he would die of this pain. He welcomed death, but it did not come. "Oh, God, she left me." His whole body shook, forlorn and abandoned, again.

Davianna's grief mirrored his own, she sat up with her hair a tangle. "She left me, too."

He stood up and staggered to the porch for a cigarette. The letter left behind on the table.

Josiah joined him a few moments later, another cup of coffee in his hand. Peter took it, with thanks this time.

"I'm sorry." Josiah took the seat beside him.

Peter exhaled. "Not your fault, Cousin. This one is on me."

Josiah nodded, but said nothing, just sat there with him, watching the ocean.

Because of You

An hour later, Peter shuffled to the restroom. When he came out, the ashtray was empty, the whiskey bottle gone. Davianna ordered him to eat. The food stuck in his throat. His stomach felt like a cauldron of boiling acid. He pushed the food away and headed to the bar.

Josiah stepped in front of him, the letter in his hand. "You need to read it, waiting will not make it easier."

The self-hatred Josiah read on Peter's face was infinite.

Peter took the letter, waving it. "You see, Cousin, there is a problem with that. Dyslexia." He covered his eyes, rubbing his forehead. "It is hard to read, in the best of circumstances, and these are not the best of circumstances."

Josiah's eyes widened in shock.

"You never figured it out when we were in class?" Peter gave him a sarcastic smile. "I am damn good at hiding it."

Pushing past Josiah, Peter went to the bar. "I know why she left me. I do not need that... that letter." He poured a shot and downed it. "She saw what a fucked-up, twisted mess I am and did the only thing a sane person could do, she got the hell away from me."

Josiah nodded to the booze, Peter poured him a shot and downed another. Josiah sipped his. "You are not a mess, Peter. You grew up in one, but you did not turn out to be one."

"Pft," Peter scoffed, "little you know."

"I know a lot more than you think I know." Josiah finished his shot and pushed it back toward Peter who filled it up again. "I know what you have done to get us this far."

Peter waved him away, in no mood to hear it.

Josiah pressed, "I know you could have run, at any point in the last few years, but you did not."

Peter shrugged. "I just did not want to be the Ruling Prince. I figured I would fix it, so I did not have to do it. Do not assign noble motives," he raised his glass in salute, "purely selfish on my part."

"You weren't selfish when we were kids. You saved my life then, and you saved us all on New Year's Eve."

Peter shrugged and staggered against the bar. "Again, I do not want to reign. And I certainly did not want any more of those freaking monsters stalking around."

"What about Astrid? What selfish reason did you have to save her?" Josiah pressed.

Her name made him flinch, but he covered it up with a flippant retort. "Because she looks like my mother, and I wanted to spite my father."

Exasperated, Josiah continued, "The ambulance, the medical equipment, all that was selfish?"

"I just did not want some strung out junkie throwing up all over my car."

Undaunted, Josiah downed his shot. "The escape plan, The Resistance, your life's work? You never mention what it took to put it together, the sacrifices you made, or the danger you were in." Josiah shook his head when Peter started to protest. "We are all alive because of you. We have a shot at taking back Alanthia because of you." Josiah held his eyes. "Because of that genius brain of yours, that understands computers, and tech, and financing. Your political campaign, the framework to build our team, and everything else it is going to take to bring Korah down. It is all brilliant, Prince."

Josiah pointed at himself, brimming with self-disgust. "I

planned to head in there with an army, which would have caused untold bloodshed, but because of you, we might not even have to fight." Josiah leaned over the bar. "So, I do not want to hear that you are a fucked-up mess. If I had not survived, you would have made an extraordinary Ruling Prince, and it is quite clear to me now that I cannot do this without you."

Peter let out a deep shoulder drooping sigh. "I think therein lies the problem, Cousin."

Their eyes held.

Peter scrubbed at his face. "Give me the damn letter. I will go read it and probably cry like a baby." He took a full bottle. "Maybe drink another bottle of booze, and when I am done wallowing, we will get your kingdom back." Staggering off, he murmured, "And I am going to settle the score."

Nobody Knows

He looked at the letter for a long while, considered taking a shower before he read it, but her body was still on his, the pillow still held her scent. He lay down beside her ghost and tore open the envelope. Her handwriting was large and loopy, which surprised him, he imagined it would be angular and exact, but she was full of contradictions. To his shock, the letters did not jumble, and he was thankful for small mercies.

Dear Peter,

This is the hardest letter I will ever write because I know I have to tell you goodbye, but I also know that I must tell you why and set you free. I have to say all these things while my heart breaks in two separate pieces, one I leave with you, and the shriveled half I take with me, for you have always deserved the best part of me.

I take with me, the worst part of you. I take the pain of your childhood and all the horrors you endured and survived. I take the grief of the little boy who lost his mother, too soon and too violently. I take the broken man, and all the shame that goes with it. I've pulled that out of you. Do not take it back. I'm strong enough to hold it. You are free.

The man I leave behind is whole and redeemed. You are set apart for something great. Alanthia is your destiny, and it always has been. You will be a wise and great ruler, whether you are at the head or by Josiah's side, it is where you belong.

To accomplish all that you are meant to, you need the blessing of the Iron King. I would keep that blessing from you, for I cannot say that our love is a sin, nor could I confess that I am sorry for it. Perhaps, I am not a true believer. In that way, I am too much my father's daughter. I know that sounds strange, considering the journey we have been on, all that we have seen. But I know my heart, and it is not right with him, at least not now. I cannot be false, to you, to myself, and if the Iron King is who they say he is, I cannot be false to him.

That is why I got so angry. Not because I don't love you, I am dying with it. But it would be selfish of me to hold on to you, as I dearly want to, and live that dream of you and I, free. Alas, you are not an ordinary man and my love cannot hold you down or keep you from becoming who you were born to be.

Be strong, be courageous, but most of all, be great. Make me proud.

I will love you every day of my life. I left "Nobody Knows" on the iPod, it says all the things I have not been able to say. Carry it with you as you go home, to fight, and to win. Know that my love follows you.

Forever,
Astrid

His hands shook as he put in the ear buds and pressed play. The words of the song, known since he was eight, had a poignant and terrible meaning now.

Peter wept.

Part 14 - Destiny

February 10, 1000 ME

Not Going

"What do you mean you are not coming?" Josiah demanded. "Of course, you are."

Peter regarded him from his beach towel. "I believe I was precise in what I said, I am not coming."

Josiah's pinched lip expression did little to hide the pulsing muscle on the side of his jaw. For the hundredth time in four days, he cursed Astrid ben Agnor's stubborn impetuousness for the tangled wreckage she left behind.

He was on the verge of retaking his kingdom, instead of celebrating, he was living in a house of mourning. He took solace in the fact that at least Peter seemed sober, a vast improvement over the first seventy-two hours. Taking another tack, he said, "Our audience with the Iron King has been granted. You are summoned, Peter. You do not ignore such a summons."

Peter raised a sardonic eyebrow. "I have been ignoring royal summons my entire life." He shrugged and put a towel over his head, dismissing the subject and Josiah.

For a blinding instant, Josiah wanted to kick him, to fall on him with pummeling fists, and beat some sense into him. "We have too much at stake to let a mere girl stand in the way."

"Go away," came the raspy voice under the towel.

It would be so easy, to lie down beside him, to stroke his taut stomach, to touch him. He was right there, and Astrid was a fool for watching him. They would be gone soon, but until he left, she would come. The draw was too great, the addiction too strong. When Josiah approached, she suppressed a wild notion to run into the house. She wanted Davianna, feeling her loss as deep as Peter's, but she made her choice. This was her own private hell.

She knew she should just leave and not come back, but each day she returned. She could not help herself. It would be easier to tell her heart to stop beating or her lungs not to breathe. She loved them all enough to let them alone, let them heal. She knew she would never heal, so she watched.

Peter could feel her. Yesterday, in his drunken stupor, he thought he imagined it, today he was sure. He reached for his phone and typed, "I need a status update."

"Status quo," Himari typed back from The Resistance bunker. She spun the coffee stained lace doily, Auntie G's latest addition to her desk. "New orders?"

Peter sighed. "Watch, protect, and follow."

"It's bad here, Falcon. Tell Doc to hurry. There won't be much left if he doesn't."

February 11, 1000 ME

Parting

The coarse black hair of the horse's mane felt cool under his unshaven cheek, Peter inhaled the comforting smell of hay and manure. The only pleasant memories of his life after his mother's death were spent among the horses and the people who loved them, and him, his refuge. His time in the saddle had dwindled to nothing, and his battered soul ached to ride. Three mounts arrived with the summons yesterday, two would make the journey.

"I should have known this is where I would find you." Josiah's wry voice came from the stable's entryway.

Peter gave the stallion a firm pat on the neck. "And so, you have." He took up a brush and began grooming the pristine animal.

Josiah leaned on the wooden stall door with an air of resignation. "We depart within the hour. I cannot change your mind?"

Peter continued brushing the horse. "No, there is much to do here. I will take care of it whilst you are gone."

Their argument rocked the villa yesterday, but Peter remained adamant, he was not going with them. Davianna surmised Peter's reasons were the same as Astrid's. Astrid's letter to Davianna dove deep into the painful reasons she left. Chief among them, her refusal to repent of her relationship with Peter, and her stubborn insistence that she would not be a suitable wife for him.

Josiah shook his head with a pained expression. "I do not know how long this will take, at least a week, perhaps longer." He started to turn, then stopped. "Peter?"

For the first time, Peter met his eyes, dull with pain, their golden bursts of sunshine no longer visible. "Josiah."

"I wanted you by my side. You get yourself together. I will have your vow on that, Prince."

"My Esteemed, I will do my best." Was all Prince Peter would commit to.

An hour later, they were gone.

Backfire

"Why aren't you leaving with them?" Astrid silently screamed. "Why are Davianna and Josiah riding out without you, Peter? This is wrong! Why aren't you going?" Her fists clenched and unclenched at her sides in silent fury. "Damn you! You are supposed to go with them!"

She stormed away. Angry tears blurred her vision as she pushed through the crowded tourist street, back to her small hotel room. She closed the door with a satisfying slam, her chest heaving.

Insufferable, stubborn, self-destructive man, how dare he throw away her sacrifice, her gift? Astrid wanted to tear his eyes out.

As the fury abated, she fell onto the green and white bedspread, beginning to question whether she had done the right thing. The sure knowledge that she was setting him free, doing the noble thing, sustained her through her own personal pain. If he rejected the gift, if he did not seek the Iron King, then it was all for naught, and she had lost him for nothing.

A steel band of pain tightened around her chest. She rolled over, taking a can of flat soda off the water stained dresser. She finished the drink and took a gulp of air.

Damn him!

Valley of Aijalon

The landscape stretched before Davianna and Josiah, lush green and eternal spring. No curse or drought touched this land, it bloomed with the heady scent of fennel and lilac. Daubs of yellow, blue, and purple adorned the Valley of Aijalon as they rode at a leisurely pace along the path.

Josiah led the way. Comfortable on the giant stallion, he exuded confidence and rode with a natural grace. They were alone. While he remained vigilant, there was an easy set to his jaw, and he relaxed in the saddle. His peaceful expression was reminiscent of how he looked when he slept. The worry lines between his eyes softened, and if she touched him, he would smile dreamily. In the early morning, beard stubble shadowed his strong jaw, transforming him from regal Prince to dark pirate. He always looked younger when he slept. His hair had grown and curled around his collar in blue-black waves. The muscles in his thighs and arms flexed with the gentle gait of the horse. Josiah was strong of body, mind, and purpose. The Prince was imposing, noble, and magnificent. Her husband was also bossy, overbearing, and all too often treated her like a child.

Josiah reigned up beside her. "Shall we stop for a few moments? The Golden City lies an hour ahead."

Davianna felt a spike of impatience. "You forget, Husband, the skills of your own wife. I know the direction, perhaps better than you. I am no wilting flower, even though you would make me into one."

He heard the teasing exasperation in her tone, though there was a hard set to her jaw when she wheeled around to face him. In the golden light, she was both strong and delicate, enchanting and primal. Dressed in her Gune Black, armed from ankle to wrist, she controlled her blonde mare with expert skill, a warrior Princess. The thought twisted his guts in pride and fear.

His Princess silently challenged him from behind quick intelligent eyes. His mouth lifted in a half smile and he said, "Aye, my intrepid minx, you are a worthy Princess, indeed."

She acknowledged him with a regal bow of her head, the royal mantle upon her shoulders seemed as natural as if she were born to it. She had shed no tears since the royal summons. Davianna became resolute and determined, exhibiting an iron core and self-assurance he first glimpsed that long-ago night on Waterloo Bridge, yet even then, there were traces of a fearful girl. They were no longer present. Her fear had burned away in the fire. Davianna dismounted of her own accord and tended to the horse. Her capable actions were designed to send him a message.

Josiah strolled over to a low-hanging branch, plucked a ripe fruit, and presented it to her on one knee, his head bowed. "My lady, a gift from the King."

Her chestnut hair hung down her back in thick waves. A floral breeze lifted the curling ends, framing her face. She smiled at the proffered fruit, a grain apple. "Ah, thank you, Prince. 'Thou art not alone' is perhaps a message for you this day."

He rose to his feet, towering over her.

Davianna met his eyes, as an equal.

He grinned and answered her in the court speech they had been practicing, "Speak plain, good wife, for thou knowest I am a simple man."

"Thou art not simple," she touched the side of his neck, "thou art stubborn."

He leaned his head into her hand with a rueful smile. "Aye, but thou art loved." Josiah gathered her in his arms, kissing her gently. "Thou art cherished, above all else."

"As well, I know. Alas, I was created to be more than just cherished, more than just protected, for I was given unto thee as thy *ezer kenegdo*. Josiah, dost thou knowest the meaning of that?"

The shriek of the alarm in her pocket shattered the moment. Music blared and skipped in random order, with no visible hand controlling it. Davianna's hand convulsed over the device. Josiah pushed her behind him, whirling with his dagger at the ready.

Lucifer stepped from his hiding place behind the grain apple tree. "Such a touching scene." His bored tone belied the menace he exuded as he approached.

The songs continued to skip in her pocket, discordant and violent.

He regarded them with contempt. "Our very own Millennial super couple," he sneered. Then his eyes lit on Davianna, his voice dripped with disgust, "with a baby."

His veneer of boredom evaporated into a quivering force of such eternal and vicious hatred toward Davianna that her hair blew back. Life giver, beauty and love, the pure essence and manifestation of the Most High, embodied in woman, he hated it above all else in the universe, had sought to destroy it since Eve.

Josiah moved in front of her, the Holy Spirit upon him.

"'Sun, stand still over Gibeon, and you, moon, over the Valley of Aijalon.' Begone foul beast, for thou art defeated, and thou shall die as thy servants did in this valley."

Lucifer's eyes narrowed. The ground their feet trod witnessed his great defeat in the First Age, the slaughter of the Amorite kings. It was the day that the sun stood still so the Israelites could continue their pursuit that resulted in a complete annihilation of his faithful servants. "I knew Joshua ben Nun." A wicked smile showed pointed teeth. "I watched him die, as you will this day, Josiah ben Eamonn."

"Yet Joshua sits in the presence of the Most High, one of the twenty-four elders around the throne, while you bleed like a man under your coat," Josiah countered.

Lucifer roared, his face transforming into a black dragon. "I am no man!"

Davianna wrenched herself free and stood beside Josiah. "True! There are no fingerprints of the Most High upon you."

The dragon roared, shooting flames out of his mouth.

Josiah pulled Davianna to his side prepared to be incinerated. They watched in fascination as the fire raged around them. They were untouched.

The dragon charged.

But Davianna ben David shouted, "By the blood of the Lamb!" The dragon hit an invisible wall and bounced backward.

Josiah shouted, "It is written, surrender to the Most High, resist the Devil, and he will flee from you."

"I do not flee before man!"

The countenance of the dragon changed, he became beautiful, clothed in ebony and jet. However, it was a facade, a remnant of who he had been. It lay upon him like a caricature, a fabrication of his own remembrance. Davianna saw through it, to the eternal evil and unredeemable beast behind the mask.

She did not raise her voice; she did not scream or rail against him. "You are defeated, whether we live or die in this valley, it does not alter your destiny. For it is written, wicked serpent, that your head was crushed at Calvary, destroyed by the seed of the woman and the blood of the Lamb."

"Oh, Lucifer, son of the morning, thou art fallen." Josiah bore himself up under the blazing hatred the wicked creature blasted at them.

"Lies." Lucifer raised a black eyebrow, oozing confidence.

The discordant music coming from inside her pocket continued unabated and ominous. In the distance, they heard the cacophony, saw smoke rising to the heavens. The Devil smiled.

"I have taken possession of the Black Key, Davianna ben David, all your struggles were for naught. And you, Josiah ben Eamonn, should have taken me up on my offer. You will never sit on the Alanthian throne. I win."

"Nay," Josiah shook his head. "Thy destiny was determined long ago. Thou will burn for eternity in the Lake of Fire."

"Wrong! The kings of men rally to my side. I will lead the people of Earth, they will follow me, and rise in numbers greater than the sands on the shore. No force can withstand the onslaught of my wrath."

He pointed at Josiah. "Alanthia will be first, I will wreak utter destruction on your land. I have seen their hearts. Even now, your streets run with blood, and that is just a taste of what is to come."

"Yet," Davianna's voice sounded small, but steady, "we stand before you, and you are not victorious."

Josiah held her tight. Side by side, they faced the Devil together. In the stillness, the songs continued.

"Ah, the small minds of men, you are so easy to deceive, promise power, freedom, and your own way. They always come. It has always been so." He grinned, horrible and wicked. "Do you know who is being unleashed, Davianna ben David?"

She felt a cold serpent of fear slither down her spine. The screeching music haled darkness and destruction. Her hand tightened on the cursed device, willing it to be silent.

Lucifer pointed to the south; a stench of rotten fish blew on the wind. "There, rises Isis in Egypt." A shriek split the clear sky.

To the north, he gestured. "In Russia, there is Gog." His very words brought a chill to the air, the roar of an enraged grizzly bear.

To the east, he swept an arm. "In India, there is Cali." He turned and flicked a horrible forked tongue. "The goddess of destruction."

He held Josiah's eyes and wagged a pointed claw, his countenance that of the fallen, Satan. "And I have a very special present waiting for you in the west, they are ready for her, Josiah ben Eamonn, they worship her." The smug satisfaction on his face chilled Josiah to the bone. "She is loosed." Satan threw his head back and shouted to the sky, "My servants are free!"

Abruptly the music stopped. Silence reigned in the Valley of Aijalon.

Lucifer looked from Josiah to Davianna. "You should have joined me when you had the chance."

Josiah's voice was cold and vehement. "The Lord Jesus rebuke thee, Satan."

For a fleeting moment, fear flashed in his black eyes. Then the superior, bored demeanor returned. "We are done here. I do hope you enjoyed the music."

With a flash of sulfuric black smoke, he disappeared.

Return to Eden

They turned to each other, speechless. Josiah seized Davianna in a huge hug. "Oh, baby, are you okay?"

Davianna squeezed as hard as she could, tears falling down her face. "Yes, but Josiah, I failed."

"No, you were magnificent."

"Well done, good and faithful servants," said a voice behind them.

Josiah and Davianna's eyes locked in momentary paralysis and reverential fear. They fell to their knees before The King.

Josiah murmured to the ground, his head bowed, "My Lord."

Davianna's voice was quiet, her voice soft. "Yeshua, Savior."

He placed a strong hand on each of their heads, supernatural peace and clarity calmed their pounding hearts. "Come, let us walk in the garden. It is the cool of the day."

They rose.

With her head bowed, Davianna held out her hand. "My King, you have caught me again with nothing save a grain apple."

He lifted her chin, smiling. Yeshua's hazel eyes were full of love, his nose prominent, his jaw square and strong. "I never eschew those that offer what they have, Daughter."

In a husky whisper, she murmured, "I am humbled, my Lord."

Yeshua turned to Josiah and said, "I believe thy wife asked of thee a question. Doest thou knowest the meaning of *ezer kenegdo?*"

Josiah looked from his wife to his Lord. "I fear, my Lord, I do not. Wilt thou tell me?"

Yeshua smiled fondly at Davianna as they strolled. "'Twas what Eve was called at her creation. She was to be beside Adam, his alter half, his helper, especially in times of great trouble."

Josiah remembered Davianna standing by his side. "Thou art not alone. Thou chose wisely for me."

"Aye, since I laid the foundations of the Earth, ye were chosen for one another and for this day. Ye have always been destined. For thou stood before thy wife to protect her, thou didst not give her over to the foul tempter, as Adam did to Eve, not in the Palace, not in the bayou, nor in this valley. For in Eden, Adam was not deceived by the serpent, but reasoned in his heart that he could willingly participate in the great sin then claim his *ezer kenegdo* deceived him. He sought to place the blame upon her and plead his own innocence. Thou hast not done so.

"When Davianna came unto thee, thou sacrificed thine own desires, and valued her over the lust of the flesh. Thou did not sin, nor seek to place blame, nor revile her as tempter."

Davianna's face flamed bright red.

"Instead, Josiah, thou protected her and thyself, doing what was right in my eyes."

"Forgive me, Lord." Davianna hung her head in shame.

"Daughter," Yeshua lifted her chin, "as a father has compassion for his children, so I, the LORD, have compassion on those who fear Me. I know thy frame, and I am mindful that my children are dust." He smiled. "Thy sins are forgiven."

Davianna blinked back tears.

"Davianna, thou hast fulfilled my commandment to protect what I gave thee to carry. Thou hast protected my gift from man and beast. Thou didst not falter under the coercion of Korah and stood stalwart against the temptation of Satan. Even in the face of death, thou didst not falter but called my name.

"Ye both have withstood and prevailed, turning neither to the left nor the right, in faithfulness to Me. And because ye have done what is right in mine eyes, Davianna took her place beside thee, Josiah, as thy *ezer kenegdo*. Ye have set right the relationship between husband and wife, between man and woman, that ye may once again live in harmony."

He smiled at them both with love so boundless that it saturated them with peace and joy. He was not a mere observer in their lives. He had directed and guided them, for their good, by His own hands. They had not understood why they found themselves on the path He set them on but in his presence, they understood.

Davianna hung her head and said, "My Lord, I fear the enemy took control of the device entrusted to me for safekeeping." With trembling hands, she pulled it from her pocket and offered it to him.

He did not take it from her, instead his lips narrowed, and he shrugged, "Twas foreordained. Keep it as a token, thou shalt tell thy children the tale."

She blinked in surprise but bobbed her head in ascent.

Yeshua gestured forward. "Come, I will ride with ye into the Golden City."

Loosed

The chaos sweeping the planet since the London attacks was a mere pebble in the ocean compared to the flood that swamped the landscape at the release of the elohim. Madness, murder, rape, and every violent and vile action hidden in the heart of man erupted in a frenzy that bathed the planet in blood and tears.

Alanthians rose by the millions, thousands descended upon Korah's Palace. Only a massive military guard kept them at bay, sealing Korah inside. His Palace became a prison.

Bubba and Zanah watched with growing horror as the scenes unfolded on the television screen. They huddled together, safe and secure in Peter's remote cabin in the mountains. Those in The Resistance went underground, into hiding.

Satan gloated; his army was free!

Dark Visitor

Astrid heard the glass door slide open. Leaping from her bed, her weapon clicked open as her feet landed. Her heart thundered in her ears, ready to fight.

A cold voice from the shadow behind the curtain said, "Put the knife down, Red."

She closed her eyes, relieved that he was not an assassin. "Damn you, Peter. You scared me to death."

He stepped into the darkened room and pulled the door closed behind him.

Inevitable reckoning crashed on the room. Six days of hell separated them, full of fury, agony, and longing. The air crackled with tension, raising the hair on their bodies, like the second after a lightning strike.

He moved across the room in an instant, pinned her against the wall, and delivered a bruising kiss.

Fire erupted between them.

To touch him, to kiss him, when she thought she would never see him again, it was too much.

He tore his mouth away and bit her ear. His voice sounded ragged, full of anger and pain. "You do not get to decide, not like that, not alone."

She tried to push him away, but he was prepared for it. They played this game before.

Their bodies, as familiar to each other as their own, reacted in primal and elemental passion, heedless of the storm brewing between them. Their bodies simply knew, my mate is here. He cupped her and growled. She was already moist and hot under his hand. Her breath came in short pants of excitement, of need.

"You were supposed to go!" Astrid said through gritted teeth.

They were nose to nose, he held her pressed against the wall, burning hot. "Not without you," he growled, and fumbled with his pants.

She felt him, pressing against her. With his knees, he forced her legs apart.

Poised at her apex, he panted, "Never without you!"

He entered her, and she welcomed him, like the opening notes of a favorite song.

"Never without you!"

She banged against the wall.

He thrust harder. "Ever!"

She sobbed and clung to him, desperate to hold him, but afraid if she gave in, she would never have the strength to leave him again. A cry ripped from her throat as she surrendered. She was lost in him, had been from the first moment. She called to him in the darkness, "Peter."

"Not without you." His climax came hard and violent. He never took his eyes off her as he pumped his seed into her body. "Astrid."

He claimed her, took her, sealed her.

Then he left as quickly and quietly as he had come, leaving her a crumpled wreck on the floor.

February 14, 1000 ME

Return of Prince d'Or

The burned-out rubble that greeted Peter in the New City, while not surprising, was breathtaking to behold. Acres of desolation marred the landscape, the smoke from the conflagration still hung in the gray air, sick with the smell of charred ash and shattered dreams. His motorcycle was perfect for navigating the abandoned torched cars and looted trucks. He put on his helmet and took off.

The citizenry was quiet after days of intense rioting and fighting. With the collapsing government, there was no authority to rein in the chaos. Alanthians hunkered down, hiding from themselves.

He heard the mob before he saw them, surrounding the Palace, screaming for Korah's head. Korah's security force set up a secondary perimeter outside the walls, dozens of bodies lay between it and the gates, a stark warning to those who might seek a direct frontal assault.

Peter had no intention of making such a foolhardy move. The remote control on his motorcycle opened the cave entrance a half mile away from the perimeter, the bike set to full electric was silent as he entered the pit of his own personal hell.

Welcome Home.

Surrender

For three days, Astrid tore herself apart, down to the atomic level. It began the moment the glass door closed behind the stranger. He looked, sounded, and smelled like Peter but was missing something fundamental. She knew in her heart; she took it from him.

How had it all gone so wrong? How had she come to this?

An image flashed in her memory. She was eight, sitting atop the landing, fiddling with the ribbon of her favorite purple and white pajamas, listening to her parents argue.

Her mother cried, "Bubba, we can't keep going on like this. You have lost the house? Where will Astrid and I live when you go off on your next scheme?"

Another memory fell in her mind, she was ten. "Daddy, are you going to church with Momma and me?"

Bubba's bloodshot eyes, peered at her from the pillow in her parents' room, "Ain't got time for that con, sweetheart. Religion is for suckers. Trust your daddy on that one."

Then she was twelve, and Frank, from church, had brought groceries. He sat in the kitchen with Momma while she cried. "Thank you, Frank. I don't know what we would do without you."

Another memory hit her. Ginny ben Arnold, skinny mean-girl, looking her up and down at Youth Group. "Have another cupcake, fatty." The church girls dissolved into laughter and pointed at her, Astrid stormed away in humiliation and fury. She never went back.

Frank, red-faced and angry, rose like a specter in her mind. "I don't care what you say, young lady. We are packing up and heading to the Golden City. Alanthia has fallen. This is no place for good people."

Astrid screamed back, "I hate you! I hate all of you!" Then she collapsed in tears in the yellow bedroom Daddy bought her.

It all came back, the memories.

For years, she tucked it all away, emotions, sadness, and pain to be dealt with another day. When the day came, it crushed her under the weight of it all. Grief, terror, torture, abandonment, fear, addiction, it swamped and swallowed her up in murky green slime.

It took every bit of her strength to bathe and dress. The only food she ate was a leftover sandwich and a container of cold take out mashed potatoes.

Utterly miserable, she realized her actions, while wrapped in a cloak of self-righteous sacrifice, had been selfish and stubborn. Fear and pain had governed her, not love.

However, the pain was more fundamental than that.

Her daddy had left her. He abandoned her, walked out of her life, and never came back. Daddy, who she loved more than anyone, taught her to guard her heart, because you cannot trust those who say they love you. It was why it was so easy for her to believe the worst about Davianna and Guan, and she had been wrong.

And Peter, oh Peter, from the moment Davianna screamed she was nothing but a piece of tail to him, she knew it would be over. The moment they were safe, the moment she could flee, she had run.

Astrid had fled them both, both people who said they loved her.

In so doing, she delivered a grievous wound to the ones she sought to protect. She left Davianna to traverse the treacherous waves of royal society on her own. And she knew, the soulless man who came to her in the dark was in mortal danger.

The weight of it crushed her to the floor, and she cried out in surrender.

Korah's Reckoning

Korah stalked the empty hallways of the Palace, disheveled and unshaven. He called for servants who had long ago abandoned their posts. He saw ghosts of the long dead and argued with the voices that tormented him. Disappointments and long-forgotten dreams haunted him.

He cried out over the desertion of the Dark Master and raged against the Iron King. Cursing his treacherous son, he damned his nephew to Hell. Tormented and bedeviled, the madness that hovered in the corners of his brain overtook him. Insanity chased him through the empty Palace halls.

The dark mob outside chanted for his blood. They were coming now. He heard their footsteps marching. Dark music filled the corridors. They would sacrifice him on that altar, as the dream predicted, as he had done to Eamonn. He heard the drums. They were here.

Korah screamed in terror and ran.

Moment of Truth

The light that filled the musty hotel room was not the golden halo of Tel Aviv, but pure white power. Astrid scrambled to her feet, stumbling backward in fearful dread.

"Astrid ben Agnor, daughter of my heart, I have longed for you, to gather you under my wing, like a hen gathers and protects her chicks, but you have not been willing!"

Falling to her knees, she buried her face in the carpet, weeping. "I could not. I know what I have done, who I am," she sobbed.

"Tell me true, do you surrender your proud heart and humble yourself before me now?"

"I do! Please help me. I am so sorry."

She rose from the floor like a helium balloon, weightless.

He embraced her and stroked her head. "Courageous, Astrid, with the heart of a lion. I am the LORD your God, who takes hold of your right hand and says to you, do not fear; I will help you."

Then, the light that had blinded her, scared her, enveloped her. Surrounded by His love, all her defenses of anger, pride, and willfulness crumbled at his feet. She wept in the

Savior's arms.

After a time, Astrid did not know if he held her for seconds or hours, he looked into her eyes and said, "Beloved, your actions, while well intentioned, have set Peter on a path to destruction. You must stop him from committing this grievous sin and giving over to the darkness in his own heart. Go now, with this message. 'Vengeance is mine, sayeth the Lord.'"

I Saw What You Did

Peter became the stalking monster of his nightmares. He abandoned himself to it, let it take control, and let the beast hunt. With his heart set on murder, he gave himself over to wrath.

Relishing Korah's cries of terror, he chased him through the corridors, taunting him from invisible places. Peter set the course, directing Korah, sending him to Hell with poetic justice and sweet revenge. Clothed in the despicable black robe, Peter ran like a demon, pursuing Korah down a dark hallway.

Korah panicked, slipped on the marble floor, and went down hard. Peter heard his wrist snap under the impact. He howled like a wounded animal and staggered. His gait became awkward as he fled, cradling his arm against his chest. Losing his balance, his shoulder clipped a corner, and he spun several times before sprawling on the floor.

Peter howled with wicked laughter, and in a perfect imitation of Marduk's guttural voice, he shouted, "Spinning! It is just a game."

Korah cried out in terror and scrambled away.

Peter threw off the robe and ducked into the passageway, hunting. He had no light, needed no guidance, he knew where they were going.

He emerged through the panel in his mother's room full of black wrath and pulsating death. His father, a wild-eyed, broken madman, huddled in the corner whimpering, just as his mother had.

Peter threw back his head and roared. Blood lust surged through his veins. He fell upon his father in a berserker's rage, beating Korah with fury held at bay for a lifetime.

His knuckles found purchase: blood, bone, and teeth. He smashed Korah's head against the floor, pulled away great hunks of hair and scalp. Korah fell unconscious, yet Peter kept beating him.

He rose from the floor, looked at the broken bloody mess, and spit. Unsheathing his dagger, he raised both hands above his head, and prepared to pierce the black heart of his father.

A voice halted the knife's descent.

He froze, certain it was a hallucination born of blood lust and fury. "I am doing this for you!"

"No, Peter, you are not. Darkness has overcome you, and you have let it reign in your heart tonight. The Lord sent me to tell you that vengeance is His. You are not to commit this grievous sin, my love."

"I have to protect you!" Peter cried, never taking his eyes from the crumpled heap at his feet, the knife still held above his head. "He killed my mother." His brain superimposed his mother's body over his father's. It shifted, erratic and disorienting. He closed his eyes. Dizziness made him falter, and he staggered.

He smelled her perfume before he saw her. In a blinding moment of clarity, he recognized the unidentified scent that dark night in his penthouse, when he held the gun to his mouth. He opened his eyes and found blue cat eyes full of love staring back at him.

"Put the knife down, Peter."

He stumbled back in shock. The knife fell to the floor as he stared at her in awestruck wonder.

Astrid moved to Peter's side, taking his limp hand. She paled, staring at the mirror image before her.

Princess Alexa's shimmering visage reached out and

stroked Peter's cheek. "My golden Prince, what a strong and handsome man you have become." Her smile radiated maternal pride. She ran her palms over his broad shoulders, touching her beloved son.

"Mother." Peter's chest constricted.

Alexa glanced at Astrid and her grin broadened. "I see you have not forgotten me. I approve."

Peter, spattered with blood, hair standing on end, looked between them and back again, settling on his mother. "I did not protect you." The magnitude of his heartbreak and grief reverberated in his chest.

Alexa cupped his cheek, wiping away a bloody tear. "You were just a boy. It was my job to protect you, which is why I have come. Leave this place, Peter." She looked down at Korah, "Leave him to his fate."

Peter stood transfixed.

Alexa turned a steely blue gaze to Astrid. "You must leave. There is a mob coming. Love him and guard his precious heart. Promise me."

Astrid nodded convulsively. "Yes, ma'am. I will."

The angry shouts of the mob grew louder. Alexa glanced toward the window, seeing them surge. "Go! They are coming."

Astrid pulled Peter's arm toward the exit in the wall.

He stood anchored, unmovable. With a cry, he broke free and engulfed his mother. She was small, unlike the last time he held her. He crushed her to his chest, inhaling her scent, burying his face in her glorious red hair. "I love you."

Astrid heard Alexa's muffled sob. She turned away, holding her heart, tears burning her eyes.

"I love you too, Peter."

Peter did not look back as he ducked under the passageway, but Astrid did. Princess Alexa held Peter's discarded knife raised above her head.

Balm in Gilead

Peter led her through the dark corridors. Memories of their last terrifying retreat dropped like carpet bombs behind her as they ran. They reached the end of the tunnel, escape vehicles and weapons were still positioned, untouched and undiscovered.

He curled around her, enfolding her in his arms. "What are you doing here?"

"I came to save you." Glass shattered above them. Astrid held his face between her hands. "Now, you need to save me. That mob has broken through."

Peter cast a dubious look at the ceiling. "I am driving."

Astrid wiped a tear away from her eye and gave him a tremulous smile. "Of course, you are, love."

He mounted the motorcycle behind her, before donning his helmet he kissed the hollow below her ear, a firestorm raging inside him. She settled into his arms and let him take her to safety.

An hour later, the motorcycle arrived at Gilead, the long unused Palace of the Princes, forty miles outside of the New City. Nestled among thousands of acres of woods and streams and sitting on the banks of a clear blue lake, the vast estate remained untouched by the ravages of rebellion and destruction. The ancient seat of Alanthian power had not hosted a royal visitor in years.

Jarrod ben Adriel met them in the cavernous receiving hall. "My Esteemed, welcome to Gilead."

Peter grabbed his manservant around the shoulders and pulled him in for an exuberant hug. The dignified valet's arms flailed, at a loss over such a breach in protocol, though Astrid caught a glimmer of unshed tears in his old gray eyes.

Peter smiled down at him and reached toward Astrid, pulling her to his side. "Jarrod, may I present the love of my life, Miss Astrid ben Agnor, of Alanthia."

Astrid gave a formal curtsy, thrilled to meet the man she and Davianna dubbed the Wonder Servant. She was indebted to him for his amazing care while they ran. "I am pleased to meet you, sir. May I thank you for your thoughtfulness toward Davianna and me while we have been traveling?"

Jarrod blinked rapidly, seeing a ghost.

She smiled at him with patience and understanding.

He shook himself imperceptibly and in a hoarse voice, demurred, "No trouble at all, my lady. It was my pleasure."

Peter surveyed their surroundings. "I was born here." Old fashioned oil lamps lit the entryway, and the flickering lights illuminated stone walls covered in gilded swords and accoutrements of war. "I suppose we have plenty of weapons in the event that mob follows us."

He pulled off a riding glove and winced, his hand swollen and bloody beneath. Astrid's quick intake of breath prompted Peter to send Jarrod a sardonic smile. "I do not suppose this place has running water does it?"

Jarrod looked offended. "Certainly, my Esteemed. We did not have computers, but we were not savages."

Astrid giggled, and Peter shot her a sideways glance that told her he had been teasing.

Jarrod, well acquainted with Peter's humor, ignored him with stoic dignity. "I will see you to your chambers. You will find a rather large contingent of staff at your service. I took the liberty of evacuating them here when circumstances," he cleared his throat, "became untenable at the former residence."

Peter cocked a blood-spattered golden eyebrow. "That is putting it mildly."

He guided Astrid by the small of her back, following Jarrod down a long hallway filled with priceless art and portraits from long ago.

The Master's Chamber was richly decorated with warm wooden furnishings, woolen rugs, and masculine paintings of harvest and hunt. A fire crackled in a huge stone hearth.

Astrid hung inside the door.

Jarrod bowed formally. "Miss, if you would like to follow me, there is a lady's chamber down the hall that will suit your needs."

Peter reached out to stop her. Astrid took his wounded hand and brought it to her lips. "Jarrod, if you would have it readied for me and a bath. I would appreciate it, but give us a moment, please."

Peter's face darkened. "What are you doing? You are damned well not sleeping somewhere else tonight."

Astrid moistened the tip of her thumb with her tongue, rubbing a smudge of blood on his forehead. "I hadn't planned on spending my wedding night anywhere other than in your bed, Prince Peter ben Korah. However, I will not do it with you covered in blood and me without a bath."

Peter's face transformed from a scowl to beatific joy. With a great whoop, he picked her up. "You mean it, Red? You will marry me?"

"Yes, but I have decided that I will not be a Princess."

His emerald eyes sparkled with humor. "And what have you decided you are going to be?"

"Other than your wife?"

He nodded, grinning with boyish glee.

"I would like to be a Duchess. They sound like they have more fun than Princesses."

"You can be whatever you want, as long as you do it by my side." He let her slide down his body, kissing her with gentle tenderness, and murmured, "But I have to ask, do you still have reservations, doubts?"

She rested her cheek against his chest, his heart thumping hard and strong under her ear. "I laid them down." She tilted her chin, looking up at him, serene. "Where they belonged, at the foot of the cross."

"'Tis a good place to leave them." He smiled, and there was light and peace in his eyes. "Hurry back, Duchess."